The
First Puritan
Settlers
of
Connecticut

The
First Puritan
Settlers
of
Connecticut

Royal R. Hinman

foreword by
Christopher C. Child

NEW ENGLAND HISTORIC
GENEALOGICAL SOCIETY

First published in 1846
Foreword copyright © 2015 by the New England Historic Genealogical Society

ISBN: 978-0-88082-328-9
Library of Congress Number: 2015939574

Cover design by Carolyn Sheppard Oakley
Cover image: *Reverend John Davenport (1597-1669/70)*, by "Davenport Limner," ca.
1670. Courtesy of Yale University Art Gallery.

Printed in the United States of America

NEW ENGLAND HISTORIC
GENEALOGICAL SOCIETY

AmericanAncestors.org

Boston, Massachusetts • 2015

FOREWORD

Other than Vermont, the five New England states had significant European-derived settlements in the early colonial period. In the late nineteenth and early twentieth centuries, "genealogical dictionaries" were produced for the states of Rhode Island, Massachusetts, and Maine and New Hampshire (together), by John Osborne Austin, Charles Henry Pope, and Charles Thornton Libby, Sibyl Noyes, and Walter Goodwin Davis, respectively. Such a dictionary was not completed for Connecticut, but Royal Ralph Hinman had made an earlier attempt in the mid-nineteenth century, which serves as an initial reference when researching seventeenth-century families of Connecticut.

A Catalogue of the Names of the First Puritan Settlers of the Colony of Connecticut is Hinman's "first attempt" at such a catalogue. It was published serially in five numbers beginning in 1846 and ending before 1852. Hinman did not write the volume entirely as a "dictionary" but more as a variety of lists and other items.

In 1852, Hinman started a similarly titled volume, *A Catalogue of the Early Puritan Settlers of the Colony of Connecticut* (the only difference being his replacement of the word *First* with *Early*). This work was certainly Hinman's attempt at a more straightforward dictionary of families in Connecticut, with many families being brought down nearly to the present time (although with no sources). The first four numbered sections go only through the surname Danielson, however, and in 1856 he jumped ahead to the letter H with *A Family Record of the Descendants of Sergt. Edward Hinman*, which is paginated as if it is a continuation and labeled "No. 5." Then Hinman abandoned the second catalogue project. He moved from Hartford to New York City and died in 1868. His papers were given to NEHGS and organized by Anson Titus into eleven large folio volumes, which contain valuable information "obtained from manuscripts since lost, and some of it from the recollection of persons now dead" [*Proceedings of the New England Historic Genealogical Society at the Annual Meeting, January 4, 1888* (Boston: NEHGS, 1888), 26].

Had Hinman continued with his "second attempt," the result would be a more standard Connecticut genealogical dictionary. But this, his first attempt, with lists for the entire alphabet, is our best general reference for early Connecticut genealogy.

Two overall lists are given in this volume, "First Settlers of the Colony," on pages 12 to 109 (going from A to Y), with an appendix (pages 110 to 159) containing additions and corrections. A second list, with surnames from A to W, follows the appendix, on pages 182–247. Together, these lists serve as a reference to all of Connecticut. While generally focused on the seventeenth century, they mention occasional events in the eighteenth century. Because sources are generally not given, the researcher needs to infer the primary records Hinman consulted— probably original state and town records that he had immediate access to, having lived in Hartford and having served as the Secretary of State of Connecticut from 1835 to 1842.

The remainder of this volume includes lists generally relating to Connecticut, for example, a short piece on chimney viewers; town-centric lists relating to first settlers of Windsor, Hartford, Wethersfield, and Enfield; a list of *Mayflower* passengers; a transcription of the tobacco law of Connecticut in 1647; and a list of officers of the first general court.

Although it is regrettable that Hinman never carried through on his second, more thorough "catalogue"—which would have been enormous, as the letters A–Da comprised nearly 800 pages—the volume reprinted here serves as a very useful reference, in conjunction with primary sources. The overview of early Connecticut genealogy and history makes *First Puritan Settlers* a good first stop for anyone with Nutmeg State ancestry.

Christopher C. Child
Senior Genealogist of the Newbury Street Press
NEW ENGLAND HISTORIC GENEALOGICAL SOCIETY

CATALOGUE OF THE NAMES

OF THE

FIRST PURITAN SETTLERS

OF THE

COLONY OF CONNECTICUT;

WITH THE

TIME OF THEIR ARRIVAL IN THE COLONY,

AND THEIR

STANDING IN SOCIETY, TOGETHER WITH THEIR PLACE OF RESIDENCE,
AS FAR AS CAN BE DISCOVERED BY THE RECORDS.

....

COLLECTED FROM THE STATE AND TOWN RECORDS,
BY R. R. HINMAN.

....

No. I.

~~~~~~~~~~~~~~~~~~~~

HARTFORD:
PRINTED BY E. GLEASON.
1846.

INTRODUCTION.

A GREAT portion of the population of Connecticut have the curiosity to learn how their ancestors firstly reached this country, where they landed, when they came to Connecticut, and what was their condition when they started in the wilderness, to begin to live,—surrounded by the beasts of the forest and by savage men, vastly more dangerous to their property and lives than the beasts could be.

The object of the writer is to issue several Numbers, giving the names of such of the settlers as can be found on record, who came into the Connecticut Colony previous to the Union of the Colonies of New Haven and Connecticut in 1665, together with their standing and condition, as far as can be ascertained. In the few remarks I shall make, I shall not go into an investigation of the titles under which Connecticut was settled.

In 1631, Governor Winslow, of Plymouth, appears to have had his attention drawn to the settlement of Connecticut, and he made a journey to Connecticut soon after, and discovered Connecticut River— [*Dr. Trumbull.*] In 1632, some of the people of New Plymouth were in Connecticut, and soon after determined to erect a trading-house at Windsor, as an advantage to commencing the future colony. The Indian name of the River was Quonehtacut, (long river)—from this the Colony took its name. So anxious was Gov. Winslow, in 1633, for the settlement of the rich land upon the Connecticut, that he made a journey to Boston with Mr. Bradford to consult Gov. Winthrop and his council upon the subject, and to join with them in erecting a trading-house upon the River, and gave his reasons for his anxiety upon the subject. Gov. Winthrop then gave his reasons why it would be an unsafe step, and declined the offer. Gov. Winslow and his people were at once determined upon erecting a house, and settling a company of men at their own risk upon the Connecticut. Soon after Mr. Holmes, of Plymouth, and a company of men with him, prepared a frame for a house, and obtained all the necessaries to cover it, placed them on board of a vessel and sailed for Connecticut River. He soon reached his place of destination, and erected his house on the west side of Connecticut River — south of the mouth of Little, or Farmington river, in the present town of Windsor. This was the first house built in Connecticut, and was the first act towards settling the Connecticut Colony. The house was soon protected by palisadoes. Soon after the Dutch at Dutch point erected another trading house, which was the second house built in the Colony.

In 1634, and for many years after, all the settlers for New England landed in the colony of New Plymouth, or Massachusetts, and emigrated from thence to Connecticut. For several years after 1635, there were no settlements by the English in the Colony, except in the towns of Windsor, Hartford and Wethersfield, and a few at Saybrook, In 1634, some of the Watertown settlers came and erected a few houses in what is now Wethersfield. (Mr. Weeks in his manuscript claims Wethersfield to be the oldest town on the river.) In 1635 the congregation of Mr. Warham at Cambridge, settled upon moving to Connecticut, and some few came to Windsor, and made preparations to move their families. The people of Watertown also many of then moved to Wethersfield, and the people of Newtown were preparing to move to Hartford in the Spring of 1636 — though some had come in 1635. John Winthrop, a son of Gov. Winthrop, of Massachusetts, arrived at Boston in 1635, as agent for Sir Richard Saltonstall and others, for the purpose of erecting a fort at the mouth of Connecticut River, and was appointed by the Company, (whose agent he was) Governor of the River Connecticut, for one year after his arrival. He soon built the fort and erected houses — which was the commencement of the building up and settling Saybrook. Many of the Dorchester people who had settled in Windsor occupied land near the Plymouth trading-house — this greatly disturbed Gov. Bradford, as the Plymouth people had purchased the land of the Indians, and taken possession of it by building their trading-house upon the land. About October, 1635, the Dorchester people commenced moving to Windsor; about 60 men, women and children started through the wilderness with their horses, cattle, swine, &c., without roads, bridges, or even huts to cover them, sleeping in the open air — but they arrived safely, though the journey was long and tedious. Much of their provisions and household furniture had been sent round by water, to Dorchester (Windsor) and were cast away and lost. The sufferings in the Colony in the winter of 1635 were most severe; — their provisions failed, and bedding lost, so that many to save life returned to Boston for the winter. But those who remained in the Colony through the winter came near perishing by famine, notwithstanding all they could procure of the Indians and get by hunting. Much of the winter they subsisted on acorns, roots and grains. Many of their cattle died. How changed the scene!

In the spring of 1636 the emigration began again in companies from Massachusetts to Connecticut, and sent their provisions by water. In June, 1636, the Rev. Thomas Hooker, Mr. Samuel Stone and about 100 others, of all ages and sexes, started through the wilderness, guided only by a compass, to Hartford—with no covers but the heavens, and no lodging but the ground, and subsisted on the milk of the cows which they drove with their other cattle, numbering 160 in all. They carried their packs upon their backs, and their arms for protection in their hands. Mrs. Hooker was so feeble in health that she was carried the whole journey upon a litter, and they reached Newtown (Hartford) in about two weeks. In September, 1636, as many of Mr. Warham's people had moved to Windsor, he started for Windsor to take charge of his church, but left his family at Dorchester until he could prepare to receive them; so that at this time the three towns upon the River were permanently settled by many inhabitants, with Mr. Warham in charge of the church at Windsor, Mr. Hooker and Mr. Stone at Hartford, and the Rev. Henry Smith at Wethersfield. All emigrants to Connecticut, until the settlement of New Haven, came first to Hartford, and afterwards settled other towns, as they did Stratford, Fairfield, Norwalk, &c.

It will be recollected by the reader, that Mr. Warham and Mr. Hooker had been ordained, one at Dorchester and the other in Newtown in Mass., before they and their churches moved to Dorchester and Newtown, in Connecticut. They gave the towns where each resided in this colony the same names of the towns from which they had removed; Hartford was called Newtown—and Windsor, Dorchester—and Wethersfield, Watertown. But at the General Court of the Colony, in February, 1637, (as time is now reckoned) they gave the several towns their present names. Mr. Phillips, who had been ordained in Watertown, Massachusetts, over the church which settled at Wethersfield did not move with his church, and Henry Smith became their pastor in Wethersfield.

It will be discovered then, that here were three towns located in the wilderness, with a large number of inhabitants, (as many must have come into the colony, before either of the churches moved as a colony) without any law to govern them, either civil, military, or criminal; and the principles and much less the practice and forms of an independent government, in a great measure unknown to men who

had been educated under the Crown of England and had learned only
to obey. The first year (1635) no courts were organized, not even a
town organization formed, and much less any thing like a General
Court formed to enact laws and punish offences. The officers of the
several churches governed their own members according to the rules
and discipline of the church; and as no other law existed in the
Colony, all offenders, if any, were tried before 1636, must have been
tried by the Mosaic law, by the churches. But as the law of Moses
made no provision to punish a white man for selling a gun to an
Indian—it therefore became necessary that some civil body of men
should be so organized as to enact such laws as would prevent or
punish offences not provided for in the Bible. The placing of fire-
arms in the possession of the Indians was considered one of the most
culpable offences in the Colony, which endangered not only the property but the safety and lives of the English settlers. At this time it
was discovered that Henry Stiles had traded a gun with the Indians
for corn. Therefore on the 26th day of April, 1636, a court was organized by five of the best men in the Colony—whether they constituted themselves a court or were elected by the people, the record gives
no account. The court consisted of Roger Ludlow, as chairman,
and Mr. Westwood, John Steel, Andrew Ward, and William Phelps,
as his associates. The first act of the Court was to try Stiles for
the offence. He was found guilty, and ordered by the Court to regain
the gun from the Indians in a fair and legal way, or the Court should
take the case into further consideration. The Court then enacted a
law, that from henceforth no one within the jurisdiction of the Court
should trade with the Indians any piece or pistol, gun or shot, or
powder, under such penalty as the Court should see meet to inflict.—
This was the first Court, the first Trial, and the first Law ever enacted
or had in Connecticut.

As the members of the court resided in the three towns before mentioned, they assumed the power (as no law had been enacted by them,
and the Mosaic law had not provided for it,) to appoint and swear
constables for Dorchester, Newtown and Watertown, for the then
ensuing year, or until new ones should be chosen. This it appears
was considered by the Court as an organization or incorporation of
the three towns. For many years after, and long after the Confederation of Hartford, Windsor and Wethersfield, all that was done by
the General Court to incorporate a plantation or town, was to appoint
and swear a constable, and the remainder was left to the inhabitants of
the plantation to finish its organization or incorporation. Even as late

as 1662–3–4, in many of the towns upon Long Island, also at West-chester, where they were claimed by the Colony, or placed themselves under the government of Connecticut, a constable was appointed or approved by the General Court, and the towns at once became liable to be taxed by the Colony, and had the privilege of being represented at the General Court. The Court thus formed for the trial of Henry Stiles was continued from session to session and from year to year, and was called the General Court until the Union with the New Haven Colony in 1665—after which it was styled the General Assembly: so that the reader will see that the origin of the present General Assembly of the State of Connecticut was the formation of a Court of five men, in 1636, to try Henry Stiles criminally, (without law) for selling a gun to an Indian.

The General Court soon discovered the propriety of adding a House of Representatives to the first Court formed in 1636, particularly upon great occasions. Therefore in May, 1637, the several towns were represented at the General Court by the name of Committee, by three from each town—and took their seats with the magistrates who had previously constituted the Court. The object at this time of enlarging the number of the General Court, was an event which has never been surpassed in importance to the Colony or State since. It was whether they should declare war against the most warlike and powerful tribe of Indians in New England. The future safety of property and life in the Colony depended upon the result. The Pequotts had stolen not only the property of the English, and murdered some of the inhabitants, but had abducted from Wethersfield two young ladies, and carried them among the Indians by force. But not to add to this interesting narrative further. The General Court, feeble as the inhabitants were in numbers, and deficient in means, trusted in God for the result, and boldly declared war against the Pequotts. Ninety men were ordered to be raised—munitions of war were at once prepared—Samuel Stone was selected as chaplain for the little but valorous army. They went down Connecticut River in three small vessels, with Captain Mason as commander, (and to be brief,) they met the enemy at the Mystic Fort; and though the colonists lost two, with sixteen wounded, they fought like men who were fighting for the future welfare of the Colony—for the lives of their wives, children, and their own lives and property. When all was closed nearly 600 Indians lay dead upon the battle ground—about 60 or 70 wigwams burned to the ground, and the Fort in ashes. So valorous and complete was the victory that the Pequotts became extinct as a nation. Sassicus fled with a few of his warriors to the Mohawks : others united with other tribes, particularly with the Mohegans.

It will therefore be seen that what is now styled the Senate, originated, as has been stated ; and the formation of the House of Representatives originated in the necessity of having more councillors in the declaration of war against the Pequott Indians. After which meeting of the Committee, in 1637, the Committee met in the General Court as the House of Representatives, and the two houses were styled the Commissioners and Committee until after the Union of Windsor, Hartford and Wethersfield, in 1639, when the government was formed by adding a Governor and Deputy Governor. The Upper House was styled the House of Magistrates, and during 1639 the Lower House retained the name of Committee; but in April, 1640, the Lower House, or popular branch, was styled the House of Deputies.

[*Records of Conn., Winthrop's Jour., Dr. Trumbull.*

From the organization of the Gen. Court in the Colony, in 1636, to the confederation of the three towns upon Connecticut River, in 1639, being three years—there was no other court in the Colony, except the Particular Court of 1637 which did little business. The General Court took cognizance of divisions in churches—of all criminal offences—of all civil matters—the appointment and confirmation of all officers in the jurisdiction—declared war—regulated commerce—formed and governed the militia ;—indeed every thing in the Colony came under their supervision. They ordered that no young unmarried man, unless a public officer, or he kept a servant, should keep house alone, except by license of the town, under a penalty of twenty shillings per week ; and that no head of a family should entertain such young man under a like penalty, without liberty of the town. The object of this law probably was, to compel early marriages, to aid in settling the colony, and to prevent their keeping bad company.

As early as 1640 the General Court intended that the inhabitants should measure their apparel by the length of their purses—the Court being the judges. The constable in each town was ordered to take notice of all persons, and if he judged any persons exceeded their rank and condition in life, in their attire, to warn them to appear before the Particular Court to answer for the offence. All excess in the price of labor, in 1640–41, was expressly forbidden by law. All artificers and other laborers were priced, as well as the labor of horses and oxen. Most of the penalties attached to the criminal laws, were accompanied with flogging and pillory ; so much so that a law was enacted in 1643, which made it imperative upon all the towns on

9

Connecticut River to appoint a whipper to do execution upon offenders.

As Massachusetts and Plymouth were settled a few years earlier than Connecticut, and had become somewhat organized as a government, many of their laws were copied into the code of laws enacted by Connecticut. Labor and dress were regulated by law in those colonies before it was in this. Their laws upon these subjects were much more severe than in this jurisdiction. They had a law that ladies dresses should be made so long as to cover their shoe buckles. They prohibited short sleeves, and ordered the sleeves to be lengthened to cover the arms to the wrists. They forbid by law, immoderate great breeches, knots of ribbon, broad shoulder bands, silk roses, double ruffs and cuffs. Even as late as 1653, John Fairbanks was solemnly tried for wearing great boots. He probably shewed he was afflicted with corns on his toes, and therefore he could not comfortably wear small ones, as he was acquitted on trial. The colonies were poor, and it appears the object of the law was to prevent all kinds of extravagance, and to compel the inhabitants to govern their living, strictly by their means.

As there were no printing presses in the colony or country in the early settlement of Connecticut, the laws enacted at each session of the General Court, were promulgated to the inhabitants of each town, by copies of the laws being made out by the Secretary of the Colony, and sent to the constables of each town, and read by them at public meetings to the people. This inconvenient practice was continued in the Colony nearly forty years, until 1672. This year all the laws in force were prepared and sent to Cambridge to be printed, and bound with blank paper interspersed in the book, to enter the laws which should be afterwards enacted. It was a small folio. The book is now a curiosity of ancient days. Its introduction to the public is vastly better fitted for Watts's Psalms, than a code of laws. After the book was printed, the General Assembly ordered that every family in the Colony should have a law book. The blank pages in the book were not filled until nearly thirty years after. The New Haven Colony at a much earlier period, procured a code of laws to be printed for that Colony, of about 100 pages, entitled " New Haven's Settling in New England, and some Laws for Government; published for the use of that Colony." This early and first volume of laws was printed in London, for the New Haven Colony. I know of only two copies extant of the edition of 500 that were printed.

CHIMNEY VIEWERS.

As the office of Chimney Viewer is attached to the names of some of the first settlers, I take the liberty of explaining the cause. Immediately after the organization of the town of Hartford as a town, or rather as a company of land holders—a law was enacted that all chimneys should be cleansed by the owner once in a month, upon a penalty provided by law. Therefore that the law should be strictly obeyed and carried out by the inhabitants, for several years a committee of respectable men, (for no others held offices at that day) were appointed to see that all house-holders fully obeyed the law. It was also a law that each house-holder should provide a ladder for his house, where there was not a tree standing by his house which reached within two feet of the top of the chimney. This law also came within the duties of the viewers of chimneys.

At the time these laws were in force, men were selected to fill every office, high or low, with a single eye to the fact, that men who held the offices, should be of such standing in society, as the men should honor their offices, and not the offices the holders of them. To effect this object you find men who had filled a seat at the General Court, the next year filling the office of hayward or chimney viewer. It was this practice of our worthy ancestors, which caused an officer, either civil or military, who held any place of power, to hold on to his titles with a tenacity, that living or dead, he never lost them. You find them now upon ancient tomb-stones of more than 200 years standing, and upon the Colony, State and Town Records as far back as 1637. Even a sergeant or corporal never lost his title—they were entombed and recorded. These days existed before spoils-men were known in the land of steady habits, when the love of country was the primary object of all; and when political partizans were unknown in the Colony or country—when leading men were honest—when principles were of more importance to our country than party.

THE FIRST PURITAN SETTLERS

OF

WINDSOR.

The first settlers of Windsor were, Mr. John Warham, who laid the foundation of the church there, in 1635; Henry Wolcott, William Phelps, John Whitfield, Humphrey Pinny, Deacon John More, or Moore, Deacon Gaylord, Lieut. John Ffiler, Matthew Grant, Thomas Dibble, Samuel Phelps, Nathan Gillett, Jonathan Gillett, Richard Vere, or Vose, Abraham Randall, Brigget Egglestone, George Phelps, Thomas Ford and Jobe Drake.   Others arrived at different times until 1639, when the Rev. Ephraim Huit came from England and was settled as a colleague with Mr. Warham, at Windsor, in 1639. A part of his church came with him, viz Edward Griswold, John Bissell, Thomas Holcomb, Daniel Clark, and Peter Tilton.   On his way to Windsor he was joined in Massachusetts by others, who accompanied him, viz: Joseph Newbury, Timothy Loomis, John Loomis, John Porter, William Hill, James Marshall, John Taylor, Eltwed Pomeroy, William Hosford, Aaron Cook, Elias Parkham, Richard Aldage, Henry Stiles, John Stiles, William Hayden, George Phillips, Thomas Stoughton, Owen Tudor, Return Strong, Captain Mason, Matthew Allen, John Hillyer, Thomas Barber, Nicholas Palmer, Tho. Buckland, Isaac Selden, Robert Watson, Stephen Terre, Bray Rossiter, Thomas Dewey, William Hurlbut, Roger Williams, Thomas Bascomb, Nicholas Denslow, Thomas Thornton and Simeon Hoyt. Several of the last class had been to Connecticut before they came with Mr. Huit in 1639; but they may all be considered as the first Puritan settlers of Windsor.   Mr. Huit was spared to his people but a few years—he died in 1644.   Mr. Warham was continued longer with his church.   He lived to see much of the forest removed—roads made passable—a house for worship built—himself and family and friends comfortably situated in this new country—the two Colonies united, and the title of their lands confirmed, with his family rich in new land, and died in 1670, after a ministry there of about 35 years.

FIRST SETTLERS OF THE COLONY.

A.

ADAMS, ANDREW, of Hartford, school teacher for the town of Hartford, £16 per annum, 1643.

Adams, Jeremy, of H., 1639, to purchase corn with Capt. Mason of the Indians, in 1638—a juror and deputy.

Adams, John, Hartford, died in 1670—children, Rebecca, Abigail, Sarah, Jeremy, John, Jonathan, and one ensient.

Abbott, Robert, of Windsor, juror in 1640–41.

Abbott, Henry, of Wi., a servant man in 1640, fined £5 for selling a pistol and powder to an Indian.

Addies, William, of New London, 1660.

Allen, Nathaniel, of H., 1639.

Allen, John of H., 1645, secretary of the colony, and held many other places of honor and trust.

Allen, Thomas, of H., 1636, one of the first settlers.

Allyn, Samuel, of Wi., juryman, 1644, died in 1648.

Allyn, Matthew, of Wi., he was a man of high standing in the colony—held many town offices—was juror, deputy, magistrate, assistant, and a member of the congress of U. C. in 1660 and 1664. He died in Windsor in 1670. His children were, John, Thomas and Mary. Mary married Benjamin Newberry. He gave all his lands in Hartford to his son John as a marriage portion. He also had a grandson, Matthew Allyn—a granddaughter Mary Newberry, and another granddaughter, Mary Maudsley. He was the ancestor of the Hon. Job Allyn, of Windsor, and Timothy M. Allyn, Esq., of Hartford.

Alcocks, Thomas, of H., 1639.

Alcott, Abijah, 1658.

Abell, George, 1647.

Andrews, William, of H., 1639, original proprietor.

Andrews, Francis, of H., in the land division.

Andrews, William, of H., 1645, 1639.

Aiken, Joseph, 1648, viewer of chimneys and ladders.

Alexander, George, 1644.

Alford, Benedict, married Jane Newton, of Wi., 1640.

Alford, Alexander, married Mary Vere, or Vose, 1646.

Arnold, John, of H., 1639, in the division of lands. He died in '64, eft children, Josiah, Joseph, and Daniel—had a granddaughter, Mary Buck.

Ashley, Nicholas, lived at 30 Miles Island, and owned the little Island at the lower end of the cove, and a six acre lot towards Saybrook, supposed to be near Middletown.

Almer, Benedict, 1643.

Anadacom, Roger, 1643.

Abbot, George, 1648. ·

Askwood, 1641, a committee with Fowler and Cappe to settle the bounds between Poquonnuck and Uncoway.

Avery, James, of N. L., 1660.

B.

Bradford, Governor of Plymouth Colony. He united with Gov. Winslow in conferring with Gov. Winthrop, in 1633, about building a trading-house on Connecticut River, at Windsor, to deal with the Indians, and for commerce, and to prevent the Dutch taking possession of the River and land. Gov. Winthrop declined. Mr. Bradford was Governor in 1635, and wrote to the men who left Dorchester, a reprimand for settling at Windsor, Conn., as it was an injury to the Plymouth Colony, after they had purchased land, built a house there, and taken possession.

Brewster, Jonathan, 1648.

Boltwood, Robert, do.

Burnham, Thomas, do.

Basly, John, was in the land division in '39—died in '71—his children were, Mary Burr, Lydia and Elizabeth—Elizabeth married Mr. Peck.

Beale, Thomas, 1639, landholder.

Bloomfield, William, 1640.

Bridgeman, James, do.

Biddolph, John, do.

 Baldwin, Timothy, of Milford—died in '64, and left children, Mary, who married Benjamin Smith—Sarah married Mr. Buckingham—Hannah and Timothy.

Bacon, Andrew, was juror Sept. and Dec. 1641, and frequently afterwards. He was in Hartford at the division of lands in '39—was assistant of the General Court of the colony in 1637-8—was several times elected deputy to the General Court, and was a highly useful citizen. He was a committee with Mr. Steel and Boosy to provide in Hartford, for the comely meeting of the Commissioners of the United Colonies. He was frequently honored with offices of the town, and was selectman in 1640.

Burr, Jehu, one of a committee to collect money to aid students in Cambridge College in 1644, with Robert Band of S. Hampton—collector of rates at Agawam in 1637, and juror often.

Beaumont, William, of Saybrook, 1659.

Bushnell, William, of   do.   do.

Backus, William, 1663.

Brockway, Woolston, do.

Borden, John, 1664.

Burlant, Thomas, 1647.

Blackman, was a committee with Mr. Ludlow and Gov. Hopkins to settle the line at Uncoway.

Birchwood, Thomas, original proprietor, 1639.

Blumfield, William, proprietor in   do.

Buckland, Thomas, a juror in 1644.

Belden, Richard, 1643.

Boarman, William, 1645, of Wethersfield.

Barrett, Samuel,   do.

Barrows, Robert,   do.

Bramfield, William, do.

Beedle, Robert, whipt and branded in 1644.

Barlow, Thomas, juror in '45, settled in Fairfield county, and was the ancestor of Joel Barlow the Poet.

Bradfield, Lesly, 1643.

Beckwith, Matthew, fined 10 shillings for using ardents, 1639.

Bailies, Thomas, 1642.

Bissell, James, deputy, 1648.

Beardsley, William, deputy, 1649—went to Fairfield county.

Baradell, John, married Ann Denison, sister of Geo. Denison.

Beebie, John, 1662.

Blatchford, Peter, 1639—he moved to Haddam, where he died in 1671.   His children were, Peter, 4 years old, Joanna 5, and Mary 1.

Bartholomew, 1643.

Bassett, Peter, 1644.

Baker, Lanslet, shipwright, 1649.

Beckwith, Stephen,   do.

Bartlett, William,   do.

Blackleach,   do.

Bushmore, Thomas,   do.

Barley, Thomas,   do.

Billings, Richard, 1640.

Barnes, Mary, of Pequett.

Butler, William, 1639. He was brother of Richard—had a sister who married a Mr. West, in England—died in 1647 or 8, and left three score pounds to the church in Hartford. He had no family. He was one of the proprietors in the division of lands in 1639.

Buck, Emanuel, selectman of Wethersfield.

Buck, Enoch, of Wethersfield, 1648.

Bishop, John,   do.

Bennett, Joseph,   do.

Barding, Nathaniel, 1645.

Bush, James, a deputy to the General Court, 1640, also in '46.

Burr, John, a deputy in   do.   do.

Branger, Abigail, 1648.

Barber, Thomas, came to Windsor in 1639, with Rev. Mr. Huit—married in 1640.

Buckland, Thomas, came to Windsor in 1639, with Mr. Huit.

Bascomb, Thomas, came with the 2d colony to Windsor, in 1639—juror in '44.

Benjamin, Samuel, died in 1669, and left children, Mary, Abigail, and Samuel.

Banks, John, 1640, juror in '45.

Bancraft, Samuel, of Windsor, 1647.

Bradfield, Lesly, 1640.

Brundish, John, of Wethersfield, 1639—died in '40—left a widow, one son, and four daughters.

Beebe, John, 1662.

Burnham, Samuel, 1648, of Windsor.

Browning, Henry, 1639.

Brunson, Mary, wife of Nicholas Disborough, punished for improper conduct with I. Olmsted, J. Rudd and John Pierce, in 1639.

Brundish, Rachel, of Wethersfield, 1639.

Buckley, Enoch, of Wethersfield, 1648.

Bruen, Obadiah, town recorder of New London, 1653, 1662, assistant, and one of the principal men of N. L. He moved to New Jersey.

Bocker, William, 1640.

Birdge, Richard, Windsor, 1640—married Elizabeth Gaylord, '41.

Buell, William, 1640, after some years went to Litchfield county.

Bancraft, John, Windsor, 1645.

Buell, Samuel, Windsor, 1660.

Brown, Peter, married Mary Gillet, of Windsor.

Branker, John, 1640, '43.

Brooks, John, Windsor, juror in 1643.

Bul, Thomas, Lieut., 1637—one of the five brave men in the Pequott battle, to whom the General Court gave 500 acres of land for their valor. He found the gun of John Wood after he was murdered, marked on it I. W.—he found it when he was in pursuit of the Pequotts. He was juror, townsman, and held other offices of trust. He was the ancestor of the different families by that name in Hartford.

Beers, Thomas, 1645—constable of Hartford, 1647.

Bunce, Thomas, Hartford, 1645—a committee to view chimneys and ladders—resided in H. in 1639.

Barnard, Francis, 1646—viewer of chimneys and ladders.

Bassett, Thomas, 1643.

Bassaker, Peter, do.

Bissell, John, juror in 1640–43—came to Windsor in 1639—deputy and ferryman, in '40.

Blingfield, Peter, fined 5 shillings for not training, in 1644.

Blacklee, Thomas, 1641.

Barnard, John, 1634, selectman in '44, also in '46—deputy and juror in '42–3.

Barnard, Bartholomew,	Hartford,	1645.
Bigelow, Jonathan,	do.	do.
Brunson, John,	do.	1639.
Betts, Widow,	do.	do.
Bunce, John,	do.	do.
Barnes, John,	do.	do.
Burr, Benjamin,	do.	do.
Bearding, Nathaniel,	do.	do.
Blisse, Thomas, sen'r.	do.	do.
Blisse, Thomas, jr.	do.	do.

Butterfield, of Saybrook, was taken by the Indians and tortured to death by them, in October, 1636; and the meadow where he was taken was afterwards called Butterfield's meadow, and is so named until this day.

Bennett, John, 1639, whipt for bad conduct with Mary Holt.

Boosy, James, 1639, clerk of the train-band in '45, juror, deputy, assistant in '39, '41 and '42.

Barber, Thomas, 1637, apprentice to Geo. Stiles, made freeman, '45.

Betts, John, 1648.

Biddall, John, 1639—landholder.

Barnes, Thomas, 1639.

Butler, Richard, townsman of Hartford, 1644, juror in '43.

Baily, John, 1648, viewer of chimneys and ladders.

Blynman, Rev. Richard, came from Gloucester, and settled in New London, in 1643. He was the first minister of the town—several settlers had been there before and had left, but in 1648–9 there were about 40 families, which consisted of some of the best and most active men in the colony, viz: Gov. Winthrop, Thomas Minot, or Miner, Samuel Lathrop, James Avery and Robert Allyn. Mr. Winthrop, Thomas Minot and Samuel Lathrop, in '49, were formed into a court for Tawawag, for the trial of small causes. New London and what is now Groton, was called Pequott; soon after the name was changed to New London. Mr. Blynman was ordained there, and remained as their pastor about 10 years; he then went to New Haven, and from thence he returned to England.

Brooks, Thomas, who had moved to Haddam—died in 1668. His children were, Sarah, Thomas, Mary and Alice.

Bird, Thomas, Hartford, 1647.

Bartlett, Robert, Hartford, 1649, viewer of chimneys and ladders—freeman in '45.

Bascum, William, Wethersfield, 1636.

Birchard, juryman in 1639.

Banbury, Justus, died in 1672. Children, Elizabeth Plumb, Mrs. Butler, Hannah Cutler and Deborah Green.

Blackman, Adam, was ordained at Stratford about 1648, the town was settled about 1639. The principal men who first settled Stratford were, Mr. Fairchild, who was the first civil officer of the plantation, Samuel Hawly, William and John Curtiss went from Roxbury, Massachusetts; Joseph Judson and Timothy Wilcoxon were the leaders of the church and town of Stratford. After the town got started, John Birdseye removed there from Milford; Samuel Wells, of Wethersfield, also removed to Stratford, with his three sons, John, Thomas and Samuel. Mr. Blackman was eminently pious, and many of his church in England followed him and settled with him at Stratford.

Birdseye, John, resided in Stratford in 1645.

Boarman, Samuel, Wethersfield, died in 1673. He left a wife Mary, and children, Samuel, Joseph, John, Sarah, Daniel, Jonathan, Matthew, and Martha.

Bulkley, Gershom, Wethersfield, 1674.

Briant, Richard, 1674—went to Milford.

Berding, Nathaniel, Hartford—wife Abigail—son in law Thomas Spencer, Elizabeth wife of Samuel Andrews—children of Thomas Spencer, Sarah, Hannah, Mary, Martha, and Jerred Spencer—John and Thomas, sons of his wife Abigail.

3

Butler, Thomas, Hartford, 1645.
Buckingham, Thomas H. do.

C.

Cullick, John, was one of the original proprietors of the town of Hartford, in 1639. John Ince, who died at sea, was a landholder in Hartford ; his land the town settled upon Mr. Cullick. He was in the division of the town lots in 1639—was selectman and deputy in '44, secretary of the colony from '48 to '57, and assistant in '48. He married Elizabeth, the daughter of George Fenwick, Esq., of Saybrook. He was frequently a member of both houses of the Gen. Court—was a commissioner to the Colony Congress in 1652–3–5. After he removed to Boston, his wife being the heir to the estate of Geo. Fenwick, then deceased, the settlement of the estate with this colony, for the purchase of the lands on the Connecticut River, and the Fort, &c., devolved upon Mr. Cullick and Leverett, of Boston. Mr. Cullick died in Boston, in 1663, and left a large landed estate, and two children, John and Elizabeth. John Leverett possessed his lands in Hartford, after his decease. Upon the final adjustment of the different claims between the estate of Mr. Fenwick and the colony, a balance was found of about £500 in favor of the colony which was soon after appropriated by the General Court, for the expenses and charges of Gov. Winthrop, in his voyage to England, to procure the Charter or Patent for the Colony of Connecticut.

Clark, John, Hartford, 1642, surveyor of roads, land holder, deputy in 1649, juror, in '42, in land division '39.

Caloug, Nathaniel, or Kellogg, Hartford, 1639.

Chester, Mrs. Dorothy, owned land in do. do.

Crowe, John, Hartford, 1630, in division of lands.

Coles, James, do. do. do.

Clark, Nicholas, do. do. do.

Church, Richard, 1639, viewer of chimneys in '47—was an original settler, but moved to Hadley, Mass. He was the ancestor of Judge Church and most others of the name in the State.

Clark, William, Hartford, 1642, land holder, hired servant in '39.

Calder, Thomas, Hartford, 1645.

Catlin, Thomas, Hartford, 1646, viewer of chimneys and ladders, in '47, and constable in '62.

Carter, John, Hartford, 1645, in the division of lands in '39.

Chapin, Clement, deputy in 1639 and '42, in land division in '39.

Crabb, Richard, 1639 — was often deputy and assistant to the General Court, juror, &c., one of the principal men.

Coe, Robert, Wethersfield, 1636, with Andrew Ward, purchased in 1640, for a company, of New Haven, Rippowams.

Coop, Thomas, 1637 — an apprentice to Geo. Stiles, carpenter.

Chappel, George — apprentice to George Stiles in 1637.

Chalkwell, Edward, died in 1648.

Cornwell, Thomas, 1639 — fined 30 shillings for immoderate drinking — came to Boston with Thomas Hooker, Sept. 4, 1633, an eloquent divine.

Crosby, William, a white servant in 1641.

Clark, Henry, Windsor, 1642, often a deputy, assistant and juror — was a gentleman of high standing in the colony.

Cattell, John, deputy in 1642.

Chester, Leonard, a grand juror in 1642, juror in '43-4-5, captain in 1640.

Coleman, Thomas, 1639, juror in '41 and '45.

Craddock, Nathaniel, 1639.

Chapman, John, 1639.

Crowe, Philip, deputy to the General Court in 1642.

Cheesebrough, Samuel, New London, 1653.

Cook, Aaron, settled in Windsor in 1639, under Mr. Warham — juror in 1643.

Churchil, Joseph, juror in 1643.

Cook, Nathaniel, Windsor, 1645.

Clark, Daniel, came to Windsor in 1639, with Mr. Huit in the 2d colony.

Collins, Mary, Windsor, 1640.

Carter, Joshua,   do   do.

Cooper, Thomas,   do   do.

Coult, Joseph, Windsor, 1648.

Cook, Sarah, 1647.

Chaplin, in 1643, was fined £15 for signing a paper which defamed Mr. Smith, the minister of Wethersfield. An address was drawn up and read in each town in the colony, which exculpated Mr. Smith — and it was ordered if any one repeated or divulged any charges against him, after it was publicly read, he should be fined 40 shillings.

Carrington, John, 1644.

Coltman, John, 1645.

Cole, Susan,   do.

Cross, William, 1645 — a mariner, of Fairfield, '49.

Chaplin, Clement, was one of the noble band, who declared war in 1637, against the Pequotts — deputy in 1637, also in '42 and '43—assisted in settling Oldham's estate — treasurer in the colony in '37 — elder of the church in Wethersfield. He was the first treasurer of the colony — died in 1643.

Carter, Joseph, was a juror in 1643.

Comstock, Samuel, 1648.

Chappell, George, 1640.

Cook, Richard,   do.

Cables, John,   do.

Chapman, Edward, Windsor, died in 1675. His children were, Henry, 12 years old, Mary 10, Elizabeth 8, Simon 6, Hannah 5, Margaret 3, and Sarah 1.

Castle, John, died in 1641, and left some estate.

Curry, William, 1643.

Cappe, of Milford, 1641.

Chapman, R., Clark, G. and Capt. Mason, of Saybrook, were appointed to press men for a war expedition, in 1653.

Caulkins, G., and Capt. Denison, appointed in 1653 to press men at New London.

Chester, John, 1642 — juror.

Coleman, Ephraim, 1644 — juror.

Comstock, William, 1644.

Cynker, John,   do.

Cornwell, William, 1639.

Clark, Joseph, of Saybrook, made his will in Milford, in 1658, and died soon after.

Coake, Richard, 1648.

Chichester, owned a vessel in 1649.

Collins, Thomas, 1644.

Capell, John, 1649.

Curturs, or Curtis, John, 1645.

Cornell, William, 1640.

Cadwell, Thomas, constable in 1662.

Crowe, John, jr., died in 1667, wealthy.

Corbin, or Corby, William, died 1674. His children were, William, 18 years old, John 16, Mary 12, Samuel 9, and Hannah 6.

Coles, J., died in 1664.

Champion, Henry, 1664.

Coggen, John, 1640.

Colefax, William, 1645.

Curtiss, John, one of the early settlers of Stratford, in the colony of Connecticut, 1640.

Curtiss, William, 1640, one of the early settlers of Stratford.

Crump, Thomas, 1643.

Coldicot, Richard, 1646.

Carpenter, John,   do.

Codman,   do.

Carwithy,   do.

Chancut, Thomas, 1647.

D.

Day, Robert, Hartford. He was viewer of chimneys and ladders in 1643. He died in 1648, and left a comfortable estate for his widow and several children. He had been a good citizen in the colony. He was the first ancestor, who came to Connecticut, of President and Secretary Day, and of the Day family in this State.

Dewey, Thomas, came to Windsor in 1639, with Mr. Huit — died in '48. He left a good estate to his six children — Thomas, 8 years old, Josiah 7, Israel 3, Jedidiah an infant, Mary Clark 12, and Anna, 5 years old. He was juror in 1642 and '44 — was frequently a juror and deputy to the General Court.

Desborough, Nicholas, Hartford, 1639. He was an original and early settler — chimney and ladder viewer. He died in 1683, and left four children, Mrs. Obadiah Spencer, Mrs. Samuel Eggleston, Mrs. John Kelsey, and Mrs. Robert Flood.

Davey, Fuller, Hartford, 1639.

Davis, Philip, Hartford, 1645.

Daggett, 1640.

Dibble, Abraham, died at Haddam.

Deane, Thomas, 1643.

Daniels,   do.

Denslow, Elizabeth, Windsor — died in 1669. One of her daughters married Nicholas Buckland, and had children, Nicholas, Hannah, and Temperance; another daughter married Edward Adams; another daughter Joanna, married Mr. Cook, and had children, Elizabeth, Samuel and Noah.

Daves, Stephen, 1646.

Davis, John, 1647.

Diggins, Jeremiah, Windsor, 1648.

Davie, Even, left Hartford, but was an early settler.

Dickinson, Nathaniel, grand juror in 1642–43–44, also deputy.

Denison, George, captain, New London, 1660.

Denison, John, son of George, married Ann Lay, daughter of Robert Lay of Six Mile Island, 1665–6.

Denison, Elizabeth, New London, 1660.

Drake, Job, one of the puritans who came to Windsor in 1635–6.

Drake, Job, jr., married Mary Wolcott, of Windsor, in 1646.

Drake, John, married Hannah Moore, in 1648 — juror in '43.

Drake, Jacob, married Mary Bissell, all of Windsor, 1649.

Dibble, Thomas, came to Windsor in 1635, in the first colony.

Dewey, Thomas, jr., married Frances Clark, of Windsor, in 1638.

Deynton, 1640.

Demmon, or Deming, John, Wethersfield, 1636. He was at an early period one of the principal men in the town and colony. He was frequently upon the jury, and grand jury, selectman, and deputy to the General Court, and assistant.

Dyke, Leonard, 1645.

Deming, Thomas, 1649.

Day, Stephen,   do.

Doxy, Thomas,   do.

Dement, Thomas, a deputy in 1648.

Denison, William, 1647 — moved to Pequott.

Denslow, Nicholas, came to Windsor with Mr. Huit, in 1639. He died in 1667, and one of his daughters married Timothy Buckland.

E.

Endicott, John, arrived in New England in 1629, with 300 settlers, and located at Salem, which was the first town settled in Massachusetts. Capt. Endicott, (with 90 men) was sent from Boston, in 1636, to avenge the murderers of Oldham, Norton and Stone, who had been killed by the Indians. The Narragansetts had restored the two boys taken from Mr. Oldham, and made such satisfaction as had been accepted by the English — but no compensation had been made by the Block Island & Pequott Indians. Mr. Endicott was therefore ordered to go to Block Island and put all the men to the sword — to spare the women and children, and take possession of the Island; after which to go and demand of the Pequotts the murderers of Captain Stone, Norton and others who had been murdered on Connecticut River — to demand of them several of their children as hostages, and 1000 fathoms of wampum for damages, for the delivery of the murderers, and if refused, to take them by force of his arms. The Indians at Block Island at first resisted their landing, but at a show of their arms the Indians took to the woods, thickets and swamps, and could not be found ; but the troops burnt their wigwams, destroyed their corn, broke their canoes, and then sailed for Pequott. When arrived, they informed the Pequotts the object of their visit—many gathered upon the shore, and as soon as they had withdrawn, they shot arrows at them. Endicott burnt their wigwams, killed a few of them, and returned to Boston in September, all well. The names of Endicott and Indicott are the same, as Capt. Endicott was the ancestor of Mr. William Indicott, of this city, upon the male line of his ancestry—and the change has grown out of some strange fancy—as it has in the name of Hurlbut, which is the original name, yet it is spelt by some of the name, Hollabird, Hollaburt and Holleburd.

Ely, Nathaniel, Hartford, 1635—a constable in 1639—townsman in '44, also in'49—juror in '43—was in the division of land in '39. He was one of the settlers of Norwalk, but afterwards removed to Springfield, Mass. He was a loss to the colony.

Elmer, Edward, Hartford, 1639—land holder.

Eldridge, Nathaniel, Hartford, 1642. Children, David, Joseph, Mary wife of William Smith—grandchildren, Mary, Sarah and John Rockwell.

Ensign, James, Hartford, 1639—constable in '45, also in '48—one of the original settlers. Died in 1670.

Easton, Joseph, Hartford, an original proprietor in 1639.

Edwards, William, Hartford, 1647.

Edwards, Richard,   do.   1645.

Edwards, Joseph,   do.   1650.

Edwards, Edward, 1645.

Edwards, John—juror and deputy in 1643, juror in '40—died in '64, at Wethersfield. His children were, Thomas, John, Easter, Ruth, Hannah, Joseph, and Lydia.

Edmand, John, censured by the court in 1639.

Eggleston, Brigget, one of the first Puritans who settled Windsor with Mr. Warham in 1635—land holder—died in '74. Children, Benjamin, Joseph, James, Samuel, Thomas, Mary, Sarah and Abigail.

Eggleston, Thomas, son of Brigget Eggleston, Windsor, 1645.

Eggleston, James, 1645, son of Brigget.

Eason, John—juror in 1644.

Enno, or Enos, James, Windsor, 1640.

Elmore, Samuel, 1645.

Edwards, John, Hartford—died in 1675.   He left no children—
was a brother of Joseph Edwards.

Edson, John, 1644—juror.

Ewe, John, in 1643 the jury found he had been the cause of the
death of Thomas Scott by misadventure, and he was fined £5 to the
country, and £10 to the widow Scott.

Evans, John, 1645.

Elson, John, on the jury, in 1645–6.

Elson, Abraham, Wethersfield—died in 1648.

Ellison, Laurence, 1643.

Elsworth, John, 1646.

Eggleston, Hester, married by major John Pynchion, son of William
Pynchion, of Springfield, in 1684.

Eaves, John, 1643.

Ellyt, or Eliot, William, 1646.

F.

Fenwick, George, Esq., was a gentleman of character in England,
and was one of the proprietors of the River Patent with Sir Richard
Saltonstall and others, who sent John Winthrop from England as agent
of the company of Lords Say and Seal, Brook and others, to build a
fort at the mouth of Connecticut River in 1635.   The company appointed Mr. Winthrop not only an agent for the above named purpose,
but appointed him Governor for one year after his arrival, of the river
Connecticut, and of the harbors and places adjoining.   Mr Fenwick
within a short time after came to the Fort (Saybrook), but for several
years did not acknowledge the territory over which he had control as
strictly under the government of the Connecticut colony.   Though
the fort at the mouth of the river was a great protection to the river
towns, against the Dutch and Indians, yet Mr. Fenwick gave great
trouble to the Connecticut colony, by offering to sell not only the Fort,
but all the lands of the company upon the river, to the Dutch.   In
1644 an agreement was made by the Connecticut colony with Mr.
Fenwick for the purchase of the fort, guns, &c. ; also that all the lands
upon the Connecticut River should be under the jurisdiction of the
Connecticut colony.   The mode of payment having failed in some
measure on the part of the colony—a second contract, or an alteration of the first took place in Feb. 1646, when it was agreed that the
colony should pay to Mr. Fenwick, or his assigns, for the term of ten
years, £180 per annum—one third in good wheat, at 4 shillings—one

third in peas, at 3 shillings and 2 pence — one third in rye or barley at 3 shillings per bushel, with some other considerations. In 1644 he was made an assistant. In 1642 the General Court requested Mr. Fenwick to unite with the Connecticut colony, in answering letters which had been received by the colony from some Lords in England. In 1639, Mr. Fenwick was nominated for a magistrate in the colony, and was to have been appointed the next April, provided he should then be a freeman of the colony of Connecticut. He was afterwards a magistrate, and was an assistant in the General Court, in 1644–5–6–7 and 8. He was twice a member of the Colony Congress, in 1643 and 1644 — was also appointed on several important committees by the General Court at different times. The first few years of his residence at the Fort (Saybrook) he was not a favorite of the colony, but after he disposed of his lands and the fort to the colony, he was shown all the honors and favors due him from Connecticut. No taxes had been paid by the inhabitants at the fort, or in Saybrook, to the colony, until after the fort and lands were sold by Mr. Fenwick to Connecticut, in 1644, as the town had been entirely independent of the colony. Many of the inhabitants of Windsor and Hartford moved to Saybrook in 1646–7. After this Mr. Fenwick was much noticed in the colony. In 1643, the object so much desired by the colonists of Connecticut and New Haven, viz: the Union of all the New England Colonies in a General Congress was effected, and met at Boston for the first time; Gov. Haynes and Mr. Hopkins appeared there for Connecticut, and Mr. Fenwick from Saybrook, represented his own jurisdiction.— Amongst the many salutary provisions contained in the Articles of Confederation of the United Colonies, it was provided, that each colony should send to their conventions two Commissioners only, who should in all cases be members of the church. At the time of the death of Mr. Fenwick, the purchase of the fort and the lands upon the River, had not been closed between the contracting parties — and was afterwards closed by his son-in-law Mr. Cullick, whose wife was the principal legatee of the personal property of her father.

Fenwick, Mrs. Mary, was slandered by Bartlett, in 1646; for which he was ordered to stand in the Pillory during Lecture, whipt, fined £5 with six months imprisonment. This was not the day to speak evil of dignitaries.

Friend, John Hartford, 1639, an early settler—ancestor of F. Humphrey, of Albany, on the female side.

Field, Zachery, Hartford, 1639—viewer of chimneys in '49—in the land division in '39.

Fellows, Richard, 1648, Hartford—made a freeman in '45, collector for Cambridge students in '44, and often a juror.

Fitch, Samuel, Hartford, 1645.

Foster, Nathaniel, Wethersfield, 1637—furnished by order of court, 20 pounds of butter, and 50 pounds of cheese, for the war against the Pequotts.

Finch, Daniel, constable of Wethersfield in April, 1636 — aided in settling John Oldham's estate in '36.

Ford, Thomas, settled in Windsor, with Mr. Warham, in '36, elected deputy in '37–8–9 and '40 to the General Court, grand juror in '43, juror in '44.

Ffiler, Walter, Lieut., one of the first settlers of Windsor,—came from Cambridge with Mr. Warham, in 1635, deputy in '47, juror in '40, '42, '44.

Fitch, Joseph, 1655.

Fowler, Ambrose, 1646, married Jane Alford, both of Windsor.

Filly, Eddy, Windsor, 1640.

Filley, William, 1640.

Finch, John, Wethersfield, was killed by the Indians in 1637.

Fryes, Michael, 1640.

Foot, Nathaniel, deputy in 1641 from Wethersfield, juror in '43–44, and died in '44. He left a widow and five children, viz : Nathaniel 24 years old, Robert 17, Francis 15, Sarah 12, and Rebecca 10.

Fish, Ruth, 1645.

Fitch, Rev. James, Saybrook, 1646.

Fitch, William, 1647.

Franklin, William, 1649.

Flye, Robert,   do.

Fetchwater, John, 1653.

Fuller, Elizabeth, 1646.

Fisher, Thomas, 1639— forfeited his lands in Hartford.

Flood, Robert, married Abigail Disbrough, of Hartford, 1646.

Ffayrchild, Thomas, a deputy in 1646—one of the first and principal settlers of Stratford.

Frink, Charles, 1644.

Fynch, Abraham, 1640.

Fenner, Thomas, deceased in 1647.

Fford, Nathaniel, a grand juror in 1643.

Ffishe, Windsor, 1642.

Fish, William, 1646.

Ferris, Jeffery, juror in 1639.

Ferris, Peter, Fairfield, 1662 — was made a freeman with Richard · Hardy, John Green, Joseph Mead, Richard Webb and Joseph Weed.

Fowler, Ambrose, 1641, one of the committee to settle the bounds of Uncoway and Poquonnuck.

G.

Gallup, John, in passing by water from Connecticut to Boston, discovered John Oldham's vessel filled with Indians, and several Indians in a canoe carrying goods from the vessel — he hailed them, but received no answer. He at once suspected they had murdered Mr. Oldham; he bore down upon them, and though he had but three with him, two of them boys, yet being a bold and daring man, he fired duck shot so fast and thick, that the deck was soon cleared. Some of the Indians jumped overboard, others crowded below, and some hid under the hatches; but Capt. Gallup run down with a brisk gale upon her quarter, and gave the vessel so severe a shock, that those who leaped overboard were drowned. He repeated running against the vessel twice or thrice, and upon the third shock, other Indians leaped into the water and were drowned. He then boarded the vessel, and bound two of them, and threw one overboard ;— two or three were in a small room in the cabin, armed with swords — these he could not drive out—(he probably fastened them in)—and he found on board the corpse of Mr. Oldham, with his head split and his body badly bruised and mangled; he cast the body into the sea, and took Mr. Oldham's vessel in tow, after stripping off her rigging, and put what few valuables the Indians had left, on board of his vessel; he set sail, but night coming on and a high wind, she was set adrift, with the Indians on board; she of course soon went to pieces. This was unquestionably the first man by the name of Gallup that came into the colony, and he proved himself a brave ancestor to those now in the country.— Capt. Gallup was educated in a military school in Holland, and rumor has said he was in Holland with Major Mason, and that they were intimate friends after they arrived in this country.—*Colony Rec. and Dr. Trumbull.*

Gaylord, Lay, married Elizabeth Hull, of Windsor, 1646.

Gaylord, Samuel, 1640.

Gibbs, Giles, Windsor, 1640 — his children were, Gregory, Samuel, Benjamin, Sarah and Jacob.

Gibbs, Francis, 1640.

Gunn, Thomas, Windsor, 1643—juror in '44, and often afterwards.

28

Gardner, David, came to the Fort at Saybrook, in 1635, and was the principal architect and builder of the fort, and buildings erected under the care of Mr. Winthrop. Being an engineer he not only assisted in building, but planned the fort, and was afterwards made a Lieutenant there. He was induced to come to New England for the Company, by the Rev. Mr. Davenport, who afterwards settled at New Haven.

Gould, of Fairfield, 1658 — one of the principal men — in '60 he with Hill and Knowles were appointed to settle the affair of Norwalk and the Indians.

Goodrich, John, fined 40 shillings for signing a paper defaming the Rev. Mr. Smith.

Green, Bartholomew, left Hartford, and forfeited his land — which fell to John Crowe.

Gray, Walter, 1644.

Griswold, Matthew, first of Windsor, afterwards at Saybrook — deputy in 1649. He with the Deputy Governor were ordered to loan to N. London, two great guns and shot from the fort. He was in court in '47, and deputy and assistant frequently. In 1662, he with Thomas Tracy and James Morgan, were appointed to aid and establish the bounds of New London, assisted by the most able man in N. London, by order of court. The same year Mr. Griswold had a severe lawsuit with Reinold Marvin, concerning a large number of horses. The arbitrators awarded that one-half the horses should be equally divided between them, and the other half should go to the colony, and Marvin should look them up, and appointed a committee to sell the horses and execute the award. (The arbitrators must at least have resided at *Dutch Point*, if they were not Dutch justices). Mr. Griswold was the ancestor of Gov. Griswold, and many of the leading men of Connecticut, viz: Griswolds, Parsons and Wolcotts.

Green, John, a freeman in Fairfield, in 1662.

Gilbert, Jonathan, Hartford, 1635 — came in the first colony. In '46 he took the place of Thomas Stanton as interpreter. In '53 he had liberty of Hartford to build a ware-house at the little meadow landing. He held several offices in the colony — was the first collector of customs at Hartford, in '59 — was marshal of the colony—appointed in '62 to keep a tavern at his house at Cold Spring, to relieve travellers. In the same year the colony granted him a farm of 300 acres.

Gifford, John, one of the committee who declared war against the Pequotts in 1637 — died in '68.

Goodwin, William, deacon, was one of the first settlers in Hartford. He was one of the purchasers of the town for a company, of the Indians; he also purchased large tracts of land up the river; he aided in some measure in purchasing Farmington. Being an elder in Mr. Hooker's church, he was as active in matters of the church, as he was in the affairs of the town and colony. In '44, as no gallery had been built in the church, he was appointed to build it, and stairs to enter it. In '39 he with Mr. Stone, deacon Chaplin and George Hubbard, were appointed by the General Court, " to gather those passages of God's providence, which had been remarkable, since the first undertakings of the Plantations, and report them to the General Court." In the early part of the settlement, he was one of the most active as well as useful settlers in the colony. During the great dissension in the church at Hartford, which lasted for a considerable period of time, and caused much anxiety not only to the church in Hartford, but to all the churches in New England; for some cause about this time deacon Goodwin moved his family to Hadley, but afterwards returned into the colony, and died at Farmington in '73. He left a large estate to a daughter, his only child; she afterwards married John Crowe, of Hartford. The Crowe family has now become extinct in the colony.

Goodman, Richard, Hartford, 1639, was townsman in 1641 and in '46 — surveyor of common lands and fences in '47 — fence viewer in '49 — member of the civil court in '37 — juror in '43 and '45, and held other offices. He was a valuable citizen.

Gibbins, William, Hartford, 1639 — land holder, selectman in '42, constable in '46, also in '39, juror in '43, often deputy and juror — an active and useful man.

Goodwin, Hosea, Hartford, 1639.

Garwood, Daniel, do. do.

Griffin, John, married Ann Bancraft, of Windsor, in 1647. In '63 he satisfied the General Court that he invented the art of making pitch and tar. The Court gave him 200 acres of land, where he could find it not taken up, between Massacoe and Waranock, including 40 acres of meadow, as a present for his invention.

Gardiner, Samuel, fined 10 shillings for insulting the watch in 1644.

Gower, 1641.

Graves, Philip, deputy in 1646 and '48 —removed to Stratford, and was one of the court there in '54.

Gridley, Thomas, Windsor, 1639 — was surveyor of highways in '48, strong suspicions of drunkenness, refused to watch, struck Stiles and ordered to be whipped in '39, at Hartford, for the offence.

Gibbs, Joseph, committee to the General Court, in 1637 — one of the first colony to Windsor in '35, with Mr. Warham's church.

Gibbs, John, appointed to treat with Indians for corn.

Goff, came to Boston, September 4, 1633.

Gildersleve, Richard, of Hartford or Wethersfield, 1636,—deputy at New Haven from Stamford in '43.

Gilbert, Joseph, 1645.

Grant, Matthew, settled in Windsor in 1635, in the first colony — held several offices.

Grant, Seth, a land holder in 1639.

Griswold, Edward, settled with Mr. Huit in Windsor, in 1639.

Goodman, Richard, Hartford, married Mary Terre, of Windsor, in 1649.

Goodwin, Nathaniel, Hartford, 1645, cobbler.

Graves, George, Hartford, 1649 — townsman, deputy in '46, was in the land division in '39, and died in '73. Children, John, Josiah — Deming son-in-law, Mary Dow, and Priscilla Marcum.

Grimes, Henry, Hartford, 1645.

Gaylord, William, deacon — was one of the first colony to Windsor — was committed to the General Court in 1639, in April, August, and in September and January, '42, and frequently afterwards; died in '73. He left sons Walter and Samuel — Mrs. Birge, Mrs. Elizabeth Hoskins — grandsons, John Birge, and Hezekiah Gaylord.

Gregory, E., Windsor, 1641.

Gridley, Thomas, Windsor, 1639 — land holder.

Gutteridge, John, 1646.

Gennings, Joshua, do.

Gree, Henry, 1647.

Gymnys, John, do.

Gates, William, 1646.

Garrit, Daniel, 1640—jailor or prison-keeper at Hartford, in '54, and was the first that kept the new jail.

Graham, Henry — surveyor of ways in Hartford, in 1662.

Goodrich, William, lived in Wethersfield in 1664 — he came early.

Geffers, Gabriel, died in 1664.

Goodfellow, Thomas, 1639.

Ginnings, John, do.

Greenhill, Samuel — died early.

Grouts, G., appointed with G. Thornton to press men in Stratford, in 1653.

Griswold, Samuel, died in 1672.

Gunn, Jasper, 1648. He was a physician, for which he was exempted from training in '57.

Gibbs, Gregory, 1649.

Goodheart, Isbrand, 1650.

Goffe, Philip, Wethersfield, died in 1674—children, Jacob 25 years old, Rebecca 23, Philip 21, Moses 18, and Aaron 16.

Gardiner, B., 1648.

H.

Harrison, John, Wethersfield, died in 1664—children, John 22, Joseph, Thomas, Mary and Sarah.

Hallaway, John, 1640—viewer of chimneys in '48.

Hallet, James, 1644.

Hastlewood, Richard, mariner in 1649.

Hayes, Jacob, 1649.

Hawley, Samuel, one of the settlers in Stratford in 1640.

Hart, Stephen, deputy in 1646–48–49.

Haward, Robert, 1649.

Hammon, William, 1640.

Hawks, John, Windsor, 1640.

Hawkins, Anthony, first of Windsor—he moved to Farmington, and died there in 1673. Left Ann, his widow—and children, John 22, Ruth 24, Sarah 16, Elizabeth 14, and Hannah 12 years of age.

Harvey, Edward, deputy in 1646, juror in '47.

Hale, Nathaniel, 1645.

Hale, John, made a freeman in 1645, surveyor of highways in '44.

Hardy, Richard, a freeman in Fairfield in 1642.

Hall, John, Hartford, 1639—collector of customs at Middletown, in 1659.

Hall, John, jr., Middletown—a carpenter—died in 1673, aged 89.

Hall, Thomas, Hartford, 1639, viewer of chimneys in '45.

Hale, Samuel, Hartford, 1639—juror twice in '43—and in '45 was fined 30 nobles for drinking ardents contrary to law.

Haynes, Joseph, Hartford, 1644.

Hayden, William, Windsor, 1639—came in the 2d colony in '39—juror in '43; he was frequently a juror, deputy and assistant.

Harris, Richard, Wethersfield, 1644.

Harwood, James, 1647.

Hews, John, Hutchinson, Edward, and Richard Smith were appointed selectmen for Westchester (now in the State of N. Y.) at Smith's trading house, in July, 1663. Richard Smith, jr., was appointed constable, and sworn by Richard, sen'r, by order of the General Court—and the place was named Wickford—and was taken under the jurisdiction of Connecticut; which was effected by John Talcott, Esq., as agent of the General Court.

Hemsted, Richard, Hartford, 1644.

Heyton, William, Hartford, 1639.

Heyton, Thomas, 1642.

Hewit, John, 1645.

Hillyer, Benjamin, 1648.

Hillyer, John, Windsor, came in 1639 with Mr. Huit.

Higley, Edward, 1649.

Higginson, John, Pastor at the Fort, in Saybrook in 1638—land holder in Hartford in '39.

Hill, William, Windsor, came in the 2d colony in 1639. Was appointed in '39, to view arms and military provisions in each town—deputy in '39–41 and '44—auditor of public accounts in '39; after which he was assistant—and collector of customs at Fairfield, in '59. He was a prominent man in the colony.

Hill, Luke, Windsor, 1651.

Hills, William, Hartford, constable of Hartford in 1644—fined £4 for burying a gun and breaking open the cobler's hogshead in '40.

Higginson, John, Hartford, 1642.

Hitchcock, Luke, a juror in 1649.

Hoyt, Walter, Windsor, 1640.

Hoyt, or Hoyette, Simon, 1639—came to Windsor in the 2d colony in '39.

Hoyt, Nicholas, Windsor—married Susannah Joyce in 1646.

Horton, William, 1645.

Holton, William, was in the division of land in Hartford, in 1639.

Hopkins, William, assistant in 1641–2.

Hopkins, Thomas, Hartford, 1639.

ERRATA.

On page 5th, where speaking of Rev. Henry Smith having the charge of the church at Wethersfield, in 1636, I should have stated they had no ordained minister. Mr. Smith *was not* installed or ordained over the church at Wethersfield until about 1640 or '41. Peter Prudden, who was ordained at Milford in 1640, preached at Wethersfield in 1638. He was preparing, in 1638, to locate at Milford as soon as a sufficient number of settlers had moved there from New Haven and other places. It appears from all the facts which can be gathered, that no regular preaching was had at Wethersfield until the ordination of Mr. Smith, as he was the first ordained minister there.

Hopkins, Edward, Governor—was born at Shrewsbury in England, in 1600. He was a merchant by profession and practice, in London, and came to New England with Mr. Davenport who settled at New Haven in 1638. If Mr. Hopkins made any stay at New Haven, it could not have been long, as he was a member of the Committee of the General Court of Connecticut in 1638. This was his first appearance officially in the Colony. When the General Assembly convened in April, 1639, under the Articles of the Confederation of Hartford, Windsor and Wethersfield, Mr. Hopkins appeared as one of the house of magistrates, and the same year was chosen Secretary of the Colony, and performed the duties of both offices. At this time no man in the Colony was more popular than Mr. Hopkins. In 1643-5-7-9 and 1651 and '53, he was elected Deputy Governor of the Colony, and in 1640-4-6-8-1650-2 and 4 he was Governor of the Colony, and performed the duties of the high, honorable and responsible offices in which he had been so early placed to the satisfaction of the people. In 1643 he was a Committee with Major General Mason and Mr. William Whiting to press men to defend Uncas with arms. He was united with Gov. Haynes to form a combination with Massachusetts. He was one of a Committee of seven to build the first vessel in the Colony. He was one of the Committee of three persons to consult with the Elders concerning the sin of cursing father or mother, incorrigibleness, banishment and contempt of ordinances, lying and breach of promise, and to form laws against such offences. This was probably the Committee who formed the code of Criminal Laws of 1642, punishing twelve different offences with death, most of which laws remain in the statutes of Connecticut, with such alterations in language and punishments as the times have required. He was elected a member of the United Colony Congress in 1643-44-46-57-48-49 and 1651.

The General Court were uniformly liberal to all their public officers, and gave them lands, and bestowed upon them privileges denied to others. The General Court gave to Gov. Hopkins the exclusive trade in beaver with the Indians at Waranock, and at all places up the Connecticut River for the term of seven years.

Governor Hopkins was not only one of the best, but one of the most able and efficient men in the new world at that day. He finally returned to England, and died in London, March, 1657, aged 57 years. He had disposed of his property in New England, by will, to public and charitable uses—£1000 of which he gave for the support of grammar schools at Hartford and New Haven, and this fund is yet kept entire for the worthy object for which it was given by the testator. Those who have received their instruction under this liberal bounty of Gov. Hopkins, even at this late period, will not forget their liberal benefactor.

Hopkins, John, Hartford, 1639, selectman in '40—in the land division in '39—juror in '43. The name of Hopkins has been respectable in the colony from its first settlement.

Hancock, George, 1663.

Hanford, Rev. Thomas, the first minister at Norwalk, 1654.

Howell, John, deputy in 1662—assistant and magistrate.

Hosmer, Thomas, Hartford, was constable in 1636, '39 and '63—selectman in '42 and '46—often a juror and deputy—once fined 5 shillings for being tardy on the jury, and was a magistrate in '47. He was several sessions a member of both houses of the General Court. He was a gentleman of good standing in the town and colony. He was the ancestor of Stephen Hosmer, Esq., and of Chief Justice Hosmer, deceased, and of the Hosmer family of Hartford. He was a brother of James, of Concord, Mass., and came from the county of Kent, in England. James came with his wife and two children in the ship Elizabeth to Massachusetts, from England, and settled at Concord.

Hosmer, Stephen, Hartford, 1674.

Hayes, Nicholas, Windsor, married in 1646, and had sons, Samuel, Jonathan, David and Daniel—perhaps son of Jacob.

Hoskins, Anthony, married Isabel Bowen, in 1656—children, Isabel, John, Robert, Anthony, Rebecca, Grace, Jane, Thomas and Joseph.

Hoskins, John, Windsor—he was a Committee to the Gen. Court in 1637. He died in '48, and left a widow and son Thomas, with a fair estate for his family. He was probably the same who was admitted freeman in Massachusetts in '31 or '34.

Hoskins, Thomas, Windsor, married Elizabeth Birge—died in 1666, and left a son John, and a widow, who died in '75. He came from Dorchester early to Windsor.

Hillyer, John, (in No. 1,) resided in Windsor near the mill south of Little River—was in Windsor as early as 1640. He was the ancestor of those of the name in Granby, Hartford, and other towns in the State. Left children, John, Mary, Timothy, James, Andrew, Simon, Nathaniel, Sarah, and Abigail, who was born in 1654. He died in 1655 or '56.

Harris, Daniel, Lieutenant, 1660.

Howlton, Josiah.

Huntington, Thomas, is found first upon the land record at Windsor, in 1656—he probably came there some time before. He left Windsor and moved to Saybrook, and at or after the settlement of Norwich he moved there. Thomas is the only one of the name who came into the colony before 1663.

Huntington, Simon, or Simeon, made free under the Charter, 1663.

Houltan, William, Hartford, 1639.

Hart, John, died in 1666, and left a son and other children. He probably came from Cambridge, and the son of Stephen who came to Hartford before 1639. Constable in '64.

Hart, John, Farmington, juror in 1730, supposed son of Stephen.

Hart, Thomas, made free under the Charter, 1663.

Henbury, Arthur, land record, Windsor, 1669.

Holmes, William.   In 1633–4 he resided in Plymouth, Mass., and was about to erect a trading-house on the Connecticut River, (in the present town of Windsor.)   He procured the frame, boards, and other things necessary to put up a house, and put them on board a vessel, and with his men sailed for Connecticut.   He held a commission from the Governor of Plymouth to accomplish the work.   When he had gone up the river as far as Dutch Point, where Hartford now is, he found the Dutch were before him, and had made a small fort, and had planted two cannon.   The Dutch officer forbid Holmes passing, and ordered him to strike his colors, or he should fire upon them.   Holmes replied, he had a commission from the Governor to go up the river, and passed the fort without injury or a gun's being fired.   He soon landed his materials and put up the house a little below the mouth of Little River, in Windsor.   It was fortified with palisadoes.   The land where the house was erected was immediately afterwards purchased of the Indians.   This was the first house built in the colony.—*Dr. Trumbull.*

Hale, Thomas, Hartford, in 1639—was viewer of chimneys in '45. John, 1644.   Nathaniel, 1645.

Hall, Richard, had his cider stolen by three men in 1664, each was fined £2 for the offence.

Hall, John, Hartford, 1639, (in No. 1,) moved to Middletown, died 1673.   Son Richard had children, Samuel and John, Sarah his daughter married Thomas Wetmore.

Hall, John, Middletown, grand juror 1661—perhaps son of Stephen.

Hall, Timothy, is found on Windsor land record, 1664.

Hull, Cornelius, deputy in 1663.

Hardy, Richard, Fairfield county, made free in 1662—supposed of Stamford.

Haughton, Morton, at New London in 1662.

Haughton, William, Hartford, 1649.

Humphrey, Michael, 1645, in the land record, Windsor.   Married P. Grant, 1647.   Children, John, Mary, Samuel, Martha, Sarah, Abigail and Hannah.   As he was the only person of the name who came early into the colony, he was probably the ancestor of those of the name in Simsbury, Granby and other parts of Connecticut, and of the Hon. Friend Humphrey, of Albany.

Hyde, William, Hartford, surveyor of highways in 1641—he was in the colony in 1639.

Hyde, Humphrey, Windsor, 1640—on land record of Windsor.

Hayward, Robert, Windsor record, 1643—probably Howard.

Hosford, William, came to Windsor early—he was Committee to the General Court in 1637.

Hull, Josias, formerly of Windsor—was made free in 1662, from Fairfield county.

Haynes, John, Governor—came from Essex, England, to New England, in 1633, with Rev. Thomas Hooker and others. He located first in Massachusetts, where he was made a freeman in 1634, and as he had been known in England as a gentleman of high standing, by many of the settlers in the new colony, he was the same year elected an assistant, and the following year was made Governor of the colony. It has been stated by some historians that Gov. Haynes removed to Hartford in 1636, but his first appearance, upon the record is, that at the November General Court of 1637, he was a member of that Court, and presided over their deliberations, for the first time. He continued president of the House of Magistrates during the remainder of 1637, and the whole of 1638. Mr. Ludlow had uniformly presided at the General Court from its formation until Gov. Haynes was placed in his seat in November, 1637. At the time of the organization of the Colony Government in 1639, by Articles of Confederation by the towns of Windsor, Hartford and Wethersfield, Mr. Haynes was chosen the first Governor of Connecticut, in April, 1639. He resided in Hartford, and continued to be elected alternately Governor of the colony eight years, viz. in 1639–41–3–5–7–9–1651 and '53. He was also elected Deputy Governor in 1640–4–6–1650 and '52. Previous to the year 1647 no salary had been allowed or claimed for performing the duties of governor, but the services had been rendered entirely for the good of the public. But in 1647 a law was enacted giving the governor of the colony an annual salary of £30. The General Court were liberal to Gov. Haynes, and though there was a great scarcity of money, so much so that they were obliged to resort to wampum for a circulating medium in business, and at one time made wheat and peas a lawful tender for debts, yet they were rich in public lands. And in 1642 the General Court made a grant of 1000 acres of land in the Pequott country to Gov. Haynes. The same year he was appointed with Mr. Hopkins to go to the Bay, to intercede for a combination of the New England colonies. During the year 1642 he was associated with Mr. Whiting and others to build a ship by the aid of the towns. In 1639 he was appointed by the General Court with a large committee, to agitate the business of another Indian war (against the Quinnipiacs,) with power to press 20 arms, 2 shallops and 2 canoes for the service ; and 40 men had been ordered to be raised in the three towns upon Connecticut River. In 1640 Gov. Haynes and William Goodwin, as agents for the town of Hartford, purchased Farmington of the Indians, which included Southington, and was bounded West upon the Mohawk country. In 1641 he was one of a Committee to consult with George Fenwick, Esq. for the purpose of obtaining liberty of him to manufacture salt upon Long Island Sound, and take fish there. While he was Governor, he presided not only over the deliberations of the Gen. Court, but acted as Chief Judge of the Particular Court, which was holden five and often six times in the year, besides attending to his own private concerns, and the business of the various committees on which he was appointed by the General Court.

Gov. Haynes was one of the great and good men of his day in the colony and country. His whole time appears to have been occupied in the service of the public until his death. In addition to his other important places of trust, in 1646, while he was acting as Governor, he was appointed a Commissioner to the

United Congress of the Colonies. A vast deal more might be said of the public honors conferred by Connecticut upon Gov. Haynes, but enough is here collected to satisfy the object of the writer in this publication.

Governor Haynes had married two wives, by whom he had eight children, viz. Robert, Hezekiah, John, Roger, Mary, Joseph, Ruth and Mabel. The four eldest sons settled in England; Hezekiah occupied Copford-Hall, where his father had formerly resided in Essex, before he came to New England; Joseph settled in Hartford as pastor of Mr. Stone's church, after Mr. Stone's decease—he married a daughter of Richard Lord, of Hartford, and many of the descendants of Joseph are yet in Connecticut; Ruth married Hon. Samuel Wyllys, of Hartford; Mabel, the youngest daughter of Gov. Haynes, married James Russell, of Boston.

The name of Haynes is not now in the State, as known to the writer, though the blood of the Governor circulates in the veins of many in Hartford, yet but a single family have honored their worthy ancestor with even the Christian name of Haynes, (Haynes Lord Porter.) Joseph, Ruth and Mabel were by the second wife of the Governor. Joseph married and had sons; his son John was a gentleman of importance in the colony, and for a time was a magistrate and judge—and the name became extinct in the colony in this generation. He had no sons who left sons.

Haines, Joseph, Wethersfield, 1664.

Hanmer, William, came late to Windsor.

Hawkins, John, died in 1676, unmarried—was brother in law of John Judd, cousin of Joseph Judd—had a sister Ruth Hawkins and Mary Judd, and sisters Sarah, Elizabeth and Hannah.

Harris, Richard, (in No. 1,) died in 1666, unmarried. This is an ancient and early name in Wethersfield—there are many of the name in Massachusetts and Rhode Island. Andrew was in Massachusetts as early as '39. Thomas was at Providence in '37. Toleration was killed by the Indians in '75. The name was common in Massachusetts in the early settlement.

Harris, Samuel, taverner at Middletown in 1659.

Harris, John, came to Boston from London, in the ship Christopher, in 1634.

Holt, Mary, Hartford, whipt, and ordered to leave the conoly in '39.

Hackleton, Hannah, in January, 1665, was indicted for three offences against the laws of God and man. To the first she pled guilty. On the charge of murder and blasphemy she pled not guilty—but confessed she had said "there was as much mercy in the devil as in God"—was found guilty on the first charge, and on the third, that she had been guilty of express, direct and presumptuous blasphemy against God—but acquitted on the charge of murder.

Hagborn, Samuel, 1663.

Holridge, Mary, Fairfield county, 1661.

Hooker, Rev. Thomas, was born at Marfield, in Leicestershire, Eng. He was educated at Emmanuel College. He had preached at Chelmsford, but was silenced for his religious opinions, and fled to Holland. His church in England were anxious to be again under his instruction. They emigrated to Cambridge in Massachusetts, in 1632; when they wrote to Mr. Hooker in Holland, inviting him to come to New England, and again become their religious instructor. Mr. Hooker at once engaged Mr. Samuel Stone who was a Lecturer in England to become his assistant in the ministry, and took passage for America. He landed at Boston upon the 4th day of September, 1633. Governor Haynes, Rev. John Cotton and others came with him. Soon after his arrival he met his church and friends at Cambridge; as he met them, he exclaimed with the Apostle, " Now I live, if ye stand fast in the Lord." He at once became pastor of his old church, and Mr. Stone took his place as teacher. Soon after this time the Watertown, Newtown and Dorchester settlers began to talk of emigrating to Connecticut; and the spirit for removal soon spread through the church at Cambridge. Many of the people of Dorchester and Watertown had moved to Connecticut; and in June, 1636, as liberty had been granted them to remove, Mr. Hooker with his family, Mr. Stone, and about 100 others, men, women and children, started through the trackless wilderness, guided by a compass, for Hartford. They reached their destined home with many hardships in due time in safety. They found themselves located in an immense forest, surrounded by savages, and deprived of all the conveniences and comforts to which they had been habituated in England, and the savages jealous of the new intruders upon their corn fields and hunting grounds only the more excited them to revenge the wrong, and make them greedy for blood. The settlers soon prepared themselves against the dangers from the Indians, by watch and ward, day and night. Mr. Hooker and Mr. Stone were soon organized with the church, and became the principal advisers in all matters both civil and religious. They were strictly the pioneers of Hartford. Though Mr. Hooker did not appear to seek after civil appointments, yet such was the confidence of the General Court placed in his integrity and ability, that he was occasionally appointed upon important committees. In 1639 Mr. Hooker and Mr. Wells were appointed by the General Court to consult with Mr. Fenwick " concerning the Bay's aiding Connecticut in an offensive and defensive war; also relative to the bounds of Patents on Connecticut River." In 1640 a long controversy had subsisted between Lieut. Robert Seely and the Plantation of Wethersfield, he with Mr. Wells were appointed arbitrators to close the controversy. He received other appointments from the General Court.

Mr. Hooker closed his usefulness in the colony and the world by his death, which occurred in 1648. He left an estate of about £4000 to his family. His children were, John, Samuel, Sarah, Joannah and Mary. Joannah had married Mr. Shepard, and Mary Mr. Newton, and had children before the death of Mr. Hooker. Sarah married Rev. John Wilson. In his will he laid a special injunction upon his son John, forbidding him settling in England, yet he gave him leave to marry there, but enjoined upon him to return and settle in New England, which fully proved his attachment to his religion and his adopted country. Samuel succeeded Rev. Roger Newton, first minister of Farmington, in 1649, and preached there 40 years until his death. He was the ancestor of nearly all, (if not all) of the name in New England, and well may they be proud of their ancestry, so long as they sustain his reputation by their own equally meritorious acts.

Hungerford, or foot, Thomas—on the record is spelt Hungerfoot until October, 1664, after which it is spelt Hungerford—the last is the name in England. He held land in Hartford before 1639. He died in '62, and left children, Thomas aged 15, Sarah 9, and Hannah 4 years old. He moved down the river, probably to Haddam or New London. Ancestor of William Hungerford, Esq. of Hartford.

Horton, Barnabas, of Southhold, L. I., in 1663 was appointed a Commissioner for Southhold with John Young. The Commissioners on Long Island were vested with the power of magistrates upon the Island, with orders from the General Court to administer the oath to all the freemen there under the Charter of Connecticut. Thomas, Springfield, 1639.

Hamlin, Giles, Middletown, 1663—was an assistant in 1685, and as early as '73. At a special session of the General Court held at Hartford in '73, to prepare against an apparent war with the Dutch, the Governor with Giles Hamlin, Capt. Benjamin Newbury, William Wadsworth, Capt. William Curtiss, Lieut. William Fowler, and Lieut. Thomas Munson, assistants in the colony, were appointed to act as a Grand Committee of the colony, in establishing and commissionating military officers, pressing men, horses, ships, barks, or other vessels, arms, ammunition, provision, carriages, &c. as they should judge needful for defence ; and to manage, order and dispose of the militia in the best way for the safety of the colony.

Hurlbut, Thomas, Wethersfield, one of the first settlers, juror in 1645 —appraiser of Elson's estate in '48—was fined 40 shillings for excess in prices in '42—clerk of training band in Wethersfield in '40. He was a man of good standing, often on the jury and deputy—supposed to be the brother of William at Windsor. He was the ancestor of many of the name in Litchfield county. Constable in '64.

Hurlbut, William, Windsor—went to Windsor in the 2d colony in 1639. Gideon, Fairfield, juror in 1730.

Hopewell, Thomas, 1671.

Hutchinson, Capt. Edward. A letter was sent by the Council to Narragansett, informing the people there, that Richard Smith, senior, Capt. E. Hutchinson and Joseph Hewes were appointed selectmen at Smith's trading-house, and that Richard Smith, sen'r. was appointed constable by the Council, for the town, and named the town Wickford. [This was an error in No. 1—it should have been as above.] Edward, of Boston, opposed the law of 1658, punishing Quakers with death for returning to the colony of Massachusetts after they had been banished.

Hutchinson, William, died in 1643, and left a widow.

Holcomb, Thomas, came to Windsor in the 2d colony with Mr. Huet in 1639. He was a member of his church in England, and came with him. In 1649 Mr. Holcomb, E. Griswold, J. Bartlett, F. Griswold and G. Griswold resided in a remote section of Windsor, called Poquonnock, near the Indians. The General Court allowed one soldier to be exempt from training, that he should remain at home on military days to protect these families from depredations by the Indians. They resided by the brook about a quarter of a mile south of the present meeting house at Poquonnock. (There was no settlement in East Windsor until 1659. The first settler there was Edward King, an Irishman from Windsor—he built a house there, and afterwards gave one half of it to his son.) Mr. H. died n 1657. His widow married again. His children, Abigail, Joshua, Sarah, Benajah, Deborah, Nathaniel and Jonathan. His son Joshua married Ruth Stanwood in 1663, and had three children. Benajah married Sarah Eno, and had Benajah and James.—*Hayden. Record.*

Hull, George, Windsor—surveyed Wethersfield in 1636—deputy in April, August and September in '39—was a magistrate and member of the General Court often. He was allowed to trade for beaver on the river—was one of the Gen. Court that declared war against the Pequotts in '37 ; and he surveyed Windsor and Wethersfield by order of court the same year. He was a man of great worth in the colony.

Hull, John, married Elizabeth Loomis, of Windsor, in 1641. He came from Dorchester. A committee of the General Court in 1637–8–9.

Hull, Josiah, Hartford, 1640.

Hudson, or Hudgson, John, an atttorney at Hartford.

Hussey, Stephen, 1663.

Hunt, Ephraim, 1642.

Hunt, Thomas, was made free, 1663. Edmund, Cambridge, '34.

Howard, Robert, Windsor—juror in 1643 and '49—land record in '46. His descendants are several of them now in Windsor—though there are few of the name in the State—they have sustained a good reputation.

Howard, Robert, Hartford—a miller, admitted an inhabitant 1661.

Hurd, John, Stratford, 1648—deputy from Stratford, constable of the town in 1657. He was one of the principnl men there.

Hubbard, Thomas, Wethersfield—licensed to trade for beaver in 1638. He moved to Middletown, where he died in '71. Children, Mary 17, Thomas 10, Ebenezer 7, John 4 and George 1 year old.

Hubbard, George, jr., died in 1775, unmarried.

Hubbard, William, Windsor, 1640.

Hubbard, William, resided in Windsor, within or near the public palisadoes.

Huntly, John, New London, 1671.

Huet, Rev. Ephraim, in 1639 he came from England to act as colleague with Rev. Mr. Warham at Windsor, and was so settled there over the church. He was accompanied by several members of his church from England. He was a gentleman of education and of exemplary piety. He died in 1643 or 1644, and left a widow and four daughters, viz. Susannah, Mercy, Lydia and Mary, with a large estate.

Hollister, Joseph, was one of the early settlers of Wethersfield—he was juror in 1644—was deputy five sessions of the General Court, and was a leading man in Wethersfield, and held many offices. He died in '74. He probably came from Weymouth. He was a brother of John and Thomas. The name is yet in Glastenbury, Washington and other places in the State.

Hollister, John, Wethersfield, 1664. His children were, John, 22 years old—Thomas, Joseph, Mary and Sarah.

Howell, John, assistant in 1647–8–9, probably a descendant of Edward, of Lynn.

Hobart, Thomas, 1643. Caleb, of Braintree, was probably his ancestor, perhaps the son of Edmond.

Holyoke, Elizur, brother in law to Edward Stebbins. I find him in the colony, but it is probably Elizur who resided at Sprinfield, the son of Edward, of Springfield.

Hobby, Jonathan, Greenwich—juror.

Hill, William, (in No. 1, of Windsor,) moved to Fairfield in 1658, and was appointed Collector of Customs there in '59. (Hill, Thomas, Fairfield, juror in 1730.) William Hill, N. Gold and Mr. Sherman, of Fairfield county, were ordered to examine a letter which had been sent to Bridget Baxter from her husband in England, (she having petitioned for a divorce from him,) and compare the letter with his other writings, and if they found a strong similarity in the hand writing—then to declare to the said Bridget that the Court frees her from her matrimonial bond with said Baxter.

Harrison, John, Wethersfield—died in 1666, and left children, Rebecca, Mary and Sarah—left no sons. He left to his widow and three daughters an estate of £929. He was an early settler in Wethersfield, and came from Watertown to Wethersfield.

Harrison, Catherine, (spelt Kateram) Wethersfield, tried for witchcraft in 1669, and acquitted.

Hayden, William, (in No. 1.) He is said to have been one of the little band of brave men who fought the bloody battle against the Pequotts, under Capt. Mason, and exterminated the tribe. About 1665 he removed from Windsor to Killingworth, and died there in 1669. He was the father of Daniel, who was the father of Samuel, who was the father of Nathaniel, who was the father of Nathaniel the father of Levi.—*Jewett.*

Higley, John, supposed the son of Edward of Windsor, (in No. 1,) married Hannah Drake, in '71, and had Jonathan, Hannah, John and Rebecca.

Higginson, John, (in No. 1,) the 2d minister of Guilford, removed 1659.

Hensdell, Robert. Hinsdel.

Howell, Baker and Mason, magistrates in 1664.

Howe, Mr., was elected magistrate in 1647.

Harvey, John, 1664.

Husted, Robert, made free under the Charter, 1663.

I.

Ince, John, was a land holder in Hartford in 1639. He died at sea. He had resided at Boston. His claim to the land in Hartford was forfeited, and voted by the town to the Hon. John Cullick, which afterwards greatly enhanced the value of his estate.

Ingersoll, Dorothy, married Mr. Phelps, of Windsor, 1676.

Ingersoll, Hannah, married Mr. Kelsey, 1676.

Ingersoll, Margery, was not married in 1676—(these three are suppossed to have resided at Windsor.) There were Ingersolls at Westfield or Springfield in the early settlement of those towns. Jonathan, of Fairfield, a juror in 1730. Jonathan, of New Haven, Lieut. Gov. from 1815 to '23. Hon. Ralph I., and Charles A. of New Haven, 1846. Jared, 1765, of New Haven, stamp-master, ancestor of Hon. Charles J., and Joseph R. of Philadelphia, 1846. All of whom perhaps originated at Springfield.

Ireland, Samuel, fined 10 shillings for contempt of Court, in 1639.

J.

Judd, Thomas, Hartford, 1639 and '41—deputy in '46-8-9. He probably is the same Thomas Judd who came from Cambridge to Hartford, and from thence to Waterbury in the first settlement of the town. Deputy and grand juror in '62—was frequently a deputy— a deputy in '63—freeman in '63. He had a grant of 400 acres of land if it could be found between his and the land of Anthony Hawkins, in '61. Perhaps of Farmington. (Thomas, of Waterbury, was the great grandfather of Jonathan, the first minister of Southampton, Mass.) He was an original proprietor of Hartford, and in the land distribution in '39.

Jessup, John, 1637. This name is yet in Fairfield county.

Johnson, Mary, 1646. In '48 being arraigned before the court for witchcraft, she confessed herself guilty of familiarity with the devil. This is the first case for witchcraft found upon the colony record. There is no record of either a sentence or execution in her case to be found. Perhaps she might, in the frenzy of that day upon this subject, have been executed.

Johnson, Thomas, died in 1642. This has been a name of great note in this State since the days of Dr. Johnson, of Stratford.

Johnson, Isaac, 1630.

Judson, Joseph, came early to Hartford from Concord, Mass., and soon after became one of the first settlers in Stratford about 1639 or '40. He was the son of William, who had resided at Concord. He came from England in '34. Deputy in Stratford, '62–3. Appointed with John Hurd in '63 to settle the bounds of Norwalk and Fairfield. Jeremiah, of Hartford, 1730.

Judson, William, of Stratford, probably father of Joseph—in 1645 was the collector for the town of Stratford, of the annual funds to support students in Cambridge College. J. Farmer says, " he was of Concord, 1635, came to New England in '34 with his sons Joseph, Jeremiah and Joshua. He removed to Hartford in '39." He with his family soon moved to Stratford.

Jackson, Christopher, 1656.

Jackson, Thomas, do.

Jones, Richard, died in 1670. Children, David, Elizabeth, Mary and Patience.

Jones, William, Deputy Governor from 1692 to '98.

Jones, Thomas, Fairfield, 1655, moved from Concord to Fairfield in '55.

James, Joseph, Fairfield county—had trouble with Mary Holridge, 1661.

James, Thomas, 1639. Probably the same man who went missionary to Virginia in '43, and afterwards moved to New Haven.

Jennings, Nicholas, Hartford, 1639.

Jennings, Joseph, died in 1676—left no family.

Jennings, John, Hartford, 1639. There are some persons of this name in the west part of Connecticut. He was employed by the town of Hartford in '64, to sweep all the chimneys in Hartford, at 6 pence for brick, and 3 pence for clay chimneys.

Jennings, Joshua, Hartford, 1688.

Jacob, Peter, 1647.

Jecoxe, or Jacocks, in the colony, 1647.

Jeffries, Gabriel, Saybrook, 1663. Robert Jeffries, with his wife and three children came to New England with William Hillier, in the Elizabeth and Ann—Cooper, master.

June, Jonathan, Hartford, 1639.

K.

Kirby, John, Hartford, 1645—of Middletown in '70, where he died in 1671. He left a widow, son Joseph 21 years old—his son John died before he died. Mary, aged 31, married Emmanuel Buck, of Wethersfield—Elizabeth died before her father—Hannah 27, married Thomas Andrews—Hester 25, married Benajah Stone—Sarah 23, married Samuel Hubbard—Dethiah 18—Susannah 13, and Abigail, were unmarried at his death. David Sage appears to have married one of the daughters, as he appeared as legatee or heir in the distribution of the estate.

Kelsey, William, was in the colony in 1639. It is a common name at Milford. He was in the distribution of lands in Hartford in '39, and had 16 acres. After his decease, his widow, Bethiah, married David Phillips, of Milford. The town of Hartford, in '64, offered him £10 to remove from Hartford with his wife.

Kilbourn, John, Wethersfield, was the son of Thomas, who came to New England in the ship Increase, Robert Lea, master, and brought with him his wife Margaret, and daughthers Lydia, Maria and Frances, and moved from Massachusetts to Wethersfield, when his son John was, quite young, in the early settlement of the town. Thomas was nearly sixty years of age when he moved his family to Wethersfield. John became an active and useful man in the colony. He was juror, grand juror and deputy in 1663, and held other offices in the town and colony. He settled many estates of deceased persons.— George Kilbourn, of Rowley. The names of several persons who came to this country with Mr. Kilbourn and his family are names yet familiar in the town of Wethersfield, viz. Buck, John Warner, &c., who probably moved to Wethersfield in company with him.

Keeler, Ralph, Hartford, 1639, viewer of chimneys in '45. The name of Ralph is a family name in Ridgefield. Samuel Keeler, a juror in Fairfield, 1730.

Knowles, Alexander, resided in Fairfield in 1654, and was appointed an asssistant there, to aid the magistrates in holding courts, and to marry persons—to press horses by warrant on sudden emergencies, and other duties. He was an important man in that section of the Connecticut colony. He came from Massachusetts, where he was made a freeman in 1636. He with William Hill and N. Gold were appointed by the General Court, in 1660, to try and settle the dispute between Norwalk and the Indians.

Kelting, Thomas, 1644.

Kellogg, Nathaniel, 1639.

Kitwell, Samuel, fined 10 shillings for drinking ardents contrary to law and good morals.

Kircum, Thomas, Wethersfield, 1646.

Kimberly, Eleazer, Wethersfield, 1673. Secretary of the Colony from 1696 to 1709—grand juror, 1672. Nathaniel, of New Haven, was accepted as an inhabitant of Hartford, 1659. Nathaniel, of Wethersfield, 1663.

King, John, 1656.

Knap, Thomas, died unmarried, in 1669.

Kempe, Daniel, 1663.

Keeny, William, a land holder about New London in 1650—deputy in '62. Alexander, Wethersfield, '76.

Kecherell, 1644.

Kessar, or Kessan, William, juror in 1641.

L.

Lathrop, Samuel, in 1647 was one of the principal men of New London. The town had been slowly settling before this time, but the removal of the Rev. Richard Blynnman to New London added greatly to the importance of the place. They had as settlers at this time not only Mr. Lathrop and Mr. Blynnman, but John Winthrop, James Avery, Thomas Minot, Robert Allen, and many others. Mr. Winthrop was appointed to superintend the affairs of the new settlement, and the inhabitants were exempted of all colony rates for three years. In 1648 a court for the trial of small causes, consisting of Mr. Winthrop, Mr. Lathop and Minot, was formed there by the Gen. Court.

Law, Richard, Wethersfield, in 1638. The General Court gave him permission to trade with the Indians. He moved to Stamford, and became an important man there. He early came out in favor of Stamford's being under the Connecticut Charter and colony, and in favor of paying taxes to the colony. He was the ancestor of Jonathan Law, Governor of Connecticut from 1742 to 1751, and Deputy Governor from 1725 to 1742—of the former collector of customs at New London—of Judge Law—of Hon. Lyman Law, and the Law family in Connecticut, which has done the State so much honor in high places of public trust.

Law, George, 1641. The connexion of Richard, George and William is not found, if any ; from the Christian names in the Law family there appears to be only one family of the three first settlers.

Law, William, Hartford. In 1639 he was in the colony, and was selectman of Hartford in '40 and '44.

Lay, Edward, was in the second land division of Hartford, and had six acres of land, with liberty to fetch wood and keep swine and cows on the common.

Lamberton, Deliverance, 1663.

Larraby, John, 1674.

Lake, Thomas. There have been several Thomas Lakes in Massachusetts. The name of Thomas appears to be a family name. Persons of this name resided at Stratford.

Lay, Robert, resided at Six Mile Island, in the vicinity of New London, in 1665. His daughter Ann married John Denison. He was ordered, in '60, to take charge of Mr. Fenwick's estate, and to account for it to the court. John Lay, an executor in '64.

Lay, Peter, was probably a son of Robert.

Langdon, Anthony, 1647. There have been several eminent men in New Hampshire and Massachusetts by this name; but there is no record in the colony which shows that Anthony was allied to those families.

Langdon, Andrew—a juror in 1643, with Andrew Landon. He resided in Hartford as late as '64.

Lampson, Edward—as he was from Cambridge, probably came with the other settlers of Hartford. And Barnabas residing there in 1635, and Edward coming from Cambridge in '44, he might have been the son of Barnabas.

Lattimore, John, was fined 15 shillings for drinking ardents, in 1639, contrary to law.

Lattimore, Mrs. Wethersfield, 1662.

Latham, Cary, 1649. He went to New London in the early settlement of the town—was an active man, and received appointments from the town and General Court. Some of his descendants now reside at Groton—one of them was a State Senator in 1845.

Latham, John, New London, 1664.

Landon, Andrew, Hartford, was juror in 1643—probably the ancestor of John Landon, formerly sheriff of Litchfield county. Few of the name are in Connecticut at this time.

Lanson, Samuel, was tried in 1670 for robbing a mill at Wethersfield, and another at Branford, at several different times, and breaking prison at New Haven, then hiding a half year in the wilderness to escape punishment—for which he was fined £20, and sold in Barbadoes as a servant for four years.

Leonard, Robert, on the jury, 1645.

Lettin, Richard, 1647—removed to Huntington, Long Island, and in the difficulty there in '63, about submitting to the Charter of Connecticut, the General Court ordered him to depart from Huntington for his turbulent conduct.

Lettin, Mrs., had liberty to move to Fairfield in 1662, if the town would receive her.

Lee, Edward, 1647. This name was in Massachusetts earlier than in Connecticut.

Lewis, William, Hartford, 1639—juror in '42. In '49 he was a sergeant for Farmington to train the men there. Some families of the name now reside there, and are probably the descendants of William. He came from Cambridge, and was in the land division of Hartford, in 1639.

Lewis, Philip, Hartford, 1645.

Leverson, Sanders, 1663.

Lindsly, Sarah, 1663.

Lord, Thomas, came to Hartford from Cambridge, Mass., in 1636. His ancestor was John Lord, and was in the division of lands at Hartford in '39. His children were, Thomas, Richard, William, Dorothy, Robert, John and Amy. He is the ancestor of the Lord family of this State. Robert Lord, Fairfield, 1730.

Lord, Thomas, Jr., Hartford. In 1652 was a surgeon and physician, and thought of leaving Hartford ; to prevent which the General Court contracted with him, that if he would remain in Hartford one year, and use his best skill with the inhabitants of the towns upon the river, both for setting bones and in the practice of physic, that the Court would pay him a salary of £15 ; and that he should in addition receive for visiting at any house in Hartford, 12 pence as reasonable pay ; any house in Windsor, 5 shillings ; any house in Wethersfield, 3 shillings ; any in Farmington, 6 shillings, and in Mattabeseck, (Middletown,) 8 shillings. Dr. Lord informed the Court he required no more. A law was therefore enacted to this effect, confirming the contract. The Doctor was also by the law freed from watching, warding and training, but not from finding arms. He was the first physician mentioned upon the record, and was probably the first regular bred surgeon in the colony, or he would not have been thus by the General Court solicited to remain in Hartford upon a salary paid by the public. Some of the Lord family settled at Haddam, Saybrook and New London. The next surgeon employed by the public was Daniel Porter. In 1655 the General Court ordered him to be paid out of the public treasury, a salary of £6, and 6 shillings a journey to each town on the River, to exercise his art of Chirurgery (surgery.)

Lord, Richard, son of Thomas, constable of Hartford in 1642, and selectman in 1644—was fined £5 for drawing his sword with threats, about trading for corn with the Indians. He with Mr. Thomas Stanton were licensed to trade with the Indians on Long Island for corn for the period of 12 months, in 1642. He was a man of great energy, and an original settler. In 1657 he was appointed captain of the first troop of horse ever raised in the colony. All troopers on duty could cross ferries free of toll, by law. The officers and men were paid a salary by the public for doing military duty in the troop. He was in the land division at Hartford in 1639. He came from Newtown in Massachusetts with the other emigrants to Hartford in its early settlement. After several years spent in Hartford, he removed to New London, where he died.

Lord, John, 1648—a brother of Thomas, jr., and son of Thomas, sen'r., was one of the first settlers.

Lockwood, Robert, came as early as 1649 to Connecticut from Cambridge, and probably was one of the settlers of Norwalk. There are now in Norwalk some ancient and respectable families of the name. He was confirmed by the General Court as a sergeant at Norwalk as early as '57.

Ludlow, Hon. Roger, came to Massachusetts, and settled at Dorchester in 1630. He became an assistant in that colony for three or four years —was then elected Deputy Governor of the colony, and removed as early as 1636 to Windsor. He probably came to Connecticut in the autumn of 1635, as he presided at the first Court organized to try Styles in April, 1636. It would have been difficult for him to have arrived in the colony thus early in the spring of 1636 either by land or water. Mr. Ludlow was uniformly a member of the General Court from its first organization in April, 1636, until the Confederation by Constitution, of Windsor, Hartford and Wethersfield in 1639, and presided at the General Court until March or November, 1637, when Gov. Haynes was made the presiding officer until he was elected Governor of the Colony, and Mr. Ludlow Deputy Governor, in 1639. He had been a member of Mr. Warham's church, in England, and came with him to New England, in 1630. He presided at the Court of Magistrates and Committee in 1637, that declared war against the Pequotts. He held the office of Deputy Governor in the Colony during the years 1639-42 and 48, and was at the head of the Court of Magistrates in 1649—was repeatedly on committees to produce a Union of the New England Colonies. He was one of the most useful men as well as able pioneers of Connecticut, and greatly benefitted the progress of the colony in the early settlement. In 1646 he was appointed by the General Court to form a code of laws. As early as 1639 Mr. Ludlow aided in settling a few families at Uncoway, in Fairfield—after these families had moved there from Windsor, another company joined them from Wethersfield, and soon after another from Massachusetts, which were shortly after formed into a town under Connecticut. In 1640 Mr. Ludlow purchased that part of Norwalk which was located between Saugatuck and Norwalk rivers, and Captain Patrick purchased the tract of land immediately west of the land so purchased by Mr. Ludlow ; and the few planters who had moved there purchased the west part of Norwalk—all of which was purchased of the Indians. The exact time of his removal to Fairfield is not known to the writer, probably about 1650. He is first found on the record at Fairfield in 1652-3. He remained there but a few years before he removed to Virginia, (1654) where he died.

Lyman, Richard, Hartford. He came into the colony as early as 1639, and held several offices—was a juror, &c., but died in '40, and left a competent estate to his widow and children. His sons were, Richard, Robert and John ; and his daughters, Sarah, and Phillis the wife of William Hills. He probably came from Northampton, and a brother of John and Robert.

Leffingwell, Thomas, of Saybrook, 1637, afterwards of Norwich. Upon the settlement of Norridge, (Norwich) he with Major Mason, Thomas Tracy, Baldwin, Reynolds, Backus, Hyde, Post, &c., settled in Norwich with Mr. Fitch, nearly at the same time. He was one of the original contractors with Uncas and his sons and others for the town of Norwich in 1659. He appeared as attorney for John Gager at Norwich, in a case where Gager had been robbed by the Indians in 1673. He was a deputy in 1662. Dr. Trumbull says, that during the war of Uncas and the Narragansetts, his fort was beseiged and his provision nearly exhausted. Uncas gave notice to the scouts who had been sent from the fort ; upon the intelligence reaching Mr. Leffingwell, who was an ensign at Saybrook, he loaded a canoe with provisions, and under cover of the night, paddled his canoe into the Thames and lodged it safe in the fort of Uncas. For this noble act he gave a deed of all or a large part of Norwich to Mr. Leffingwell.

Loomis, John, settled in Windsor in 1639. He came with Mr. Huet, and was a juror in '42. Col. James Loomis and some other persons in Windsor possess lands there which their ancestors purchased of the Indians, when the town was first settled. All the persons by this name in the State appear to have descended from those who came to Windsor on its first settlement.

Loomis, Timothy, came to Windsor from Massachusetts with the second colony in 1639. He was afterwards recorder of the town for several years. There are no persons of the name of Loomis who came into the colony except those who came to Windsor.

Loomis, Joseph, married Sarah Hill, Windsor, 1646. Juror in '44.

Loomis, John, 2d., married Elizabeth Scott, Windsor, 1648—son of John.

Loomis, Samuel, constable of Windsor, 1664.

Lockman, Govert, 1649.

Lobdell, Simon, 1649. Sued Jared Spencer in '60.

Loveland, Thomas, 1670. There was a Robert Loveland in Massachusetts in 1645.—*Farmer.*

Loveland, John, died in 1670, and gave his estate to his widow.

Loveland, Robert, 1664, Westchester.

Loveridge, a deputy in 1661.

Lyon, Richard, Fairfield, 1653.

Lyon, Henry, Fairfield, 1657.

Luxford, Stephen, died at Haddam in 1676. There were two by the name of Luxford in Massachusetts—one in '34, and the other in '74—both by the name of Reuben.—*Farmer.*

M.

Mason, Maj. Gen. John.   Of this extraordinary man of early days, Dr. Trumbull remarks, " that he was bred to arms in the Dutch Netherlands, and came from England to Massachusetts with Mr. Warham in 1630, and settled at Dorchester ; that he came to Windsor as early as 1635 with the pioneers of that settlement.   He was made a magistrate as early as 1642 in the new colony, and held the office until he declined it.   He was elected Deputy Governor in 1660, and held that place until 1669.   In 1647 he removed his family to Saybrook, to have the oversight of the fort, and in 1659 removed with several other families to Norwich, where he resided until his death.   He was tall and portly—full of martial fire—neither feared or avoided danger—shunned no hardships where the colony had an interest.   He possessed not only prudence and heroism, but great wisdom in all his military movements."   He was one of the fathers of the colonists.   He afterwards, with Mr. Hooker, Gov'rs. Haynes, Hopkins, Webster, Welles, Talcott, and Messrs. Ludlow, Warham, Wyllys, Whiting, Wolcott, Phelps, Swain, Steel and Mitchell, all of whom were magistrates, (except the clergy) in the direction of the affairs of the colony, religiously and civilly.   In 1637 he commanded the little and valorous army who conquered and exterminated the Pequott nation of Indians (in the southeast part of Connecticut.)   For this expedition ample provision was ordered by the General Court, among which were one good hogshead of beer for Capt. Mason, the minister, (Mr. Stone,) and sick men—three or four gallons of strong water, and two gallons of sack.   He was made the first major general in the colony in 1637, and was called upon the record, " the Public Military Officer to train the Military men in each Plantation 10 days in a year," with a salary of £40, payable quarterly from the public treasury.   In 1637 the General Court sent him with 20 men to reinforce the garrison at Saybrook, but soon after his arrival Capt. Underhill came with 20 men from Massachusetts for the same purpose, and Major Mason returned with his men to Hartford.   In 1637, in November he was a member of the General Court, and was frequently a member of both Houses of the General Court previous to his being Deputy Governor. At the time he was deputy in 1638, he with other members, were not present at the opening of the General Court, for which each of them were fined 1 shilling for failing to be at the House at 7 o'clock in the morning at the roll-call. In 1637 he was allowed by the Court to trade with the Indians for himself, and for such as were in want of corn.   The same year he was sent by the Court to Waranock to treat with the Indians to pay their tribute—to aid in defraying the expense of the Pequott war—to the amount of one fathom of wampum a man. He was also one of the Committee to establish the bounds of Poquannock plantations.   In 1639 he was of the Committee to agitate the question of declaring war against the Quinnipiac Indians, with power to press fire arms, shallops and canoes for the service—forty men having previously been raised by the three towns on Connecticut River for the expedition.   In 1641 the General Court gave him 500 acres of land at Pequott for his valor at Mystic, and at the same time gave to his officers and soldiers 500 acres, who had left nearly six hundred wounded and dead red men upon the battle field at Mystic, in 1637.   In 1642, such was the confidence of the General Court in the good judgment of General Mason, that they appointed him with two others, to procure some pieces of ordnance from Piscataqua, and erect fortifications at the discretion of the Committee. The same year he and Mr. Whiting, were sent to Long Island and upon the Main, to collect tribute of the Indians. He was one of the Committee to build a ship by the towns. He was twice appointed with Jeremy Adams to settle a trade with the Indians for corn. He was of the Committee to treat with Hon. G. Fenwick for liberty to make salt and take fish upon Long Island. He was one of the Committee to press men with fire arms to defend Uncas.

No act of his life more fully shows the esteem in which he was held in the colony, than when the General Court was applied to by the colony of New Haven to obtain the services of Major Mason to head their troops for the purpose of driving the Dutch and Indians from their Delaware lands, and settle there with promises of great reward ;—to see the General Court so promptly and peremptorially refuse all rewards to him as any inducement to spare him to settle in any other colony upon any terms. So high did he stand in the colony not only as a brave officer but as a statesman, that in 1647 he was appointed a Commissioner to the Congress of the United Colonies; also in 1654-5-6-7 and 1661.

It would require a volume to recapitulate the services Gen. Mason rendered the colony, and the honors and rewards bestowed upon him by Connecticut. No man in the colony was more serviceable, and all things considered, as much so, as Maj. Mason, particularly in all transactions with the natives. The bloody battle at Mystic had terror-stricken every Indian in the land, and no man was as much feared, and at the same time revered by them. He was in fact the General Jackson of his day, as an Indian fighter; and as a civilian he held many places of power and trust in the colony, the duties of which he discharged in such a manner as proved him as safe a counsellor in the cabinet as he was efficient in the field. In one other respect his character resembled that of the Hero of New Orleans, whose military glory was so resplendent, that though he was afterwards President of the United States, he never lost the title of General: so with the Hero of Mystic, though he was Deputy Governor, assistant, and member of the Colony Congress, his titles of Captain and Major have been preferred by his friends before all his other appointments, so much so that he is often familiarly recorded, when speaking of him, as " the Captain," " the Major," without any name being attached to his title.

Major Mason closed his most useful life at Norwich, in 1672, at the age of 72 years. He left seven children, viz. Priscilla, who married James Fitch in 1664 ; Samuel, who left no sons ; his son John was wounded in Philip's war, and died in 1676—he left a widow and children, viz. John and Ann—the last John, the grandson of Major Mason, married the daughter of Samuel Mason, (a relative) and by her had a son Samuel. The other children of Major Mason were, Rachel, Ann, Daniel and Elizabeth. Daniel married Miss Hobart, and had a son Samuel. Jeremiah Mason, LL. D., of Boston, is a descendant.— Robert, the proprietor of New Hampshire. The posterity of Major Mason are at this day numerous in Connecticut, particularly in New London county. In Hartford several of the Wadsworths, and Nathaniel and Harvey Seymour, Esq'rs. are the direct descendants of General Mason.

Mason, John, Robert Chapman and John Clark, of Saybrook, in 1654, were appointed to press men for an expedition against the Dutch.

Mason, Edward, 1639–40.

Marvin, Matthew, was surveyor of highways at Hartford, in 1639 and '47—was an original propritor and settler in Hartford before '39. He came from England in the ship Increase, R. Lea, master. He removed to Norwalk, and was freed from training and watching there in '59, and was a deputy to the General Court from Norwalk in '54. The family were of some distinction in Fairfield county for many years.

Marvin, Reinold, died at Saybrook in 1665. He moved early to Saybrook, and in 1662 the Court ordered the marshal to go to Saybrook and distrain £50 of him for disobeying an order to look up some horses which had been in litigation between him and M. Griswold—and awarded half to the plaintiff and defendant equally, and the other half to the colony. He moved to Saybrook in 1639, from Hartford. He left a son Reinold, (he was in the colony in 1637.) His daughters were, Hannah, Mary and Sarah. Hannah married Francis Barnerd in 1644; Sarah married William Goodrich, and Mary married Richard Bushnell in 1648.

Martin, Anthony, died at Middletown in 1673, and left three children—John 11 years old, Mary 7, and Elizabeth 2. He probably was the son of Samuel who came early into the colony. The principal settlers of Middletown were either direct from England, or from Hartford and Wethersfield, but principally from Hartford—some were from Chelmsford, Rowly and Woburn in Massachusetts. In the fall of '51 it had many settlers, and in '53 was called Middle Town.

Martin, Samuel—was in the colony in 1645—juror in '47.

Martin, Thomas. The townsmen of Hartford refused to receive him as an inhabitant in 1660.

Mascall, Thomas, Windsor, died in 1671, and left three children.

Marsh, John, Hartford, 1639. In '60 the town of Hartford gave the Jews who lived in the house of John Marsh, liberty to remain in Hartford seven months. He signed the agreement to remove to Hadley in '59.

Markham, William, Hartford, signed the agreement of the 60 to remove to Hadley, in 1659.

Maudsley, John, Windsor. He is not found as early as the name is found in Windsor.

Marvin, Richard, 1662.

Manvill, Matthew, in the colony in 1639.

Mayo, Samuel, in 1653 complained to the General Court that Baxter had seized his vessel and goods under a pretended commission from Rhode Island, for which Baxter was tried.

Maverick, John, came to Massachusetts in 1630 with Mr. Warham, and was chosen teacher and pastor with him over the church which came with him, and settled awhile at Dorchester, Mass. He did not move to Connecticut.

Maybee, Nicholas, 1664.

Marshall, Samuel, Windsor, magistrate in 1638—deputy in '37. He died in '75. His children were, Samuel, Lydia, David, Thomas, Mary, Eliakim, John and Elizabeth. He was often a juror and deputy, and held other offices of trust and honor, and was a leading man in the town. He was licensed to sell liquors by retail, not to be drank in his house, in '63. Samuel, son of Daniel, married Mary Wilson in '52, and had Samuel, Lydia, and seven other children.

Marshall, Thomas, was in the colony as early as 1637. He died in '71, and left a son and two daughters. He came from England in the ship James, John May, master, in company with Samuel Bennett, R. Palmer, Solomon Martin, John Hart and William Hill—all appeared to have settled in Connecticut.

Marshall, James, came to Windsor with Mr. Huet in 1639—perhaps a brother of Samuel. James Marshall was grand father of deacon Daniel Marshall, born in 1706.

Marshall, Ann, Windsor, 1639.

Maskell, Thomas, married Bethia Parsons in 1660. Children were, Thomas, (died) Abigail, Thomas, John and Elizabeth.

Maynard, John, was in the colony at Hartford as early as 1639—surveyor of highways in '41 and in '48—had 14 acres of land in the distribution of up-land in '40, at Hartford.

Marshfield, Thomas, appears to have left the colony in 1643. He came as early as '39. He was a gentleman of good standing, but had difficulty in the church.

Marks, Richard, 1647.

Meigs, John, constable in 1663. The family moved to Middletown. So far as I have known those of the name in Connecticut, they have originated from John Meigs, who settled at Middletown. He might have been John, of Weymouth. The family have not been numerous —but of high reputation.

Merrick, Thomas, was appointed in 1638, with Major Mason and Jeremy Adams to treat with the Indians for corn. Whether he resided at Hartford or Springfield in '38 is not asserted—but it appears it is the Welchman who came to Springfield about the time it was settled by Mr. Pyncheon and his company in '36. He had a suit at law in Connecticut a few years after.

Mead, John, at Hartford in 1640—moved to Fairfield. Gabriel was of Dorchester in '38. The name continued in Massachusetts as late as '90, and has been frequent in Fairfield county, Connecticut.

Mead Joseph, was made a freeman in Fairfield or Stamford, 1662.

Messenger, Edward, 1663—supposed of Windsor.

Merrills, John, Windsor—grand juror in 1672-7—chimney viewer in '63.

Meggs, John, was held by the Court in the office of constable over those constables appointed by the town, though they had submitted to the government, in 1663.

Miles, Moor, free in 1663.

Mills, Simon, Windsor, married in 1639. The name of Mills was in Massachusetts as early as '30. Simeon was early in Connecticut, and the name is now common in this State.

Mills, Simon, jr., married Mary Buell, 1650 ; and had Mary, Simon, John, Hannah, Sarah, Abigail, Elizabeth, Prudence, and Simon born in '78—son of Simon, sen'r.

Mills, Richard, 1644.

Mills, Samuel, made free in 1663.

Mills, Richard,   do.   do.

Minor, Thomas, at New London in 1665—he was at New London previous to 1665. He came from Massachusetts where he was made a freeman as early as 1634. There are many of the name in Connecticut at this time, and I find no other person of the name who came into the colony in its early settlement. His son was the first prepared and educated missionary among the Indians in this colony. Mr. Minor with M. Griswold and William Waller were appointed in 1663, to settle the line between the town of New London and the land of Uncas. He was a strict puritan, and had much to do in church affairs.

Mitchell, Matthew, Wethersfield—a member of the General Court in November, 1637—March, 1637—April, 1638—February, 1637, and deputy in May, 1637. He was on the General Court who declared war against the Pequotts, and held many offices in the colony. He had a controversy with Deacon Chaplin, and was ordered by the Court to make him satisfaction in some public meeting, or own his fault ; not having done either, the good people of Wethersfield elected him constable, but as he was under censure of the Court—his election being reported for confirmation by the Court—he was found incapable of holding the office, and was fined 20 nobles for accepting the office, and those who voted for him were fined £5.

Middleton, Thomas, 1663.

Milbourn, Jacob,   do.

Minot, Thomas, a principal settler at New London in 1647, and a judge of the first Court constituted in New London, with Winthrop and Lathrop.

Miller, Thomas, Middletown, in 1663—probably the same Thomas Miller who came to Massachusetts with his wife from London in the Elizabeth, and ancestor of the Hon. Asher Miller, deceased, and H. L. Miller at Hartford.

McLord, David, 1664.

Moore, J., Capt. Newbury and E. Griswold were ordered in 1662, to lay out all the undivided lands in Windsor, at Massico, to such persons in Windsor as needed it. He was one of the early settlers of Windsor—and was a juror in 1639-42-43 and 44—deputy in '43. He was deacon of Mr. Warham's church, and died there in 1677. He left a son John and four daughters; John Drake, sen'r married one of them; Nathaniel Loomis, Thomas Bissell, and Nathaniel Bissell married the other three daughters. He had two children, Mindwell and John born after he moved to Windsor. A John Moore came in the ship Planter from England to Massachusetts, in 1634—perhaps the same.

Moore, Thomas, Windsor—juror in 1639 and '42—perhaps a brother of deacon John.

Morrice, John, Windsor, 1639—died in '68. His children were, John, Joshua or Joseph, and Mary. He was an original settler, and in the land division in '39—he was a brother of Robert.

Morgan, James, New London, 1658. In '56 Gov. Winthrop applied to the General Court for a grant of 1500 acres of land—the grant was made,—and the Court appointed James Morgan, Deacon Caulkins and James Avery to lay it out to the Governor, at the head of Paugatuck Cove, for a plantation. He was an efficient and active man in New London—was a deputy in 1662-3. He appears to have been the ancestor of the Morgans in the colony. He received many appointments from the General Court.

Morgan, Evan, 1656.

Moody, Deacon John. The town of Hartford ordered that the watch, who were under the direction of the constable, should ring the (large cow) bell every morning one hour before day break—to begin at the bridge (over Little River,) and so ring all the way, forth and back from Master Moody's, (Wyllys Hill) to John Pratt's, and see that one should be up with a light in every house, within fifteen minutes after the ringing of the bell, on the penalty of 1 shilling and 6 pence. At this time there were no other bells in the colony except large thin cow bells; and some towns used these bells to call together the inhabitants to attend public worship and other meetings. The town of Farmington used for several years for this purpose a large drum, which could be heard at quite a distance from the church. This drum has been carefully preserved by the good people of Farmington, and is now owned by the Connecticut Historical Society.—Mr. Moody was townsman in 1639—lieutenant in 1640. He was frequently honored with the offices of the town and colony—was an early settler of Hartford—an original proprietor, and in the first division of lands there in 1639.

Moody, Samuel, Hartford, supposed son of John,—agreed to move to Hadley in 1659.

Moore, John, jr., married Hannah Goff, 1664. His children were, John, Thomas, Samuel, Nathaniel, Edward, Josias and Joseph.

Moses, John, Windsor, an early settler, and father of John, jr.

Moses, John, married Mary Brown in 1653, and had nine children.

Morton, William, Windsor, 1649.

Moore, Isaac, Norwalk, 1664.

Morehouse, Thomas, Fairfield, 1653.

Montague, Richard, Wethersfield, 1646. This name has continued at Wethersfield since the early settlement of the town. The name is also found in Massachusetts. He signed to move to Hadley in '59.

Moulton, Samuel, 1660.

Munn, Benjamin, viewer of chimneys and ladders in Hartford in 1647—was in the colony in '39, and in the 2d division of lands had eight acres.

Mulford and Baker, of East Hampton, L. I., 1661.

Murwin, Miles, Windsor, 1640, afterwards moved to Milford.

Mudge, James, 1644.

Mudge, Jarvis, married the widow of Abrahnm Elson—she had two daughters.

Mynott, Thomas, sergeant at Pequott, 1649. He held many offices and possessed the confidence of the General Court—was judge and magistrate at New London, and was an important early settler there.

Myles, Richard, 1644.

Mygatt, Joseph, Hartford—townsman in 1639–41—fence viewer in '49—frequently juror, and held other offices. He was the ancestor of the Mygatts in Fairfield and Litchfield counties. He was a valuable man in the colony.

Mygatt, John, 1648—perhaps son of Joseph.

N.

Nash, Joseph, constable of Hartford, 1660. Timothy admitted an inhabitant of Hartford, 1659. John was an assistant in 1662. The name was frequent in Massachusetts in the early settlement. Thomas, Fairfield.

Newbury, Thomas, married Ann Ford—supposed to be the son of Joseph.

Newbury, Joseph, (Mr. McClure says) came to Windsor in 1639. He was the ancestor of Gen. Newbury, formerly of Windsor. He was an early settler and a respectable family.

Newbury, Benjamin, married Mary Allyn, of Windsor, 1646—son of Joseph.

Newton, Rev. Roger, the first minister in Farmington about 1642, after about 9 years he moved to Milford, where he was installed. Rev. Samuel Hooker, son of Rev. Thomas Hooker succeeded him, and preached at Farmington about 40 years. He married the daughter of Rev. Thomas Hooker, of Hartford. He was installed at Milford in '60, and died in '83.

Newton, Thomas, elected deputy of Fairfield in 1644.

Newton, Benjamin, Haddam, 1673.

Newman, Robert, 1656. There were several of this name in Massachusetts in the early settlement of that colony. Antipas Newman married the daughter of Gov. Winthrop, of Massachusetts.

Nichols, Isaac, Fairfield, 1653—deputy in '62—supposed to be from Stratford.

Nichols, John, do. do.

Nichols, a sergeant, ordered to train the men at Hartford in 1639. Supposed to be Siborn Nichols.

Niccolls, Siborn—juror in 1661—appraiser of Dix's estate in '76. Ancestor of Cyprian Nichols, of Hartford. The name of Nichols is spelt differently by those of the same original ancestor. He settled an estate also, in 1670. Cyprian, of Hartford, juror in 1701. Cyprian has been a family name. There were many of the name of Nichols came to Massachusetts in the early settlement of that colony.

Northum, James, 1644. Signed the agreement in '59 to remove to Hadley. He moved and died there ; and the name is yet at Williamstown and other towns in Massachusetts, and one family at Hartford.

Norton, Capt. in 1634, was barbarously murdered with Stone and others of his crew, by the Indians on Connecticut River. (See John Endicott in No. 1.)

Norton, Francis, Hartford, 1639—juror in '44—fined £5 for a libel in '43. His ancestor was the agent of Capt. Mason.

Norton, John, made free in 1663.

Norton, James, 1640.

Norton, Thomas, 1647. The name is not numerous in the State at this time. John, a juror in '71.

North, Sarah, applied to the General Court to be divorced from her husband. The Court decided, that if she did not hear from her husband within seven years, she should be divorced, (six years having then expired.) It appears from this case, that seven years unheard of, has been a cause for divorce in Connecticut from its early settlement by the Puritans.

8

Nott, John, Wethersfield—on the jury in 1640—deputy in '62–3. Some distinguished men from this ancestor.

Nowell, Thomas, Windsor—died in 1648, and left a widow without children. He was a kinsman of Robert Wilson and Tabbe Phelps. He left an estate of £368. He came from Yorkshire.

Noyes, Nicholas, clergyman at Haddam as late as 1684.

Noyes, Richard, Haddam, 1674–76.

Noyes, Rev. James, Stonington—was the son of James who was from Wiltshire in England, and came to New England in 1634.

Noyes, Moses, Lyme, was a brother of James. He was the first minister in Lyme—lived to be aged, and preached there over 50 years.

O.

Oldham, John. In 1633 he resided in Dorchester, and came to Connecticut the same year, through the wilderness with three others, to trade for beaver with the Indians. The Indians on the Connecticut River made him most welcome, and gave him some beaver skins. He traded with them for hemp, which spontaneously grew on the low lands of Connecticut. Mr. Oldham was afterwards killed by the Indians near Block Island, and his estate was settled in the Connecticut colony. He had with him when killed, two boys and two Indians—these the murderers took with them. Capt. Gallup afterwards found Oldham on board of his vessel, (filled with Indians) with his head split and his body badly mangled. Capt. Gallup put the body into the sea—stripped the vessel of her rigging—and took from her what the Indians had left, and then took Oldham's vessel in tow, but night coming on with a high wind, he let her adrift, and she was lost.

Olcott, Thomas, 1640, constable of Hartford—died in '54—left a widow Abigail who died in '93. The children were, Thomas, Samuel, John, Elizabeth and Hannah. Thomas was the only one of the name who came to Connecticut in the first settlement. The biography of this family has been traced by N. Goodwin, Esq. from Thomas to the present descendants.

Olcott, Samuel, Hartford, 1676, son of Thomas.

Oldage, Richard, came to Windsor with Mr. Huet in 1639.

Olcoke, Thomas, 1639, 1643.

Olmsted, James, Hartford, came into the colony as early as 1639. He resided at Cambridge in 1632, and was a constable and freeman there. He died in 1640 or '41. His children were, Nicholas and Nehemiah. Nicholas married Miss Loomis, of Windsor. He had a cousin Rebecca Olmsted—Richard was also a kinsman as well as John. He left a large estate, and gave in his will £50 to the church in Hartford. The family, some of them, particularly Nicholas, must have come to Hartford as early as 1636.

Olmsted, Richard, Hartford, 1640—constable in '46—fence viewer in '49—deputy in '62-3. He moved to Norwalk, and was made a military officer. In 1661, he with John Banks and Joseph Judson were appointed by the General Court to run the town lines between Fairfield and Stratford. He and Nathaniel Ely were two of the first and principal settlers of Norwalk. And though Norwalk had been purchased some years previous and some few families had settled there; yet in 1650, Mr. Olmsted and Nathaniel Ely petitioned the General Court for a settlement of it—the Court so ordered, and called the town Norwalk, afterwards gave them town privileges. He was a leading man in that section of the colony.

Olmsted, Nicholas, Hartford, 1639—surveyor of roads in '46—a soldier at Mystic against the Pequotts in 1637, and son of James. In 1673 Lieut. Nicholas Olmsted with Capt. B. Newbury and John Wadsworth, Ensign, were appointed, if any forces were sent out of Hartford county for the relief of other counties, in case of a war with the Dutch, to command such forces so sent. Nicholas, grand juror in 1672.

Olmsted, Nehemiah, 1649, son of James.

Olmsted, Ensign, Hartford. The General Court granted him a farm of 300 acres in 1662.

Olmsted, John, Hartford, 1639—made free in '62.

Orcot, Thomas, Hartford, appointed with J. Talcott and W. Pantry to set off the meadow fences, and order the proportions between proprietors.

Orton, Thomas, Windsor, married Margaret Pell at Windsor, 1641, was a juror in '63-4—perhaps a son of Thomas, of Charlestown, Ms., 1642.

Osborn, Richard, Fairfield, 1653. There was a Richard Osborn at Hingham in '35—perhaps the same. The name was early at E. Hampton, L. I.

Osborn, John, 1643, married Ann Oldage, of Windsor, '45. He probably was the son of John of Weymouth.

Osborn, James, died in 1676. His children were, James, Sarah, Samuel, Elizabeth, Arnold and Mary Brace.

Orvis, George, died in 1664.

Owen, John, married Rebecca Wade, of Windsor, 1650. John Owen came to New Haven in 1641 or '42. Rev. John resided at Groton. The family came first to Massachusetts. John Owen had children, Josiah, John (died,) John, Nathaniel, Daniel, Joseph, Mary, Benjamin, Rebecca, Obadiah and Isaac—Josiah married Mary Osborn. Josiah in Simsbury, 1682. Hon. Daniel, of Rhode Island, Lieutenant Governor.

P.

Patrick, Daniel, and Robert Feaks first purchased Greenwich, as agents of the New Haven Company; and by the management of the Dutch Governor of New Netherlands, and other causes, the first settlers placed themselves under the government of the Dutch, and received their incorporation as a town of Peter Stuyvesant, the Governor of New Netherlands. In the Indian war with the Dutch, the settlers were driven from their homes, and did little more towards settling Greenwich until they were taken under the protection of the government of Connecticut after they had obtained the Charter.

Packer, John, New London, 1664.

Packet, John, 1665.

Palmes, 1663.

Panton, Richard, made free in 1663.

Parker, William, Hartford, an original proprietor in 1639—supposed moved to Saybrook or New London.

Parkman, Elias, owned a vessel in the colony in 1637. He came from Dorchester to Windsor in '35 or '36.

Parsons, Thomas, married Lydia Brown, of Windsor, 1641. There have been some men of distinction in Massachusetts and Connecticut by this name.

Parsons, Ebenezer, Windsor, 1676. Joseph and William, of Simsbury in 1682.

Park or Parks, Robert, a juror in 1641-2-3, and a grand juror in '43—deputy in '41,

Parks, Thomas, 1649—probably a son of Robert.

Pantry, William, Hartford, 1639. In land division in '39—juror '42-'44—grand juror in '43—viewer of chimneys in '49—townsman in '45—constable in '48—to set off meadow fence and proportion between proprietors in '43. He was from Cambridge, possibly the same William who was at Cambridge and admitted freeman there in 1635.

Patrigg, William, Hartford, (so spelt by himself,) was one who signed the agreement to move to Hadley in 1659.

Patrick, Capt., who commanded a company of men at the Mystic Fort, in 1637. After the close of the action, he started with 40 men, in company with Major Mason, with 20 men for Saybrook, through the woods, a distance of about twenty miles, while Capt. Underhill went by water and took with him the Indian prisoners and the men who had been wounded in the action. This took place upon the 27th of May, 1637, which was on Saturday. The Sabbath was spent at the Fort with Lieut. Gardner, who treated them with the kindness they so richly merited.

Palmer, Edward, Hartford, 1645. The name of Edward has been a family name in Massachusetts in the Palmer family. The name is common in the centre and eastern part of Connecticut.

Palmer, Nicholas, went to Windsor in 1639 with Mr. Huet—and is found in the colony in '61.

Palmer, Henry, 1648.

Palmer, Walter, 1658.

Palmer, William, juror in 1642—made free, '60.

Patridge, John, 1656.

Patridge or Partridge, William, 1656, was an important man in the early settlement of Fairfield county. William Partridge is found a chimney viewer at Hartford in '59—perhaps the same.

Payne, John, Hartford, 1639, constable. No man in Connecticut held the office of constable as early as 1639, unless he was a man of high standing in his town. They were the principal directors of town affairs. A constable was the first officer appointed by the General Court in forming a new town —a kind of confidential adviser of the General Court in town matters.

Payne, M. 1664.

Peck, Deac. Paul, Hartford, 1639—held some offices in the colony, and was an early settler, and resided in Hartford. Richard Peck and his wife Margery and family, came to New England in the Defence, of London. Paul Peck was of great use in the town and colony in its early settlement. Some of the family moved to Milford.

Peck, Joseph, moved to Saybrook.

Pearce, John, Hartford, 1639.

Perkins, William, had liberty of the Court at Boston, with William Sergeant, Thomas Hardy, Thomas Howlet, Robert Coles, and five others, under John Winthrop, jr., to plant at Agawam, about 1632— (Ipswich.)

Perkins, John, 1646, came from Massachusetts. There was a John Perkins who came to Massachusetts in '31—two other John Perkins' were admitted freemen there as early as '33 and '37. John Perkins, (spelt on the record Purkis) had 6 acres of land in the division of the up-land east of the river.

Pette, John, first found upon the land record in Windsor, 1666— probably son of John of Springfield.

Pete, and Alexander Knowles, appointed assistants, Fairfield, 1661.

Peters, Rev. Thomas, came to Saybrook with Mr. Fenwick, and was the first minister there. There had been but a few settlers there previous to the arrival of Mr. Fenwick, and those who came with him, except the officers and men of the fort. It had been little more than a military post. Many of the inhabitants of the three old towns, after 1644, moved to Saybrook and cultivated farms. It had progressed slowly as a settlement until the colony purchased the fort and lands upon the river in 1644. Upon the settlement of Norwich many of the principal men of Saybrook, with Mr. Fitch, the minister, moved to Norwich, viz. Major Mason, Thomas Tracy, and others.

Pell, Thomas, New London county, was made free, 1662. It was ordered, that those who wished to be freemen should present themselves in person, with a certificate under the hands of a majority of the townsmen where they resided, that they were persons of civil, peaceable and honest conversation, and of the age of 21 years, and had £20 estate, exclusive of the poll, in the list. With such certificate and the approbation of the General Court, they could be made free. A Doctor Pell, supposed to be Thomas or his father, who resided at the fort as physician under Lieut. Gardner, went with Major Mason as surgeon for the little army to meet the Pequotts in the battle in 1637—but proved himself cowardly by remaining on board the vessel, instead of going up to the battle to the relief of the wounded. Probably the same Thomas Pell who came to Massachusetts in the Hopewell.

Penfield, William, Middletown, 1663.

Perry, Richard, Fairfield, 1649.

Perry, Francis, 1663.

Pettibone, John, is first found on the records of lands in Windsor, 1666. The family probably settled in what is now Simsbury, on first coming to Windsor. John, of Simsbury, '82. Samuel, do. 1730. Owen, do. 1846.

Pettibone, John, Simsbury, married Sarah Egglestone in 1664—his children were, John, Sarah and Stephen.

Pepper, William, was brought before the court for an offence. He confessed he had committed several robberies in 1661. Had broken prison and was punished for it in May, 1661. In 1663 committed several robberies on Long Island and Shelter Island, and tried for it at Southhold, and was banished and sold in Barbadoes for three years as a servant.

Phelps, William, Esq., Windsor, came with Mr. Warham's church to Windsor, in 1635. He married before he came from England, and had four children before he moved to Windsor, viz. William, Samuel, Nathaniel and Joseph—Timothy was born at Windsor in 1639, and Mary in 1644—the latter married Thomas Barber. He was a member of the first Court held in the colony in 1636, to try Henry Stiles; he was also a member of the Court of Magistrates in 1637, which declared war against the Pequotts; also in 1638 and '39, 1640-1-2-3, was an assistant (in the Upper House). He was foreman of the first grand jury in 1643, that attended the General Court—and deputy in 1646. He aided in enacting the first law in the colony, in 1639, after the compact of the towns on Connecticut River, and was afterwards an assistant to the Governor in the General Assembly. He was a member of the General Court for twelve sessions. He was one of a Committee to consult the Elders, and form a law against lying—was a Committee with Haynes, Hopkins and Welles to form criminal laws for the colony—to treat with George Fenwick for liberty to make salt on the Long Island Sound—and was on the war Committee against the Quinnipiac Indians. Mr. Phelps was one of the most efficient and valuable officers in the colony—his whole time must have been occupied in the service of the public. He was a brother of George and Samuel Phelps. Mr. Phelps, with Roger Ludlow, Henry Wolcott, Mr. Warham, John Mason, Thomas Lord, and Matthew Allyn were some of the leading men of Windsor and in the colony for many years.

Phelps, George, came to Windsor with Mr. Warham in 1636—brother of William and Samuel Phelps. From William, George and Samuel—the three brothers, who settled at Windsor, came the Phelps's of Connecticut. William was a magistrate in 1636. George married Miss Randall, daughter of Philip—she died in 1648—children, Isaac, Abraham and Joseph—by a second wife, Jacob, John and Nathaniel, and died at Westfield, 1678.

Phelps, Samuel, brother of William and George Phelps—came to Windsor in the early part of the settlement, and died in 1669. Left children, Samuel, 17 years old, Sarah 15, Timothy 13, Mary 11, William 9, John 7, Ephraim 6, Abigail 3, and Josiah 2. William Thrall appraised his estate. The Phelps's brothers came from Dorchester—George went there in 1630.

Phillips, William, Hartford, viewer of chimneys and ladders in 1643—appointed to designate the location of a fence at Podunk the same year—selectman in '45.

Phillips, Ann, died in 1669 without issue. She was a sister of John Rogers, of England—moved to Hadley before the death of her husband, and owned land in Hartford at her decease.

Phillips, George, Windsor, settled in 1639.

Phiax, of Pequott, 1649.

Physic, Thomas, 1649.

Pierson, Rev. Abraham, was the first clergyman settled at Branford. He united with Davenport in opposing the union of the two colonies in 1665 with great inflexibility. He was rigid to excess in church communion, and disapproved of the liberality of the clergy in the Connecticut colony in this respect; he differed with them upon the ordinance of infant baptism, &c., as no person in the New Haven colony could be made a freeman unless he was in full communion with the church. He fully agreed with Davenport and some others in that colony, that no other government than that of the church should be maintained in the colony, and opposed any union with Connecticut for the reason that a good character and an orderly walk, with £30 estate, or had held office in the colony, was all that was required to make a man a freeman in the colony of Connecticut, which would mar the order and purity of the churches. And he unquestionably feared it might weaken the power of the clergy, who had possessed the entire control of the government over the people of the colony of New Haven. Indeed Mr. Pierson was so much dissatisfied, and most of his church and congregation united with him, (Dr. Trumbull says) that they soon left Branford and removed to Newark, N. J., and carried with them, not only the records of the church but the town records also. After it had been settled about 25 years, he left the place nearly destitute of inhabitants; and Branford was not resettled until about 20 years after Mr. Pierson left it. Some of his descendants are now of the best families in New Haven and Hartford. He was from Yorkshire, England, and came to Boston and was there a member of the church—he went from thence to South Hampton, L. I., as their minister, and from thence he removed with a part of his church to Branford, and for the cause before related, he with his church removed to Newark, where many of his descendants now reside. (He is noticed in this work because South Hampton had been under the government of Connecticut.)

Pierson, John, Middletown, died in 1677, and left one son.

Pierce, Edward, Wethersfield, 1640. There are many of this name in different parts of Connecticut, viz. Southbury, Cornwall, Bristol, and Litchfield. Edward and John came from Watertown, Mass.

Pierce, John, 1639—ancestor of Rev. George Pierce, President of Hudson College, Ohio—of the Hon. John Pierce, of Southbury, former Senator of Connecticut, brother of George.

Piddell, Corbit, 1649.

Picket, John, Wethersfield, 1660.

Pinkney, Philip, Fairfield, 1654.

Pinson, Andrew, 1669.

Pinney, Humphrey, was one of the first settlers at Windsor in 1639. He was a juror in 1645. He was from Dorchester in Massachusetts, and was probably the ancestor of the few persons of the name now in Connecticut. One of the sons moved east of the river, the remainder of the family continued on the west side. He was the ancestor of Judge Pinney, of Ellington, and of Sidney, of Hartford. He married Mary Hall in Dorchester. His children were, Samuel, Nathaniel, Mary, Sarah, John, Abigail and Isaac.

Pinney, Nathaniel, son of Humphrey, died at Windsor, 1676—left children, Nathaniel and Sarah.

Pin, Richard, 1656.

Piper, of Haddam in 1676.

Piser, of Saybrook, 1669.

Plant, John, was in the colony in 1639. It appears he did not remain at Hartford—probably went to Fairfield county, it being about the time Stratford was settled. The name is now at Stratford, in the person of the Hon. David Plant, former member of Congress and Lieut. Governor of Connecticut.

Plumb, Joseph, Wethersfield, came there in 1636, and was a member of the Court in '37, also in '38 and '41. He was fined £10 for signing a paper against Rev. Mr. Smith. He aided in settling Oldham's estate in '36–7—was often a juror and member of the General Court as magistrate and deputy.

Plumb, John, 1639—perhaps son of Joseph.

Plummer, of Wethersfield, 1638—probably the ancestor of the Hon. George Plummer, of Glastenbury, which once was a part of Wethersfield. The name is sometimes spelt Plumer. Francis Plummer came from Wales to New England in '63, and settled at Newbury.—*Farm.*

Pitkin, William, was early in the colony. He was a lawyer by profession, and often appeared in defence of criminals. He was the first attorney general appointed for the colony in 1662—and the first that induced the court to suffer a change of pleadings upon a change of jurisdiction, on an appeal to a higher court. He for a time was Treasurer of the colony. William Pitkin, Governor from 1766 to 1770—Deputy Governor from 1754 to 1766. He was often deputy and a magistrate. Either the first William must have had a son William, who was sent by Connecticut, in 1693, to Governor Fletcher of New York, respecting the militia of the colony, or he was aged when he performed the service. It has been a respectable family from Mr. Pitkin the first to the present period. As he was the first and only person of the name who came early into Connecticut, he undoubtedly was the ancestor of William who was Governor and Deputy Governor of Connecticut for 15 years; also of Rev. Timothy, minister at Farmington, and Timothy, LL. D., formerly member of Congress. The first William settled at Hartford. He taught school at Hartford from October to April, 1662, for £5—probably was poor when he began life.

Pomeroy, Eltwed or Edward, Windsor, had his horse killed by the Indians in 1637. His sons in 1640 were, Caleb, Eldad, Joseph, and Joshua. Caleb married Hepzibah Baker, and moved to Northampton. He was the ancestor of a respectable family in Hartford, and of Ralph Pomeroy of the Revolution. He was the only one of the name that came into the colony in the early settlement. The public remunerated him in part for his horse killed by the Indians in the early settlement of Windsor, but not until 1660. He then received £10 in wampum at 6 a penny.

Pond, Nathaniel, Windsor, died in 1675. Thomas Pond and Wm. Reeve came from England in the Elizabeth and Ann to N. England.

Porter, John, Windsor, came in the first settlement of the town—juror in 1641—grand juror in 1643—recorder in 1640—constable in 1639-40. He was ordered by the Court to keep Starks with locks and chains, and to hard labor and coarse fare until called for. He was an important man in the colony. He died at Windsor, 1618, and left a large estate to his children, viz. John, James, Samuel, Nathaniel, Rebecca, Rose, Mary, Anna and Joseph. To Joseph he gave 20 shillings. He was the ancestor of several of the name in Hartford.

Post, John and Thomas, made free in 1663.

Porter, Joshua, a juror in 1641.

Porter, Daniel, received his salary as physician out of the public treasury in 1661—was in the colony in '44.

Porter, Jonathan, 1639. Hezekiah, 1645.

Porter, Samuel, signed the agreement to move to Hadley in 1659. He was the son of John.

Porwidge or Periwydge, William, 1644.

Post, Stephen, Hartford, 1639—constable in '41—was in the division of lands in Hartford in '39. Some of the family moved down the River.

Pratt, John, Hartford, 1639—townsman in '41—constable in '44—deputy in '39 in April and August—member of the first grand jury in '43—juror in '42; he was a juror, deputy and a magistrate, and was an important man in the colony. He came here amongst the first settlers of Hartford.

Pratt, William, Hartford, one of the first settlers, as early as 1639. There are many of the name in the county of Hartford. He moved to Saybrook, and was made a lieutenant there in 1661—he became a prominent man there.

Pratt, Abraham, came early into the colony.

Pratt, Thomas, juror in 1643.

Presson, Edward, 1643.

Preston, William, probably was an officer, as he was ordered by the court in 1642, to take into his custody, James Hullet, Thomas Gilbert, George Gibbs and Lydia Bliss, and keep them in gins, with coarse diet, hard work and sharp correction. A William Preston came from England in the ship Truelove, James Gibbs, master—this may be the same William Preston. John Preston came with him.

Prentice, John, N. London, fined £5 for notching a colt's tail, 1664.

Price, William, 1636—probably a brother of John who married a daughter of Henry Wolcott, Esq. of Windsor.

Prior, Humphrey, 1646.

Provost, David, 1647.

Prudden, Rev. Peter—had charge of the church in Wethersfield, in 1638—he left there in 1639 or '40; after which Rev. Henry Smith took the charge of the church there. At this time (1640) a settlement was commencing at Milford, to which place Mr. Prudden removed, and took with him a few of his congregation from Wethersfield. They purchased of the Indians all the land between New Haven (west line) and Stratford, the river being the west line of Milford. The town of Milford was greatly aided in its first settlement by emigrants from the towns of Windsor, Hartford and Wethersfield. It was claimed by Connecticut as within her jurisdiction, as other towns were, where the early settlers went from Connecticut, as was Stratford, Fairfield and Norwalk. It was also claimed by New Haven.

Putman, Elias, 1642.

Purcase or Purchis, John, 1639—perhaps the same that was at Boston in 1656.

Pyne, James, 1647.

Pyncheon, William, came to New England as early as 1630. He was one of the principal settlers and founders of the church at Roxbury (near Boston.) He was made an assistant and treasurer of that colony. In 1636, he with a company from Roxbury and vicinity, removed and became the pioneers in settling Springfield. For a few years Springfield was united with Connecticut, and was claimed by it as one of her towns. Mr. Pyncheon was made a magistrate and judge of the Court of Connecticut as early as November, 1636. He attended the General Court, as a member, at three different sessions in 1636–7–8. His vessel was applied for by the General Court in 1637, to transport the men and munitions of war in the expedition against the Pequotts. In 1638 he was fined by the General Court 40 bushels of corn for his carelessness in the purchase of corn of the Indians. He was allowed by the General Court to trade with the Indians for beaver—a privilege given to only eight persons in Connecticut. Mr. Pyncheon was questioned, while a member of the Court, as to Mr. Plumb's imprisoning, whipping and freezing an Indian at Agawam; and the Court decided "to overlook the failings of Mr. Plumb against an Indian." In 1637 he was employed by the General Court to purchase and deliver 500 bushels of corn at 5 shillings per bushel, conditioned that if the Indians brought corn down the river, only 4 shillings per bushel should be paid them, and if paid in wampum, to be at 3 a penny, or beaver at 9 shillings a pound. He probably had a storehouse at Hartford, as he owned a vessel, and was an active business man, and employed by the colony as agent for the purchase of corn on the river. He was a thorough business man, and as a civilian he ranked with the most prominent and efficient settlers. He at length refused to have the people of Springfield pay duties for their exports down the river, to Mr. Fenwick in payment for the fort at Saybrook, which impost had been laid by Connecticut, and which occasioned at last much controversy between the two colonies of Connecticut and Massachusetts, in which Mr. Pyncheon espoused the cause of the latter. In 1652 Mr. Pyncheon returned to England. He had two wives—the first died before his return, and his second at Wainsbury in Buckinghamshire, in 1657. He died in England in 1662. His children were, Major John, Anna, Margaret and Mary. John remained at Springfield and became a prominent military man as well as civilian in that colony. He became one of the council of Sir Edmund Andross in 1687. He married the daughter of Hon. George Wyllys, of Connecticut—by whom he had sons, John, Joseph and William, and daughters, Mary and Mehetibel. The family have maintained a respectable standing since the first settlement of Roxbury and Springfield.

Q.

Quinby, John, made free in 1663.

R.

Rayner, Thurston, one of the pillars of the church in Wethersfield, and one of the chief men in civil matters in the town and colony. He was a committee to the General Court in 1637, and fined 5 shillings for absence—was again committee in 1648, and deputy in 1639—to preserve Mr. Oldham's corn, 1636—and held many offices in Wethersfield. He removed to Stamford, and in 1643 was nominated with Mr. Mitchell for magistrates in Stamford. Mr. Rayner was appointed judge, and Capt. Underhill, M. Mitchell, H. Ward and Robert Coe were appointed his assistant judges, which was the first court in Stamford, composed of men from Wethersfield who had removed there.

Ramon, a witness in 1670.

Randall, Abraham, at Windsor in 1635—he came in the first colony—juror in '71.

Randall, Philip, 1643.

Rawlins, Joseph, 1640.

Read, Giles, 1663—William, George and Ralph Read came to N. England in the ship Defence.

Reemes, Joseph, a carpenter under Stiles, 1636.

Remmington, 1676.

Renolds, John, made free in 1663.

Renolds, James, 1646.

Reynolds, Robert, Wethersfield—went to the fort, and died in Saybrook in 1662. His children were, Reinold, Mary and Hannah.

Reeves, Robert, chimney viewer of Hartford, 1660.

Rice, Jonathan, New London, made free in 1663.

Rice, Michael, do. do. do.

Richards, James, was an assistant in 1664–71–72, and held many important posts in the colony before and after '70—selectman of Hartford in '62. Mr. Richards, in '64 was appointed with Matthew Allyn, Nathan Gold and Captain Winthrop, by the Assembly, to accompany Gov. John Winthrop, of Connecticut, to New York, together with Capt. John Young and Mr. Howell, of Long Island, to meet his Majesty's Commissioners, regarding the claim of the Duke of York to Long Island and Connecticut.

Richards, Nathaniel, of Hartford, was in the colony in 1639—constable in '41 and '49—orderer of the town in '44—deputy in '43. In '73 James Richards and Mr. Roswell were appointed by the General Court to go forthwith to New York, with a letter prepared by the Court for the Dutch commander-in-chief at Manhatoes, and bring his answer. In case Mr. Roswell could not go, Major Robert Treat was appointed. Had 26 acres of land in the division of up-lands, east of the river, 1640.

Richards, Widow, died in 1671. She left sons, John, Thomas and Obadiah, and a daughter, Mary Peck, of Milford.

Richards, Samuel, Hartford—deputy in 1643.

Richards, Thomas, 1640.

Richards, John, 1663.

Riley, Richard, had resided at Hockanum, but moved to Wethersfield, where he died in 1648. He left sons and daughters and a large estate. The children were placed, by his will, in charge of William Hill, of Windsor, to be educated.

Rising, James, 1676.

Riley, John, Wethersfield, a carpenter—juror in 1649 and '71—died in '74. His children were, John, Joseph, Mary, Jonathan, Grace, Sarah, Jacob and Isaac. Jacob, of Windsor, 1730.

Risley, Samuel, 1645—died 1670.

Robbins, John, Wethersfield, deputy in 1643.

Robbins, Samuel, Wethersfield, 1663 The Robbins' family settled in Wethersfield early, and have many descendants yet there.

Robbinson, Thomas, 1640.

Rockwell, Simon, Windsor, died in 1665. His estate fell to the children of his two sisters. The wife of Robert Watson had children, Mary, John, Samuel, Hannah, Ebenezer and Nathaniel Watson. His second sister married Zachery Sanford, and had children, Zachery, Hannah, Ruth and Ezekiel.

Rockwell, Samuel, 1647.

Rockwell, John, Windsor, died in '73. His children were, Elizabeth, 37 years old, Sarah 20, Ruth 19, Lydia 17, Hannah 8, and Joseph 5. I also find a John Rockwell, jr., in '49.

Rogers, James, New London, who had located 150 acres of land at or near New London, in 1659, by liberty of the General Court, with liberty to improve the lands which Uncas had given him. Richard Rogers, Stratford, 1730. Samuel Rogers, N. London, 1664. James is supposed to be the person by the name, who came to this country from England in the ship Increase, with Matthew Marvin, the Bucks, Kilbourns, &c. A deputy in '62–63, and grand juror in '62. He was an important settler at New London.

Rood, Sarah, 1673.

Roscose or Ruscoe, Nathaniel—surveyor in Hartford, 1661—died in '73, and left a son Nathaniel. He was an early settler.

Roscoe, William, 1639—juror in '44.

Rose, Robert, Wethersfield, was one of the first settlers—was constable in 1639—juror in '41—deputy in '42, and had frequent manifestations of the confidence placed in his capacity and integrity by the town and General Court, by the repeated offices bestowed upon him by both.

Rose, John, juror in 1649.

Root, John, 1656, juror in '71. John, of Farmington, made free in 1663.

Root, Thomas, Hartford, 1639—in the land division in '39.

Rowe, Henry, Hartford, courier, admitted an inhabitant in 1659.

Rowe, Hugh, leather sealer in Hartford, 1663.

Rowley, Thomas, Windsor, 1640—a land holder in '76.

Rossiter, Bray, Windsor—came with Mr. Huet, in 1639, and was an ensign and recorder in 1640—also a juror and deputy in 1643—afterwards he was frequently a juror, deputy, and held other offices. In 1662 he purchased land on Stratford river (Housatonic) at Paugassette, of which the Court approved, and gave him liberty to purchase 100 acres more. He was a physician, and was allowed by the General Court £5 for visiting Mr. Talcott in his sickness, to be paid out of the treasury, in 1660. He was also allowed in 1662, by the Court, £20 for doctoring the Deputy Governor and Mr. John Talcott, and a post-mortem examination of Kelley's child. Public men were public property, and the public paid the physician's bill to attend them.

Rowland, Henry, Fairfield, 1649.

Royce, Robert, Saybrook, 1669.

Rudd, Jonathan, 1639.

Rudd, John, was appointed commissioner for the town of Hastings, with the power of a magistrate, by the General Court of Connecticut. In October, 1663, the General Court united Hastings with the town of Rye, N. Y. and was incorporated as one town, and has remained so since.

Rugg, Robert, 1646.

Ruscoe, William, came from England in a vessel called the Increase, Robert Lea, master, to Massachusetts, with his family, and was among the first settlers of Hartford in the settlement of the colony. He was juror in 1664, and at the division of the lands in Hartford in '39.— (See Roscoe.)

Russell, Jonathan or John, second minister of Wethersfield in 1665, dismissed in '67—signed an agreement in '59 to remove to Massachusetts—did afterwards move and died there.

Russell, John, deputy in 1646–8.

S.

Saddler, John, an early settler of Wethersfield, 1643—died in '75, and left a widow, Deborah, and no children.

Sadd, Thomas, Windsor, 1645.

Sage, David, Middletown, 1675, married a daughter of John Kirby.

Saltonstall, Sir Richard, settled at Watertown. He was one of the magistrates who came to Massachusetts with Gov. Winthrop in 1630. Many of these people were the first settlers of Wethersfield, in Connecticut, in 1635-6. Sir Richard was one of the associates and owners of the large tract of land upon the Connecticut River, of which John Winthrop as Governor and Agent took possession in 1635. It is supposed he afterwards located at Saybrook or New London.

Saltonstall, Robert, 1641.

Salter, John, died in 1673—left no children.

Samoy, Richard, 1640.

Sanders, George, Windsor, 1671—came some time before '71.

Sanford, Robert, sen'r., died in 1676—left a wife and children—Zechariah, Robert, Hannah, Sarah, Abigail, Elizabeth, Colio, Ezekiel, and Mary Camp.

Sanford, Peleg, 1656.

Sanford, Zechariah, Hartford, 1645, son of Robert, selectman of Saybrook, '64.

Sanford, Robert, 1640, son of Robert.

Sanford, Nathan, surveyor of roads in 1662.

Sables, John, Hartford, 1639–48. Held land in Hartford, '39, by liberty of the town, with the right of wood, and to keep cows and swine—not being an original proprietor of Hartford.

Samwis, Richard, 1649.

Savill, John, viewer of fences, 1645. The name is in Massachusetts.

Sawyer, Richard, died in 1647.

Saxton, Widow, of Windsor, died in June, 1674. Her children, John 25 years old, Richard 20—Sarah was married—Mary married George Saunders—Patience, 16.

Scott, Thomas, in 1635 or '36 he kept a bridge over brick-kiln brook, in Hartford, at 5 shillings per annum. He died in '42—left a widow, one son and two daughters. A man of good character.

Scott, Edmond, 1649.

Segar, Richard, Simsbury, 1680.

Segar, Elizabeth, wife of Richard. In 1665 she was indicted for entertaining a familiarity with Satan, the grand enemy of God and mankind, and practising witchcraft against the laws of God and the Corporation ; to which she pled not guilty. But the jury on trial returned a verdict of guilty. The Court found the verdict did not legally answer the indictment, and discharged the prisoner. She had before been tried for witchcraft, and acquitted.

Sedgwick, Ebenezer, Hartford, 1644. He was the ancestor of several noted families of this State, and Hon. Theodore, of Massachusetts. A part of his descendants reside in West Hartford, Sharon and Cornwall, in this State—also in New York.

Selden, Thomas, Hartford, 1639—constable in '49—an original proprietor in Hartford in the land division in '39.

Selden, Isaac, Windsor, 1639.

Sension, Nicholas, Windsor, 1645. He came from England in company with Joseph Alsoppe in a vessel called the Elizabeth and Ann, and was an early settler in Windsor.

Senchion or St. John, Matthias, 1640.

Seely, Lieut. Robert—resided in Wethersfield in 1636—came from Watertown. He was ordered in 1636, to look up the property of John Oldham—was a lieutenant and commander under Major Mason in the Pequott battle in 1637. After the conquest, he was sent with 30 men under him, to settle and hold possession of the territory, with an addition of 10 men, afterwards ordered there. He with Major Mason, Stanton, Adams, Gibbs, Henry Starks and Tho. Merrick were appointed by the General Court to treat with the Indians for corn. He was for a time an officer at the Fort after it was purchased by Connecticut. He was a useful man in the colony as an Indian fighter as well as a civilian. He is supposed to be the ancestor of those of his name in Fairfield county, and New York. In 1663 he was a captain and chief military officer at Huntington, L. I., to exercise the men there ; and the same year was appointed a commissioner for the town of Huntington, L. I., by the General Court of Connecticut.

Sessions, Matthew, juror in 1643.

Seymour, Richard, Hartford, 1639—chimney viewer in '46. He held land by liberty of the town, and had the privilege of fetching wood and keeping cows and swine, with many others who were not original proprietors.

Seymour, Zechariah, Hartford, 1645. This family were connected by marriage with the best families in the colony.

Sexton, Richard, Windsor, 1643. Richard Sexton, Robert Lewis, Barnabie Davies and Christian Buck embarked in England in a vessel named the Blessing, John Lester, master, for New England, previous to the settling of Mr. Sexton at Windsor.

Shaddock, Elias, died at Windsor in 1676, and left a widow and one child.

Shears, John, died in 1669 and left a son John.

Sheldon, Isaac, Windsor, 1640. Thomas, Hartford, '41.

Shelly, Henry, 1663.

Shepard, Edward, father of John—he appears to have resided in Hartford. He had a son John, a daughter Deborah Fairbanks, one Sarah Thompson, and another Abigail.

Shepard, John, Hartford, son of Edward. He became a man of consequence in the colony.

Sherman, Joseph, Wethersfield, 1636—often a juror and deputy. Daniel Sherman was a grand juror in '72. The Sherman family have been respectable since the first settlement.

Sherman, Thomas, Fairfield, 1651.

Sherman, Samuel, John Howell, Nathan Gold and John Mason were of the Particular Court in 1664. Sherman, Gold and Canfield were appointed to hold a Court at Fairfield, under the Charter, in '62, and Stamford, Greenwich and Westchester were allowed to try their cases at Fairfield. John, 1644.

Sherwood, Thomas, 1645—had a son John, who moved to Stratford, and in '54, he with Thomas Fairchild were appointed by the Court to press men for an expedition against the Dutch.

Sharpe, 1645.

Sherlock, John. 1663.

Sherrall, Thomas, juror in 1649.

Sherwington, Thomas, 1651.

Shore, Samson, 1649.

Simonds, Rev., 1663.

Sipperante, Joanne, 1649.

Skidmore, Thomas, do.

Skinner, John, Hartford, juror in 1639—an original proprietor of Hartford—had 22 acres in the division of up-land east of the river in '40. Joseph, Windsor, '46. Richard, '48. John, juror in '71.

Slater, John, Simsbury, 1682, register of the town.

Sly, Robert, 1648.

Smith, Rev. Henry, was the first settled minister at Wethersfield—he had been a clergyman in England, and most of his congregation in Wethersfield came from Watertown, in Massachusetts, in 1635 and '36, where they had been under the charge of Mr. Phillips, who did not move to Wethersfield with his church and congregation. Rev. Cotton Mather Smith, who was born at Suffield, 1731, and settled in Sharon, Connecticut, was the son of Samuel Smith, who was a grandson of the Rev. Henry Smith, of Wethersfield. Hon. John Cotton Smith, former Governor of Connecticut, was a son of the Rev. Cotton Mather Smith, and the present John Cotton Smith, Esq., is the grandson of the late Gov. Smith. The children of Rev. Henry Smith were, Samuel, Peregrine, Noah, and other small children, and two daughters who were married at his decease.

Smith, Lieut. Samuel, New London. The General Court ordered, in 1662, that the inhabitants at Mystic and Pawkatuck should exercise no authority by virtue of any commissions from any other colony, (Massachusetts); and in case of difficulty in obeying this order, were ordered to apply to the Deputy Governor—and were ordered to choose a constable for the town, and to pay to Mr. Avery, Samuel Smith and James Rogers £20 as their share of the expense of procuring the Charter for the colony.

Smith, Samuel, 1640—deputy in April, '38–41, also in '44. He owned a vessel in '49—was deputy in November and March, '37—and was also a magistrate. Supposed of New London.

Smith, Arthur, Hartford, 1639—fence viewer in '39—deputy in '43, constable in '40. Whoever reads this "Catalogue," may well suppose all the Smiths were Puritans. Arthur Smith was a soldier in the bloody battle with the Pequotts at Mystic Fort in 1637, where he was severely wounded, and was rescued from the flames of the fort by some of his brother soldiers.

Smith, Thomas, died at Haddam, 1674.

Smith, Rebecca, in 1667, was divorced from Samuel Smith, by the General Court, for his three years wilful absence from her. This law is yet in our statute book, with little alteration.

Smith, Quince, New London, (probably an officer)—complained to the General Court, that Uncas refused to pay a fine imposed upon him by the commissioners of New London. The Court referred it to Mr. Tinker to see that Uncas paid it, '60.

Smith, William, Farmington, died in 1669. Left children, Jonathan, Jobana, Joseph, Benjamin, William, Samuel, Susannah, Elizabeth and Mehitabel.

Smith, Joseph, died in 1673, and left children, Jonathan 10 years old, Samuel 7, Lydia 19, and Joseph 13.

Smith Giles, 1639. George, '40. Simon, '46. Edmond, '43.— Patience, '48.

Southmead or Southmayd, 1645—probably moved to Middletown, where the name has been known from the early settlement of the town.

Spencer, Thomas, Hartford—a committee to view the land where the fence had been made at Podunk, and locate the fence to be made there in 1644—viewer of chimneys in '49—was in the colony in '39 —in the land division in '39. He was an original proprietor.

Spencer, William, Hartford, deputy in August and September, 1639 —committee to inspect arms once in three months, and provide powder for Hartford in '39. He was appointed with Mr. George Wyllys and Mr. Welles to revise the laws of the colony in '39—selectman in '39—an original proprietor of Hartford—ancestor of Hon. Joshua Spencer, of Utica, N. Y. Samuel Spencer, Hartford, 1670.

Spikes, Gerrard, Hartford, 1645.

Sprague, John and Lydia.

Stafford, Thomas, near New London in 1671.

Stairs, Thomas, Windsor, 1640.

Starkey, George, Fairfield, 1649.

Standish, Thomas, juror in 1649.

Stanley, Timothy, Hartford, townsman and juror in 1639 and '42. He died in '48, and left a good estate to his widow and children, viz. Caleb, Isaac, Lois and a younger daughter. Nathaniel Stanley was treasurer of the colony. Caleb Stanley was secretary of the colony from 1709 to 1711 inclusive.

Stanley, Thomas, Hartford, 1639—constable in '47—juror in '39 and '43. He is supposed to be the Thomas Stanley who came to Massachusetts in the vessel called the Planter, as he was one of the early settlers of Hartford soon after.

Stanton, Thomas, Wethersfield—in 1638, was appointed by the General Court a public officer to attend all the courts or meetings of magistrates, as an interpreter for the English and Indians, with a salary of £10 per annum for his services. In 1638 he was allowed to trade with the Indians on the river in Wethersfield for beaver—was constable in 1644. The same year the General Court granted him free trade with the Indians upon Long Island for 12 months. He was an active and useful man in transactions with the Indians. He was an original proprietor in Hartford, and was a great friend and supporter of Captain Mason.

Stark, Henry, Hartford, 1640—he was a man of worth, and after a few years died, and gave by will, a clock to the church in Hartford.

Starks, Aaron, Hartford, 1639. (This case is inserted to show the extreme severity of their punishment for bastardy.) He was placed upon the pillory on a lecture-day during the lecture—then tied to the tail of a cart, and whipped in Hartford, (probably through Main-street)—then taken to Windsor, and at the tail of a cart again whipped—then had the letter R. burnt upon his cheek, and fined £10, to be paid to the parents of Mary Holt, and then ordered to marry her. The punishment of the girl for her offence was referred to Mr. Ludlow and William Phelps to decide. She was afterwards whipped. In 1643 he was again whipped for another offence, and ordered to serve Captain Mason during the pleasure of the court.

Stanley, Caleb, son of Timothy, Hartford, 1645—became a man of much consequence in the colony, and received by his worth repeated honors from his town and the colony. Indeed the Stanley family maintained a high reputation in the jurisdiction for many years after the union of the two colonies. In 1709 Caleb Stanley was elected, or rather appointed secretary of the colony, which he held three years, and honorably discharged its duties. The descendants of the family are believed not to be numerous, but respectable. He was grand juror in 1672 and '77.

Staples, Thomas, with Philip Groves, Robert Warner, Joseph Judson, Walter Hoyt, James Avery, J. Morgan and Robert Chapman were deputies or made free in 1661. Staples deputy and juror, '49.

Stanborough, Josiah, died in 1659. His children and estate were taken into the possession of the selectmen.

Stebbins, Francis, died in 1673. His children were, Sarah Rockwell aged 20, Ruth 19, Lydia 17, Hannah 8, Joseph 5, and Elizabeth 3. Stebbins, New London, constable, '61.

Stebbins, Deac. Edward—juror in 1639 and '43—deputy in '39–41 and '48—selectman in '47—collector of funds for the students of Cambridge College, by order of the General Court, in 1645. He died in 1663, and left a grand child Edward Cadwell—his daughter married Mr. Cadwell—another daughter married Gaylord, who had children, Joseph, Benjamin, Joanna and Mary Gaylord—another daughter married Wilson, who had two sons, John and Samuel. He came among the first settlers from Cambridge to Hartford.

Stedman, Robert, Windsor, 1647. Thomas.

Stedman, Lieut. John, 1645—died in '75, and left his land in Hartford to his son John. He had other children.

Steel, John, Hartford, deputy in April, Sept. and Jan. 1639, and March, '37—was a member of the Upper House of the General Court in April, June, July and Feb. 1636, and in May and Nov. 1637, and deputy in Dec. 1637, in April, 1640, also in June and Feb. 1640, also in Sept. Nov. and Jan. 1641, also in April and August, 1642, in March, April, Sept. Nov. and Feb. 1643, in April, Sept. Nov. Dec. and Feb. 1644, in April, July, Sept. and Oct. 1645, in April, 1646, in May and March, 1647, in Sept. and Oct. 1648, and many sessions afterwards. Mr. Steel was of the Court that declared war against the Pequotts. He was the town register in Hartford in 1639, which office he held until he removed to Farmington. He was a valuable man in the colony, and was the ancestor of the Steels in Hartford, Farmington and Woodbury. He collected the debt for the drum used in Farmington instead of a bell, to call the people to church on the Sabbath and other times. He died in 1665, and left a son Samuel, who married Mary Boosy, of Wethersfield—his two daughters married William and Thomas Judd. He must have removed from Cambridge to Hartford in 1635, or very early in the spring of 1636. Samuel Steel, son of John, 1649.

Steel, George, was an early settler, and a brother of John. He was surveyor of highways in Hartford in 1639-43 and '49—selectman and juror in 1644. He died in 1664. His children were, Elizabeth Waite and Mrs. Harrison—grand children, Martha Harrison, and James and Mary Steel. He had a son James.

Steel, James, 1645—he with Samuel Boarman were appointed by the General Court, in '63, to lay out and define the bounds of Middletown.

Stevens, Nicholas, Stamford, 1664.

Stevenson, Thomas, 1646.

Stiles, Henry, came to Windsor in 1635 or 6—one branch of the family early moved to Stratford, then to Woodbury, where many of the descendants now reside. (Southbury was made a town since Stiles moved there.)

Stiles, John, came to Windsor as early as 1639. He came from Milbroke, in Bedfordshire, England, in '34. His son John, (Farmer says) was the father of Rev. Isaac Stiles, of North Haven, whose son Ezra Stiles, D. D., LL. D. was President of Yale College.

Stiles, Francis, fined £50 in 1642, for resisting an officer in his duty—carpenter in '37—juror in '42-44. Some of the Stiles family moved to Stratford, and with Edward Hinman, of Stamford, were the pioneers in settling Woodbury, where at this time many of their descendants reside.

Stiles, Henry, Hartford, was the first man tried in Connecticut, for an offence, viz. for selling a gun to an Indian. He was tried by the first Court ever formed or held in the colony, on the 26th day of April, 1636. In 1634, Francis Stiles, Thomas Stiles, John Stiles and Henry Stiles came to Massachusetts from London, in the ship Christopher, John White, master. These probably are the same men. The Henry last mentioned settled at Windsor—the first in Hartford, and not of the family at Windsor.

Stoddard, John, sergeant, of Wethersfield, 1639—juror in '42–3. He died in 1664, and left children, Mary, John, Josiah, Mercy, Elizabeth and Nathaniel. Anthony, Boston, 1639—Ebenezer, 1664—Solomon, Northampton, married Mrs. Mather, 1672—Anthony, Woodbury, 1702—John and Simeon, brothers, Boston, 1675—Hon. Anthony, 1697—Hon. Ebenezer, Woodstock, Lt. Governor, 1833—Hon. Jonathan, N. Haven, 1845—Hon. Henry, Dayton, Ohio. Most of these men appear not to be descendants of John, but of Anthony, of Boston.

Stoddard, Joseph, 1643.

Stocking, Samuel, had a daughter Bethiah.

Stocking, George, one of the first settlers in the colony—townsman in 1647. He came from Cambridge, and was one of the original proprietors of Hartford in '39.

Stolton, Thomas, a deputy in 1641.

Stone, Rev. Samuel, came to Boston in 1633, and was soon after ordained teacher with the Rev. Thomas Hooker, in Cambridge. He had been a lecturer in Torcester, in England, and was there well known by Mr. Hooker, and came to Boston by his request. He came with John Cotton, Gov. Haynes, Goff, Mr. Hooker, and about 200 emigrants. He remained with Mr. Hooker at Cambridge until June, 1636, when he came with him and the colonists to Hartford, where he continued until his death. He was chaplain in the little army of 90 brave men under Major Mason, in 1637, who by their valorous deeds exterminated the Pequott nation of Indians. Tradition says, the night previous to their starting down the river, was entirely spent in prayer by Mr. Stone, for the success of their arms in the expedition. Mr. Stone died July 20, 1663, and left a widow, Elizabeth, and children, Samuel, Elizabeth, Rebecca, Mary and Sarah. One daughter married Joseph Fitch. He owned land in Stratford, which he gave mostly to his son. Mr. Stone, William Goodwin and others, were the original purchasers for a company, of the the town of Hartford, of the Indians, which was divided in 1639, amongst the original proprietors.

Stone, John, Hartford—died early.

Stolion, Edward, 1663.

Storm, Samuel, Hartford, 1639.

Stoughton, Thomas, came to Windsor with Mr. Huet in 1639. He was deputy in '39 and '43—juror in '42—lieutenant in '40.

Stoughton, Ancient—deputy in 1636—often a juror and member of the General Court. John, '46.

Stores, Thomas, 1643.

Stowe, Rev. Mr., had much trouble in the church at Middletown in 1664. The General Court ordered his parish to pay his salary of £40. He was dismissed—and the town were ordered to provide another able, orthodox minister, to be approved by Messrs. Warham, Stone and Whiting, aided by th Governor and Mr. Wyllys, and give him such testimonial letters as the aforesaid persons should direct in the premises. Mr. Stowe was settled at Middletown in 1657.

Strickland, John, son of Thwait. The original contract or purchase of Hartford, by William Goodwin and others, of the Indians, appears to have been lost, which in 1670 was renewed between the Indians, and S. Wyllys, J. Talcott, James Richards and others as agents for the proprietors of Hartford, and witnessed by John Strickland and others.

Strickland, Serg't. Joseph, Wethersfield, in 1636 was a member of the church there—came from Massachusetts.

Strickland, Thwait, Hartford—died in 1670. Daughter Elizabeth married Mr. Andrews. His other children were, John 21, Joseph 15, Jonathan 10, and Ephraim 7. Elizabeth Andrews was 23 years old.

Strong, Return, came to Windsor in 1639.

Strong, John, Windsor, 1645—juror in '71—supposed to be the son of Return. John had 18 children, 15 of them married and had families. He was the ancestor of J. Strong, D. D., of Randolph, Dr. Strong, of Hartford, Dr. Strong, of Norwich, Gov. Strong, of Massachusetts, Judge Strong, of Amherst, and Hon. Henry Strong, of Norwich. A noble sire of more noble descendants.

Swain, William, moved to Branford in 1644, (Farmer.) The division in the church at Wethersfield where he first settled, had become so great that Mr. Swain determined on leaving the place and colony. He therefore purchased Branford, and at once commenced a settlement there. Mr. Abraham Pierson, then at Southampton, L. I., united with him with a part of his church and congregation in the settlement at Branford. Mr. Swain was afterwards a magistrate of the New Haven colony. He came to Massachusetts from England in company with Francis, in the ship Rebecca, and was one of the first settlers of Wethersfield. He was a member of the Court in the Connecticut colony in April, 1736-7-8, and continued a leading man while he remained at Wethersfield—assistant in 1644—deputy in 1641—a member of the first Court that tried the first offender—enached the first law—declared war against the Pequotts in 1637—was often a juror, deputy and magistrate.

T.

Talcott, Dorothy, the mother of John and Samuel—died in 1669.

Talcott, John, with Gov. Haynes, Thomas Hooker, Samuel Stone, George Wyllys, Edward Hopkins, William Whiting, Thomas Welles, Thomas Webster, Thomas Hosmer and William Goodwin were the leading men of Hartford in its early settlement, though some of them were not here until after 1636. John Talcott was one of the Court which declared war against the Pequotts in 1637, and one of the General Court in 1637-8-9—a juror in 1641—selectman in 1643-4 and '48—surveyor of common lands and fences in 1647—to set off meadow fence and order proportions in 1643. He received many other marks of confidence from the colony. He was a member of the Colony Congress in 1656-7-8 and '62 and '63. This was the highest office in the gift of the colonies. He had also been treasurer of the colony, and frequently an assistant to the General Court. He was the ancestor of the Talcotts in Hartford, and of the former attorney general of the State of New York. John Talcott in 1673, was appointed a major, to act in case of a war with the Dutch. Governor Tallcott's third daughter, Jerusha, married Doct. Daniel Lathrop, of Norwich—she was a lady of great intelligence. Joseph Talcott was Deputy Governor in 1724, and Governor from 1725 to 1741 inclusive, and treasurer of the colony.

Talcott, Samuel, son of Dorothy—was a gentleman of less distinction than his brother John. John, jr., 1645.

Talcott, Gov. Joseph, a grandson of Dorothy—became a gentleman of distinction in the colony. He was appointed treasurer, and was also in 1724, made Deputy Governor of the colony, and in 1725 was elected Governor, and was continued in the office until 1742. He well kept up and sustained the early reputation of John, who had preceded him in the first settlement.

Tappin or Toppin, Thomas, and two other magistrates, with several deputies from Long Island, appeared at the General Court of Connecticut, and took their seats in May, 1663, as members of the colony and the General Court. Assistant in '63.

Tappin, was appointed with John Talcott to apportion the rates in 1639.

Taynter, was a deputy in 1643 and '46—frequently held offices.

Taylor, William, Wethersfield, 1664.

Taylor, John, Windsor, came with Mr. Huet in 1639. Juror in '41 and '44. George Taylor came to Massachusetts in the Truelove, George Gibbs, master.

Taylor, Stephen, married Ann Hosford, of Windsor, 1642.

Taylor, Stephen, also married Ann Nowel, of Windsor—grand juror in '72. (Perhaps the same person as above.)

Terre or Terry, Stephen, Windsor—was among the first settlers of Windsor, and in 1638 was appointed one of a committee with H. Wolcott, jr., William Westwood and Nathaniel Ward to lay a highway for cart and horse upon the upland, from Hartford to Windsor. Grand juror in 1643. Thomas Robert and Richard Terry came from England in the ship James, John May, master, to Massachusetts. John Terry, probably a son of Stephen, united with John Case in settling Simsbury, by enforcing the owners of lands at Massacoe to build on and settle them. Hon. Nathaniel Terry, late deceased, had been a member of Congress, eminent in his profession, and a gentleman of distinction in the State.

Terry, John, son of Stephen, married Elizabeth Wadsworth, in 1662. His children were, Elizabeth, Stephen, Sarah, John, Rebecca, Mary, Solomon, and another Rebecca.

Thomas, Serg't. of Mystic, in 1663 applied to the General Court for directions how to conduct himself there under the authority ;—he was advised to keep quiet, and if abused by them, to apply to the Deputy Governor, but not to obey those who held commissions under other colonies.

Thompson, widow of Thomas, married Anthony Hawkins, of Farmington. John, of Fairfield, 1650. William, free in 1660.

Thomson, John, 1670. In '63 had a controversy with the church at Stratford, and Messrs. Jones, Wakeman and Hanford were appointed by the General Court as advisers in the matter.

Tilliston or Tillotson, John, resided near Saybrook in 1671.

Tillerson, John, married before he came to Windsor. His children were, Mary, John, Elizabeth and Abigail. In 1667 he charged the wife of Matthew Griswold, of Lyme, of being a witch, and induced others to suspect her of witchcraft ; for which Mr. Griswold caused him to be arrested and arraigned before the Court. He stated the cause of his suspicions and jealousies. The Court decided she was not a witch, and that he had no cause to be jealous of her—that he had greatly sinned in harboring such jealousy against so good a neighbor, who had done him many favors. But as he was poor, the Court, to recompense Mrs. Griswold for the wrong, and to clear her of all suspicions of the offence—ordered that the opinion of the Court should be published by the constables in Saybrook and Lyme, at some public meeting—and ordered Tillerson to pay 7 shillings for the express warrant, and 5 shillings for the constable.

Tracy, Thomas, Wethersfield, juror in 1644—was often a juror and deputy, and held other posts of honor. He moved to Saybrook, and from thence to Norwich. He was a gentleman of importance in the colony. Deputy in 1662-3—auditor of the accounts of J. Rogers and Lieut. Smith on the corn rate for the expense of the Charter, 1663. He was a thorough business man. The name has been uniformly respectable. Some of his descendants were of high reputation. Hon. Uriah Tracy, former Senator of the U. S., and Hon. Albert H. Tracy, late Lieut. Governor of New York.

ERRATA.

Upon further examination into the genealogy of the Loomis family, I am satisfied that only the family of Joseph came to Connecticut. I was led into the error by the Lecture of Dr. McClure, delivered at East Windsor some years since. It will be corrected in No. 3—when the whole Catalogue will be published, including a large number of names since found, and not printed in either of the two Numbers before the public, in their proper places.

Tanner, Rebecca, was a sister of Thomas Shaylor, and was married and had sons previous to 1690.

Talcott, Capt. Samuel, Wethersfield, died in 1691—wife Mary, and children, Joseph, John, Elizur, Benjamin, Nathaniel, Hannah Chester, and Rachel.

Talcott, Col. John, died in 1689, and left an estate over £2000—his lands being over 2000 acres.

Taylor, Stephen, jr. His children were, Stephen and Mercy.— Their mother Patience, removed to Colchester, and resided there in 1719.

Mrs. Taylor, widow of Stephen, jr., Windsor, died in 1689.

Terre or Terry, Richard, of Southold, L. I., 1662. The descendants of Stephen, of Windsor, claim Richard, of Southold, to have been a brother of Stephen. Tradition says they came to Massachusetts in company; Stephen settled in Connecticut, and the other on L. I. It was probably as claimed by them—being found one at Windsor, the other at Long Island.

Terry, Lieut. John, Simsbury — died in 1691 — son of Stephen, of Windsor. Children, Stephen, 25, Elizabeth, 27, Sarah 22, Mary 17, Abigail 15, Samuel 13, John 7. He owned a mill, and left an estate of £518. Widow Elizabeth — son Stephen.

Thrall, Timothy, Windsor, grandson of William, 1713. The town of Tolland was originally the east part of Windsor, and in 1713 the town of Windsor appointed Matthew Allyn, Roger Wolcott, and Timothy Thrall to lay out a settlement on the east side of Windsor, on lands purchased of the Indians, which the committee performed and reported. Joseph Benton who had emigrated to Tolland from Hartford, made the record as town clerk in 1719. Notwithstanding in 1715, M. Allyn, R. Wolcott, T. Thrall, and John Ellsworth petitioned the General Court to lay out a township, to be bounded east upon Willimantic river, &c., to contain 36 square miles, and to be called Tolland. The petition was granted, and a town 6 miles sqare, called Tolland, allowed to the Windsor petitioners. In May, 1719, the four petitioners conveyed the town of Tolland to 53 persons, but reserved to each of themselves 300 acres, and these 53 became the actual settlers of Tolland, some of whom had been settled there as early as 1713 or '14. Amy Hatch was born there a early as 1713. Joseph Hatch the son of Joseph, was the first white *male* child born in Tolland in 1715. In 1719 Joseph Benton was one of a committee to build a meeting house there; the same year he was appointed to procure a minister to preach there, and the Rev. Stephen Steel officiated at Tolland in 1720. Mr. Benton was sworn first town clerk in 1719, and Shubael Stearns in 1720. Delano, West, Cobb, Steel, Shepard, Chapman, Wells, Lathrop and Grant were among the early settlers of Tolland. Timothy, sen'r. was an early settler at Windsor. He died in 1697. Children, Deborah, Moses, Elizabeth Cornish, Mehitable Carter, Martha Pinney, Abigail Thrall—Timothy, John, Thomas, and Samuel Thrall. He had an estate of nearly £800.

Thrall, William, Windsor, 1640 — juror in '64 — died in '79. Son Timothy, daughter Phillis Hosford—had a grandchild, Mary Hosford.

Tilly, Capt. In 1636, the Indians murdered five men at Saybrook, while they were at work in the meadows; and in November of the same year assassinated another, and most cruelly tortured Capt. Tilly to death. In December, 1636, six of the inhabitants of the town were attacked by the Pequots, two of whom were tortured to death by them; during the same month four others were killed there; the January after they assassinated one citizen and took two others, who they split in twain. These murders and other outrages committed by the Indians in 1636-7 caused the war against the Pequots in 1637. When the people of Saybrook attended church at the tap of the drum, the males carried their guns, and stacked them in the corners of the church with a sufficient guard the outside to secure the worshippers from surprise and danger from the Indians.

Tinker, John — in April, 1660 was made an assistant at N. London, with O. Bruen, J. Rogers, Lieut. Smith and John Smith as commissioners, with the assistance of Maj. Mason, to hold courts there for the year. William Douglass was also confirmed as packer at the same time for N. London—assistant in 1661. In 1660 the General Court licensed Mr. Tinker to retail liquors distilled by himself until October, 1662, if he would use his exertions to suppress others from selling by retail in N. London. Mr. Tinker died about 1662. Left children, Mary, John, Amos, Samuel and Rhoda. The expenses of his sickness and funeral were paid from the public treasury by order of the General Court. He was a gentleman of distinction at N. London, and throughout the colony.

Thompson, John, Middletown — died in 1693-4. He left a widow and children.

Thompson, John and Thomas, sons of John Thompson, of Wethersfield, 1680.

Thornton, Thomas, Hartford — died in 1703. Wife Hannah, and son Samuel, only child. He had a brother Nathaniel Farren. He left an estate of £498. He owned a part of a warehouse at the landing on the river in Hartford.

Thornton, G., moved to Stratford before 1653.

Thornton, Thomas, came to Windsor in 1639, and was juror in '43.

Throcmorton, 1640.

Trill, Thomas, an unseasonable night walker, 1664.

Tillerton, Daniel, went to Stratford as early as 1649.

Treat, Richard, Wethersfield. In March, 1637, was a member of the lower house of the General Court. He died in 1668-9. His children were, Richard, jr., Robert, James, a daughter Hollister, another who married Hon. Matthew Canfield or Camp, another married a Johnson, and two others married Robert Webster, son of Gov. Webster, and John, son of Hon. John Deming, (were mentioned in his will as sons, and shared in his estate). He gave Mr. Perkins's book to his son John Deming. He was a cousin of Samuel Wells, and of John Deming, sen. Some men of distinction by this name. The family ranked high in the colony.

Treat, Richard, Wethersfield, 1663, a magistrate in '63, son of Richard.

Treat, Richard, Wethersfield, died in 1713, son of James, deceased (his mother Rebecca). · He left but one child, Katherine Treat, to whom he gave all his estate, being £636. He had a sister Jemima Chester, and Mabel Treat — had a brother Salmon, of Boston — his brother Joseph resided at Wethersfield.

Treat, Thomas, Glastenbury — died in 1709 — wife Dorothy. His son Richard was in poor health. Left other sons, and several daughters, and an estate of £770.

Treat, Henry, Hartford — died in 1681. Left several children, and some estate for them.

Treat, James, sen'r., Wethersfield — died in 1708—wife Rebecca, sons James, Samuel, (to Salmon he gave 200 acres on the road to Colchester), Richard, Joseph—Jerusha, wife of Capt. Thomas Wells, (who had a son Wm. Wells), Rebecca wife of Ebenezer Deming. (had a son Joseph Deming), Mabel Treat. He gave 200 acres of land and the stone house beyond the bounds of Glastenbury to James and Samuel Treat. He left an estate of £1,235.

Trott, Richard, Wethersfield—juror in 1642, grand juror in '43— one of the committee with Mr. Hopkins and others to build a ship — to collect funds for the students of Cambridge College in '44 — deputy in '44–5 and 8. He was often a juror and deputy. The family probably afterwards settled at New London. Matthias Trott, Wethersfield, 1646.

Trumble, John, Windsor, 1647.

Trumble, Ammi, Windsor, 1648. Joseph Trumble resided at Suffield in 1704. He married Hannah Higly and they were the parents of the first Gov. Trumbull.— *Phelps.*

Tomlinson, Thomas — died in March, 1685 — wife Elizabeth — children Sarah Bishop, 20 years old, Mary 18, Ruth 15, Phebe 12, Elizabeth 10, Hannah 6, and Thankful 1. No sons.

Towsey, Thomas, sen'r., Wethersfield — died in 1712. He was the father of Elizabeth Churchill the wife of Josiah Churchill. To his son Thomas he gave his house, shop, barn and all his land. He gave to John Northway 40 shillings. He gave his apprentice John Wells one weaver's loom and gears to weave serge and kersey; all his other property he gave to his daughter Churchill. He owned a fulling mill in partnership with Mr. Bulkley. He left an estate of £387 sterling. He was a widower at his death, and probably aged—it is uncertain how long he had resided at Wethersfield. His son Thomas was educated a clergyman, and settled in Fairfield county, at Newtown, and was the ancestor of Gov. Toucey, of Hartford ; since which time all by this name have uniformly originated at Newtown, where Rev. Thomas Tewsey began to preach about 1712 or '13.

Tucker, John, 1642 — died in '62, at New London.   Children — Mary, John, Amos, Samuel and Rhoda.

Tucky, George, was fined 40 shillings for using improper language to Mrs. Eggleston.

Tudor, Owen, came with the 2d colony to Windsor, in 1639. He married Mary Skinner in 1641. He was the ancestor of a respectable family in Hartford, also in East Windsor, and in Vermont. He died in 1690. Had sons Samuel and Owen; Samuel had a double portion. He also had daughters.— Doct. Elihu Tudor, of East Windsor, was a son of Rev. Samuel Tudor, and a great grandson of Owen, he graduated at Yale College in 1750. In 1757 he entered with great spirit into the French war as a surgeon. He was with Gen. Wolfe in Canada —and was at the capture of Havanna ; after the war closed no man in New England was more eminent in his profession than Dr. Tudor.   He went to London, and for a long time practised in the hospitals, to become eminent in his profession.   He was made a half pay officer during life, and died at the advanced age of 93 years.   Rev. Samuel, the grandfather of Samuel, of Hartford, graduated at Yale College in 1728. Owen, jr., died unmarried, and left no issue.   Rev. Samuel married the widow Bissell — her maiden name was Filley.

Tully, John.   The time Mr. Tully came to Saybrook is uncertain, yet he is considered one of the early settlers.   He published an Almanac there in 1681, which he continued to do until 1702.   He was called the great mathematician of the day.

Turner, Daniel, in 1649 was twice publicly whipt on lecture days, then imprisoned one month, and again whipt and gave bonds for his future good behavior—for slandering Mrs. Chester.   The Puritans appear to have punished offenders by whipping, with the same object that a parent corrects his children, only to improve their habits, morals and manners, and not to disgrace them, unless the offence committed was a great immorality and violation of law.   Men who had been publicly whipped, are found afterwards holding places of honor in the colony.

Turner, Nathaniel (see Underhill).   He went with Capt. Endicott to reduce the Indians on Block Island, for the murder of Capt. Oldham, and from thence to the Pequots, to demand the murderers of Capts. Stone and Norton, 1636.

Turner, Ephraim, Hartford—died in January, 1705.   Wife Mary. Cyprian Nichols, administrator.

Turner, Capt., New Haven, as agent for New Haven, in 1640–1, made a large purchase of lands upon the Delaware river. Capt. Turner appears not to have been of the family of the name who settled in Connecticut.

Tuthill, John, with Rev. John Young, William Wells, Barnabas Horton, Thomas Mapes, and Matthias Corwin, who were the first and most important settlers at Southold, L. I., after the purchase of the town by New Haven—continued for a time under the strict discipline of that colony, and in October, 1640, Mr. Young renewed his church there. They however became dissatisfied that no person could hold office or be a freeman but those who were members of the church. In consequence of this fundamental principle of the New Haven Colony, Southold afterwards united with the Connecticut Colony, and Young and Horton became important officers under Connecticut.

Turney, Robert, Fairfield, 1654.

Tylerton, Daniel, deputy in 1646—went to Fairfield county.

U.

Underhill, Captain John, in 1636, sailed from Boston under Capt. Endicott, for Block Island, to put the Indians to the sword and take possession of the Island, with orders to spare the women and children; after which to sail to the Pequot country, and demand of the Pequot Indians, the murderers of Capts. Norton and Stone—which mission was performed. In the same year he was directed to reinforce the Fort at Saybrook with 20 men. In 1643 Capt. John Underhill was a deputy from Stamford with R. Gildersleeve at N. Haven, and after a residence of a few years at Stamford, he moved to Long Island, where he died about 1673. Probably the same man who accompanied Capt. Endicott to Block Island. He took the Indian prisoners and wounded men by water, in 1637 from Mystic to Saybrook, while Maj. Mason and Capt. Patrick went through the woods with the soldiers to Saybrook, after the Pequot action.

Ufford, Thomas, was a juror 1644, at Hartford—and probably was the same Thomas Ufford who resided at Roxbury in '33, afterwards at Springfield, and in '44 in Fairfield.

Ufford, Benjamin, a juror at Hartford in 1643—probably a relative of Thomas.

Upson, Thomas, Hartford. In 1640 had four acres of land in the division east of Connecticut River. Soon after 1700, Stephen Upson resided at Waterbury, who was the ancestor of the Hon. Stephen Upson, late of Georgia, deceased.

Usher, Robert, was a constable in 1662–3 in Stamford.

V.

Varlet, Jasper, in 1661, brought a Dutchman and his wife, by the name of Bolters, to Hartford, without any security to the town; upon which order was taken against him.

Vandict, Gisbert, 1649—a Dutch officer of Hartford, '36.

Vantine, Cornelius, Hartford, 1649.

Veats, Francis, Windsor, 1663. This name is yet in the north part of Hartford county.

Vere, Voare or Vose, Richard, came to Windsor with the first settlers as early as 1636. He came from Cambridge with Mr Wolcott—and was the ancestor of some of the Parsons' family. The name is spelt various ways, but more generally Vere, upon the record. He died in 1683. Wife Ann—children, Abigail, wife of Timothy Buckland—wife of Nathaniel Cook, Mary, wife of Thomas Alvord, Sarah Parsons, wife of Benjamin Parsons, of Springfield. His name is spelt Vere by himself in his signature to his will. Benjamin Parsons above was the ancestor of Major Gen. Parsons so much distinguished in the revolutionary war.

Ventris, Moses, Sen'r., Farmington—died about 1697. Children, Sarah, wife of John Brunson, Grace, wife of John Blakely, Mary Ventris, Moses and——Ventris.

Vincent, Richard, 1647.

Vincent, William, is supposed to have come from Dorchester to Windsor before 1647.

W.

Wade, Robert, Hartford, 1639—of Saybrook in '57. He was divorced from Joanna his wife, who had refused to fellowship with him in England and America for 15 years. This was the second divorce granted in the colony. He held 10 acres of land in Hartford, in '39. This was a highly respectable name in Massachusetts and Connecticut.

Wadsworth, William, Hartford—selectman in 1642, also in '47, collector in 1637, deputy in 1642, and frequently afterwards. He was an original proprietor of Hartford, and in the division of the land of the town in 1639.—He was a valuable man in the town and colony. (He is supposed to have been the ancestor of Joseph Wadsworth of Charter notoriety.) He died in 1675. His sons were, John, Samuel, Joseph, and Thomas. He had a daughter who married a Mr. Stoton—another Terry—another Jonathan Ashley, and left Rebecca unmarried—he also had a granddaughter Long. He was a gentleman of wealth and of high reputation in the colony. This Wadsworth was of the blood of him who told Col. Fletcher when he demanded the command of the militia of Connecticut, that if he was again interrupted by him, " he would make the sun shine through him in an instant."

Wadsworth, Elizabeth, widow of William—died 1680. Her children were, Samuel, Joseph, Thomas, Elizabeth Terry, Jonathan Ashley, Rebecca and John Wadsworth.

Wadsworth, John, Hartford—died in 1689, (Sarah his wife.) He gave his negro man to his wife. Children, Samuel 29, Sarah Root 31, Hezekiah 6, John 27, William 18, Nathaniel 15, James 12, Thomas 9—he had grandchildren, Timothy 8, and John 4 years old.

Wadsworth, Samuel, son of William, of Hartford, 1682, brother of Joseph, Thomas and John. He was a cousin of William Wadsworth, 2d, and died unmarried.

Wadsworth, John, Farmington, 1670.

Wadams, John, Wethersfield, 1664—he died in '76, and left a widow and son John. He might have came into the colony earlier than '64. Perhaps ancestor of those of the name in Litchfield Co.

Wainwright, Thomas, 1643.

Wakeman, Samuel, the first constable of Hartford, 1636—surveyor of Dorchester and Watertown with George Hubbard in 1636. He was directed by a law of the landholders, to attend to the watch, and warn them in their turn to do duty as a watch against the Indian depredators upon the lives and property of the settlers. He with George Hubbard, sen'r., in 1636, were appointed to survey the breadth of Windsor, and say how far it should extend above the house of Mr. Stiles; he was also to survey the breadth of Watertown. He died in 1645, and left one son and three daughters. He was an original proprietor of Hartford, and in the division of the land in 1639.

Wakeman, Samuel, a clergyman at Fairfield in 1665. His name is rarely found in the State except in Fairfield county.

Wakelee, Henry, Hartford, 1639—the first lawyer of record in the colony.

Waldo, John, Windham—died in 1700. This family appears to have come late into the colony. He had a son John in Windham—perhaps other children. He left an estate of £292. It was a family of respectability, and probably he was the ancestor of L. P. Waldo, Esq., of Tolland.

Walker, Rev. Zechariah, Stratford—was first settled at Jamaica, L. I., and preached there for a time, and about 1668 removed to Stratford, where he had a severe contest with Rev. Mr. Chauncy, and a part of the congregation at Stratford. The controversy closed by Gov. Winthrop's advising Mr. Walker and his friends to remove and settle a new town, with which he engaged they should be accommodated, and Mr. William Curtiss, John Sherman and others were authorized to locate at Pomperaug (now Woodbury); therefore Mr. Walker with his friends moved there from Stratford about 1672-3. Woodbury was settled by several different companies at different times, and embraced a large territory.

Walker, Jacob, Stratford, about 1665. Josiah and Joseph Walker, went from Woodbury to Litchfield to settle.

Walkeley, Henry, Hartford, 1639. In '63 appeared in court as attorney for James Wakelee. He held land in Hartford by liberty of the town in '39.

Walkeley, James, a brother of Alice—improved land in Hartford in 1639, with the right of wood and pasture, not having been an original proprietor of Hartford.

Walkeley, Alice, sister of James—in court in 1663.

Walkeley, Richard—died at Haddam in 1681. It appears by the record that Richard's property was given to his two sons and one daughter. Alice the daughter died in '83. The name is spelt Walkley and Walkeley. Alice left an estate of £348. The sons were James and Henry, and were brothers of Alice. Richard was the father of the family.

Waller, Matthew, Lyme, 1674. William Waller had moved to Lyme in '64.

Ward, Andrew, was amongst the first Puritan settlers who came to Wethersfield. He was one of the five persons who held the first Court in the colony, in April, 1636—tried the first cause, and made the first law. He was a member of this court seven sessions in 1636, and five sessions in 1637. He was a member of the Upper House in May, 1637, when war was declared against the Pequots. He was twice a member of the Committee or Lower House of the General Court in 1637, and of the same House again in 1638—four sessions he acted as deputy after the Confederation of the three towns into a Colony in 1639—was frequently made a member of both branches of the General Court afterwards—collector of rates in 1637, and a magistrate in 1639. He was a member of the church in Wethersfield. He held other offices in Wethersfield. He was frequently united with the Governors and the most important men in the colony on committees of the General Court. He was a gentleman of great worth in the colony, and was the ancestor of a respectable and wealthy family who reside in Hartford; also of the Wards in Southbury and other parts of Connecticut, and of a few families in Pennsylvania. In 1653, Ward and Hill were appointed by the General Court to press men in Fairfield for an expedition. In the fall of 1640, Mr. Ward and Robert Coe, of Wethersfield, for themselves and several others, purchased the town of Stamford of the New Haven Company—all of which purchasers obligated themselves to move there within one year; and in the spring of 1641, Matthew Mitchell, Thurston Rayner, Robert Gildersleeve, Robert Coe and others moved to Stamford, Mr. Ward also moved to Stamford, but whether at this time, is not known to the writer. These with their pastor, Mr. Denton, were the leading men of Stamford. Within a few years Mr. Denton left Stamford and moved to Hempsted on Long Island. Mr. Ward also removed to Hempsted within a few years—but about 1650 he returned and settled in the town of Fairfield, where he closed a long and useful life.—(See Denton.)

Ward, Nathaniel, was an early settler in Hartford, and a gentleman of good standing in the colony. In 1642 he was a juror, and frequently afterwards. He was a member of the first grand jury in 1643, held in the colony, and held other offices of trust and honor in the town and colony. In 1645 he was one of the committee appointed by the General Court to collect funds for the students in Cambridge College. He was townsman in 1639-44 and 47, and constable of Hartford in 1636—juror in 1643. He moved to Hadley, where it is supposed he died without issue, and gave no part of his estate to any person of his name. A Nathaniel Ward was at the Emanuel Institution in England, in 1618. Mr. Ward was one of the leaders with Gov. Webster and others, in procuring the settlement of Hadley, by emigrants from Connecticut, in 1659.

Ward, Joyce, Wethersfield—died in 1640. Her children were, Edward, Anthony, William, Robert and John. She had a son-in-law, John Fletcher, who perhaps resided at Guilford. Robert had given to him by his father, £20 in England, in the hands of Edward his eldest brother's son. Robert was put to a trade.

Ward, John, Middletown—died in 1683, and left an estate of £446 to his family, viz.: John, 18 years old, Andrew 16, Easter 14, Mary 11, William 9, Samuel 4, and one unborn.

Ward, William, was confirmed a sergeant by the General Court for the train band at Middletown in 1664.

Warham, Rev. John, was the first Elder of a church who came into the colony in 1636. His church had been located with him as their pastor, at Dorchester, in Massachusetts—but in 1636 the minister and church all moved to Windsor, where he lived until April 1, 1670, when he was called from his people by death; he however lived to see not only *his church* but many others in the colony prosperously located. He had lived to witness much of the dense forest he found there in 1636, by the industry of the good men he brought with him, removed. He left a large estate in lands to his family, and saw some of them happily located in life before his decease. He had preached at Exeter, in England, before he came to New England. He had four daughters. After his decease, his widow married Mr. Newbury, and had two children, both daughters. After the death of Mr. Warham, Easter or Hester one of his daughters, married Rev. Mr. Mather, and had children, Eunice, Warham and Eliakim. After the death of Mr. Mather, she married Mr. Stoddard, and had six sons and six daughters—three of the sons lived to adult years, Anthony, John and Israel; Israel died in prison, in France—John settled at Northampton—was a colonel, chief judge of the court of common pleas, and was a leading politician (or rather statesman) in Massachusetts. His brother Anthony settled as the 2d minister at Woodbury, Conn., and died there in 1776, at the age of 82, after having been the only officiating clergyman there for about 60 years. Anthony left a son Israel, who resided in Woodbury until his death. Israel had a son Asa, who married and had a son Henry, and two daughters. Asa and his children moved to Dayton, Ohio, about the year 1817. Hon. Henry Stoddard is now a gentleman of high standing in that state. Asa the grandson of Anthony, died a few years since, in Ohio, far advanced in years.

Warham, Abigail, widow of Rev. John Warham—died in 1684. She was a cousin of Miles Marwine or Merwin, for whom she had formerly done much—that in her will she declared "that if she had thousands she would not give him a penny—no, not a pin's point."

Merwin attempted to persuade her to give him her property in exclusion of her children.

Ware, Nathaniel, Hartford, 1648. Several of this name settled in Massachusetts.

Warner, Andrew, Hartford, 1639. He came to Cambridge in '32—was one of the committee with Webster, Talcott, Timothy Stanley and others to divide the lands east of the river—surveyor of lands and fences in '47—in the land division of Hartford in '39—signed to move to Hadley in '59.

Warner, Robert—deputy in 1663, and often afterwards. Supposed son of Andrew.

Warner, John, 1639—had six acres of up-land in the division east of the river in '40.

Warner, John, Farmington—made free in 1663, and died in '78–9. Left sons, John, Daniel, (Thomas did not reside in Farmington), and William Higginson—a son-in-law—father of John, of Waterbury, who died in 1707. He was a soldier at Pequot, for which the colony gave him a tract of land, which he gave to Higginson.

Warner, John, sen'r., Waterbury—died at Farmington in 1707. His children were, John, Jr., Ephraim, Robert, Ebenezer, and Lydia who had married Samuel Brunson before the death of her father.

Warner, Daniel—signed to move to Hadley, in 1659, son of John.

Warner, Andrew, Middletown—son of Andrew, of Hartford—died in 1683–4. Children, Andrew, 19 years old, John 11, Joseph 9, Abigail 21, Mary 17, Hannah 13, Rebecca 6. It is supposed this Andrew, jr., moved to Windham.

Warren, William, sen'r., Hartford—surveyor of highways at Hartford in 1663, and died in 1689. He resided at Hocanum on his farm. He left a widow, and children John, William and Thomas. He appears to have had four younger children. He married two wives, and ordered his girls to be bound out until they were 18 years of age, and Abraham until 21.

Wastall, John—deputy in 1643—juror in '43—selectman of Saybrook in '63–4 with Zachariah Sanford and John Clark.

Wasby or Wasly, William, Hartford, 1645.

Way, Elizur—died in 1686. His wife Mary had over £200 in his estate. His children were, Ebenezer, Sarah (married Ichabod Wells), Elizabeth (married Joseph Wells), and Lydia Way. He left an estate of £867.

Watts, Capt. Thomas, Hartford—died in 1683—wife Elizabeth—her brother's son, Samuel Hubbard, lived with her, and shared largely in his

estate ; he was a kinsman of Samuel Steel, jr., who shared in his property.—
His sister Hubbard's children were, Joseph, Daniel, Nathaniel, Richard,
Elizabeth Hubbard and Mary Ranny. His brother Brown's children were,
Nathaniel, John, Benoni Brown, and Hannah wife of Isaac Laine; to the last
five she gave her land in Middletown.· He was a brother of James Steel
who had sons James and John Steel. He gave £20 to the poor of the church
in Hartford. Martha Harrison shared in his will. He made some provision
for the south church in Hartford—owned a grist mill in Hartford.

Watts, Elizabeth, who died in 1684, widow of Thomas Watts, was
a sister of James Steel, who had four daughters, viz. Elizabeth,
Sarah, Rachel Steel, and Mary Hall—she was a cousin of Martha
Henderson, and had a sister Willet.

Watts, Richard, Hartford—an early settler, 1639—not an original
proprietor of Hartford. Had 14 acres of land, with liberty of pasture on the common and to fetch wood, &c.

Watts, William, Hartford—held four acres of land in Hartford, in
1639, with the liberty of wood and pasture of cows and swine.

Watts, Elizabeth, widow of Richard—her daughter married Hubbard ; she was a cousin of Daniel and Elizabeth Hubbard, of Hannah
and Nathaniel Brown, and had a daughter Brown.

Watts, Elenor, 1646—selectman of Hartford in '61.

Waterhouse, Isaac, New London—fined £5 for upsetting Tinker's
warehouse. Thomas Waters married Sarah Fenn, of Milford, a
daughter of Benjamin and Mary Feen, 1696. Waters, Watrous and
Waterhouse appear to have been the same name.

Waterhouse, Jacob, 1639.

Waterman, 1647. Richard, of Salem, '37, was one of the founders
of the first Baptist church in America—. *Farmer.*

Waters, Peter, (a Dutchman) 1672.

Watson, Thomas, 1644. Robert Watson came to Windsor in '39,
in the 2d colony—he died July, '89. Widow Watson signed to move
to Hadley in '59. John, of Hartford, '44—surveyor of highways in
'46—juror in '44—signed to move to Hadley in '59.

Watson, Margaret, Windsor—died in 1683. Children, Sarah
Merrills, wife of John—Mary Seymour, granddaughter Sarah Merrills— grandchildren Mary Seymour and Margaret Seymour—grandson John Watson.

Webster, Gov. John. This gentleman probably came into Connecticut in 1637, or in the autumn of 1636. His first appearance as an officer of
the court was in April, 1637. He was then one of the committee, who for the
first time sat with the Court of Magistrates for the purpose of declaring war
against the Pequot Indians. He was again the same year elected to the General
Court and was also elected as one of the committee (deputy) in 1638. He was

elected a member of the Court of Magistrates at the first General Court holden by Gov. Haynes, in April, 1639. From this time forward for many years he was a member of the General Court as a magistrate or assistant. That the public may appreciate the arduous services of Gov. Webster, I take the liberty of stating, that in 1639 he attended four sessions of the General Court—three sessions in 1640—four in 1641—three in 1642—five in 1643—five in 1644— five in 1645 ; and held five sessions of the Particular Court in 1639—four in 1640—two in 1641—two in 1642—six in 1643—five in 1644—six in 1645, and four in 1646—and so continued faithfully to discharge all the duties of the responsible and important offices bestowed upon him by the people for years. He was uniformly a magistrate or assistant while he remained in the colony after 1638. He was appointed with Mr. Ludlow and Gov. Welles to consult with their friends in the New Haven Colony, respecting the Indian murders which had been committed, to learn of them whether they would approve of a declaration of war as a reparation of the injury, in 1640 ; he was appointed with the Hon. William Phelps, to form a law against lying, and to hold a consultation with the elders upon the subject. He was of the committee with Wm. Phelps, &c., who formed the noted criminal code of laws for the colony, reported and approved by the General Court in 1642—several of which laws yet remain in our statute book with little alteration, except in punishment. In 1655 Mr. Webster was elected Deputy Governor of the colony, and the following year was made Governor. In 1654 he was appointed with Maj. Gen. Mason a member of the Congress of the United Colonies— Enough is already said to show the elevated position held by Gov. Webster in the colony, while he remained in it. He was the first in this country who gave the high character for talent to the name of Webster, which has been since so nobly and amply sustained by Noah as a man of literature, and Daniel as a statesman and orator. Many of his descendants yet reside in Connecticut and Massachusetts. Gov. Webster was from Warwickshire, in England, and was an original settler in Hartford as early as 1637, when he was a member of the General Court. He greatly aided and improved the new form of government in the colony. The severe quarrels in the churches at Hartford and Wethersfield so disgusted, not only Gov. Webster, but 59 others of the settlers in the colony, that upon the 18th day of April, 1659, they signed an agreement, in which they engaged to remove themselves and families out of the jurisdiction of Connecticut, into Massachusetts. Gov. Webster headed the list of names. About three-fourths of the signers did remove to Massachusetts, and purchased and settled the town of Hadley, which then included what is now Hadley, South Hadley, Granby and Amherst, east of Connecticut river, and Hatfield and a part of Williamsburg west of the river. Gov. Webster became a Judge of the Court in Hampshire. He died in 1661, and left four sons, Robert, Matthew, William and Thomas. He also left three daughters. Matthew settled in Farmington, William in Hadley, Thomas moved to Northampton, afterwards to Northfield, and was driven from the latter place by the Indians, he then located at Hadley, but finally returned and died at Northfield. His daughter Ann m. John Marsh, of Hadley ; the other two married Markham and Hunt. Robert, the eldest son, appears to have remained in Hartford, where he died in 1676. Robert left six sons and four daughters. The daughters were connected by marriage with the families of Seymours, Mygatts and Graves, some of the most respectable settlers. Robert was the branch of Gov. Webster's family through whom Hon. Noah Webster, LL.D., late deceased, traced his ancestry.—(See Robert Webster.)

Webster, Robert, the eldest son of Gov. Webster—probably came into the colony in 1637, with his father. He appears to have been a man in active life in the early settlement of Connecticut. He received many marks of respect, showing his fair standing as a citizen; but like most young men who have a father of wealth and distinction, he borrowed some of the plumes of his father's greatness. As is often the case with young gentlemen in his situation in life, he fell short of arriving at the eminence to which Gov. Webster had attained; yet he was above a mediocrity in talents and standing in the colony. In 1659, he with 59 others, his father at the head of the company, signed a contract to remove from Connecticut to Massachusetts; but from all the facts, it appears that Robert did not remove his family, but continued in the colony until his death. The children of Robert, Jr., the grandchildren of Gov. Webster were, Robert, born October, 1689, Abraham, September, 1693, Hannah, Nov. 1695, Matthew, April, 1698, Joshua, March, 1700, Caleb, January, 1702, Mary, December, 1704, Abigail, January, 1710.

Robert married Hannah Bockly, daughter of John, Sept. 1689. Jonathan Webster married Easter Judd, daughter of Benjamin, Dec. 1704. John Bracy married Mary Webster, daughter of Jonathan, 1705. Joseph Webster married Mary Judd, 1695. Benjamin Webster, supposed the greatgrandson of Gov. Webster, after 1717, moved to Litchfield, where he located, and where the name yet continues. Jonathan resided on Wright's Island in 1730.

Webster, Matthew, made free in 1645.

Webb, Richard, Hartford, 1639—on the first grand jury at the General Court in the colony in 1643—also juror in '43-4—selectman in '48—surveyor of highways in '49. He soon after moved to Stamford, was made free there in '62, and he was sworn by Judge Gold, at Fairfield court. He was an original proprietor of Hartford in '39, and was a gentleman of standing in the colony. Henry Webb, '42, John, Hartford, '48 and '63. William, Hartford, in '40. Richard was the ancestor of John Webb, Esq., of Hartford.

Weed, Joseph, Fairfield—made free in 1662. Jonas Wethersfield, 1636—juror in '39. Perhaps the father of Joseph.

Weeks, Thomas, John Ketchum and Mr. Ridgebell, in the reception and organization of the towns of Huntington, Setauk and Oyster Bay, on Long Island, in 1662, were appointed constables of those towns under the Charter of Connecticut. All the towns upon Long Island were also notified by Capt. Sylvester and Lieut. Gardner, to attend the General Court of Connecticut by representatives, the next May session. Mr. Weeks appeared and took the oath with 22 others. After he returned to Long Island he revolted, and made great disturbance in Southold—to quell which the General Court appointed Mr. Allyn and S. Wyllys to go to Long Island, and with the assistance of the magistrates there, to settle the affair.

Welles, Gov. Thomas, came into the colony and located himself at Hartford in the autumn of 1636, and upon the 28th day of March, 1637, he became a member of the Court of Magistrates. In April following an important crisis had arrived. The inhabitants of the colony had been constantly annoyed by the Indians, and particularly by the Pequots, by robberies, murders, and the abduction of two respectable young ladies from Wethersfield, who had been carried among the Indians—which outrages could no longer be submitted to by the English settlers. To redress these grievances a General Court of Magistrates were convened, and the three towns which then formed the colony, were ordered, for the purpose of adding safety to the counsels of the court, to send a committee of three persons from each town, to set as advisers with the General Court. Gov. Welles was one of the Court of Magistrates held on the 7th day of May, 1637, who declared an offensive war against the powerful and warlike nation of Pequots, for the redress of the many grievances they had visited upon the English settlers. It was a most important meeting and decision not only to the colony, but to all the settlers in New England. The Indians had not only murdered many of the English, but had driven away their cattle, and committed other gross wrongs. After mature deliberation, war was declared and the result saved the colony, and was of immense advantage to all the other colonies, and much credit was due to Mr. Welles for his course taken in this important step. After this time he appears to have become an important man in the colony. He was uniformly a member of the Court of Magistrates after March, 1637, until he was elected Deputy Governor, in 1654. In 1640 he was appointed secretary of the colony, which office he held until 1649, and performed the duty of both offices during the whole period. For a time he also performed the duties of treasurer for the colony in 1639. At the session of the General Court in 1653, in March and April, the Governor being absent, Mr. Welles performed the duties of the Governor as Moderator of the General Assembly under the Constitution of the Commonwealth. In 1654 he was elected Deputy Governor, in 1656-7 and 1659. He was also elected Governor in 1655 and 8. In 1649 he was a Commissioner to the Colony Congress. Gov. Welles was frequently associated with Haynes, Ludlow, Mason and other leading men upon important committees appointed by the General Court. He did much in the formation and union of the colonies in 1643, for the mutual benefit and protection of each other. No one of the distinguished men of his time was more uniformly attentive to all his official duties than Gov. Welles, from his first appointment in 1637, until 1659. He was a constant attendant upon the General Court, except when employed in other public duties. His whole public life being fairly examined, he was as important a prop to the new colony as any of the principal men, except Gov. Winthrop—He died in 1668, and left a large estate to his children, viz. Thomas, Ichabod, Samuel, Jonathan, Joseph, Rebecca and Sarah. Samuel settled at Wethersfield. The descendants of Gov. Welles are numerous in Connecticut at this time. The most prominent of whom are Hon. Gideon, of Hartford—since his late appointment, at Washington—Thaddeus, Esq., of Glastenbury—Hon. Martin, of Wethersfield, and Doct. H. Welles, of Hartford. Gov. Welles came to Massachusetts in a vessel named the Susan and Ellen, E. Payne, master, in company with Richard Saltonstall, Esq., and family, Walter Thornton and others.

Welles, Capt. Samuel—died in 1675. His children were, Samuel

16 years old, Thomas 14, Sarah 12, Mary 10, Ann 7, and Elizabeth 5. John, son of Samuel, 1664. Edward, 1644. Thomas, son of Thomas, born 1690.

Welles, Wid. Elizabeth, Wethersfield—died in 1683. Children, Robert Foot, (died before her), Sarah Judson, deceased—left children, daughters Churchill, Goodrich, Barnard and Smith. Nathaniel Foot's eldest son Nathaniel and his brother and their children shared in her will, Daniel and Elizabeth—grandson John Stoddard—grandsons Joseph and Benjamin Churchill. She was a sister of John Deming, sen'r. and had a grandson Henry Buck.

Welles, Samuel, moved from Wethersfield to Stratford, with three sons—Thomas, Samuel, and another, perhaps other children. He was the son of Gov. Welles. Perhaps the same Capt. Samuel who died in 1675.

Weller, Richard—came early to Windsor. He married Ann Wilson in 1639. Children, Rebecca born May, 1641; Sarah in '43; William in '45; Nathaniel in '48; Ebenezer in '50; and Thomas in '53. This name is yet known in Litchfield county.

Westover, Jonah, sen'r., Simsbury, father of Jonah, jr., died in 1708. Samuel Case married his daughter. Children, Jonah, Jonathan, Margaret, Hannah, Jane, Mary and Joanna.

Welton, Richard, 1656.

Welton or Wilton, David—juror in 1644—deputy in '46.

Westley, William, Hartford, 1639—held 14 acres of land there, with liberty to fetch wood and keep swine and cows on the common. Widow Westley signed to move to Hadley in '59.

West, of Saybrook, 1669. John West, '49.

Westcoat, Richard, 1639.

Westwood, William—selectman of Hartford in 1636—member of the General Court in April, June, July, November and February, '36 —aided in declaring war in '37—deputy in '42–46—selectman in '39. He was one of the first settlers and leading men of the colony—an original proprietor of Hartford, and in the land division in '39. In '59 he signed a contract to remove his family to Massachusetts with those who settled the town of Hadley.

Wakelin, Henry, Stratford, 1650.

White, John—one of the early and principal settlers of Hartford, before 1639—was a juror in 1643–4—orderer of the town in 1641 and '45— fence viewer in 1649. He was an original proprietor of Hartford, and in its land division in 1639. He was one of the 60 persons, in 1659, who signed an agreement to remove to Massachusetts for the settlement of Hadley. He removed, and died there in 1683. His children were, Nathaniel, (who resided at

Hadley,) Daniel, Jacob, John, Sarah Gilbert, Mrs. Taylor, and a daughter who had married Mr. Hixton. Nathaniel had a daughter Sarah. Mr. White in his will gave Rev. John Whiting £5 in silver. He had intended to have given Stephen Taylor a select tract of land, but he found himself bound for a large sum to redeem his son Taylor's house and home-lot; he therefore ordered the land originally designed for Taylor to be sold to redeem his house and lot. He gave property to the children of his daughter Hixton—to his grandson Stephen Taylor, to be received at Nathaniel White's at Hadley — to his granddaughter Sarah, (a daughter of Nathaniel) he gave £5. The remainder of his estate he gave to his grandchildren, viz. Jonathan Gilbert, and to the children of his sons Nathaniel, John and Daniel, also the children of Sarah, (who had three sons)—his grandson Gilbert was the son of his daughter Mary. He owned a share in a mill at Hadley. His son Nathaniel was his executor. Mr. White was a strict Puritan in all its forms, and left the colony in consequence of a division in the church at Hartford.

White, Nathaniel—confirmed an ensign at Middletown in 1664— deputy in '63. Philip, 1646.

Whaples, Ephraim, Wethersfield—wife Mindwell—died in 1712. His children were, Ephraim and three daughters. He ordered his daughters to be paid out of his estate £10 each, by his son Ephraim, and to have a share of the movables. The will was signed in the presence of Eliphalet Whittlesey and Joseph Hurlbut. Jabez Whittlesey was made overseer of the will. He was a brother of Thomas

Whaples, Thomas, 1644—died in '71, and left children, Rebecca, Hannah, Joseph, Jane, Ephraim and John—resided in Hartford in '64. Thomas, son of Thomas, of Hartford, died in 1712–13. Children, Nathan, Joseph, Abigail, Rebecca, Mary and Elizabeth. Elizabeth was learning the trade of a tailor.

Wheatly, James, 1644.

Wheeler, John, from Concord in Massachusetts—went to Fairfield in 1644. He was one of the early settlers of the town. Moses, Stratford, '50. Samuel, sen'r., of Hartford, had children in 1712— Rachel 14, Elizabeth 7, Isaac 17, and Moses 9 years of age. Thomas of Fairfield, 1653. John, juror at Stratford, 1730. Ephraim, collector for the students of Cambridge College in '45—from Fairfield or Stratford. Farmer says, 30 distinct families of the Wheelers lived in Concord, Mass., between 1650 and '80—a prolific race of men.

Whelpley's fine remitted in 1661.

Whitefield, Thomas, removed from Dorchester to Windsor, 1635–6. Henry, first minister at Guilford, from Surrey, England, '39. John, came to Windsor as early as '36.

Whitehead, Samuel, had owned land in Hartford before 1639. Richard, jr., juror in '40.

Whiting, William, Hartford—was a member of the General Court in 1637. The Court ordered him to supply 100 pounds of beef (for Hartford) to carry on the Pequot war, in 1637. He was treasurer of the colony in 1641 to 1647. In 1638 he was allowed to trade with the Indians; and was appointed with Maj. Mason, &c., in 1642 to erect fortifications; he was also appointed with the Major in 1642 to collect tribute of the Indians on Long Island and on the Main;—on a committee to build a ship, and also to defend Uncas—foreman of the jury in 1640. He was a magistrate as early as 1639, and a leading man in the colony. His estate at his decease was over £9000 sterling. In 1649 he made his will. His children were, William, John, Samuel, Sarah, Mary, and Joseph. Joseph appears to have been born after the will was made, and he provided for him by a codicil to his will. He had a sister Wiggins who had children. He gave £10 to Margery Parker, £10 to Mr. Hopkins; £10 to Mr. Webster; £10 to the children of Mr. Hooker; £10 to the children of Mr. Stone; £10 to the poor of Hartford; £5 to the town of Hartford; £5 to the poor of Windsor; £5 to the poor of Wethersfield, and £5 to the children of the Rev. H. Smith, of Wethersfield. His son William was a merchant in London, and sold the lands he received by his father to Siborn Nichols, of Witham, in England.

Whiting, Rev. John. His children were, Sibbel Bryan, aged 34, Martha Bryan 28, Sarah Bull 26, Abigail Russell 24, William 30, Joseph 8, Samuel 19, and John one year old—(probably had two wives.) Ordained at Hartford in 1660. In '69 the church divided, and Mr. Whiting became pastor of the south church, and died in '89.

Whiting, Joseph—was the third treasurer of the colony. John was afterwards also treasurer. William was an original proprietor of Hartford, and in the land division in '39.

Whiting, Giles, 1643. Samuel, educated at Emanuel College in 1613, Anna married Nathaniel Stanley in 1706.

Whittlesey, John, 1662—the first of the name who came into the colony. He was located at Saybrook, not however as early as many others. The name was next found at Middletown and Wethersfield. It has been a most prolific race. The family have been uniformly respectable, generally wealthy, and produced some men of high standing and reputation, viz. Hon. Elisha, of Ohio. He has through a long and constant public life, from early manhood, retired to private life, and carried with him the reputation of an *honest man* -the fate of few politicians. John Whittlesey and William Dudley, of Saybrook, in 1663, contracted with the town to keep a ferry across the river at Saybrook, from Tilley's Point, for which the town gave them all the toll received of strangers, (except the inhabitants of Saybrook,) 20 acres of up-land, 10 acres of meadow, and £200 of Commonage—£100 on each side of the river. Whittlesey and Dudley contracted to build a road to the Point—build a horse canoe or boat large enough to carry over 3 horses at a time, and such passengers as desired to cross the river. They made the contract with John Wastall, John Clark, William Pratt, William Waller and Robert Lay, agents for the town.

Whitmore, Thomas, Middletown, 1654—was a gentleman of good character, and received appointments of the General Court. The name is spelt differently by the same family. It has been an ancient name at Middletown and in Stratford. Seth and William, of Middletown, were jurors as late as 1730.

Whitmore, Thomas, sen'r., aged 66. He was a carpenter by trade, and gave his tools to two of his sons. He died at Middletown in '81, and left a wife Katherine, and children, viz. John aged 36 years, Beriah 23, Thomas 29, Hannah Stowe 28, Samuel 26, Elizabeth 32, Abigail 3, Israhiah 25, Nathaniel 20, Joseph 18, Josiah 13, Sarah 17, Mehitabel 13, and Benjamin 7. I find the name spelt Whitmore, Whetmore, Whittemore and Wetmore, apparently the same name.— John, of Hartford, 1665.

Whittemore, John, Stamford, was murdered by the Indians previous to 1649.

Whitcombe, Job, Wethersfield—died in 1683. Wife Mary. His children were, Mary, aged 12 years, Job 9, Jemima 6, and John 4. This name is yet in New London county.

Witchfield, Margaret—died at Windsor in 1663. Her daughters were, Hannah and Abigail. They married two men by the name of Goff at Wethersfield. Her son married Miss Hayward. Margaret was a sister of Jane Winship, who left a daughter Joanna. Samuel Goff had children, Edward and Deborah.

Whitefield, Henry, the first minister at Guilford. He left preaching there in 1650, and was succeeded by Rev. John Higginson.

Wickham, Sarah, Wethersfield—died in 1699. Children, Thomas, Wittin, Sarah Hudson, Samuel, Joseph and John—perhaps others. She had a grandson John Cherry, the son of Sarah Hudson.

Wilcox, John, Hartford—surveyor of highways in 1642 and '44—selectman in '49—juror in '45. He had moved to Middletown in '54 —and died in '76. His children were, Sarah Long, aged 28 years, Israel 20, Samuel 18, Ephraim 4, Hester 2, and Mary 1. He was an original proprietor of Hartford, '39. John, of Middletown, (wife Mary died in 1671.) His children were, Joseph, Samuel and Mary. Israel, sen'r., died in '89. Children, Israel aged 10, John 8, Samuel 5, Thomas 3 years, and Sarah one month. Mary, widow, of Hartford died and left a cousin Sarah Long, a daughter, Ann Hawley, and a son-in-law John Bidwell.

Wilcocks, Ephraim, Middletown—died in 1712—son of John, and grandson of Andrew, of Middletown.

Wilcoxson, Samuel, Windsor, deputy in 1646. William, '47—perhaps the same who was made free in Massachusetts in '38. Timothy moved to Stratford as early as '40. William, of Stratford, '50—had sons, Joseph, John and Timothy.

Wickham, Thomas, Wethersfield, 1671.

Wild, Edmond, 1663. John, a grand juror in '43.

Wilkinson, Josiah, about Saybrook in 1664. Thomas, '49.

Willard, Josias, Wethersfield—died in 1674—juror in '71. Joseph, Wethersfield, '70, and died in '74.

Willet, Nathaniel, Hartford—constable in 1644. Elizabeth, '48.

Willer, Richard, Windsor, 1640.

Williams, Roger—juror in 1642–44 and 45—deputy in '37. He came to Windsor as early as '36. He was often a member of both branches of the General Court, and was a gentleman of importance in the colony.

Williams, William—a landholder at Podunk, an early settler, 1646. Arthur, of Windsor, '40—juror in '43. David, died in '84, and left a small estate. Matthew, of Hartford, '46. James, son of James and Sarah, born in '92, Hepzibah in '98, Sarah in '99, Samuel in 1700, Abigail in 1707, Daniel in 1710. John, of Windsor, married Bethia Marshall, in 1672. John and Ebenezer born in '73, another in 75. (John, of Hartford, '37. See Aaron Starks.)

Williams, Amos, an orphan. The magistrates ordered the little Bible and a paper book, left by his mother, to be delivered to him, in 1663. He died in '83. Children, Amos 13, Samuel 8, Elizabeth 6, and Susanna 3 years old.

Willey, John, Haddam—died May 2, 1688. He left an estate of £169 to his wife and 7 children, viz., Isaac 18 years old, Isabel 17, John 14, Miriam 12, Allyn 9, Mary 7, and Abel 6 years. Thomas, 1664. Isaac, 1649, about N. London in '71.

Wills, Joshua, Windsor, 1647. This was a common name in Massachusetts in its early settlement. Henry, a Pequot soldier in '37.

Wilton, Nicholas, Windsor—died July, 1683.

Winterton, Gregory—constable of Hartford in 1642—selectman in '45—juror in '40 and '42—surveyor of common lands in '47. He was an original proprietor of Hartford, and in the land division in '39. Signed to move to Hadley in '59. He was an uncle of John Shepard, and gave John £34. John was a brother of Thomas Greenhill, 1654. *Record*, p. 118.

Willoughby, Jonas, Wethersfield, 1666. This was a reputable name in Massachusetts in the early settlement of the colony, as it was in Connecticut.

Wilson, Anthony—deputy in 1646. Phineas, of Hartford—died in '92, and left a large estate. He had an only son Nathaniel, and daughters Hannah and Mary. Had 3 sisters, Hannah, Margaret and

Jane, who then lived in Hull, in Yorkshire, England. His wife had a daughter Abigail Warren. Samuel married Mary———, May, '72. and had a daughter in '74, and another born in '75, and Samuel in '78.

Wilton, David—moved to North'ampton from Windsor, in 1660, where he died. He left a grandson, Samuel Marshall, to whom he gave much of his property at Northampton. Joseph Hawley was about to marry his granddaughter Lydia, at Northampton, to whom he gave a share of his estate, provided he married her, and built a house on the land at Northampton, and lived there four years—if not, he gave it to Samuel Marshall, his grandson. He provided for his wife Katherine. Samuel Marshall, sen'r., married his daughter, and died before him. He was a brother of Nicholas Wilton—had a sister Joan Welton. He gave a silver bowl to the church in Northampton—£10 to the College—gave his wife the sawmill at Northampton. His grandson Thomas Marshall lived with him at Northampton. Medad Pomeroy was overseer of his estate at Northampton. Daniel, 1644. Nicholas, of Windsor, died July, 1683.

Wimbell, Robert, a distributor of the estate of Thomas Dewey, 1648.

Winchell, Robert, Windsor—a juror in 1644. In '37, was appointed with Mr. Ludlow and William Phelps as agents for the purchase of corn, &c. He came early to Windsor. His children were, Phebe born in 1639, Mary in 1641—David, Joseph, Martha, Benjamin.—Robert died in 1657. Nathaniel, son of Robert, married Sarah Porter, and had Nathaniel, Thomas and Sarah, born 1674, and Joseph 1677. Jonathan Winchell married Abigail Brunson, and had a son Jonathan, 1663. David married Elizabeth Filly, 1669, and had Joseph and two daughters. Nathaniel Winchell, 1664— probably the same who was at Westfield in 1686.

Winthrop, Gov. John, who first came to Saybrook, in 1635—was the son of John Winthrop, the Governor of Massachusetts. He arrived at Boston in the autumn of 1635, with a commission from Lord Say and Seal, Lord Brook and others, who were interested in a Patent of a large tract of land adjoining the Connecticut River, as agent of the Company—to erect houses and build a Fort at the mouth of the river, not only for self-protection against the savages, but to command the navigation and prevent the Dutch from taking possession of the lands. Mr. Winthrop brought with him from England, men, ammunition, ordnance and money, furnished by the Company, to carry out their design. He was directed by the Company, on his arrival at Boston, to repair at once to Connecticut, with 50 men, to erect fortifications and build houses for the garrison, and the houses for the men of quality within the Fort. He was also directed that such as should locate there in the beginning, should plant themselves either at the harbor or near the mouth of the river, for their own safety, and that they should set down in bodies together, that they could be better entrenched; also to reserve to the Fort 1000 or 1500 acres at least of good ground as near to the Fort as could be obtained. The Company also, before Mr. Winthrop left England, appointed him Governor of the Connecticut River, in New England, and of the harbors and places adjoining, for the space of one year after his arrival there. Gov. Winthrop soon learned that the Dutch at New Netherlands intended to seize upon the mouth of the river, and he immediately despatched 20 men from Boston to his place of destination, (now Saybrook) to get command of the river, and repel the Dutch if they should appear. Soon after the arrival of Mr. Winthrop's men at the mouth of the Connecticut, the Dutch who had been sent from New Netherlands arrived to take possession, but Gov. Winthrop's men had in season planted two of their cannon in so favorable a position that the Dutch troops were prevented from landing. Mr. Winthrop soon went to Saybrook and fulfilled his commission as agent for the Company, He and Mr. Fenwick did not consider either themselves or the lands within their grant, as strictly under the government or within the jurisdiction of Connecticut, until after the colony of Connecticut had purchased the land upon the river, and the Fort of Mr. Fenwick, in 1644; for which reason Gov. Winthrop is not found very frequently upon the records of the colony for some of the first years of its settlement. Even Mr. Fenwick was not a magistrate in the colony until 1644. Gov. Winthrop the younger applied to the General Assembly of Connecticut, in 1640, for a grant to him of Fisher's Island. The Court decided that so far as it would not hinder the public good, either in fortifying it for defence, or fishing, or making salt, that he had liberty to proceed therein. He therefore took possession of it, and his heirs hold it to this day. Gov. Winthrop did not become a member of the House of Assistants in the colony until after 1650; after which time he became the favorite of the colony, and received apparently any appointment he desired. He was elected Governor in 1657, 9 and 1660 to 1675. He was the first Governor of the colony who was ever elected previous to 1660, two years in succession—the old law upon this subject, owing to the universal popularity of Mr. Winthrop as Governor, was repealed. In 1662 he procured the Charter for the colony, for which he was agent, which greatly added to his popularity in Connecticut, but gave much offence to the colonists at New Haven; yet at the Union of the two Colonies, in 1665, Mr. Winthrop was continued as Governor of the colony, and Major Mason, deputy Governor. To give the honors and incidents of the life of so valuable a man as Gov. Winthrop would require volumes, it therefore will not be expected even an outline can be detailed in this small pamphlet.

In September, 1647, the General Court "thought meet" to give Mr. Winthrop a commission to execute justice, at Pequot, according "to their laws, and the rules of righteousness." Previous to 1660 no person was eligible by law, two years in succession to the office of Governor. But the people had now become so much enamoured with the good management of the affairs of the government by Mr. Winthrop, that the General Court, at the April term, proposed repealing the law, that Gov. Winthrop should be eligible the second year to the office of Governor. To do which it was propounded to the freemen, and inserted in the warrants for the choice of deputies, which was effected, and Gov. Winthrop triumphantly elected, not only two years in succession, but many years after. This was a year full of great and happy events in the colony. Mr. Winthrop had been elected Governor, and Gen. Mason, Deputy Governor; two of the most popular, deserving and able men in the colony, and better acquainted with the affairs of the country than any others. Gov. Winthrop was deemed by the people as a learned, safe and judicious statesman, while it appeared to be a conceded point by all that no man could be as familiar with the condition of the various tribes of Indians as Maj. Mason—and in this respect was viewed as peculiarly fitted for his new and responsible office of Deputy Governor. In the repeal of the law, the freemen had wisely discovered that the first year of holding an office was wasted more in learning its duties than in performing them acceptably to the public. Lhere for brevity, skip over that part of the record which appointed Gov. Winthrop agent to procure the Charter for the colony, and much of their distress in meeting the expense of his mission. In July, 1662, it was discovered that the £500 which had been appropriated for the expenses of Gov. Winthrop, had proved altogether insufficient for the object, and a part of that even then, unpaid, and the expenses had far exceeded their expectation. All was now consternation and excitement—a new and unexpected debt had been added to their misfortunes, while they were ignorant of the progress or success of their petition to the King—yet never daunted, the General Court at once appointed committees to notify those persons who were yet owing Mr. Cullick any part of the £500, to pay it at once, and the collectors for the country to prepare for payment without delay, to discharge the sums required by the Worshipful Governor. The General Court, in case those indebted as aforesaid, failed to pay as directed, appointed a committee to procure corn or other provisions, and compel such as were indebted towards the £500 so appropriated, to pay for it. The distress continued through the summer. But when the General Court convened at Hartford on the 9th day of October, 1662, all was hilarity and excitement in-doors and out, such as had never before been witnessed in the colony, and probably never since, when the people were notified that Gov. Winthrop had succeeded in the object of his mission to England, and that the Charter had arrived full of liberty for the people, confirming their titles to their lands, extending their territory, with the confidence of the King in the loyalty of his new subjects. They were publicly notified that it was then in the possession of the Court. It was then publicly read to both Houses of the General Court, with an immense concourse of the freemen and people present—when one of the Court, (probably Major Mason) held it out in his hand, and declared it to be *theirs* and *their successors!* It was viewed by all as a full confirmation, not only of all the titles in the colony, but of the colony itself. Gov. Winthrop at this time had not arrived, but remained in England for some time after he forwarded the Charter. The question in the House at once arose, who should take charge of and hold an instrument that was the Palladium of every man's liberty in the Colony, and the safeguard to the title of every foot of soil in the jurisdiction of Connecticut. The Court selected Mr. Wyllys, John Allen and John Talcott to take the Charter into their custody and keeping, in behalf of the Colony. An oath was then administered to them in open Court, for a faithful discharge of so important a trust.

It now became necessary for the General Court to prepare to legislate in conformity to and under the provisions of the Charter. The General Court, therefore, established and confirmed all civil and military appointments in the colony—all orders and laws not at variance with the provisions of the Charter were also confirmed. The Colony Seal was declared to be continued in the hands of the Secretary as the seal of the colony under the Charter. The town of Hartford was decreed by the freemen as the settled location for the convocation of the General Assembly for all future time, (except when visited by epidemic diseases.) The people throughout the country at once saw the advantages which

Connecticut necessarily must possess under the Charter, over other colonies, and particularly over the New Haven Colony. Towns from all parts of the country soon began to apply to the General Court to become members of the colony under the new government. Capt. John Young and others applied for the admission of Southold, on Long Island, into the colony, and submitted their persons and property under the Charter, which was accepted, with a promise of protection. South and Easthampton had before united with the colony. Capt. Young was declared a freeman, and a commission given him to act in Southold as the General Court should require. Their citizens were required to meet and elect a constable for the organization of the town. The inhabitants of Guilford applied for admission, and tendered themselves and estates, and were accepted upon the usual terms. The towns of Stamford and Greenwich also applied, and were received as other towns had been. The inhabitants of Mystic and Paugatuck had until this time held their commissions under Massachusetts, but the Court now ordered that "henceforth they should forbear exercising any authority by virtue of commissions from any other colony than Connecticut;" and ordered the inhabitants to elect a constable and organize the town, and pay the sum of £20 towards defraying the expense of procuring the Charter, as their proportion.

Gov. Winthrop executed his will in Boston, at the time of his sickness, where it is supposed he died. His sons were, Fitz John and Wait Still. He had five daughters, viz : Elizabeth, Lucy, Margaret, Martha and Anne. He gave his sons double portions compared with his daughters, and made all his children executors and executrixes of his will. He also appointed John Allen, Mr. Humphrey Davie, James Allen and his brother John Richards, to settle any difficulty that might arise in the settlement of his estate, or any three of them. His will was proved in court by Thomas Hatch and John Blake, July 25, 1676.

Winthrop, Fitz John—son of Gov. Winthrop, of Connecticut. He early became an important man in the colony, and was a magistrate when young. He depended not so much upon the exalted reputation of his honored father as upon his own exertions, for preferment and honors. His doctrine was the same as that of the Wolcotts—that all men were self-made who became eminent—that the son of a great man was no better than the son of a pauper, except that his advantages were preferable for accomplishing the object. Fitz John appears early to have imbibed a military spirit, and possessed every qualification for an important military officer ; he was educated in the art of war—was bold, brave and daring to a fault, and received the commission of Captain when young. The first important appointment which brought him particularly before the public, was an appointment by the General Assembly of Connecticut in 1664, with his honored father, Matthew Allyn, sen'r., Gold, Richards, Howell, and Young, some of the most important men in the colony, to meet his Majesty's Commissioners in New York, and hear the differences and settle the boundaries of the Patent of the Duke of York and the colony of Connecticut, by which decision Long Island was awarded to the Duke of York, &c., and the boundaries of Connecticut settled. We next find Mr. Winthrop, in 1683, appointed by the King of England, and associated with Cranfield, the Commander-in-Chief of New Hampshire, with Dudley, Stoughton, Randolph, Shrimpton,

Palmes, Pynchon, jr., and Saltonstall, as a committee to quiet all disputes regarding the Narragansett country, as Commissioners of Charles II. In 1693 the colony of Connecticut found it necessary to address King William and Queen Mary with reference to the militia of the colony, and to send an Ambassador to England for this special purpose. Maj. Gen. Fitz John Winthrop was at once selected and appointed for the important mission. While in England, in 1667, he laid before the Council of Trade a memorial giving an answer to the Duchess of Hamilton's petition to the King regarding her claims to Narragansett, so far as the people of Connecticut were concerned, though this matter was not included in his instructions. He managed the affair with great adroitness and good judgment. Gen. Winthrop 'was appointed Major General in 1690 over the army designed against Canada. In 1698, such was his popularity that he was elected Governor of Connecticut, and continued to be re-elected until his death, in 1707. He was the last of the eminent men of the name in Connecticut, though Massachusetts yet has her Winthrops.

Wood, Jonas, Wethersfield, 1636—produced to the court his certificate of church-membership, dated at Watertown, Mass., 29th of March, 1636, to join a church in Connecticut; and he was at Wethersfield in '36. He came with Andrew Ward, Coe, &c. Jonas, at Southampton, L. I., in '48, (which was under the jurisdiction of Connecticut)—was custom-master there in '61—magistrate and commissioner in '63. Perhaps the same who located at Wethersfield in '36.

Wood, John, was killed in 1639, near the mouth of Connecticut river. Lieut. Bull, while in pursuit of the Pequots, found his gun marked I. W. Matthew, '63. Consider, '64, of Westchester, which at this time was claimed within the jurisdiction of Connecticut.

Woodcock, John, 1639. This name is found in Connecticut before it is in Massachusetts.

Woodbridge, Rev. Timothy, Hartford. I insert this family as a family of clergymen ; there having been seven of the name, ministers in the colony, at about the same period of time. Timothy was settled over the first church in Hartford, in 1685, and died in 1732. According to an account by T. S. Perkins, Esq., deceased, (who was a descendant,) Timothy was the 2d son of Rev. John, who married a daughter of Gov. Dudley, of Massachusetts, and was settled at Andover, in that colony, in 1644. Thomas Woodbridge was first married to a daughter of Hon. Samuel Wyllys, of Hartford, and was the ancestor of Sheldon Woodbridge, Esq., of Hartford. A daughter of Thomas married Gov. Pitkin. Rev. Samuel (was a nephew of Timothy, of Hartford,)—was settled over the 3d church in Hartford, in 1705, and died in 1746. He was a grandson of Rev. John, of Massachusetts, mentioned above—from him are the descendants of those of the name in Hartford, East Hartford, and Manchester. Rev. John Woodbridge was settled at Killingworth. Rev. Dudley Woodbridge was settled over the first church in Simsbury, and died in 1710. The 2d Rev. Timothy, son of the first Timothy, was settled also at Simsbury, over the first church in 1712, and died in 1742. Rev. Ashbel was settled at Glastenbury, in 1728, and died in 1758 ;—he was the son of the first Rev. Timothy by his second marriage to Mrs. Howell. Rev. Benjamin was settled at Amity in the town of Woodbridge, in 1742. Rev. Ephraim Woodbridge was settled over the first church in Groton, in 1704, and died in 1724—neither of whom were either dismissed or removed from their places of settlement. The first Rev. Timothy, was a member (in 1708) of the Convention which, for the better regulation of the administration of church discipline, formed the noted Saybrook Platform, of which meeting Rev. James Noyes and Thomas Buckingham were moderators, and Rev. Stephen Mix and John Woodward were chosen scribes.

Woodbridge, Benjamin, 1673—witness of Thrall's will.

Whittlesey, Ruth, Wethersfield—died in 1734. This is the first death in the family, in Connecticut, on the Probate record at Hartford. Jabez Whittlesey was administrator. Jabez, of Wethersfield, was a farmer at Newington. He died in January, 1743, and left an estate of £718.

Wolcott, Hon. Henry, sen'r., was an early settler at Windsor. He came to Massachusetts from Tolland, England, and moved his family to Windsor in 1636, to continue with Mr. Warham's church, with which he had united in England. He had married Elizabeth Saunders before he left his country, and had some family. His son Henry, jr., was about 25 years of age when the family moved to Windsor, in 1636, and soon became an active business man. Hon. Henry was a gentleman of education, wealth and distinction, and had been a magistrate before he left England. He was long a magistrate and assistant in the colony, though he had become somewhat advanced in life before he settled at Windsor. He was made the first constable of the town, which at that day and for many years after, was an office of great honor and power in the colony. In 1637 he was appointed collector of rates—deputy in 1639 and '41—juror in 1641, '3 and '4—a committee with Major Mason to locate and erect fortifications—was frequently a member of both houses or branches of the General Court, and upon many of the most important committees in the colony—was one of the nineteen signers of the Petition to Charles II. for the Charter of Connecticut, all of whom were the principal men in the colony. Mr. Wolcott was the ancestor of more Governors of the Colony and State than any other individual, not only in the State, but in the United States. He was the ancestor of three Governor Wolcotts in Connecticut, viz. Roger and two Oliver Wolcotts—two of whom had been Lieutenant Governors ; also by the marriage of his daughter to the first Matthew Griswold, of Saybrook, he became the ancestor of the two Governor Griswolds, viz. Matthew and Roger. His son Simon married a daughter of the first William Pitkin ; and by this connexion he also became the ancestor of Gov. Pitkin. The children of Hon. Henry were, Henry, jr., George, Ann, Mary and Simon. Simon's children were Elizabeth, Martha, Simon, Joanna, and the Hon. Roger—the latter was the second in command at the siege and reduction at Louisburg, in 1745, and in 1751 he was elected Governor of Connecticut. The first Oliver, LL.D., was Governor in 1796 and 7. The second Oliver, LL.D., had been Secretary of War, and Governor from 1817 to 1827. Erastus, who served as General in the War of the Revolution, was a brother of Oliver, who was also General in the same service. Erastus was a Judge of the Supreme Court of Connecticut for some years. This worthy band of a single line, were the descendants of Henry Wolcott, of Windsor. Of the same line of ancestry was the Hon. Frederick, late of Litchfield—a brother of the last Gov. Oliver—who was a gentleman no less talented and worthy than any of his ancestors. There are at this day no public men by this name in the high public stations of our country. It was well for the Wolcotts that they lived when integrity and talents were the only qualifications for preferment and high places of public trust. There are two of the sons of Hon. Frederick—one in Boston, the other in New York—who are merchants of distinction. A grandson of the last Governor Oliver, and a son of the late Col. Gibbs, of Long Island, is fast rising into notice and favor as a gentleman of literature by his valuable productions. One other of the descendants in Hartford, not of the name, but of the blood, is also by his talents, industry and acquirements, making rapid progress to public favor and preferment. Hon. Henry Wolcott died in 1680. He gave in his will his seal ring to Henry, jr. He had land at Tolland, in England, at his decease, which was in the possession of John Wolcott, and John Dart, which he gave to his youngest son Josiah, after the expiration of the estate given by his (Henry's) uncle Christopher to John Wolcott, sen'r., then deceased. He also held land at Willington, called Longforth, in England, in the possession of Hugh Wolcott at his decease. He at the close of his will changed his views, and gave his land in England to Henry, jr., for life, and to the heirs male of his body lawfully begotten, and to their heirs forever, by Henry, jr.'s paying annually for six years, £50 to his other three youngest sons. He was a gentleman of great wealth; his land at Wethersfield alone was appraised at £1234. His other property in this country at £2743, exclusive of his property in England.

Wolcott, Henry, jr., received many appointments from the General Court. George, 1640—a brother of Henry, jr., and son of Henry, sen'r. Hannah, had a sister who married James Russell, who had a daughter, Mary Russell—she also had a sister Price, who shared in her estate. She died unmarried in 1683-4. Sarah, died unmarried, or without children, in July, 1684. Simon, of Windsor—moved to Simsbury, and owned land there in 1667. Simon, son of Simon, brother of Henry, John, William Pitkin, Christopher, William and Roger. Treat, an assistant in 1663.

Woodford, Thomas, Hartford, 1639—fence viewer in '39—collector of funds for the students of Cambridge College in 1645—sexton to dig graves and ring the bell for funerals, with orders that Thomas Woodford should "attend making graves for any corpses deceased; and that no corpse shall be laid less than four feet deep; none that be above four years old shall be laid less than five feet deep; none that be above ten, shall be laid less than six feet deep. He was not an original proprietor of Hartford, but had 14 acres of land there, with the right of pasture on the common, to fetch wood, &c. He was appointed to cry all lost property at public meetings, at 2 pence paid in advance, in 1640. Joseph, made free in 1663.

Woodhull, Richard, and Thomas Pierce, were appointed officers under Connecticut, on the admission of Setauk, L. I., into the jurisdiction of Connecticut.

Woodruff, Matthew, came early to Hartford among the first settlers. After remaining awhile at Hartford, he removed with his family to Farmington; since which the Woodruffs have emanated from Farmington. Nathaniel, after 1717, moved from Farmington to Litchfield, which makes Matthew the ancestor of the name there. Matthew died at an advanced age, in 1691. His children were, Matthew, aged 23, John 19, Samuel 14, Nathaniel 5, Joseph 2, Mary 21, Sarah 17, Elizabeth 12, Hannah 10. Widow Sarah Woodruff died in 1690. John died at Farmington in 1692, and left Joseph, aged 13, John 23, Mary 25, Hannah 21, Phebe 16, Margaret 10, and Abigail 8. The family have uniformly supported the good reputation of their ancestor. Gen. Morris Woodruff was as prominent as any of the name. The Woodruffs of Connecticut are the descendants of Matthew, and not of William.

Woodward, Rev. John—was scribe, in 1708, for the Convention who formed the Saybrook Platform.

Woodward, Hartford, 1640. It was voted by the town that he should employ his whole time in killing wolves, for which he was to have 4s. 6d. per week for his board in case he killed neither wolves or deers in the course of the week, but if he killed either, to pay for his board. This name was frequent in the early settlement of Massachusetts.

Wolfe, Edward, New London, 1671. Peter was at Salem as early as 1634.—*Farmer.*

Wolterton, Gregory, Hartford—died in 1674 or in '74. He had a nephew James, son of his brother Matthew, in New London. He left no children. He was a useful citizen.

Worstall, John—juror in 1644.

Wright, Thomas—deputy from Wethersfield in 1643—died in '70, and left Margaret, his widow, and children, Samuel, Joseph, Thomas and others. A daughter of his son Thomas married Job Hillyer, and they had a son William, and daughters, Margaret and Sarah. His widow died in '71.

Wright, Thomas, Wethersfield—died in August, 1683. His children were, Thomas, aged 23 years, Mary 18, Hannah 13, Lydia 11. His estate was £673. Anthony Wright married Mary, the widow of Matthias Treat, by whom she had children. Anthony died in '79.

Wrisly, Richard—one of the first settlers.

Wrotham, Simon, Farmington—died in 1694-5. His daughter House's children were, William, Susanna and Samuel—sons Samuel, and Simon, and daughter Newel.

Wyard or Wire, Robert, Wethersfield—died in 1682.

Wyatt, John, 1646—died in '68. His children were, Mary, Hepzibah, Dorcas, Sarah, Joanna, Elizabeth and Israel.

Wyllys, Gov. George, was the son of Richard, of Fenny-Compton, in Warwickshire, in England. He was the first of the family who came to New England. He held an estate there of £500 per annum, in possession of George, his eldest son, who he left in England. In 1636, being a puritan in principle and feeling, he became anxious to remove to Connecticut with his family, he therefore to prepare a comfortable situation in the new country for himself and family, at Hartford, during the year 1636, sent his steward, (William Gibbins) with 20 men, to Hartford, to purchase and prepare for him a farm, and erect such buildings as should be needed for his reception. Mr. Gibbins therefore came to New England, and purchased that elevated and delightful plat of ground, at this day celebrated not only by the location of the *Charter Oak* upon it, but as the Wyllys Place, at the south part of the city. He erected the necessary buildings, and prepared the grounds for a garden, where the family have uniformly resided. In 1638 Mr. Wyllys removed with his family direct to Hartford. His reputation in England had been of that high character, that in the following year he was made a magistrate, and in 1641 was elected Deputy Governor of the colony, and in 1642 was made Governor. He was once elected Commissioner to the United Congress of the Colonies. Dr. Trumbull says, " he was a Puritan of the strictest kind, and lived in all the exactness of the most pious Puritans of the day." His death, which took place March 21, 1644, was deeply realized throughout the colony. He left a son Samuel, who was born in England, about 12 years of age at the decease of his father, who at the age of 22, was made a magistrate, and became a prominent man in the colony. Gov. Wyllys, as early as 1639, 'was appointed with Gov. Welles to revise the laws of Connecticut. Among the many important offices which have been held by the different members of the Wyllys family, it is worthy of remark, in this day of shifting and change, that three of the descendants of Gov. Wyllys, (viz., Hezekiah, George and Samuel) held in succession, the office of Secretary of State of the Colony and State of Connecticut 98 years. Gov. Wyllys had brothers, William and Richard. This family, ·so long and so favorably known in Hartford, are now all deceased, and the name become extinct in the State ;—and that beautiful seat occupied by them nearly 200 years, has passed, for want of Wyllys heirs, into the hands of a gentleman no less talented than its original proprietors—a regular descendant of the Hon. Henry Wolcott the first, of Windsor. He left a wife, Mary, and children, George, Samuel, Hester and Amy. His son George remained in England, and was there, as appears by the will of Gov. Wyllys, in 1644; property was given to his son George in Connecticut, provided George should move with his family to Hartford, &c., otherwise given to his son Samuel.—*Records, Trumbull, and Farmer.*

Wyllys, Hon. Samuel, son of Governor Wyllys, of Connecticut, was born in Warwickshire, in England, in 1632, and came to Hartford with his father in 1638. When only 22 years of age he was made a magistrate, (in 1654) which he held for many years. He married a daughter of Governor Haynes, and died aged about 77 years, in 1709. His son Hezekiah held the office of Secretary for the colony from 1712 to 1734, when he died. George his grandson, was Secretary from 1735 until he died in 1796, when Samuel the son of the 2d George succeeded his father in the same office, and held it until 1809, when Hon. Thomas Day was appointed, and held it 24 years. In 1659 Mr. Wyllys was appointed by the General Court to go to Saybrook and assist Major Mason in examining the suspicions there about witchery. In 1660 he was auditor of public accounts with Capt. Lord. He was a member of the Congress of the United Colonies in 1661, '2, '4 and '7.

Hezekiah Wyllys married Elizabeth Hobart, a daughter of Rev. Jeremiah Hobart, in 1704. George Wyllys, son of Hezekiah and Elizabeth—was born October, 1710—grandson of Samuel first—Samuel, his great grandson, was the last Secretary of the Wyllys family.

Y.

Young, Rev. John, of Southold, L. I., was appointed a magistrate by Connecticut as early as 1662, to assist the magistrates of South and East-Hampton. The towns of Southold, Huntington, East and Southampton, Oyster Bay and other towns on Long Island, were under the jurisdiction of Connecticut for several years ; and the Island was claimed as being within the bounds described in the Charter, as was Rye, Hastings, Westchester, Narragansett, &c., and most of them were organized as towns by order of the General Court of Connecticut, and were represented in the General Assembly of Connecticut for some years, until the bounds of the Colony under the Charter were settled by the King's Commissioners, in 1664-5. On the admission of Southold into the jurisdiction of Connecticut, a petition, signed by said Young, Richard Terre and 22 others, inhabitants of Southold, was presented, all of whom were made freemen of Connecticut. George, 1664. Capt. J. Young was appointed in 1655, to command a vessel for observation, with men from Saybrook and N. London, to prevent Ninegrate's crossing the sound to attack the Indians on Long Island, and in case he did, to destroy his canoes, and kill his men, if possible. John, of Windsor, 1640.

APPENDIX,

A.

Abbey, Samuel, Windham—died in 1698—wife Mary. His children were, Mary, 25 years of age, Samuel 23, Thomas 20, Eleazer 18, Ebenezer 16, Mary 14, Sarah 13, Hepzibah 10, Abigail 8, John 7, Benjamin 6, and Jonathan 2.

Ackley, Nicholas, chimney viewer of Hartford, 1662.

Adams, Edward, resided at Fairfield in 1653. Ephraim, of Simsbury, 1730. Edward, in 1660, married Elizabeth Buckland— whether he was the son of Edward, of Fairfield, is not known—he had a daughter Mary. Jeremiah, of Hartford, (in No. 1,)—was the only person in Hartford, in 1660, allowed to sell wine in a less quantity than a quarter cask, or other liquors less than an ancor.

Adgate, Thomas, Norwich, 1660—was a deacon of the church in Saybrook in '59. He is not found upon the colony record in any town previous to his being in Saybrook. While there he married the widow of Richard Bushnell. Was made free in '63.

Adkins, Thomas, (probably now Atkins)—died in 1694. His children were, Mary aged 22, Thomas 21, Mary 19, Jane 16, Josiah 9, Sarah 12, and Benoni 4. Estate £182. Josiah died in '90— wife Elizabeth—children, Solomon, aged 12, Josiah 10, Benjamin 8, Ephraim 5, Sarah 16, Abigail 14, and Elizabeth 3.

Andrews, John, sen'r., Hartford—died in 1681—wife Mary. His children were, Benjamin, John, Abraham, Daniel and Joseph. He had grandchildren, Thomas Barnes, John Andrews, Abraham Andrews, John Richards, Daniel Andrews, Ezekiel Buck, and Joseph, the son of his son John. He had daughters, Mary Barnes, Hannah Richards, and Rachel Buck. He gave each of his grandchildren named, a legacy.

Andrews, Edward—died in 1663—was a brother-in-law of Josiah Adkins. He left a wife and children. Josiah Howlton married his sister. Gideon, of Fairfield, juror in 1730. Thomas, of Middletown, died in 1690, and left children, Thomas, John, Samuel, Hannah, Elizabeth, Sarah and Abigail.

Allyn, Matthew, (in No. 1,)—stated by Miss Caulkins, as having been a brother of Robert, who early settled at Saybrook, and afterwards at New London. All the descendants of Matthew spell the name (Allyn,) instead of (Allen) in and about Hartford; so that their signs upon their buildings show their descent from Matthew. He so spelt his own name. He was a petitioner for the Charter of Connecticut. Robert, was one of the principal settlers of New London, 1648.

Alsope, New London, 1674. He is supposed to be Joseph Alsope who came to New England in the Elizabeth and Ann, Roger C. master. Thomas came in the same vessel at another time.

Armstrong, Jonathan, New London, 1671.

Arnold, Joseph, Haddam—died in 1691. His children were, John 29 years old, Joseph 26, Samuel 23, Josiah 21, Susannah 16, Jonathan 12, and Elizabeth 9. This name is yet at Haddam in the person of the sheriff, Charles Arnold, Esq. Samuel had his share of the estate at Machemoodus (in East Haddam,)—he probably moved there.

Ashley, Jonathan, sen'r., Hartford—died in 1704. His son Joseph was his executor. He married a daughter of William Wadsworth, sen'r. His children were, Jonathan, Joseph, Samuel, Sarah and Rebecca. He gave four score acres of land in Plainfield to his son Samuel. His family appear to have been a distinct family from that of Robert, of Massachusetts.

Atwood, Capt. Thomas, Hartford, 1664—was an early settler.

Atwood, Doct. Thomas, Wethersfield—died in 1682, and left a wife, Abigail, and children, Abigail, aged 14, Andrew 11, Jonathan 7, and Josiah 4. He was a son of Capt. Atwood, of Hartford. One of the descendants emigrated to Woodbury or Waterbury.

Avery, James, New London, (in No. 1,)—was ordered in case of a war with the Dutch in 1673, to act as captain, Thomas Tracy, lieutenant, and John Denison, ensign, for the county of New London, over such forces as should be called out. Commissioner in '63.

B.

Babcock, James—was born in Essex, England, in 1580. In 1620 he moved to Leyden, in Holland, and remained there nearly three years, and being a strict Puritan in his faith, he removed from Holland to Plymouth in 1623, and arrived in July of that year. He came to this country in the ship Ann. He had four children born in England who came with him, viz., James, John, Job and Mary. He lost his wife by death, and married a second wife in 1650. He soon had a son—he named him Joseph; this son, between 1670 and '80, emigrated to Connecticut, and settled in the vicinity of Saybrook, and was the ancestor, in this State, of the family at Hartford, New Haven and other parts of Connecticut.

Backus, Stephen, Norwich, 1660—married Sarah, a daughter of Lyon Gardiner, the first Lord of Gardner's Island. His sons, Stephen born in '70, and Timothy in '82. Stephen moved to Plainfield, afterwards to Canterbury.—*F. M. Caulkins.* · William, was early found at Saybrook, and made free in '63. The name was at Saybrook at a much earlier period, (in '38); he afterwards became a proprietor of Norwich.

Bacon, Elizabeth—died in 1670-80, widow of Andrew, deceased, of Hadley. She returned to Hartford after the death of her husband, (being old.) One of her daughters married Caleb Stanley, to whom she gave her house and lands in Hadley, and the share of Isaac, her son, deceased, in his father's estate, which was then hers. She had a daughter, Abigail Coles, wife of Samuel Coles, and Lois, wife of Thomas Porter, both of Farmington, and Elizabeth Sension, wife of Mark Sension. Nathaniel, Middletown, 1664. Andrew, (in No. 1,) signed with the 60 to remove to Hadley, in '59, which he performed, and died there.

Badger, Daniel—moved from Hartford to North Coventry. He had sons, Daniel and Moses. The first settler there was John Bissell, jr., from Lebanon, (originally of Windsor)—his deed was dated July, 1716, and his deed of land in South Coventry is dated October, 1715, ancestor of Hon. Samuel Badger, of Philadelphia.

Bailey, John, Hartford, 1648—he resided at Haddam in '76—was a fence viewer at Hartford in '66. He with Joseph Aiken were viewers of chimneys in Hartford in '48.

Baker, Jeffery, Windsor—married Jane Rockwell in 1642, and had Samuel, Hepzibah, Mary, Abigail and Joseph. Samuel married Sarah Cook in '70. Baker, Wyllys, Gold, Richard Treat, Thomas Tappin, Wolcott, Sherman, Howell and Thurston Rayner were magistrates at the General Court in '63. Joseph, of Windsor, son of Jeffery, died in '91, and left Joseph and Lydia. He was a brother of Samuel. John married a daughter of John Bailey—was chimney viewer at Hartford in '65. Timothy, of Wethersfield—died, 1709—estate £21.

Baldwin, John, Saybrook, 1659—afterwards one of the proprietors of Norwich. Miss Caulkins states in her valuable work, that John was the ancestor of Judge Baldwin; he was also of Gov. Baldwin, of N. Haven; and of Judge Baldwin, late deceased, of Pennsylvania. The name first came into the colony at Saybrook.

Banks, John, was juror at Hartford in 1645. It appears he had been some time in the colony. He probably removed to Fairfield as early as '55, as the name is found there in '53—deputy in '63.

Barber, Thomas, Windsor—married in 1640, and had John, Thomas, Sarah, Samuel, Mary and Josiah. John married Bethsheba, and had a daughter and son. Thomas married Mary Phelps, and had Mary and Sarah. Samuel married Mary Long, and had Thomas and Samuel, in '71 and '73.

Barber, Thomas, of Windsor, (in No. 1.) There was a young man of this name at Wethersfield who was a carpenter. The one at Windsor came there with Mr. Huet, in 1639, and married in '40. The name is common in Hartford county. John, '64. (See No. 1.)

Barlow, John, Fairfield, 1652—perhaps the son of Thomas, who was juror at Hartford in '45, and moved to Stratford soon after.

Barnard, John—a man of active business habits, and held many offices in Hartford. He came early—was one who signed to move to Hadley in '59. Bartholomew, a constable in '64. He was often a deputy, and held other important offices. Francis signed the agreement to move to Hadley in '59.

Beach, John, settled at Stratford previous to 1650.

Bartlett, John—one of the first settlers of Poquonnock, in Windsor, with Holcomb, Francis and Griswold. He was among the first settlers of Windsor. Edward, died in 1676, and left no family. He gave a part of his estate to Benoni Case, of Simsbury, a son of Christopher Crow. Robert, in '46, appears to have been of Windsor. He moved to Northampton, but owned land in East Hartford in 1664. The town of Hartford applied to purchase it, on condition that if he refused to sell, to call on him for security not to sell it to improper inhabitants. William, resided at New London in 1649.

Barnes, Thomas, Hartford, 1640—had land distributed to him east of the river, and resided there in '63. Joshua, deputy in '63.

Bassett, Robert, united with John Chapman and others, in 1653–4, in Fairfield county, to raise troops. The town of Fairfield held a meeting, without authority from the General Court, to raise troops to fight the Dutch at New Netherlands, and appointed Mr. Ludlow commander-in-chief of their troops, which office he accepted. This transaction, it was supposed, caused the departure of Mr. Ludlow to Virginia. Thomas, '43. A man of this name came from England in '34, to Boston—may be the same Thomas Bassett.

Basey, John, was in the land division of Hartford, 1639. He died in '71. Elizabeth his wife. He had a grandson, Paul Peck, another Joseph Baker, a brother John Baker, and a son-in-law John Baker. His eldest daughter married a Burr—his third daughter Elizabeth, married a Peck—Lydia married John Baker.

Bascom, Thomas, in 1639—had a daughter, Abigail. Thomas, in '40, and Hepzibah in '44.

Bates, John, Haddam, 1676—died in 1718. Jonathan, of Haddam, had children, John, Solomon—Joseph Graves married his daughter—Jonathan, James Ray, jr., Elizabeth Bailey. His widow was Elizabeth. John, of Middletown, 1677, and James Bates. James, '69, of Saybrook.

Baxter, Thomas, New London, husband of Bridget, 1662.

Beardsley, William, (in No. 1,)—is probably the William Beardsley who came from Hertfordshire with John and Joseph Beardsley to Massachusetts in a vessel called the Planter.

Beardsley, Thomas, at Fairfield in 1658—probably the grandson of William, who moved to Stratford before, and who was a juror at Hartford in '49. John, of Stratford, before '50.

Beaumont, William—moved to Saybrook, and resided there in 1663.

Beckwith, Nathaniel, Haddam—died in 1717, and left Sarah, his widow, with £269 estate. His children were, Job, Nathaniel, Jerusha, Sarah, Joseph and Patience. Nathaniel, of Lyme, was appointed by the court, guardian of the children of Nathaniel Beckwith, deceased, of Haddam. It is probably the two Nathaniels above, were the sons of Matthew and Stephen, brothers, who were early settlers in Hartford, neither of whom appears to have died at Hartford.

Beckly, Richard, Windsor—juror in 1664.

Beers, Thomas, came to Connecticut as early as 1645, and was a constable in '47—whether he was a relative of the brave Capt. Beers, who, in Philip's war, was killed with 20 of his men near Northfield, is not known. The name soon after '47 disappeared in Hartford, and is early found at Stratford, so that it is supposed Thomas moved to Stratford, with the flood of emigration from Hartford and Windsor. Joseph Beers who resided at Stratford in '72, is supposed to have been the son of Thomas. Joseph had a son Daniel, who, after a settlement had commenced at Woodbury, located himself there, and married a Miss Walker, either a daughter or granddaughter of the Rev. Z. Walker, who had also moved to Woodbury. They had sons Josiah, Zechariah and Lewis, born at Woodbury. Josiah was the father of Hon. Seth P. Beers, Commissioner of the School Fund of Connecticut, Josiah, of Stratford, and James, of Fairfield, were jurors in 1730. The name yet remains in Fairfield and Litchfield counties.

Bell, Francis, Stamford, 1642. Mr. Bell was one of the early settlers, and an important man in the colony—a firm Puritan in forms and principles. Rev. Mr. Denton, Mitchell, Ward, Law, Rayner, Bell and Hollys were important men in Stamford in its first settlement. Some of the descendants of Francis have a Bible which was brought to New England in the Mayflower, in which is a record of the first male child born in Stamford. Francis Bell is favorably noticed by Cotton Mather, in company with Slosson.

Bell, Robert, Hartford—was fined £10, in 1683, for selling Tucker a pint of liquor with which he became intoxicated, in violation of law. Bell died in Hartford in '84—Estate £28—children, John 6 years old, Robert 4, and Mary 1. Thomas, of Fairfield county, '70.

Belding, John, Wethersfield—died in 1677. His children were, John, 19 years old, Jonathan 16, Joseph 14, Samuel 11, Daniel 7, Ebenezer 4, Sarah 9, Lydia 2, and Margaret 6 months, at his death. John Belding, Robert Morice, John Waddams and John Stedman, jurors in 1664.

Benedick, Thomas, 1662.

Benfield or Penfield, Middletown, 1664.

Benham, Hannah, daughter of Richard, was born, July, 1683. Rebecca, was born, September, '85.

Bennet, James—moved from Concord to Fairfield in 1644. He had a son Thomas. This is a familiar name in the west part of Connecticut at this time. A man by the name of Henry Bennite—(perhaps the same name was Secretary to King Charles II., and signed the commission or letter for Col. Richard Nicolls, Sir Robert Carr, George Cartright, &c., in '64, to the Governor of Connecticut, in behalf of the King.

Benton, Andrew, Milford, in 1646—of Hartford, '66. He married at New Haven—died at Hartford, July, '83, aged 63 years. Himself and wife took a dismission from the church at Milford to the church in Hartford, in '66. His children were, Hannah, (died) Andrew, Mary, John, (died) Samuel, (settled at Tolland) Dorothy and Joseph, (his wife died)—and by a second wife he had Ebenezer, Lydia and Hannah, (named after the deceased Hannah.) See Timothy Thrall in this No. He left 7 children at his decease. Andrew, of Hartford, '64, '70—juror in '64. Edward, in '74. Edward, of Guilford, '50. Andrew held land, and was a fence viewer in Hartford, in '64. Edward, of Hartford, signed with 59 others to remove to Hadley, in '59.

Benjamin, Caleb, resided in Hartford, but appears to have died at Wethersfield, in 1709. He was a brother of Samuel, who died in 1769. He left a son John and four daughters. John had a double portion of his estate, and was executor of his father's will. Caleb was admitted a freeman with Gershom Bulkley, &c., in '69. He petitioned the

General Court in '82, to form a town in the Webaquassett country, situated probably north of the Pequot territory, perhaps in what is now Windham county.

Benjamin, Samuel, (in No. 1,)—resided at Hoccanum, in Hartford —died in 1669, and left sons Samuel and John, and daughters, Mary and Abigail. Probably was a relative of John at Watertown, one of the proprietors of Cambridge. Left his estate with his wife Mary, and made Caleb, his brother, overseer of his estate and family.

Benjamin, Richard, in May, 1664, with Jeffery Jones and others, were admitted freemen, and the oath was administered by Capt. John Young, of Southold, L. I. He appears to have resided at L. Island. The relation, if any, to Samuel and Caleb is not known.

Benjamin, John, appears to have been the grandson of Samuel, who died at Hartford, (Hoccanum) in 1669. Samuel left a son Samuel, and daughters, Mary and Abigail. The first Samuel was a brother of Caleb, of Hartford. John died in '53, and left his wife Hannah. To his son John he gave £50—to his son Caleb he gave a house and four acres of land east of the river—to his son Samuel, £50. He had a son David, who died before him, who left two children. Gideon, his son, was executor of his will, and had the residue of his estate. Gideon, or his son Gideon was the grandfather of Edwin Benjamin, Esq., now of Hartford. Jonathan, son of Gideon, married Miss Woodbridge, who was a descendant of Governor Dudley, of Massachusetts. Samuel, son of John and Hannah, of Hartford, was born, May, 1708. Caleb was born, 1710.

Beswick, George—died in 1672.

Betts, Thomas, Guilford, 1650. (See John and Widow Betts in No. 1.)

Bidwell, Joseph, Wethersfield—died in 1692. Children, Amy 14 years, Joseph 12, Benjamin 9, Ephraim 6, Lydia 3, and Mary four months old. John Bidwell died in '92, and left an estate of £1081.

Bidoll or Bidwell, John, 1673—of Hartford, '51.

Bigelow, Jonathan, sen'r., Hartford—died in 1710, and left Mary his wife, and children, Jonathan, John, Mary, Sarah, Violet, Joseph, Abigail, Daniel and Samuel. Left an estate of £549. Jonathan, son of John, married Mabel Edwards, in 1699.

Biggs, William, Wethersfield—died in 1681, and left his widow, and children, William 15 years old, Mary 14, Thomas 9, Elizabeth 8, Sarah 6, and John 4. Estate £139.

Billings, Richard, Hartford—had 6 acres in the division of land east of the river, in 1640. He was in the colony before '40, and was one of the 60 who signed to remove to Hadley in '59.

Bingham, Thomas, is first found at Norwich as a proprietor in 1660, after which he married, and had eleven children. The name yet remains in New London county. Thomas, of Windham, '97.

Birchard, John. A Mr. Birchard was a juror at Hartford as early as 1639, before any jurors came from Saybrook, which shows he must have been settled in one of the three towns on Connecticut river— perhaps John, who afterwards settled at Norwich, and became a proprietor and clerk, selectman, constable and commissioner there—perhaps the same to whom the General Court sent a warrant to enforce payment of the Charter tax against Mystic. His sons, as stated by Miss Caulkins, were, Samuel, James, Thomas, John, Joseph and Daniel. John was made free in '63.

Birdsey, John, moved from Milford to Stratford, before 1645, and became a leading man in the church there.

Bird, John and Joseph, first settlers of Litchfield from Farmington— were descendants of Thomas, (in No. 1,) who moved to Farmington, and was the ancestor of Dr. Bird and Gen. Bird, and others. James, Thomas and Joseph, 1663.

Birdge, Joseph, who settled at Litchfield in the early settlement of that place, was from Windsor, and a descendant of Richard, (in No. 1.) The present Treasurer of Connecticut is also a descendant. John, of Windsor, married Hannah Watson in 1678—in '79 had a son John.

Bishop, Anne, Guilford—died in 1676. Children, John, Stephen, and a daughter who married James Steel. She had removed from Hartford to Guilford—perhaps the ancestor of James, who was seven years Deputy Governor of Connecticut before '90. Rev. John minister at Stamford, '44.

Bissell, John, Windsor—had a son Nathaniel born in 1640. His son John married Miss Mason, in '58, and had Mary in '58, John in '61, Daniel in '63, Dorothy in '65, Josias in '70, a son in '73, Ann in '75, and another son in '75. Thomas Bissell in '55, married Abigail Moore, and had Thomas in '56, Abigail in '58, John in '60, Joseph in '63, Elizabeth in '66, Benjamin in '69, a son in '71, and other children. John, sen'r., of Windsor, died in '77—his children were, Mary who married Jacob Drake—Joyce married Samuel Pinney—John. Thomas, Samuel and Nathaniel. John, jr., was the first settler in Coventry—and received his deed of Israel Everett, of Lebanon, Oct. 1715—was the first captain in Coventry—held slaves. Though he moved from Lebanon to Coventry, he originated at Windsor.

Blachford, Peter, Saybrook, 1663.

Blackledge, John, jr., admitted an inhabitant of Hartford in 1659.

Blackleach, John, Wethersfield, (in No. 1,) slandered the authority of the colony, and was fined £30—was informed by the Court, that he deserved a penalty of £100, but owing to a weakness incident to him, they fined him only £30. He died in 1683. He had been a gentleman of estate, but left only £373 to such of his children as were supposed to be then living, viz. John, Exercise Hodges, Mary Jefferies, and Benoni. Was an early settler.

Blackley, Thomas, (in No. 1)—who resided in this colony in 1641, embarked from London in the Hopewell, Thomas Babb, master, for Massachusetts, some time previous.

Blake, John—died in 1690. Children, Mercy 17 years of age, Sarah 16, Mary 14, Elizabeth 12, Abigail 10, John 8, Jonathan 6, Stephen 4, and Richard 11 months. Nicholas, 1656.

Blanchard, Peter—collector of rates against the inhabitants of Mystic and Paugatuck, in 1662.

Bliss, Thomas, sen'r., and jr., (in No. 1,) were among the early settlers of Hartford, before 1639. It is more than probable that in the constant emigration down the Connecticut river, from the three old towns, that the Thomas Bliss who settled at Norwich in '60, was one of the above—probably was Thomas, jr., who had then grown to manhood. Thomas, made free in '63.

Bloomer, Robert, 1664.

Bloss, James, was voted not to be an inhabitant of Hartford, but he was allowed by the town to continue there until the spring of 1660.

Blumfield, William, Hartford, (in No. 1)—in 1663 had moved down the Connecticut river.

Boardman, Daniel, Wethersfield—married Hannah Wright, and had 12 children, viz. Richard, born in 1684—settled at Wethersfield—Daniel, jr., born in '87—he became a minister at New Milford, and died Aug. 1744—Mabel, born in 1689, and married John Griswold—John, born in '91, and died young—Hannah, born in '93, and married John Abbey, of Enfield—Martha, born in '95, and married a grandson of Josiah Churchill, of Wethersfield—Israel, born in '97, and died at Stamford, in 1724—Timothy, born in 1699, and died the same month, (and a second) Timothy was born in July, 1700—he married and settled at Wethersfield, and had a son Timothy, in '27—sons, Oliver, Thomas and Sherman—(Timothy died in '53, and his widow in '80)—Joshua, born in 1702—Benjamin, born in 1704, and settled at Sharon—Charles, born in 1707. Daniel, the father, died the 20th of February, 1725, and left his wife, Hannah, and most of his children living. Son Charles died soon after his father. Daniel the father of Daniel, sen'r., of Wethersfield, appears to have died in Massachusetts, and left a son Daniel, and other sons. Daniel moved to Wethersfield about 1680. About the same time the name appears at Middletown—perhaps a brother of Daniel, sen'r., of Wethersfield. Daniel in his will, gave Joshua his house at Wethersfield, and half his lands at Litchfield and New Milford—and to his son Benjamin the other half. John Bostwick and Zechariah Ferris, of New Milford, appraised the property at New Milford in 1725. Daniel was the ancestor of the Boardman family at N. Milford. The name and family are distinct from the name and family of Samuel Boarman, who was an early settler at Wethersfield. Boardman, Isaac, jr., of Wethersfield, died in 1719. Sherman, and other families of Hartford, are descendants of Daniel Boardman. Elizabeth, widow, at Middletown, died in 1730—estate £115. Samuel, of Middletown, died in 1733. Sarah, of Wethersfield, widow, died in 1733, and left children, David, Joseph and Mary Warner. She had grandchildren, William, Sarah and Hannah Warner. Isaac, jr.'s property was given and distributed to his widow Rebecca, and his children, Isaac, Edward, Josiah, Ephraim and other children. In this family there has been one Senator of the U. States, one member of the House of Representatives in Congress, a Judge of the County Court, and several clergymen.

Boarman, John and Joseph, Wethersfield—both died in 1676.

Boreman, William, Guilford, 1649.

Boltwood, Robert, signed to move to Hadley in 1659.

Booth, Richard—was an early settler at Stratford, some years previous to 1650. This family has now become numerous in the western part of the State.

Boen, Daniel, Wethersfield—died in 1693—was unmarried—he owned a sloop and other property, all of which was appraised at £85.

Boosy, James, (in No. 1,)—who was one of the principal settlers of Wethersfield, was united with Edward Hopkins, John Haynes, John Mason and John Steele, as a committee for Connecticut, to conclude articles of agreement with George Fenwick, Esq. for the purchase of the Fort, &c., at Saybrook, which was effected in 1644. He was a leading man in Wethersfield, and ranked high in the colony.

Bostwick, Arthur, Stratford, 1659. Had trouble in his family, which was submitted by the General Court, to Joseph Judson, Mr. Blackman, Beardsley and Fairchild. He settled at Stratford previous to '50.

Bowe, Alexander—died in 1678, and left children, Samuel, Anna, and Rebecca.

Bowden, John, 1663.

Bowers, Morgan, Norwich, 1660. He is said by Miss Caulkins, to have been illiterate and thriftless, and was the first case of penury in Norwich. John, of Derby, from Cambridge, Massachusetts. A clergyman by this name came later into the colony, whose descendants are of high standing at Berlin, Middletown and other places.

Bowles, Richard, at Fairfield, in 1641 and '51. Thomas, of New London, '71. Richard was chosen constable of Greenwich, and made a freeman in '62—appointed a constable of the town, of Hastings in '63. No person by this name died in Hartford until after 1700. The name is uniformly spelt Bowles upon the early record, and not Bolles.

Brace. Stephen, Hartford—died in 1692, and left a widow and children, Elizabeth, Phebe, Ann, Stephen, John and Henry. He ordered in his will, to put Henry to a trade. He owned land in the great meadow at Rocky Hill and at Pattacunk. Left an estate of more than £400.

Bradfield, Leasly.

Bradford, John, Norwich, was the youngest son of Gov. Wm. Bradford, of Plymouth, Mass. by Dorothy, his first wife. An interesting account is given of this man by Miss Caulkins, p. 100. Mercy Bradford married Samuel Steel in 1680.

Brainard, Daniel, was one of the first settlers of Haddam. Several of the family have been deacons at Haddam and East Haddam, from the first formation of a church there. Daniel, jr., was made deacon in E. Haddam in 1725—died '43, aged 77 years. Noadiah, made deacon there in 1743, and died in '46. Daniel, sen'r., died in 1714 or '15. His sons were, Daniel, James, Joshua, William, Caleb, Elijah and Hezekiah—no daughters, A respectable family.

Brewster, Jonathan, (in No. 1,) was at New London in 1648. He was the grandson of William, who came to Plymouth in the Mayflower. He was early an important man at New London, (in '49)—he afterwards, in the early settlement of Norwich, moved there. The Brewsters of Connecticut are most of them descended from Jonathan, and apparently all from William of the Mayflower. In '61 he was ordered to take his pay out of the wampum received from Narragansett.

Brinsmaid, John, first settled at Stratford, and held land there before 1651. Probably the ancestor of General Brinsmade, of Washington, Conn.

Brockway, Woolston, (in No. 1, of Saybrook, 1663)—left a son

William, and perhaps other children. He was the ancestor of Rev. Diodate, and Hon. John H., of Ellington. The family by marriage, are connected with the Spencers at East Haddam.

Brigden, Rev. Zechariah, Stonington, 1661.

Briggs or Biggs, William, of Middletown—died in 1681. His children were, William 15 years old, Mary 14, Thomas 9, Elizabeth 8, Sarah 6, and John 4.

Brown, Francis, and Lieut. Lewis had buildings burned by the Indians, at Farmington. The damage was submitted by the General Court to Mygatt, &c., in 1661. Francis Brown, constable of Stratford, in '63.

Brown, Peter, Windsor—died 1691. Children, Peter, John, Jonathan, Cornelius, Mary, Hepzibah, Esther, Isabel, Deborah and Sarah; he also had two other daughters who were married. He left for them an estate of £408.

Brundish, John, Wethersfield—died in 1639, and left two sons and three daughters.

Bruen, Obadiah, James Rogers, and John Smith were appointed commissioners in 1660 and '63, to try causes and punish offences—confined to a jurisdiction of £20. Mr. Bruen was a petitioner to Charles II. for the Charter of Connecticut.

Brunson, John, Farmington—died in 1680, and left a widow, and 7 children, viz., Israel, John, Isaac, Abraham, Mary, Dorcas and Sarah. John settled at Waterbury, and died there in 1696–7. Dorcas married Mr. Hopkins, and Sarah Mr. Kilbourn. The name on the record is generally spelt Brunson, but occasionally Brownson. Jacob, sen'r., of Farmington, died in 1707–8, and left Samuel, Roger, Isaac, Jacob, Elizabeth Harris, and Rebecca Dickinson. (See John, of Hartford, in No. 1.) John moved from Hartford to Farmington. The descendants of this family are numerous, and settled in many parts of the State and country. Judge Brunson, of the State of New York, has become the most eminent of the name ; Alvin, of Oswego, N. Y.; the family at Waterbury, Greenfield Hill, Middlebury, Southbury, and Simsbury, are descendants of John, originally of Hartford and Farmington.

Bryan, Alexander, 1664.

Buck, Ezekiel, Wethersfield, father of Enoch—was a farmer, and died in 1712 or '13. To his wife Rachel, he gave a share of his estate for her life-time—at her decease to fall to his grandson Ezekiel, the son of his eldest son Ezekiel. His children were, Ezekiel, Enoch, Jonathan, (Stephen 2 years old at this time,) Hannah, Abigail, Comfort, Rachel Brunson (was deceased,) Sarah Welton, and Mary Kelsey. He left a good landed estate to his large family. Samuel, of Wethersfield, died in 1708. Ezekiel, jr.. moved from Wethersfield to Litchfield. Henry, of Wethersfield, 1670. This family have generally been farmers or merchants, and uniformly respectable.

Buck, Roger and William, with Thomas Kilbourn and family, Matthew Marvin, William Payne and James Rogers were fellow passengers in the ship Increase, Robert Lea, master, from England—most of whom settled in Connecticut, as is supposed, from the fact that early settlers of the same names were early settlers here, and most of them at Wethersfield as early as 1636.

Buckingham, Rev. Thomas, sen'r., was a Welchman, and was not ordained at Saybrook until 1670. His parents resided at Milford. He was a Trustee of the College at Saybrook—was a strict Puritan in all forms—was one of the Moderators of the Synod which formed the noted Saybrook Platform in 1708—and died in 1709. Thomas, of Hartford, married Ann Foster, daughter of Isaac Foster, November, 1699. He was a judge at Hartford, and a man of some considerable importance in the colony. Some of the name yet reside in Hartford, and a street is called by that name in honor of the family. Others of the name still reside in Milford. Thomas came to Hartford as early as 1645.

Buckland, Thomas, Windsor—had children, Timothy in 1638, Elizabeth in '40, another daughter in '42, Mary in '44, Nicholas in '46, Sarah or Tana in '48, Thomas in '50, and Hannah in '54. Timothy married Abigail Ware, in '62, and had Timothy, Thomas, Abigail, Mary, Sarah, Hannah and others. Thomas, (in No. 1,) Windsor— died in '76.

Bulkley, Rev. Gershom, the third ordained minister at Wethersfield, 1666—married Sarah Chauncey—he also preached at New London. He resigned his ministry in consequence of ill health, several years before his death. He was eminent as a divine and scholar. He was the son of the Rev. Peter Bulkley, of Concord, Mass., who had descended from an honorable family in Bedfordshire, England. His father was Edward Bulkley, D.D., of Bedfordshire. Rev. Edward was, when young, made a Fellow of St. John's College, Cambridge. He married the daughter of Thomas Allen, of Goldington, in England, and she had a nephew who was the Lord Mayor of London. He had by two wives, fifteen children. His son John was a minister at Colchester, and father of judge John Bulkley.—*Cotton Mather, and Rec.*

Bulkley, Peter, Wethersfield—died in 1701-2—a mariner. Wife, Rachel—died without issue. His property was quit to the widow, by the children of Gershom Bulkley, by her securing the child of Charles Bulkley, deceased, of New London, if she should demand it.

Budd, John, was appointed commissioner for the town of Hastings, and Richard Bowles, constable, in 1663.

Buell, William, (in No. 1,) married in 1640, and had children, Samuel, Peter, Mary, Hannah, Hepzibah, Sarah and Abigail. His son Samuel, settled in Killingworth, and had a son Samuel. Peter, of Simsbury, in '86, was chosen sergeant of the train-band, in Simsbury, and was *orderly* proclaimed by the chief military officer there, sergeant of the train-band by 23 votes. He was also, in '87, voted 20s. for his deputyship and expenses. In Simsbury, the *deacons* published all persons for marriage, as late as 1786. Widow Mary Buell, of Windsor, died in 1684. Children, Mary Mills, Hannah Palmer, Hepsibah Wells, and Hannah, grandchildren Mary and Sarah Palmer. Thomas Buell and Edward Stebbins were ordered to take the charge and management of the estate of Mr. Hopkins, deceased, in '61. In '62 Samuel Buell married Deborah Griswold, and in '63 had a son Samuel. John Buell, moved from Windsor to Killingworth, with his father—then to Lebanon, and afterwards to Litchfield—and not William, as in No. 1.

Burnham. Thomas, (in No. 1,) purchased lands of the Indians, at Podunk, in 1660.

Burden, John, Saybrook, 1664.

Burlson, Edward, 1664.

Burrell, Charles. The first of this name I find in the colony, is Charles, 7 years old, and Jonathan 5, wards of Capt. Jonathan Westover, of Simsbury, appointed in 1728, as their guardian.

Burr, Jehu, Agawam, (in No. 1.) In 1637, a tax of £520 was imposed upon the colony to defray the expense of the Pequot war. Hartford was to pay £251; Wethersfield, £124; Windsor, £158, and Agawam, £86 : 16—payable in money or wampum at 1 a penny, or beaver at 9s. a pound. Mr. Burr was appointed collector for Agawam, (now in West Springfield.) The tax appears to have been laid large enough to cover losses. He was a grand juror from Fairfield in '61. He was a carpenter by trade. Rev. Jonathan from Dorchester, also settled in Fairfield county. Jehu first settled at Agawam as early as '37, and received many of the offices and honors of the Connecticut colony in its first settlement, early left Agawam, and removed with his family to Fairfield, where he continued to be favorably known in the colony. He is supposed to have been the ancestor of those of the name in Fairfield county, viz., Thaddeus, of Fairfield, who during the struggle in the war of the Revolution, ranked with such men as Davenport, Sherman, and Hillhouse in usefulness in that eventful struggle. Rev. Aaron Burr, who was born at Fairfield in 1715, settled at Newark, N. J., in the ministry, married the daughter of Rev. Jonathan Edwards, of Northampton, and afterwards became the first President of Princeton College. He was the father of Col. Aaron Burr, former Vice President of the United States. This, however, so far as concerns the ancestry of Rev. Aaron, and his son, Col. Aaron, has a different version by M. L. Davis, Esq., in his Memoirs of Aaron Burr. He states, that the grandfather of Col. Burr was a German, and by birth of noble parentage; that he emigrated to this country, and settled at Fairfield—perhaps so, but quere—there is now in the Hall of the Connecticut Historical Society a very ancient and beautiful *English* chest, which was presented by some one of the Burr family, of Fairfield, to the Society, as an early family relic—supposed to have been brought from England by the family who settled at Fairfield. The workmanship upon the chest has the appearance of English work 200 years since. The name of Burr is an English name, and not German. Jehu was an Englishman, as was Rev. Jonathan, born, educated and licensed in England. Perhaps Aaron was of German extract.

Burritt, William, was an original settler at Stratford, previous to 1650. The family have been uniformly respectable.

,Buttolph, George, Simsbury—died in 1696, and left a small estate, and children, John, David and one other child. David died in 1717, and left an estate of £176. John died in 1692, and his son David was his executor.

Bushnell, Susannah, Saybrook—died in 1686. She gave all her estate to her son, John Waddams, as testified by Lieut. William and Samuel Bushnell, of Saybrook. John Bushnell was townsman at Say brook in '86. The relation of the Bushnell family at Guilford and at Saybrook is not known to the writer, (if any.) Richard, of Saybrook, in '48—married Mary Marvin, sister of Reinold. Francis, of Guilford, '50. William, of Saybrook, sergeant in '61.

Butler, Richard, and Josias Bull, of Wethersfield, grand jurors, 1661.

C.

Cable, John, Fairfield, 1653.

Cadwell, Samuel, had a daughter Mary, born in 1708, and a son Samuel, born in 1710.

Calkins, Deacon Hugh—deputy in 1663, two sessions, from New London, with James Rogers. Appointed in '59, with James Morgan and J. Avery, to lay out to Governor Winthrop, 1500 acres of land at the head of Paugatuck Cove on Fresh river.

Caulkins, G., was one of the first settlers of New London, and an important man there. Hugh, of Norwich, the father of John, might have been the son or brother of Deacon Calkins, of New London, and Hugh resided himself at New London in '54. Those of the name in Sharon are of the family of Hugh. John, free in '63.

Cakebread, Isaac, Hartford—died in 1698, and left a son Isaac, 18 years of age. Isaac, jr., died at Hartford, in 1709. This probably closed the Cakebread family.

Callsey, Mark, 1663.

Camfield, Matthew. (This name is uniformly spelt upon the record, Camfield or Campfield.) He was an early and original settler at Norwalk. He was soon made a magistrate and judge, and was not only a leading man there, but in the colony As full proof of his standing in the colony, I need only mention that he was one of the 19 signers of the Petition to King Charles II. for the Charter of the Colony; and his name is mentioned in that invaluable grant to Connecticut in 1662. (It is signed Camfield.) He was in '62, appointed with Gold and Sherman, to hold courts at Fairfield. Deputy in '62. He was early a magistrate, assistant and judge.

Camp, John—son of John and Rebecca, born in 1711.

Carrington, John, Waterbury—died in 1692. He appears to have been by trade a cooper. He left no children. His brothers and sisters were, John, Clark, Ebenezer, Mary, Hannah and Elizabeth.

Case, Richard, Hartford, (E. H.)—died in 1693, and left his wife Elizabeth, to whom he gave all his estate during her life. Children, Richard, John and Mary. He was a kinsman of Thomas Olcott. He moved to East Hartford from Windsor. John Case married Sarah Spencer, and settled in Windsor—died in 1704. He moved to Simsbury before his death. Children, Mary, John, William, Samuel, Richard, Sarah, (born in 1676) Elizabeth, Abigail, Bartholomew and Joseph. John, of Simsbury, 1681 and 1667. Benjamin, removed from Mansfield to Coventry in its early settlement—probably a descendant of Richard, of East Hartford, who came from Windsor.

Case, Richard Hartford—married Elizabeth Purcase or Purchase, a daughter of one of the early settlers of Hartford. The name is yet common in Hartford county.

Catlin, John, Hoccanum, 1664, son of Thomas, who was an old and standing constable of Hartford, as well as selectman. John or his son, moved to Litchfield in its early settlement. Many of the name now reside there. John signed the agreement to remove to Hadley, in 1659. He signed his name Catling. The name is now numerous. He was the ancestor of all the Catlins in the State. Col. Catlin, of Hartford, now owns some of the real estate held by Thomas, more than 200 years since. Samuel, son of John, married Elizabeth Norton, of Farmington, in 1702.

Champion, Henry, and John Borden witnessed the will of Tobias Coles in 1664. The name of Champion, since the war of the Revolution, has been noted for wealth and good common sense, in which few excelled the late Hon. Henry, and Hon. Epaphroditus Champion, a member of Congress from this State.

Chaplin, Clement—came to New England with Mr. Swain, in the ship Elizabeth and Ann, Cooper, master. They early settled at Wethersfield, and were important men in the colony. He held land in Hartford in 1639. (See No. 1.)

Chappell, George, New London, 1671. George Chappell, of New London, Henry Stiles, of Windsor, Henry Stiles, of Hartford, John Stiles, Thomas Stiles, Edward Preston, John Harris, John Dyer and Francis Stiles came to New England, from London, in the ship Christopher, in 1634.

Chapman, Robert—deputy in 1662, and twice in '63—also an assistant in '61. He with O. Bruen and John Smith, of New London, were appointed to settle the difficulties with the Niantick Indians, for burning fence in '63—grand juror same year. The ancestor of Judge Chapman, deceased, and of Charles Chapman, Esq., of Hartford.

Chauncey, Rev. Charles, Stratfield—in 1710, was appointed guardian for his children, Robert 6 years old, Ichabod Wolcott 5, and Abiah 8. He died before 1715, and John Moore and Daniel Bissell, of Windsor, were appointed guardians for the children of Mr. Chauncey. This name has uniformly held a high rank in the State. Israel, minister at Stratford, 1665. Nathaniel, of Windsor, a witness in '77.

Cheeseholm, Thomas, 1663.

Cheesbrook, Samuel, 1664.

Cheesebrough, William. In 1657–8 a considerable settlement was made between Mystic and Paugatuck rivers; Mr. Cheesebrough from Rehoboth, was the first settler on the tract, in '49. He was charged of mending guns for the Indians, &c., and was brought before the General Court for withdrawing himself from civil society, and trading with Indians and assisting them. He confessed his fault, but claimed he had been induced to settle there by Mr. Winthrop, who claimed the land. He gave bonds for his good behavior, and was allowed to remain there.

Cherry, John—with three Milford Indians, in 1670, was ordered to pay John Brunson for cider stolen, 20s., and 10s. to Daniel Garrit, for bringing them from Milford to Hartford.

Chester, Leonard, Wethersfield—the father and ancestor of the Chester family—came to Wethersfield in 1635, from Massachusetts; he came to the latter place from Leicestershire, England, in '33. He died when young, (under 40 years of age) in '48. He had a son, grandson, great grandson, and a great great grandson, by the name of John, and the last left a son Hon. John Chester, who was well known by many of our aged men, as one of the pillars of the town of Wethersfield, and of the State. Leonard was a juror in '42, grand juror in '43, and held many places of trust in the colony. The family have been of the first respectability in the colony and State. The children of Leonard and Mary, his wife, were, John, born August 3, '35—Dorcas in November, '37—Stephen, March 3, '39—Mary in January, '41 —Prudence in February, '43—Eunice in January, '45, and Mercy in February, '47. John Chester was the first white child, of record, born at Wethersfield. Capt. John Chester married Sarah, a daughter of Gov. Welles, in '53. John, jr., married Hannah, Nov. 25, '86. Stephen, jr., married Jemima, a daughter of James Treat, in '91, and Thomas married a daughter of Richard Treat, in Dec., '84. A record is found at Wethersfield, that John Chester, the son of Leonard, was the first white child born at Wethersfield, in Aug , 1635; and another record in the same book, that he was born at Watertown, Mass.

Chester, Capt. John, sen'r., Wethersfield—died the 23d of Feb., 1697. His children were, John, Thomas, Stephen, Eunice, Sarah, Prudence, and Mary, the wife of John Wolcott. To his oldest son, John, he entailed his buildings and home-lot, and his land adjoining, to him and his heirs male. Stephen died in Feb. '97, before his father, and left heirs. Capt. Chester had a slave named Anthony, who he gave to his wife. He gave mourning rings to each of his children, and to the wives of his sons. He was a brother of Stephen the elder. He left a large estate for his family. The family held a high rank in England, and in this colony.

Chester, Stephen, was an early settler at Wethersfield, and a brother of Capt. John and uncle to Maj. John, the son of John. He died in 1705. Major John administered upon his estate. He had a warehouse at the landing on the river. The wife of Samuel Whiting, of Billerica, was a sister of Capt. John and Stephen. Thomas Russell, of Charlestown, Mass., married another sister.

Chilly, John, 1663.

Church, John, Hartford—died in 1691. Children, Richard, John, Samuel, Joseph 15 years, Deliverance 12, Sarah Knight, Mary Standish, Ruth, Ann 18, and Elizabeth 17. Samuel and Richard, both signed the contract to remove to Hadley, in '59.

Churchill, Josiah, Wethersfield—died in 1686. Wife Elizabeth. Children, Joseph, Benjamin, Mary, Elizabeth Buck, Ann Rice, and Sarah Wickham. To his son Joseph he gave his land in the west part of Wethersfield, (now Newington.) Was a juror in '64—married Miss Towsey.

Clark, Daniel—came early into the colony—though young at the time, but he became a gentlemen of distinction. He was appointed Secretary of the colony in 1658, and held the office until '64, when John Allen was appointed, and held it during the year '64. Mr. Clark was again appointed and held the office during '65 and '66, at which time John Allen was again appointed and held it until '96. Mr. Clark was removed by a charge made against him by an enemy. He was in the land division of Hartford, in '39.

Clark, Daniel—married Mary Newbury in 1644, and had children, Josias in '48—Elizabeth in '51—Daniel in '54—John in '56—Mary in '58—Samuel in '61—Sarah in '63—Hannah in '65, and Nathaniel in '66 Joseph, of Saybrook, 1658, was brother of John. He died in '63—was a relative of the Clarks of Milford, and the son of John Clark, sen'r. John, constable and selectman of Saybrook, in '64.

Clark, Mary—in 1692 " had a base born child," and accused Lieut. Hollister of being the father; " she having been constant in the charge in time of travail, and at all times," The court judged him the reputed father; and ordered him to pay 2s. per week from its birth, for the term of four years; and ordered Mary to pay a fine of 40s., and to be whipt. A portion of the present law upon this subject originated in the Puritan law of '92—the same evidence of being constant in the charge and in time of travail, is now required in this State.

Clay, Umphrey—attorney for Richard Elliot, 1663.

Clemens, Jasper—being in a probable way of marriage, in 1661— confessed he had a wife in England. The court ordered him at once to separate from Ellen Brown, until he cleared himself from his lawful wife.

Clements, Jasper, Middletown—died in 1678, aged 64 years. Wife, Eleanor. Left no children—and gave his estate to Nathaniel, John, and Benoni Brown, Hannah Long, and to the town of Middletown for the support of a school there.

Clinton, John, 1663.

Clough, John, 1663. John, jr., of Killingworth, '63. Constable of Hartford, in '61.

Cockshot, Eliza, widow at Haddam, died in 1699.

Collins, Nathaniel. The early church members in Middletown, were, Nathaniel Collins, Thomas Allen, Thomas Wetmore, John Hall, jr., Samuel Stocking, sen'r., William Harris, John Savadge or Savage, sen'r., Robert and Andrew Warner, sen'r., (and George Hubbard, sen'r., after his return from the New Haven colony.) The first meeting house erected there was in 1652—and the size of it, 20 by 20 feet. They had but one society there until 1703, when a second society was formed.

Collins, Thomas, Hartford, had his ear-mark in Hartford, for his cattle, in 1646. Timothy, of Guilford, moved to Lebanon, and from thence he removed to Litchfield. Nathaniel, of Wethersfield, in '67. Daniel, of Milford, 1730. Rev. Nathaniel of Middletown, 1668, and Nathaniel, a minister at Enfield, in '97. Nathaniel, of Middletown, died in '84. Estate £679. Left a widow, and children, John, 16 years of age—Susannah 14—Martha 11—Nathaniel 7, and Abigail 4. He gave John £146, and each of his daughters £76. Samuel, of Hartford, died in '97. Mary, his wife. Samuel, of Middletown, 1711.

Cole, Samuel, married Mary, daughter of James Kingsbury, of Plainfield, in 1693.

Coles, John, in 1661, occupied the farm in Hartford, which had been owned by Governor Hopkins.

Colefax, John, Wethersfield—died in 1681. His brother had his estate. He was a brother of the wife of Joseph Bidwell, and the wife of Henry Arnold. John, died at Windsor, in '76, and left no family

Coleman, Thomas and John, signed the agreement to move to Hadley in 1659. He was an early settler in Connecticut.

Cone, Daniel, Haddam, 1664—he then had a case in court concerning the ownership of a steer. The jury on trial disagreed. The court and jury then unitedly attempted to agree upon a verdict, but failing in so doing, the court advised the parties, to either divide the steer between them, or carry the cause to the General Court for trial. Daniel Cone, jr., was made deacon of Mr. Hosmer's church, in East Haddam, in 1704—and died in 1725, aged 60 years. His son Daniel was made deacon of the same church in 1746—he was also a justice of the peace—died in 1776.—These were the ancestors of William R. Cone, Esq., of Hartford.

Coit, John, was at Gloucester as early as 1648. Joseph was the first minister at Plainfield, in 1706. The name has been at Middletown, Haddam and New London. At a later period, during the war of the Revolution, there was a Col. Coit, and three Captain Coits— Oliver, William, &c. Capt. William was the commander of the Colony ship, Oliver Cromwell, in the Revolution. It has been a ministerial name—the name has been generally in New London county— not as early settlers as many others—but has uniformly been a name of respectability in the colony and State.

Collier, Joseph, Hartford—died in 1691. He left all his estate to his wife Elizabeth, for life—the real estate to be distributed to his sons, and the personal estate to his daughters after the decease of his wife. His sons were, Joseph 23 years old, Abel 14 (died in '97,) and John 12—daughters, Mary Phelps, 22, Sarah 18, Elizabeth 16, Abigail 9, Susannah Ann 9. His wife was sister to Zachary and Robert Sanford. She died in '95. Samuel Peck married Abigail in 1701.

Collier, Samuel, removed from Hartford to Litchfield, and became a member of the church there, with Jacob and Comfort Griswold, Dorothy Pierce, Sarah Beach, Nathaniel Hosford, Ezekiel Buck, jr,. Sarah Buck, Thankful Woodruff, John Gay, Benjamin Hosford, Nathaniel Woodruff, Joseph Kilbourn, Elizabeth Collins, Daniel Allen and James Beebe, jr., before 1736. The Parish originated in May, 1717, by a company from Hartford, Windsor, Wethersfield and Lebanon, under the direction of deacon John Buell, from Windsor, and John Marsh. The original name of the place was Bantum—and a pond there now retains the first name of the place. Their first minister, was the Rev. Timothy Collins, from Guilford, who was ordained at Litchfield, in 1723, old style. He was dismissed at his own request in 1752. His salary the first four years, was £57 annually, and was afterwards increased to £80. The May after his dismission, (1753) he was made a justice of the peace, and practised medicine at Litchfield. He died there in 1776. Samuel, was the ancestor of the Hon. John A. Collier, of Binghamton, New York.

Coke, Penfield, not accepted an inhabitant of Hartford, 1664.

Cook, Nathaniel, Windsor, married Lydia Ware in 1647, and had children, Sarah, Lydia, Hannah, Nathaniel, Abigail, John and Josiah. Capt. Aaron Cook, owned land at Massico in '61, and resided there or at Windsor. Samuel, left Middletown in '64.

Cooly, Samuel, Hartford—in 1689, was made overseer, to counsel, and assist widow Newell in the distribution of her (then) late husband's estate, to his children. He was not one of the first settlers of Hartford.

Conant, Exercise and Sarah, Windham, as early as 1697. This name is first found at Windham—perhaps the name might have been at New London earlier.

Cooper, John and Thomas, 1664. John was charged of high treason, by John Scott.

Cordent, Richard, 1663.

Cornwell, William, sen'r., Middletown—died in 1677—and was old. Sons, John, William, Samuel, Thomas and Jacob—daughters, Sarah, (unmarried) Hester Wilcox and Elizabeth Hall—wife, Mary. He had a large landed estate. Was a constable in '64.

Cornish, James, was an appraiser of R. Marvin's estate in 1662.

Cotton, John, New London, made free in 1660.

Couch, Thomas, Wethersfield—died in 1687. Children, Susannah, aged 20 years, Simon 18, Rebecca 15, Hannah 13, Thomas 12, Mary 11, Sarah 8, Abigail 6, and Martha 3. He was an early settler at Wethersfield—one of the family moved to Fairfield.

Crabb, Richard, (in No. 1)—removed first to Stamford, afterwards to Greenwich. In 1655 complaints were made to the General Court at New Haven, of the conduct of the people of Greenwich that they permitted drunkenness, harbored runaway servants, and joined persons in marriage without lawful authority. Greenwich denied the jurisdiction of New Haven over them and refused obedience to their orders. The General Court therefore ordered, that unless they appeared before the Court, and submitted by the 25th day of June then next, viz: Richard Crabb and others, who had been the most stubborn, they should be arrested and punished. They complied. Mr. Crabb had been at Hartford, one of the leading men in the colony. He resided for a time at Stamford.

Craddock, Matthew, in 1637, was indebted to John Oldham's estate, £229.

Crane, Benjamin, sen'r., Wethersfield—juror in 1664—he died in '93. His eldest son was Benjamin—he had other children. John, of Wethersfield, died in '94. Jonathan, of Windham, '97.

Crandall, George, New London, 1671, was suspected of opposing the government of the colony.

Cross, Samuel, Windsor—died in 1707. He had sons-in-law, Lyman or Simon Chapman, and was a cousin to John, Samuel and Jonathan Bates, also of Sarah Ketchum, Jonathan Jagger, Hannah Welch, James Picket, Mary Hoyt and Ephraim Phelps—all of whom shared in his estate.

Crombe, Alexander, 1663.

Crook, Samuel, 1664.

Crow, Christopher, Greenfield, in Windsor—died in 1681. Children, Samuel 21 years old, Mary 18, Hannah 15, Martha 14, Benoni 12, Margaret 11, and Thomas 5. John Crow, was an early settler, as early as '39. He signed the agreement to remove to Hadley, in '59—he did remove, and died there.

Crowfoot, Margaret, widow, Wethersfield—died in 1733. Children, Joseph, Ephraim, Elizabeth, Mahitabel and Sarah.

Culver, Edward—Roath, Sherman, Abell, Amos, Hough, Coy, Armstrong, Breed, Elderkin, Bushnell, Lathrop, Brewster, Hendy. Waterman, Wade, Leffingwell, Gifford, Gager, Egerton, Caulkins, Bowers, Gookin, Fitz, Bingham, Backus and Adgate, and some few other names, appear to have come directly to the county of New London, and a few of these names are yet found in no other county in the State—as is the case with a few names in Fairfield county, which first came there, viz., Scofield, Sherwood, &c.

Curtice, Thomas, Wethersfield—died in 1681. Estate £717.—Children, John, Joseph, James, Samuel, Isaac, Ruth Kimberly and Elizabeth Stoddard. Joseph, died in '83—wife, Mercy—estate £271. Children, Joseph 9 years old, Henry 7, Sarah 5, Thomas 3, David one.

Curtiss, Henry, Windsor, married Elizabeth Abell, in 1645, and had children, Samuel and Nathaniel, '77. Samuel married a widow, and had Hannah and Samuel. Hannah died in '80. Abraham and Daniel Curtiss, jurors at Stratford in 1730. Capt. William and Ens. John Curtiss, brothers, resided at Stratford, with their mother, in the early settlement of the town. The Curtiss and Beardslee families were, by tradition, from Stratford-upon-Avon. The Curtiss family located at Wethersfield, in 1636–7.

D.

Davis, Philip, constable of Hartford in 1659—was at Hartford in '45. John Davis is supposed to be the Sergeant Davis who, tradition says, cut the bow-string of an Indian, and saved the life of Major Mason at the battle of Mystic. The same who pursued them to a swamp in Fairfield, and cut his way into the swamp, which was the ambuscade of the fugitive Pequots. John, appointed to impound all swine over three months old, unwrung, in Hartford, in 1651.

Davie, Humphry, Hartford—died in February, 1688. He was the son of Humphry and Sarah, of Boston, a particular friend of Governor Winthrop. He held land at Boston at his death, and a part of a powder mill at Dorchester; also a small house with two acres of land near Beacon Hill, at Boston, with movables there, and a large estate in Connecticut. He had a son John. Humphry was one of the persons pointed out in the will, of Governor Winthrop, to settle any difficulty that might arise in the settlement of his estate.

Dayley, Nicholas, made free in 1663—supposed one of the descendants settled at Woodbury.

Deming, John, with William Swain, Thurston Rayner, Andrew Ward, Matthew Mitchell, &c., were the principal settlers of the town of Wethersfield.

Denslow, Henry, Windsor—died in 1676. Children, Samuel, his only son, and seven daughters, viz., Susannah, married John Hodge—Mary married Thomas Rowley—Ruth married Thomas Copler—and Abigail 21, Deborah 19, Hannah 15, and Elizabeth 11 years old.

Denton, Rev. Richard, was from Yorkshire, in England, and had preached at Halifax before he left his native country. After his arrival in New England, he preached for a time as an unsettled minister, at Wethersfield. At this time seven members constituted the church there, among whom a severe contest had arisen. The division was three and four, and it became necessary to make peace in the church —that one party or the other should remove. After some controversy, who should remove, the four members consented to yield to the minority, viz. Matthew Mitchell, Thurston Rayner, Andrew Ward and Robert Coe, when they united with Mr. Denton and others in purchasing the town of Stamford, in 1640. Mr. Denton soon organized his church, and remained in Stamford until '43 or '44, when he removed with a part of his church to Hempsted, L. I. He appears to have been a pioneer in the settlement of many towns. Rev. Cotton Mather says of him, " he was small in stature, and blind with one eye—but was an Iliad in a nut-shell." He was educated at Catherine Hall, in England, in 1623.

Dibble, Thomas, Windsor—had children, Israel, born in 1637— Ebenezer in '41—Hepzibah in '42—Samuel, baptized, in '43— Miriam, baptized, in 45—Thomas, born in '47. One of the sons married Elizabeth Hull, in '61 ; Ebenezer married Mary Wakefield, in '63, and had Mary, Wakefield, John, and Ebenezer; Samuel married Hepzibah Bartlett, and had (Abigail by a former wife in '66) Hepzibah in '69 ; Joanna in '72; Samuel in '75, (died) and a 2d Samuel in '80. Thomas, married Mary Tucker, and had Mary, born in '63, Thomas in '77, and Mary in '80.

Dibble, Ebenezer, Windsor—lost his life in the early settlement of the colony, in a war with the Indians. Left his wife, Mary, and children, Mary 12 years old, Wakefield 9, Ebenezer 5, and John 5. He was killed in December, 1674–5.

Dickinson, John, Nathaniel and Thomas—signed the contract to leave Hartford, and move to Hadley, in 1659.

Dier or Dyer, Mahon, New London, 1664. John' Dyer came to Massachusetts in '34, in the Christopher.

Dinley, John, 1663.

Dix, William, Hartford—died in 1676. His estate was appraised by Nathaniel Stanley, Siborn Nichols and Stephen Hosmer. Left no family.

Dymon, John, New London, 1671—probably the ancestor of the late sheriff Dimon, of Fairfield.

Dyx or Dix, Leonard, Wethersfield—died in 1696. Left an estate of £53, to his children, viz. Samuel, John, Mercy Squire, Hannah, Elizabeth and John Francis, a son-in law. Sarah Dix, of Wethersfield, a widow, died in 1708—her children were, Elizabeth Vincent, Mercy Goff, Hannah Renolds, Samuel and John Dix.

Dixison or Dixon, John, 1674.

Dixwell, George, 1663.

Doeman, Wethersfield, 1670.

Douglass, William, New London, 1663. He with Cary Latham were appointed by the General Court, to appraise New London for assessment, in 1663. He was one of the early settlers there, and was appointed packer at New London in '60.

Doughty, John, 1663.

Dow, Samuel, died in 1690.

Drake, Job, Windsor, married Mary Wolcott in 1646, had children, Abigail, born in '48—Mary in '49—Job in '52—Elizabeth in '54—Joseph in '57—Hepzibah in '59, and Hester in '62. John Drake married Hannah Moore, and had John in '47—Job in '51—Hannah in '53—Enoch in '55—Ruth in '57—Simon in '59—Lydia in '61—Mary in '66—Elizabeth in '64—Mindwell in '71, and Joseph in '74. Jacob married Mary Bissell in '49. These were the ancestors of Richard G. Drake, Esq., of Hartford, and those of the name now in Windsor.—The first Job appears to have had a family before he came to Windsor. He was a strict Puritan.

Dudley, William, Saybrook, 1663. (See John Whittlesey).

Dunk, Saybrook, 1669.

Dunn, Thomas, Fairfield, 1652.

Driscall, Florence, owned property at Wethersfield and Springfield. He died insolvent, in 1678.

Dunham, Thomas—probably came to Mansfield before 1700, as he died there in 1717, where he owned a large landed estate. He had 236 acres adjoining the Willimantic river—lands at Mount Hope and other places. His son was of age to settle his father's estate. Jonathan resided at Haddam in 1712—perhaps son of Thomas.

Durant, George, Middletown, the father of Edward, died in 1690.

Dwire, Mayo, or Dyer, New London, 1664.

E.

Earl, Ralph, 1665—a Scotchman or Welchman.

Easton, Joseph, hog haward of Hartford, in 1654.

Edwards, John, Wethersfield, noted in No. 1, as early as 1640—father of Joseph, Thomas and John. This name has furnished many men of distinction: two Presidents of Colleges—Hon. Pierpont, of N. Haven—Judge Ogden, of New York—Hon. Henry W. of New Haven, three years Governor of Connecticut, the sons of Pierpont. William Edwards came to Hartford when young, with his mother, who, when a widow in England had married James Cole—they settled in Hartford. Richard, who had been a minister in London, was the father of William. A sister of Gov. Talcott married an Edwards. There have been many distinguished men of this name.

Edwards, Capt. John, Wethersfield—(he is noted of Hartford in No. 1),—died in 1675, mortally wounded by the enemy when in the service as a captain—which was proved by Benj. Adams and Samuel Williams. Was a brother of Joseph—left no children.

Edwards, William, in 1663, caused the removal of Daniel Clark from the office of Secretary of the colony, by charging him with an infringement of a Royal prerogative.

Edwards, Thomas, Agawam, with the inhabitants there, were ordered by the General Court, to build two bridges at Agawam, for horses and footmen, before the next Court—by hewing three sticks of timber and laying them side by side, over each stream. Ten shillings was to be paid out of the public treasury towards the expenses.

Elderkin, John, is first found at New London as early as 1650. In '54 he appears to have been at Saybrook, contracting to build a gristmill. He appears to have been not only a carpenter, but a miller. Afterwards he moved to Norwich, and erected a mill there, in fulfillment of his previous contract. In '62, he made over in writing, to Jacob Drake and John Gaylor, of Windsor, his corn-mill and lands at Norwich, and his goods, for the use of his wife, Elizabeth ; and in '70 he sold 18 acres of land at the Neck, in N. London, to James Rogers.

Edgerton, Richard, Norwich, 1660. This name I find in no other place in the colony as early as at Norwich, yet it is now in several of the eastern towns of the State, all of whom may pretty safely look to Richard, of Norwich, as ancestor.

Eggleston, Thomas, son of Bridget, of Windsor—born in 1638—Mary in '41—Sarah in 43—Rebecca in '44—Abigail in '48—Joseph in '51—Benjamin in '53. Bridget died in September, '74. James, the son of James, born in '50—John in '59—Thomas, in '61—Hepzibah in '64—Nathaniel in '66—Isaac in '68—Abigail in '71—Deborah in '74, and Hannah in '76.

Ellsworth, Serg't. Josiah, son of John, (in No. 1,) was one of the early Puritan settlers of Windsor. Juror in 1664 Died in '89, and left an estate of £655 to his family, widow and children, viz : Josiah, born in '55—Elizabeth in 57—Martha in '62—Thomas in '65—Jonathan in '69—John in '71—Job in '74, and Benjamin, 12 years old at his father's decease. Josiah, jr., died in 1706, and left his widow, Martha, with £377 for his children. Martha, (was married) Elizabeth, Mary and Abigail, Timothy and two other sons. Jonathan, a brother of the deceased, was his executor. Lieut. John, the son of Josiah, sen'r., was deceased in 1722—he left a daughter Anne ; John and Esther were appointed her guardians. Esther and Daniel were also guardians of Martha, another daughter of Lieut. John, deceased, and of another young daughter. Lieut. John also, son of Josiah, sen's. left three daughters and two sons—the sons had the two farms in Windsor, and paid Martha and her sister's legacies.

Ellis, John, and Edward Hall, for their ill carriage the 9th time, on the Sabbath, in meeting, were ordered to sit in the stocks one hour and a half the next training day, at Wethersfield.

Ellis, James, Saybrook, in 1665, gave all his estate to William Pratt, of said town, by will—proved by Robert Chapman, &c., of Saybrook.

Elson, Abraham, Wethersfield, (in No. 1)—died in 1648. A part of his estate was given to the children of B. Gardiner, and the remainder to his two sons, Job and John Elson.

Elmer, Edward, Hartford—died in 1676, (in No 1.) His children were, John, 30 years old—Samuel 27—Edward 22—Mary 18, and Sarah 12.

Enoe, James, Windsor, married Anna Bidwell, in 1648, and had children, Sarah, born in '49—James in '51—John in '54. His wife, Anna, died in '79. His son James married Abigail Bissell in '78, and had a son James, who married the widow of James Eggleston for his second wife.

Ensign, Sarah, Hartford—died in 1676. Children, Mary Smith, Hannah Easton, David and Mehitabel Ensign ; grandchildren, Sarah, Ruth and Lydia Rockwell. James, constable of Hartford, in 1661.

Evens, Nicholas, Windsor—died, August, 1689. Left £110 to his children, viz., Samuel, aged 14—Nicholas 12—Joseph 8—Thomas 5—Benoni 1—Mercy 16—Hannah 10, and Abigail 3.

F.

Fanning, Thomas—supposed at New London.

Fenwick, Lady. or Lady Ann Butler, as she was usually styled in Saybrook, (in No. 1,) was the daughter of an English nobleman, (*Jewett.*) She married Hon. George Fenwick, before he came to Connecticut, and died in 1648—over whose ashes was erected the first table monument in the colony, at Saybrook, which is in full view from the Sound at the mouth of the Connecticut river. Mr. Fenwick was so grievously afflicted with the loss of his wife, that he soon returned to England, and received the appointment of judge. He died in Sussex, England, in '57. The moss-covered monument of Lady Ann Butler, or Lady Fenwick, who died in Saybrook nearly two centuries since, yet shows the place of her sepulture. The monument being now greatly out of repair, a gentleman of wealth and of a liberal and noble spirit of Hartford, is about to repair it, at his individual expense. A noble spirit for a man of wealth surely. He is not a relative of the family.

Fenner, Thomas, Wethersfield, (in No. 1)—died in 1647.

Ferris or Pheries, Peter, Stamford—was made free in 1662, under Connecticut.

Finch, Abraham, Wethersfield, (in No. 1)—died in 1640, and left a wife and one child. His grandfather's name was Abraham.

Filly, William, Windsor, in (No. 1,) married in 1641–2, and had four daughters, viz., Mary, Elizabeth, Abigail and Deborah, and sons, Samuel, John and William. Samuel married Ann Gillett, and had four daughters, and sons, Samuel, (died) Jonathan, Samuel, Josiah and John.

Fisher, Robert, one of the first settlers of Stamford, 1640–1.

Fish, William, 1664.

Fitch, Rev. James, was from the county of Essex, in England, and received the foundation of his education in England, though he came to this country in his boyhood, (about 16 years old.) He was placed in charge of Rev. Thomas Hooker and Samuel Stone, for the completion of his literary and religious education, where he remained about seven years. He was soon after settled at Saybrook, and remained there about 14 years, until he removed to Norwich, in 1660, with most of his church, where he closed his pastoral life in his old age, and died in 1702, aged about 80, (at Lebanon with his children.) He had two wives. His first wife was Abigail, the daughter of Mr. Whitefield, of Guilford. His children born at Saybrook were, James in '47—Abigail in '50—Elizabeth in '52—Hannah in '54—Samuel in '55, and Dorothy in '58. His wife died in '59. After he removed to Norwich, in '64, he married Priscilla, a daughter of Major General Mason, who resided at Norwich. By this marriage, his children were, Daniel, John, Jeremiah, Jabez, Anna, Nathaniel, Josiah and Eleazer, in all fourteen children, and a majority of them sons, which was fortunate in the early settlement; thirteen of them married and had families. Thomas Fitch, who was an early settler at Norwalk, and father of Gov. Fitch, was a brother of Rev James; also, Joseph, of Windsor was his brother. Mr. Fitch came to this country with 13 other young men in 1638, to prepare for and become ministers of the gospel—most of whom effected their object.

[*Record, Tombstone & Miss Caulkins.*

Fitch, John, Windsor—died in 1676, and gave his estate to support a school there, and appropriated it in such manner as the county court and the selectmen of Windsor should direct its application. Joseph Fitch was accepted an inhabitant of Hartford, in '59, selectman in '61. He died in Hartford. Samuel was a school teacher in Hartford for 3 years, at £15 a year, 1649. Thomas, of Norwalk, was the father of Gov. Fitch. The Fitch family did more for schools and schooling in the early settlement, than in any other, except Gov. Hopkins.

Fitz, Gerrald, New London, 1664.

Flower, Lumrock, Hartford—had a daughter Elizabeth, born in 1714, and a son, Elijah, in 1717. Lydia Flower married Edward Dodd, in 1705. Lydia Flower was born in March, 1686—Lumrock in March, '89—Elizabeth in March, '92—John in Feb. '94—Mary in '97—Francis in 1700—Ann in Nov., 1703, and Joseph in 1706.

Ford, Thomas, moved to Northampton. He had been a leading man at Windsor.

Foote, Nathaniel, Wethersfield, appraiser of the estate of Abraham Fynch, in 1640. His children were, in '43, Nathaniel, 24 years old—Robert 17—Francis 15—Sarah 12—Rebecca 10, and some daughters married.

Forbes, James, Hartford—died in 1692—estate £344. Children, John, Dorothy, Robert, Mary, David, Sarah, all except Francis (15 in number) were more than 21 years of age at the death of James. This name came first to Windsor.

Forward, Samuel, sen'r.—died in 1684. His wife died in '85, His children were, Samuel and Joseph. Samuel, jr., son of Samuel. of Windsor, was born in '71—another Samuel Forward, born in '74. These were the ancestors of the Hon. Walter Forward, late Secretary of the Treasury of the United States.

Foster, Rev. Isaac, Hartford—died in 1683. £200 of his estate was given to Ann Foster, and the remainder to Mehitabel Woodbridge—supposed the daughter of Mrs. Mehitabel Russell.

Foster, Nathaniel, Wethersfield (in No. 1). After the conquest of the Pequot country, the General Court found it necessary to hold the country—that troops should be sent there for this purpose—accordingly 40 men were detached from the three towns, and Lieut. Robert Seely took command of them, and provision was made for their support, viz. for Wethersfield, Nathaniel Foster's hog, 20 pounds of butter. and 50 pounds of cheese; and Mr. Wells, 2 bushels of malt. Windsor, one ram goat, 20 pounds of butter, 50 pounds of cheese, 1 gallon of strong water, and 3 bushels of malt. Hartford, 20 pounds of butter, 50 pounds of cheese, and 100 pounds of beef, from Mr. Whiting. (Other provision was made).

Fowler, Lieut. William, with Giles Hamlin, Captain Newbury, W. Wadsworth, Captain W. Curtice and Lieut. Munson, in August, 1673. were made a grand committee to commission officers, press men, horses, arms, &c., and dispose of the militia, &c., to march against the Dutch, who were suspected of approaching Connecticut. John

Talcott was made major for Hartford, Robert Treat for New Haven, and Nathan Gold for Fairfield—and other officers appointed.

Fowler, Ambrose, Windsor—married Jane Alvord, May, 1646, and had children, Abigail, John, Mary, Samuel, Hannah, Elizabeth and Ambrose.

Fox, Richard, sen'r., Glastenbury—died in 1709. His widow, Beriah, was administratrix— perhaps the same who came to New England with Isaac and Thomas Jones. The first emigrant of the name in the colony came to Windsor. Thomas, 1663. Richard, with Isaac and Thomas Janes, William Payne, John Moore, Richard Graves, Francis and Christopher Foster and Robert Sharp, came from England to N. England, in the Abigail, Robert Hackwell, master.

Francis, Robert, is first found on the records, at Wethersfield, in 1651, and was the first of the name who settled there. He had three sons, and four daughters. He died in 1711, and left a family. John, son of Robert, died also in 1711, aged 53. Estate £713—wife Mercy —children, John, James, Thomas, Robert, Joseph, Daniel, Sybbarance, Abigail, Hannah, Sarah, Prudence, Mercy, Mary Griswold, and one who died young. Of the three sons of Robert, John only left issue. John had 14 children. His sons John and Robert remained at Wethersfield—Daniel settled at Killingworth—Joseph at Wallingford—James at Berlin, and Thomas at Newington.

Freeman, Joseph, 1665.

French, Ephraim, 1676.

Frost, Daniel, Fairfield, 1649. Henry, '63.

Fry, Michael, Richard Voar, Fossaker, and Stockin, freed from training in 1660. Anthony, 1663.

Fyler, Walter, Windsor. Children, John born in 1642—Zerubabel in '44—the last married Miss E. Strong; in '69, and had a son Thomas in '69—Jane in '71—Zerubabel in '73, who died; and in '74 had another Zerubabel, and John born and baptized in '75. John, married Elizabeth Dolman.

G.

Gager, John, Saybrook, son of William, was among the earliest settlers there, and it is supposed came there firstly with Mr. Winthrop, about 1645. He removed to New London, where he continued until he united with the other proprietors and settlers of Norwich, in '60. This name is rarely, if at all, yet found in the State west of Connecticut river. John, of Norwich, in '73, was robbed of his goods by Indians. They were apprehended, and tried. The court inflicted a fine of £20, and authorized Gager to sell them in service to pay it.

Gaines, Samuel, Glastenbury—died in 1699 or 1700—wife Hannah.

Galpin, Philip, of Bristow, Somersetshire, England—a mariner, son of John Galpin, of Rye, Fairfield county, Conn. Mary was the wife of John. In 1689 he owned land near the shore in Fairfield county, he also had a deed of land and houses there in '70, and sold his land in 1700.

Gardner, David, Saybrook, (in No. 1.) By the account given by Rev. Mr. Hotchkiss, it appears, he left the Fort at Saybrook as early as 1639, and then removed to Gardner's Island and became a magistrate there, which office he held until his death, in '63. His first son was born at the Fort. As Mr. Fenwick came to the Fort at Saybrook in '39, Lieut. Gardner must have left it soon after his arrival, if Mr. Hotchkiss is correct.

Gardner, Wid. Elizabeth, Hartford—died in 1681. Before her marriage with Mr. Gardner, she was the widow of Samuel Stone, by whom she had a son Samuel. Her children were Samuel and Elizabeth. She had a grandson Samuel Sedgwick, another John Roberts; Rebecca Nash, Mary Fitch, and Sarah Butler, daughters to whom she gave legacies. She gave Mary Butler one acre of land. Samuel, of Hartford, agreed to move to Hadley, in '59. This name is spelt Gardner and Gardiner.

Garding, Nathaniel, chimney viewer of Hartford, in 1664.

Garrad, Daniel, 1664.

Gates, Deac. Thomas, was an early settler in Haddam. In 1704 he was made a deacon at East Haddam—died in 1734, aged 70 years. The Gates family were a family of deacons Thomas in 1704—Jeremiah in 1741—James in 1762—Caleb in 1795, and Ephraim in 1806, deacons in East Haddam. This was a noble name in England. Sir Thomas Gates, Kt., was one of the grantees of the Great Patent of New England, by King James.

Gates, George, a chimney viewer of Hartford in 1661. He was located at Haddam, in '75. Robert, '64.

Gaylord, William, Windsor—married Ann Porter in 1641. Walter Gaylord married Mary——in '48. Samuel Gaylord married Elizabeth Hull in '46. John Gaylord married Mary Drake in '53, and had four children. Ruth, daughter of William, born Oct. 1704—twins born, Aug. 1706—William born, Nov. 1709—Samuel and Sarah, grandchildren born afterwards. Children of John were, John, born in 1656—Mary in '63—a second John born in '67, and Elizabeth in '70. Joseph, son of Walter, married Mary Stanley in '70—his children were, Sarah, Joseph and John. Hezekiah, of Windsor—died in '77. He had no family. Was a brother of John and William, Ann Phelps and Hannah Crandall, and half brother of Joseph and Nathaniel Gaylord.

Geere, George, New London, 1664. Dennis and Elizabeth Geere and two daughters, came in the ship Abigail, from London to New England (from Thesselworth). This name is spelt on some records Geere, others Geeree and Gear.

Geffers, Gabriel. Saybrook, died in 1664.

Gibbs, Jacob, Windsor—married Elizabeth Andrews in 1657, and had children, Mary, Abigail, Jacob, Sarah and Elizabeth. Samuel, married Hepzibah Dibble in '64, and had Hepzibah, Paulina, Elizabeth, Catharine and Jonathan. Many of this name came early to Massachusetts. Giles, of Windsor, died in '41—wife, Katharine, and children, Samuel, Benjamin, Sarah and Jacob. Richard Wellar had lived with him at 40s. per annum. Giles was father of Jacob—perhaps the same who was admitted freeman in Massachusetts, mentioned by Farmer.

Gibbins, William (in No. 1), Hartford, 1636, the steward of Gov.

George Wyllys, in England, he first purchased the Wyllys place in Hartford, for Mr. Wyllys—came to Hartford in '36, for this purpose, and built his house and prepared his garden for him. In the division of land in Hartford, in '39.

Giles, John, in 1637, was ordered with Capt. Mason, Thomas Stanton, J. Adams and Thomas Merrick, to go to Waranock (Westfield), and declare to the Indians there, that the Court wished to speak to them, and hear their reasons why they had said they were afraid of them, and if Capt. Mason thought proper, to receive hostages of them, and compel them by violence, if they refused to go willingly, but to leave them two of the English as pledges during their absence; also to trade with them for corn, if possible. Jacob Gibbs, after 1717, moved to Litchfield from Windsor.

Gillett, Nathan's (children of Windsor), were, Elizabeth, born in 1639—Abia in '41—Rebecca in '46—Elias in '49—Sarah in '51—Benjamin in '53—Nathan in '55, and Rebecca in '57. He moved to Simsbury, where his wife died in '70. Jonathan, sen'r., a brother of Nathan, was one of the early settlers of Windsor—held several offices, and was highly esteemed in the colony, died in '77, and left a widow and children, Josias, John, Jeremiah, Jonathan, Joseph and Cornelius, also the wife of Peter Brown, and the wife of Samuel Filley. Joseph married, and died before his father, and left a son Jonathan, and one daughter. He came from Dorchester, Mass. Jonathan, jr., of Windsor, married Mary Kelsey in '61, afterwards married M. Dibble. He had eight children. Josiah, son of Jonathan, of Windsor, married Joanna Taintor, in '76, and had Josias, in '78, and Joanna in '80.

Gilman, Richard, Wethersfield, had a daughter Elizabeth, born in 1704—and sons, Richard in 1706—Samuel in 1708, and Naomi in 1710. This name was not as early as some others—was early in Massachusetts, and respectable in the colony.

Gishop or Bishop, Edward, was appointed a commissioner, in 1663, with the power of a magistrate in the town of Westchester.

Gipson, Roger, Saybrook—died in 1680. Estate £120. Children, Samuel, 8 years old—Jonathan 6—Roger one, and a daughter 5.

Goff, Philip, and Naomi, his wife, Wethersfield, in 1704, were prosecuted for absenting themselves from church upon the Sabbath, and were tried. Goff and his wife declared in court, that they could not in conscience attend, and would not go to meeting on the Sabbath at the public meeting house. They were sentenced by the court to pay a fine of 20s. to the county treasurer. He died in 1674. Children, Rebecca, aged 23, Jacob 25, Philip 21, Moses 18, and Aaron 16. Mr. Goff was an early settler, and had a brother with him—married sisters.

Gold, Nathan, Fairfield (in No. 1), was an assistant in 1671-2, and a magistrate also—one of the leading men of the county. Gold, Toppin, Sherman and Howell were appointed to hear the claim of Saybrook to Hommonasett (Killingworth), in '63. Gold, Fairchild and Canfield were appointed to approve of the men to be selected to compose the 2d troop of horse raised in the colony, to consist of 18 men and two officers, from the towns of Stratford, Fairfield and Norwalk; officers chosen by the company, and appointed by the General Court, in '61. The troopers were allowed a salary, officers and soldiers.

Mr. Gold, with Gov. Winthrop, Samuel Wyllys, Gen Mason, Matthew Allyn, Henry Clark, John Topping, Richard Lord, Henry Wolcott, Richard Treat, John Talcott, Daniel Clark, John Clark, John Ogden, Thomas Welles, Obadiah Bruen, Anthony Hawkins, John Deming and Matthew Canfield, Esq'rs., were the petitioners to Charles II. for the Charter of Connecticut, and their names were embodied in the King's grant to Connecticut, which is ample proof of their exalted standing in the colony. No gentleman would have been called upon to have signed the Petition, but such men as had sustained a high reputation in England before they came to New England.

Gleason, Isaac, Enfield, was an early settler there. He owned the lot now occupied by Nathaniel Prior, and died in 1698, aged 44 years, leaving two sons, viz., Isaac, born in '87, and Thomas, born in '90, who moved to Farmington, and died in 1745. Isaac married Mary Prior, daughter of John Prior, in 1712, and was one of the first settlers of the southeast part of Enfield, called Wallop. He left four sons, viz., Isaac, born in 1715, Jonah in 1724, Joseph in 1726, and Job in 1734. Joseph married Hannah, daughter of Josiah Colton, in 1746—was the father of Joseph, Solomon, and Jonah Gleason— all lived and died in Enfield. David, of Simsbury, died in 1746. Isaac, of Windsor, died in 1750. Isaac, son of Thomas, of Simsbury —his uncle Ezekiel Thompson, of Farmington, was appointed guardian, in 1752. Hannah, of Enfield, died in 1757. Jonah, of Enfield, died in 1763. Sylvanus, son of Jonah, died in 1765. The name is in various parts of the State, and of uniform respectability.

Glover, John. This name is first found at Norwich, not however among the pioneers of the town, yet a familiar name in Fairfield Co.

Glover, Mary, Springfield—married John Haynes in 1659.

Goodfellow, Thomas, Wethersfield, (in No. 1)—died in Nov. 1685.

Goodrich, John, Wethersfield, son of John—died in 1676, and left Mary, his widow, and a child. He had a sister Mary, and a brother Joseph. William, of Wethersfield, died in '76. He left his widow, Sarah, and an estate of £915 for his children, John, 24 years old, William 17, Ephraim 14, and David 10. The daughters were married at his decease—one married Joseph Butler, of Wethersfield.

Goodwin, Ozias, signed the agreement to remove to Hadley, in 1659. Hosea, (in No. 1,) should have been Ozias, yet it is spelt on the record, Hosea. He was the ancestor of Nathaniel Goodwin, Esq., of Hartford. George, of Fairfield, 1654. Abraham, who moved from Hartford to Litchfield, was the son of Nathaniel, of Hartford.

Goodall, (or ale,) Richard, Wethersfield—died in 1676, and left a son John Gill. A man of this name was the founder of the first Baptist church in Boston. A Richard Goodale came from Yarmouth, in England, in 1638, and died in Massachusetts, in '66.

Goodheart, 1659.

Gookin, Daniel, 1663.

Gozzard, Nicholas, Windsor, died in 1693, and left an estate of £83.

Graham, Lieut. Benjamin, Hartford—died in 1725. Wife, Sarah —had a granddaughter, Mary Graham; sons, Benjamin, Samuel, and Isaac. He had a grist mill, saw mill and fulling mill at Hartford, and other property. In 1733, Benjamin sold out the property he had by his father. In 1749, George, the son of Samuel, died—and gave his carpenter tools to his father Samuel—his gun to his brother James. He had a sister, Abigail Seymour. He left an estate of £111 : 10. After the death of George, the family appear to have left Hartford—perhaps not. John, of Hartford, died in 1720. Hannah Tillotson, his wife, and Benjamin, administrators. Left one child only. John appears to have been a brother of Lieut. Benjamin. He is supposed to have been the ancestor of Andrew, deceased, of Southbury. Henry, lives south of Little river, in Hartford—chimney viewer in 1659—surveyor of highways in '62.

Grant, Matthew, (in No. 1)—died in 1681, when he had become aged. He had resided with his son John for some years previous to his death. His children were, Samuel, Tahan, John, and a daughter Humphrey. Samuel Grant, of Windsor, was born at Dorchester in 1631. Samuel Grant married Anne Fyler in '83, and had a daughter Anne in '84. Tahan Grant was born in Dorchester in '33. He married Hannah Palmer in '62, and had Matthew, Tahan, Hannah, Thomas and Joseph, and a daughter and son afterwards—the son as late as '80. John, the son of Samuel, sen'r., was born in '42. He married Mary Hull in '66, and had John, Mary, Elizabeth, and others.

Grannis, Edward, leather sealer in Hartford, in 1663. This name is yet in Southington and Warren. An Edward Grannis was at Hadley in '71—perhaps the same.

Gray, Walter, (in No. 1)—often spelt Grey—appears to have had descendants who went to New London. John, of Windsor, moved from Windsor to Litchfield after 1717. Nicholas and Henry, 1664. John, Fairfield, in '49.

Green, Bartholomew, had land in Hartford in 1639, which was forfeited—probably the same who was made free at Cambridge in '34.

Greenhill, Thomas, died in 1660. Samuel, was at Cambridge in '35.

Greensmith, Thomas, Hartford, set his barn on the common land in 1660. Stephen was in Massachusetts in '38.

Gregory, John—a deputy in 1662-3. Wollerton Gregory, Hartford, died in '74—was a rich tanner—had no children.

Griffin, John, Windsor, (in No. 1)—had children, Hannah, Mary, Sarah, John, Thomas, Abigail, Mindwell, Ruth, and two sons. John Griffin and Simon Wolcott, in 1673, were ordered by the court to command the train-band in Simsbury, until further orders should be given. Hugh, at Sudbury in '45.

Griswold, Matthew, (in No. 1,) was a stone cutter by trade, in England. He appears to have remained a while at Windsor, and while there, became intimate with the family of Hon. Henry Wolcott, and married his daughter Ann. He was called to Saybrook to aid in erecting the Fort and other buildings there, and finally located his family at Lyme, where he closed his life. After the death of Mr. Wolcott, Mr. Griswold made his grave-stones, which are yet standing in the burial ground at Windsor. He was the ancestor of the two Gov. Griswolds of Connecticut, Matthew and Roger. The first Matthew, appears to have been a relative of Edward, who came early to Windsor. The Edward Griswold who owned land jointly with Matthew at Lyme, in 1681, who resided at Killingworth, must have been a younger man than Edward, of Windsor—probably the son of John, and grandson of Edward, of Windsor.

Griswold, Edward, Windsor, had children, viz. Ann, baptized in 1642, Mary in '44 (married Timothy Phelps), Deborah in '46 (married Samuel Buell), Joseph in '47, Samuel in '49, and John in '50. George Griswold married Mary Holcomb, and had Daniel, Thomas, Edward, Mary, George, John, Benjamin, Deborah, and Abigail, the last in '76. In '81 the General Assembly appointed John Tully and Abraham Post, to lay out several grants of land to Edward Griswold, of Kennelworth, and Matthew Griswold, of Lyme, 400 acres of land, which was laid out to them jointly in the north part of Lyme. This Edward was probably the son of John, who emigrated to Killingworth. George and Edward were the first settlers at Poquonnock, in Windsor. (See Thomas Holcomb). Lieut. Francis, of Norwich, in 1660, appears to have been a distant family from those of Edward, Matthew, or Samuel, of Windsor. He appears to have come from Massachusetts direct to Norwich as his first location in the colony— perhaps the same Francis who was at Cambridge in 1637. (See Farmer.)—Joseph, son of Edward, sen'r., married Mary Gaylord in 1675, and had Mary and Joseph. John, son of Edward, sen'r., settled at Killingworth, or Hammonasett. Samuel, (in No. 1,) died in 1672—had a daughter, Plumb. and a daughter, Butler.

Groves, Philip, New London county—deputy in 1662 and '3, grand juror of Stratford in '61. Philip, Elder—was probably a ruling elder in Mr. Blackman's church, at Stratford as early as '50. Simon, '63.

Guildersleeve, Richard, (in No 1,) was an inhabitant of Wethersfield within the three first years of its settlement. In 1641 he left Wethersfield, with Andrew Ward, Samuel Sherman and others, and settled the town of Stamford. The name is yet in Middlesex county.

Gull, William —agreed, and did move to Hadley in 1659.

Gunn, Thomas, Windsor—had children, Elizabeth, born in 1640, Deborah, Mehitable and John—Joseph was in Massachusetts in '36.

Gwin, Paul. 1656.

H.

Hakes, John, Windsor—had children, Isaac, born in 1650, Mary in '52, Joanna in '53, Elizur in '55, Sarah in '57, a son in '59, John in '43, Nathaniel in '44, Elizabeth in '46, and Anna in '48. He was an early settler.

Harris, Capt. Daniel, Middletown—died in 1701—had children, Daniel, Thomas, William, John—(to John he gave Mingo, his negro,) Mary Johnson, Elizabeth——, and Hannah Cook. He had a grandchild, Thankful Bidwell, daughter of Samuel Bidwell—also a grandchild, Abiel, daughter of Elizabeth.

Hart, Elisha, Windsor—died in 1683. He owned land in Westfield, the north side of Westfield river.

Harvey, Richard, resided in Stratford in 1650.

Hawley, Samuel, was one of the pioneers of Stratford as early as 1640, and was a leading man there afterwards. In '77, Joseph Hawley was in Windsor. The name has been numerous and respectable in Fairfield county from the first settlement. Joseph, was town clerk at Stratford in '51. The records of Stratford were destroyed by fire previous to '50, so that what is published of the first settlers of that town is mostly taken from the colony records, and a letter from a friend in Stratford. This family were early settlers in the colony.

Hawkins, Anthony, Windsor, afterwards of Farmington—had born at Windsor, Mary in 1644, Ruth '49, and John in '51.

Hayward or Howard, Robert—died in 1684—wife Lydia aged 70, and son Ephraim, administrators. Children, Ephraim and others.— He was one of the pioneers of Windsor.

Hayward, Ephraim, Windsor—died in 1690—children, Azor, 4 years old, and a daughter 2.

Hayden, William—had children, Daniel, born in 1640, Nathaniel in '43, Mary in '48. Daniel, married Hannah Wilkinson, and had Daniel, born in '66, Hannah in '68, Nathaniel in '71, (died) William in '73, (died) and William in '75.

Hazen, Thomas, together with H. Wells, David Hartshorn, Nathaniel Rudd, Joseph Kingsbury, Samuel Edgarton and Samuel Ladd were the first members of the church formed in 1718, at West Farms, now Franklin, and the Rev. Henry Wills was the first minister there.

Heart, Deac. Stephen, Farmington—died in 1682–3. His children were, John, Stephen, Thomas, Sarah Porter, and Mary Lee. He had a son-in-law, John Cole—grandson, Thomas Porter—grand daughter, Dorothy Porter, and a grandson, John Heart, a son of John ——. Stephen, of Farmington, died in '89, son of Stephen, deceased. Children, Stephen, aged 27, Thomas 23, John 20, Samuel 17, Sarah 14, Anne 11, and one other 7. Margaret, died about '92, and gave her property to her sons, John and Arthur Smith, and daughter, Elizabeth Thompson. She had grandchildren, Elizabeth, Thomas and Ann Thompson, and Margaret Orton. She also had a son, Tho. Thompson.

Herbert, Christian, Wethersfield—died in 1686.

Honeywell, Bridget, daughter of John, of Middletown—chose her uncle, Isaac Johnson, for her guardian, in 1706.

Hicox, Samuel, Waterbury, (appears to have previously resided at Farmington)—died in 1694. Children, Samuel, 26 years old, William 22, Thomas 20, Joseph 17, Stephen 11, Benjamin 9, Ebenezer 2, Hannah 24, Mary 14, Elizabeth 12, and——Merly. After the decease of the father, whose name is spelt Hicox—the names of his sons are found upon the record uniformly spelt Hickcock. As late as 1707, Ebenezer chose his brother William Hickcock his guardian. I also find Hitchcock spelt Hickcock—perhaps originally the same name.

Higley, John, Windsor, married Hannah Drake in 1671. Jonathan, born in '75, Hannah in '77, and John in '79.

Hills, William. Hoccanum, (in Hartford), was an early settler— died in 1683, left his wife, Mary, and children, Jonathan, Mary, William, John, Joseph, Benjamin, Hannah Kilbourn, Sarah Ward, and Susannah Kilbourn. In his will he provided, that upon the death of his son William, the property he gave him, should fall to his grandson, William Hills. By his will he made all his real estate forever liable to pay taxes to maintain a minister for the church in Hartford. He owned land in right of his wife in Farmington. The name is uniformly Hills, and not Hill.

Hilliar, James, Windsor, married the widow of Ebenezer Dibble in 1677, and had James and Elizabeth.

Hilton, John, Wethersfield—died in 1686. Children, John, aged 11, Richard 7, Mary 14, and Ebenezer 8 months.

Hinman, Sergt. Edward. From record evidence and tradition, the following facts are collected of the Hinman family. Edward appears to have been the only one of the name who came from England to this country, either in the early settlement or since. Edward came to Stamford, where he first located before 1650 (probably as early as '45). Being an unmarried man when he came to Stamford, he married Hannah, the daughter of Francis and Sarah Stiles, of Windsor, who subsequently removed to Stratford. In '51, he resided in the present Main street at Stratford, upon the west side of the street, a few rods below the Episcopal church. He had before his emigration, belonged to the body or life guard of King Charles I. He had not resided many years at Stratford, before he, with Stiles, became the principal purchasers of the south part of Pamperaug, (Woodbury), new Southbury. It does not appear that he moved to Woodbury with his wife and family, but some of his children with the Stiles family located at Southbury, where the names are yet common. He died at Stratford, Nov. 26, 1681. His will was proved at Fairfield in '82. To his son, Titus, he gave his land at Woodbury; he also noticed his son Benjamin, and daughter Sarah Roberts—his son Samuel, and daughters, Hannah, Mary and Patience—he also noticed his brother, Ephraim Stiles, of Stratford. Hannah, his wife died before him, in '77. Children, Sarah, born in '53 (married William Roberts, of Woodbury), Titus in '56, Benjamin in '62, Hannah in '66, Mary in '68, Patience in '70, and Edward in '72. By his will he directed his youngest son to be placed an apprentice to Jehiel Preston, of Stratford. Sarah, who married William Roberts, had children, Hannah, baptized Oct. 21, '77, Zechery in May '82, Sarah in '85, Hannah in May, '86, Amos in July, '89—perhaps others. That part of the family who removed to Woodbury, settled in the section of Southbury Main street, called White Oak, near where the dwelling house of John Mosely, Esq., now stands.

Hinman, Capt. Titus, eldest son of Sergt. Edward, married for his first wife, Hannah Coe, of Stamford, who had moved there from Wethersfield with her father. After her decease he married Mary Hawkins of Woodbury, January, 1701-2—he died in April, 1736, aged 80 years—(Tombstone). His will is in the records of Probate at Woodbury, in which he notices his sons, Ephraim, Joseph, Andrew, Titus, Eleazer, and Timothy, and his daughters, Mary and Hannah. His children were, Ephraim, baptized July 26, '85, Joseph in June, '87, Andrew in April, '90, Titus in June, '95, Ebenezer, born January 4, 1702-3, Titus in March, 1703-4, Eleazer in May, 1706, Timothy, baptized in March, 1708-9, Mary in Feb. 1713-14, married David Bostwick, July, 1739, Hannah in March, 1720-21, married Samuel Twitchel, Dec. 1739, Patience in July, 1722. He was a member of the General Assembly in 1715, 16, 19, 20.

Hinman, Samuel, 2d son of Sergt. Edward—lived on the place called the Dr. Graham place, in Southbury, Main street, where Nathan Hinman lately lived and died. He had a wife but no children

Sarah, his adopted child was baptized, Sept. 28, 1707 He died about 1720, and his place was purchased for a Parsonage.

Hinman, Benjamin, 3d son of Sergt. Edward, married Elizabeth Lamb, at Woodbury, July 12, 1684. He lived at Bullet Hill in the Main street at Southbury—died 1727. Children, Annis, baptized in 1685 (died young), Hannah, baptized Oct., '86, married Benjamin Hurd, jr., Adam, baptized Jan., '87, Noah in July, '89, Benjamin in April, '92, Elizabeth in Feb., '93, married John Hurd, Eunice in May, '96, married Nathan Hurd, supposed the grandmother of the Hon. Judge Smith and Hon. Nathan Smith, deceased, of New Haven, Annis in Sept., '97, married Samuel Martin, Rachel born Dec., 1700, married Ephraim Baldwin, Edward born Oct., 1702, Samuel in Dec., 1704, Wait in Oct., 1706, and Mercy in Dec., 1709.

Hinman, Edward, jr., youngest son of Serg't. Edward, drew 18 acres in the land division at Woodbury, in 1702, yet he appears to have uniformly lived in Stratford and vicinity. He was brought up, after his father's decease, by Jehiel Preston. The sons of Edward, jr., were, Samuel, John, and Ebenezer. Samuel moved to Goshen, and was the father of Lemuel, of North Stratford, and ancestor of the Fairfield county Hinmans—he removed a short time to Southbury, and then back to Fairfield county—perhaps to Trumbull. He had 5 sons, viz: Ephraim, Edward, Jonathan, Michael and Bethuel. He left two daughters, one married Gideon Perry, and was living in 1836; and the other married Jonathan Hinman, of Southbury, and is yet living. She was the mother of Gen. Robinson S. Hinman, late deceased, of New Haven, of Daniel, Simeon and John, of Betsey Canfield, and Orra Wheeler of South Britain.

Hinman, Ephraim, eldest son of Captain Titus—left no family.

Hinman, Joseph, 2d, son of said Titus, married Esther Downs, Nov. 1714, and had children, Ebenezer, born in Oct. 1715, Joseph, baptized June, 1718, Tabitha, in Feb., 1721, married Joseph Richards in 1746, Esther in June, 1723, married David Munn, Nov., 1749, Eunice in Jan., 1725, Mabel Aug., 11, 1728, mother of Justus Hinman, Amos, Nov., 1730, died young, Elijah in April, 1733, Daniel in July, 1735, and Lois in Oct., 1737, married John King, Dec. 1784.

Hinman, Andrew, 3d son of Capt. Titus, married Mary Noble, Aug. 1711. Their children were, Andrew, baptized in Aug., 1712, Hannah in Dec., 1714, married Josiah Everist, March, 1739 (ancestor of Dr. Solomon Everist, late deceased of Canton, Coe in Aug., 1718, Mary in March, 1720, married Garwood Cunningham, of Woodbury, Dec., 1751, Margaret in Aug., 1723 (died single), Aaron in Oct., 1726 (died young), Nathan in Dec., 1729, Elisha, March 10, 1734, Noble in April, 1737, he went to Nine Partners, in the State of New York, perhaps he afterwards went to New London with his brother, Elisha, who married, lived and died at New London. Elisha was commander of a government ship, called the Alfred, during the war of the Revolution, which sailed out of New London. In 1776, he took and sent into N. London, a continental armed brig of 200 tons, laden with rum, sugar, &c., bound to Scotland. In October, 1777, a prize ship laden with sugar and cotton, worth £60,000, was taken by the Alfred, Capt. Hinman, and the Raleigh, Capt. Thompson, two ships of war. In 1776, he with Capt. Shaw, carried three tons of powder into Dartmouth. In 1778, he took and carried two prize ships into France, and sold them for the benefit of the States. He made several other captures of British ships during the war. After the war closed, he was for some years commander of a Revenue Cutter. Elisha left no sons, but several daughters. One married Mr. Day—one Sheriff Dimond, of Fairfield, and one Mr. Kellogg, of Stamford—perhaps others.

Hinman, Titus, Jr., 4th son of Capt. Titus—married Sarah——. Their children were Titus, baptized in May, 1725, (died young,) Ephraim in Feb., 1727, Sarah, (Gingle) in Nov., 1728, she married Deac. David Hinman, Rachel in Oct., 1731, Titus in Nov., 1733, Amie in Sept., 1736, Prudence in Sept., 1738, married David Hurlbut, Nov., 1757, and moved to Vermont, Lucy in March, 1740, married a Hurlbut, and also moved to Vermont, Enos in July, 1742, married and moved to Vermont—he had a son Deac. Calvin, who married Miss Wheeler, Annis in March, 1747.

Hinman, Ebenezer, 5th son of Capt. Titus, married Hannah Scovil, of Waterbury. He was appointed by the General Assembly, in 1776, with Thomas Fitch, Rufus Lathrop and Samuel Bishop, Esq'rs., and others, to audit all colony accounts, and report thereon. Their children were, Jonas, baptized in Feb., 1730, John, Sept. 3, 1732, Eleazer in Dec., 1734, Dorcas in Nov., 1736, married Phineas Potter, Nov., 1757, Hannah in March, 1739, married David Hinman, Dec., 1759, Peter in Aug., 1742, Molly in 1744, married B. Bassett, of Derby, Miriam in May, 1748, married Benjamin Richards.

Hinman, Timothy, 6th son of Capt. Titus, married Emma Preston —he died Dec 11, 1769, and wife died June 20, 1794. Their children were, Olive, baptized in Sept., 1739, she married Capt. Truman Hinman, Timothy in 1741, at Fair Haven in 1755, Ruth in Nov., 1748, married Aaron Hinman Oct., 1772, Patience in Dec., 1754, married Judge Increase Moseley, of Southbury, 1769, father of Col. William Moseley, of New Haven, Mary in Jan., 1757, married Sherman Hinman, son of Benjamin Feb., 1777.

Hinman, Adam, eldest son of Serg't Benjamin, died single.

Hinman, Noah, 2d son of Benjamin, married his first wife, Anna Knowles, Feb., 1711—after her death, he married Sarah Scovil, of Waterbury. For several years he was a Judge of the Court at Litchfield. The children by his first wife were, Elizabeth, baptized in May, 1713, Gideon, born in Jan., 1715, (died young,) A dam, called after Adam Winthrop, baptized July, 1718, Thankful in Jan., 1719, Gideon in Nov., 1725. By his second wife, his children were, Edward, baptized April, 1730, (Edward resided at Southbury, and was a lawyer of eminence in his day), Abigail in 1733, Reuben in Sept., 1735, Simeon in Dec., 1737, died single, graduated at Yale College in 1762, Noah in June, 1740, Sarah in Aug., 1742, Arnole in Sept., 1746, married Elijah Booth, Oct., 1772, Damaris in Dec., 1748, married Simeon Minor, Sept., 1669 (the ancestor of Simeon H. Minor, Esq., deceased, of Stamford, who was many years State Attorney for Fairfield county). Deacon Noah above, died in 1766 (76). For 16 sessions he was a member of the General Assembly.

Hinman, Benjamin, 3d son of Serg't Benjamin, married Sarah Sherman, a relative of Roger Sherman, Dec., 1718. Died in May, 1727, in the great sickness, and his wife died the same month, aged 35 years. Their children were, Benjamin, baptized in April, 1720, Jerusha in Feb., 1721, died single, and David in March, 1722. Benjamin, his son, here spoken of, was a colonel, and served as quarter master of the troop in the 13th Regiment of the Connecticut colony against the French in Canada, as early as 1751. On the 30th day of May, 1757, he was commissioned major of the 13th Regiment; in 1758 he was made a lieutenant colonel of the 3d Regiment of foot, in the forces raised to invade Canada. On the 1st of Nov., 1771, he was made a full colonel of the 13th Regiment. Early in the war of the Revolution, on the first day of May, 1775, he was appointed colonel of the 4th Regiment of enlisted troops for the defence of the colony. He was ordered, in 1775, with five companies, to Greenwich; and the same year was ordered to Ticonderoga to hold possession of the fort, &c. In 1776 he was ordered with a regiment to New York, and was at New York at the time of its capture by the British—after which he was stationed at Horse Neck and other places on the sound. In January, 1777, he returned home in ill health, and did not again join the army. He died at Southbury, March, 1809 or '10, over 90 years of age. There were more commissioned officers during the war of the Revolution by this name than any other in Connecticut—being in all 13 from the town of Southbury. Col. Benjamin's children were, Aaron, the father of Judge William, Col. Joel, the father of Joel, Judge of the Superior Court, and of Hon. Curtiss, who died when a member of the State Senate, in 1820. Sherman, who died young, and another Sherman, who was baptized in Oct., 1752, and graduated at Yale College in 1776. Col. Benjamin was a member of the General Assembly twenty-seven sessions.

Hinman, David, a brother of Col. Benjamin, married Sarah Hinman, a daughter of Titus, jr. Their children were, Annis, who married Daniel Hinman, and moved to Vermont, Gen. Ephraim, baptized in 1753, David, jr., who lived and died at Southbury, and Capt. Benjamin, of Utica, the father of Col. John E. Lieut. Asa, who served during the war of the Revolution, was also a son of Dea. David.

Hinman, Samuel, 4th son of Serg't Benjamin, died single.

Hinman, Wait, 5th son of Serg't Benjamin, married —— ——. Children, Samuel, baptized in May, 1730, Truman, (Capt. Truman) in June, 1731, Wait in Dec., 1732, Mercy in Sept. 1735, Ann in Dec. 1737, Currence in April, 1740, and Bethuel in June, 1742.

Hinman, Ebenezer, eldest son of Joseph, married Hannah Mitchell, Jan., 1737;—she soon died, and he married for his second wife, Elizabeth Pierce, April, 1743. Children, Jonathan, baptized in 1738, died young, Rhoda in April, 1740, married Seth Mitchell, Dec. 1762, Hannah in Feb. 1744, married Gideon Hicock, Jan., 1768, Betty in April, 1746, married Seth Wheeler, Nov., 1767, Annis died young, Comfort in Oct., 1750, Daniel in Sept., 1752, married Annis, a daughter of Dea. David, and removed to Vermont. Annis in Feb., 1755, married Lieut. Asa Hinman, son of Dea. David. Esther in Oct., 1757, Jonathan in Feb., 1761, died young, Jonathan, May, 1764, the father of Gen. Robinson S., late deceased, of New Haven.

Hinman, Joseph, 2d son of Joseph, married and removed to Farmington. Children, Justus, baptized in Aug., 1750, Joseph in Aug., 1750, and Hester in April, 1753. Aaron lived and died at Guilford.

Hinman, Elijah, 3d son of Joseph, married and removed to Vermont. Children, Elijah, baptized in Aug., 1763—Amos, and other children.

Hinman, Andrew, Jr., eldest son of Andrew, married Mabel Stiles, February, 1734. Children, Betty, baptized in Sept., 1735, Margaret in Dec., 1738, (single), Mabel in June, 1740, married Shadrack Osborn, Esq., of Southbury (the mother of Mrs. Betsey Dunning, of N. Haven), Francis in Aug., 1742, David in 1744, married Hannah Hinman ;—he was a member of the General Assembly in 1725, 28, 29, 36, 39 and 40.

Hinman, Coe, 2d son of Andrew, married and removed to the State of New York. Children, Nathan, baptized June, 1751, Abner in July, 1754, and others.

Hinman, Noble, 3d son of Andrew, married and had a family in Massachusetts or Vermont.

Hinman, Titus, 4th son of Titus, married Joanna Hurd, Nov., 1757. Their children were, Solomon, baptized in Nov., 1758, Hester in Nov., 1761, and Titus—Titus removed to Wyoming, Penn., was an Ensign in the Regiment of Col. Zebulon Butler, and was killed, July 3, 1778, in the bloody massacre of Wyoming.

Hinman, Ephraim, son of Titus, married Rebecca Lee, Aug., 1750. Their children were, Andrew, baptized in February, 1751, died young, Patience in Feb. 1753 ; she married Ebenezer Strong, Jan., 1771 ; one of her daughters married Nathaniel Bacon, of New Haven.— (Ebenezer Strong was a descendant of John of Windsor).

Hinman, Enos, son of Titus, married and removed to Vermont.

Hinman, Jonas, son of Eleazer, married Sarah Downs, Feb., 1756. Their children were, Silas, baptized in Jan., 1757, Agur in Jan., 1759, Jonas, Abner, Sarah, Mary, Reuben and Currence.

Hinman, John, 2d son of Eleazer, married Abigail Graham in 1772 —she died, and he married a second wife, and removed to Bethlem.

Hinman, Eleazer, 3d son of Eleazer, married Rhoda Mitchell in 1769, and had Nathan, baptized in Feb., 1771, Patty in March, 1773, Eleazer Preston in Jan., 1776, Mitchell in Sept., 1778, and Livingston in July, 1784. This family removed to the State of New York.

Hinman, Peter, 4th son of Eleazer, married and had children, William, who married Sarah Manning, March, 1790, Scovil (Deacon Scovil Hinman, of New Haven), Nathaniel, John, Hannah and Mary.

Hinman, Gideon, eldest son of Deac. Noah, married Hannah Curtiss, Sept., 1745. Their children were, Zipper, baptized in March, 1747, Asahel in Nov., 1749, died young, Love in Oct., 1751, died, Arabel in April, 1753, Gideon in April, 1753, (twins,) Moses in June, 1755, removed to the State of New York, Love in Nov., 1757, Curtiss in April, 1761, Sarah in July, 1764.

Hinman, Adam, son of Noah, married and removed to Vermont. Their children were, Isaac, baptized in 1754, supposed to be living, Mary in Dec., 1756, Martha in March, 1758, married Frederick Hurd, Dec., 1783, Timothy in 1760, for many years a Judge of the Court in

Derby, Vermont, and is yet living, Adam, Jan. 15, 1764, now lives at Southbury, Sarah in Jan., 1764—Adam and Sarah were twins.

Hinman, Reuben, son of Deac. Noah, married Mary Downs, Sept., 1756. Their children were, Currence, baptized in April, 1760, Abraham in Sept., 1762, and others. This family removed to Williamstown.

Hinman, Noah, jr., son of Deac. Noah, married, and with his family removed to Vermont.

Hinman, Col. Benjamin, son of Benjamin, married Molly Stiles. Their children were, Aaron in 1746, Joel, baptized in April, 1748, Sherman in June, 1750, died young, Sherman in Oct., 1752, graduated at Yale College in 1776 : he married, and had Ruth Emm, who married William Forbes of Derby, Vermont, formerly of New Haven, and Clara, who married Jared Hawley, Esq. ; Sherman also died a young man a few years after he was married.

Hinman, Aaron, son of Col. Benjamin—had Judge William, Anna Drakely, Benjamin, of Vermont, George, of Bangor, and Harry, of Southbury, who are yet living.

Hinman, Col. Joel, son of Col. Benjamin, married Sarah Curtiss, (yet living.) Their children were, Daniel, (deceased) Irena, married Eli Hall, Jason, Esq., in Vermont, Sally, married Jedediah Hall, Hon. Curtiss, died in Dec., 1820, Phebe, single, Nancy, single, Robert, died in 1813, Albert, died in 1842, Sophia, married Truman Mitchell, Sherman, an attorney, died in Mississippi, in 1832, Hon. Joel is the present Judge of the Supreme Court—he married a Miss Scovil, of Waterbury, Marietta, married Isaac Johnson, and Maria married Mr. Pulford.

Hinman, Hon. Edward, (more familiarly known as Lawyer Ned), son of Deac. Noah, married Ann Curtiss, July 18, 1764. Their children were, Sarah Ann, baptized in July, 1765, married Timothy Hinman, son of Capt. Truman, July, 1792, he graduated at Yale. Simeon, Esq., in March, 1766, graduated at Yale College in 1784, was a Lawyer—he died single, in 1830, Cyrus also graduated at Yale College in 1789, was a Lawyer—he died young and unmarried. Only two of the descendants of this family are now living, neither of whom are married—twice a member of the General Court before Southbury was incorporated.

Hinman, Abijah, son of Deac. Noah, married and removed to Vermont. Their children were, Adoniram in 1757, Wait in 1760. Ruth Emm in 1762. Abigail in 1764, and Rebecca, baptized in 1766.

Hinman, Deac. David, son of Benjamin, married Sarah Hinman—he died in 1756. Their children were, Lieut Asa, who served during the war of the Revolution—he was baptized in Aug., 1750, Annis in Dec., 1751, married Daniel Hinman, and moved to Bennington, Vt., where they both died, Gen. Ephraim in March, 1753—he acted as a Captain and Quarter Master, and Assistant Commissary of Forage in the war of the Revolution, David in Jan. 1716, and Benjamin, Esq., who moved to Little Falls, N. York, afterwards to Utica.

Hinman, Samuel, son of Wait, married, and his children were, Ann, baptized in July, 1759, Olive and Wait.

Hinman, Capt. Truman, son of Wait, married Olive Hinman, and -had children, Timothy, (father of the present Edward, Esq.,) graduated at Yale College in 1784, Ruth Emm, married Thomas Bull, Olive married Nathan Judson, Dec., 1800, Col., Truman married Betty Curtiss, Nov. 22, 1798. Only two of the descendants of Col. Truman are living—both unmarried.

Hinman, Bethuel, son of Wait, married Hannah Hicock, Nov.. 1770. Removed to Greenfield, N. Y., and had several sons, and one named Shadrack.

Hinman, Lieut. Asa, son of Deac. David, married Annis Hinman. Their children were, David, who sailed in 1802, for China, and never returned—died single, Rhoda, married Elisha Pierce, and Sarah, married Nathan Rumsey, of Southbury.—Annis, only daughter of Deac. David, married Daniel Hinman, and moved to Bennington, Vermont—they had but one child, (Betsey,) she married Samuel Brown, and had one child, Samuel H. Brown, Esq , of Bennington ; Samuel H. married Sarah Brown, daughter of Park, of Southbury, and had several children.

Hinman, Gen. Ephraim, son of Deacon David, married Sylvania French, daughter of William French, of Southbury, Feb. 3, 1779, and had four children, viz.. John, died in infancy, Laura, who married, and had a daughter, (Henrietta,) both of whom soon after died. Royal R., born at Southbury, and Mary, born at Roxbury. Gen. Ephraim was several times a member of the General Assembly—he was a Captain, Quarter Master, and Assistant Commissary of Forage in the war of the Revolution. He died in Dec., 1829, aged over 77 years.

Hinman, Royal R., son of Gen. Ephraim—on the 14th of September, 1814, married Lydia Ashley, youngest daughter of Gen John Ashley, of Sheffield, Mass. He graduated at Yale College in 1804—by profession a Lawyer, and in 1827 was admitted to practice before the Supreme Court of New York—several sessions a member of the General Assembly—was several years Secretary of State, and in 1844 was appointed Collector of Customs at the port of New Haven. His children are, Jane Ashley, Royal A., Lydia Ann, Mary E., and Catherine E. Jane A. married John Bigelow, of Hartford, and removed to Boston in 1844—they had children, Jane Frances, John H., and William Henry—John H,, died at the age of 3 years—William H.. died at Boston, an infant, in 1846. Lydia Ann, married Charles E. Babcock, of New York, Sept., 1845, and had a son, Charles H., born in July, 1846. Royal Ashley, unmarried. Mary E., and Catherine E. Hinman.

Hinman, David, son of Deac. David, married Mary Ann Graham, daughter of Andrew Graham, M.D., of Southbury, and had Frederick, who married Fanny Mitchell—Nathan, married Miss Burritt—Benjamin, married Miss Minor, who died, he then married Mrs. Bacon—Polly, married Mr. Ward, of Vermont—Patty, married Deac. Nathan Mitchell.

Hinman, Benjamin, son of Deac. David, moved in early life to Little Falls, N. Y., where he married Anna Keysor, in 1779, a daughter of Capt. Keysor, of Montgomery county, N. Y.—she was born on the farm where Fort Keyser was built. Their children were Col. John E., of Utica, who married Mary Schroppel, of the city of New York, daughter of George C. Schroppel deceased. John E. was several years sheriff of the county of Oneida.

Hinman, Col. John Jay, Attorney at Law, son of Benjamin, married some lady from Connecticut, and resides in or near Rushville, Illinois.

Hinman, Benjamin, Esq., son of Benjamin—died, unmarried, at Hinmanville, Oswego county, N. Y., Aug. 9, 1844, 49 years old. Maranda, a daughter of Benjamin, sen'r., died at Utica in July, 1806, about 2 years old. Gen. William A., (son of Benjamin, sen'r.,) Attorney at Rushville, Illinois, married Miss Grace Kingsbury of Brooklyn, N. Y., Annis, 2d daughter of Benjamin, married Dr. Thomas Monroe, originally of Baltimore, but now of Jacksonville, Illinois. Benjamin, the father of this family, resided at Utica—he died in April, 1831, at Mount Pleasant, Penn., on a journey to New Jersey, where he was interred. His widow is yet living in Illinois with her sons.

Hinsdel, Barnabas, Hartford—married Martha Smith, Nov., 1793. Daniel was married to Katherine Curtiss, of Wethersfield, and died in 1737. Barnabas, son of Daniel and Katherine, died in 1737–8. Descendants of Robert, in No. 2.

Hodge, John, married Susannah Denslow of Windsor, in 1665, and had John, Thomas, Mary, Joseph, Benjamin, Henry and William.—John, of Lyme, '91. Chauncey, of Roxbury, 1846.

Holloway, John, and Thomas Root, elected chimney viewers of Hartford, in 1648.

Holcomb, Joshua, Simsbury—died in 1690. Children, Ruth 26 years old, Thomas 24, Sarah 22, Elizabeth 20, Joshua 18, Deborah 16, Mary 14, Mindwell 12, Hannah 10, and Moses 4.

Holly, John and Francis, were important settlers in Stamford as early as 1641—2, with about 40 other families.

Hopkins, Gov. Edward, in 1640, aided in purchasing Waranock, (Westfield,) and erected a trading house there. He married a daughter of Mr. Eaton, of New Haven, but appears to have left no children in America. He procured to be printed in England, the first code of Laws for the New Haven Colony, in '56, and never returned afterwards to New England. He died in 1657. Ebenezer, married Mary, daughter of Samuel Butler, of Wethersfield.

Hoskins, John, Windsor, married Deborah Denslow in 1677, and had a daughter Deborah, in '79. Anthony, sen'r., of Windsor, died in 1706–7—left Mary, his widow, and children, John, Robert, Anthony, Thomas, Joseph, Grace Eggleston, Jane Alford, (Isabel Alford died before him). He was a farmer, and aged at his decease. John had a double portion, and £20 over, as Anthony lived with his son John. He owned land at Simsbury, which he gave Robert—he also had land at Greenfield he gave to Anthony. He entailed his lands to his children. Was an early settler at Windsor, and left an estate of £984.

Hosford, John, Windsor, son of William, married P. Thrall in 1657, and had William, John, Timothy, Hester, Sarah, Samuel, Nathaniel, Mary and Obadiah. John, of Windsor, died in 1683, and left a widow. The eldest son had £225, John £121, Timothy £121, Hester £100, Sarah £100, Samuel £114, Nathaniel £114, Mary £100, Obadiah £122, Widow £85 of personal estate for life. Mr. Hosford was a man of wealth and reputation, and one of the early settlers of Windsor. Benjamin, of Windsor, after 1717, settled at Litchfield.

House, William, Glastenbury—died in 1703. Children, John, aged 30, Sarah Smith 28, Mary Hale 26, Ann 20, William 19, Joseph, 16.

Hoyt, Nicholas, married Susannah——, in 1646, and had Samuel, Jonathan, David and Daniel.

Hubbard, George, in 1665, certified before William Leete, at Guilford, the consideration paid Lowheag, by the inhabitants of Wethersfield, for six miles in breadth on both sides of the river, and six deep from the river west, and three deep from the river east, in Wethersfield. He was on the committee of the General Court in March, '37, with Talcott, Mason and others. While he remained in the colony he was an important man at the General Court, and upon committees appointed by the Court. He was one of the first settlers in the colony—was appointed with two others, in '56, to survey the town of Wethersfield—was a committee to the General Court in '37 and '38, and a deputy in '39 in April, August and September, and was one of the leading men in the colony. He resided at Wethersfield, but remained in the colony but a few years before he removed to Milford, then to Guilford, and afterwards to Middletown, where he died in 1684, aged about 80. Children, Joseph, Daniel, Nathaniel, Samuel, Elizabeth, Mary Ranny, and Richard. (His wife, Elizabeth). Joseph, of Middletown, died in '86—his children were, Joseph, 15 years old, Robert 13, George 11, John 8, and Elizabeth 3.

Hubbell, Richard, sen'r., Bridgeport. The first settlers of (now) Bridgeport, and members of the church, were, Richard Hubbell, sen'r., Isaac Wheeler, James Bennett, sen'r., Samuel Beardsley, Matthew Sherman, Richard Hubbell, jr., David Sherman, and John Odell, jr., in 1695. It was a part of the town of Stratford. Most of these names are yet familiar in the town of Bridgeport.

Howe, Capt., and others, about 1640-1, purchased for Connecticut, of the Indians, a tract of land on Long Island, from the east part of Oyster Bay to the west part of Holmes's Bay, to the middle of what was then Great Plain upon the north side of the Island, extending south half its breadth, which lands were sparsely settled before '43.

Huit, Rev. Ephraim (in No. 2), gave in his will, Great Island, at the Flatts, to the Court at Hartford, for the use of the country.

Hull, Josias, married Elizabeth Loomis, of Windsor, in 1641. Children, Josias, born in '42, John, Elizabeth, Mary, Martha, Joseph, Sarah, Naomi, Rebecca, Thomas, and one other son.

Humphrey, Michael, married Priscilla Grant, in 1647, and had children, John, Mary, Samuel, Martha, Sarah, Abigail, and Hannah (born in '69).

Huntington, Simon, Norwich, 1660, appears to have been another family from that of Thomas, of Windsor. He was made a freeman in '63, under the Charter, at Hartford.

Hunt, Blayach, Wethersfield—died in 1640—was a cousin of Mary Collins, and a nephew of Mr. Welles—was also a cousin of Mary Baylding. He died unmarried.

Hurlbut, Thomas, Wethersfield—died in 1689. Wife, Elizabeth—children, Timothy, 9 years old, Nathaniel 7, and Ebenezer 4.

Hutchins, John—died in 1681, and left a widow, and two children. viz. Sarah, 4 years old, and Ann, one.

Hyde, William, Norwich, 1660—was probably the same William Hyde who came into Hartford in '39, and was surveyor of highways in '41. After a few years residence there, he moved down the river. He had 20 acres in the division of lands east of the river (in East Hartford), in '40. Timothy, of Hartford, died in 1710—he was the nephew of Caleb Watson and wife, and of Thomas and John Olcott— was young and unmarried—and a weaver by trade. He gave his property (£186) to his uncles and aunts.

J.

Jeffery, ——, had daughters, Mary in 1664—Hannah in '70, and afterwards Elizabeth.

Jellicoe, Thomas, Middletown—died in 1684—wife, Mary.

Jessup, John, was in Hartford in 1637. On the 30th day of October, '40, he with Rev. Richard Denton, Andrew Ward, Thurston Raynor, Jonas Wood. jr., John Northend, Thomas Weeks, Matthew Mitchell, Robert Coe, Samuel Sherman, Jeremiah Jagger, Vincent Simking, Edmond Wood, Henry Smith, Richard Gildersleeve, Jonas Wood, John Seaman, David Finch, Samuel Clark, and Jeremiah Wood, purchased the town of Stamford of the New Haven Company— nearly all of whom had been first settlers at Wethersfield. They had previously purchased the Indian right. The above, all came according to the stipulation; and with the first settlers also came the following as settlers at Stamford, viz. Richard Law, John Ferris, Robert Bates, John Whitmore, John Renolds, Thomas Morehouse, Francis Bell, Richard Crabb and Robert Fisher, most of whom were also from Wethersfield. The town continued to settle rapidly, and in '61-2, as appears by the purchase of lands, and a distribution by a vote of the company, the following became settlers there, to wit: Henry Acerly, John Underhill, Thomas Slauson, Francis Holly, John Ogden, John Smith, John Miller, William Newman, Joseph Bishop, Thomas Hoyt, Daniel Scofield, John Finch and John Holly. Rev. Mr. Denton, Mitchell, Ward, Law, Raynor and Francis Bell and Hollys, were strong, influential men in the New Haven Colony, as some of them had been in the Connecticut Colony.—*Minor.*

Judson, William (in No. 2), had sons, Lieut Joseph, Serg't. Jeremiah, and Joshua, all of whom came from Yorkshire in 1634, to Concord, Mass., from thence to Hartford, and in '39 or '40 to Stratford. The Christian names of the first family are yet retained in the Judson family at Woodbury.

K.

Kates, John, Windham—died in 1697. He gave in his will 200 acres of land, by entailment, to the poor of Windham, and 200 acres for a school house for the town. He gave his negro to Rev. Samuel Whiting, of said Windham, and other personal property. To the church of the town he gave £10 in money. He made Mary Howard executrix, and gave her the remainder of his estate, unless his child, or any of his children then in England, should come to New England,

and if so, such as should come should have all his estate. He was the first of the name in the colony. This name is spelt Kates, on record, and by himself in his will—but he was the same Lieut. John Cates who served under Oliver Cromwell's administration of the British Government. -His negro Jo. whom he gave to Mr. Whiting, he procured in Virginia, where he first landed. He escaped his pursuers in Virginia, and came to Norwich, yet feeling unsafe, he went to Windham, when a wilderness, and in '89 raised the first house, where he closed his life in safety from punishment by Charles II. He gave no silver plate to any person, as has been stated by some historians.

Keeney, Alexander, Wethersfield, was an early settler, died in 1680. His children were, Alexander, 18 years old, Thomas 16, Sarah 16, twins—Joseph 14, Lydia 11, Ebenezer 8, and Richard 6. Alice, his widow, died in '83.

Kellogg, Samuel, Colchester—died in 1708—left a wife, Hannah, and children, Samuel, Joseph, Hannah and Eunice. Nathaniel, of Colchester, was appointed guardian for Joseph. They were descendants of Nathaniel, of Hartford, (in No. 2,) in 1639—who was an early settler in the colony, and had 6 acres in the land division east of Connecticut river, 1640. Samuel married Sarah Merrills, in 1687.—Ebenezer, resided in Colchester in 1708. He married Mabel Butler, of Hartford, a sister of Elizabeth Clark and Mary Butler, daughters of Daniel Butler then deceased. In 1708 they sold the house of their father to Abraham Merrills, of Hartford. The deed was acknowledged before Michael Taintor, justice, at Colchester, where they all resided, except said Merrills, in 1710.

Kelsey, Stephen, married Hannah Higginson, of Wethersfield, in 1672.

Kibbe, Isaac, was the first male child born in Enfield, May, 1683. Incorporated in '83. The town had been a part of Springfield, and continued under the jurisdiction of Massachusetts until 1750. In 1681 a grant of the town was made to nine persons, and singular as it is, not a descendant of either of the nine are now residents of Enfield. The first settlers were from Springfield in 1679, and erected houses there, at first, to hunt and fish at Fresh Water Brook. Nathaniel Collins settled there as their second minister, in 1699. In 1637, Joseph Kibbe was a member of the General Court of Connecticut, and was the first of the name in the colony.

Kilbourn, Abraham, Wethersfield—died in 1715—wife, Sarah—children, Samuel, Abraham and Sarah. Widow Kilbourn, of Wethersfield, 1640. Joseph, of. Wethersfield, moved to Litchfield, a descendant of Thomas and John (in No. 2.) The Kilbourn families at Litchfield are descendants of John from Wethersfield. Thomas and John came to Connecticut as early as '36. Thomas married Hannah Hills, of Glastenbury, in '99. John, sen'r., (in No. 2)—wife, Sarah, children, John, Thomas, Naomi Hale, Ebenezer, Sarah Crane, George, Mary, Joseph and Abraham. He died in April, 1703.

Kimberly, Eleazer, Glastenbury—died in July, 1708-9. His children were, Thomas, Elizabeth, Ruth, and two other daughters. Estate £356. The same mentioned in No. 2, of Wethersfield.

King, Edward, Windsor—died in 1702—supposed the son of John, of Windsor. He left a will which was so badly defaced and torn, and having one daughter not mentioned in his will, that the court refused to accept it. His daughter Mary married Mr. Hillyer, and Sarah married Mr. Kady, and both resided on Long Island. Perhaps he left other children. Sarah, widow of Capt. John, of Northampton, died at Windsor, in 1705. Capt. John, perhaps a son of John, and brother of Edward.

Knell, Nicholas, Stratford, 1650.

Knight, George, Hartford—died in 1699. Estate £257.

L.

Lancton, John, jr., Farmington—died in 1683. He owned a house and land at Northampton. He was a son of Deacon Lancton.

Lester, Edward, held land about New London in 1653.

Lovering, William, a hatter by trade—was admitted an inhabitant of Hartford in 1658.

Loomis, Joseph, sen'r., Windsor, 1639. From history, tradition and records, it appears, and is believed by the Loomis family, that Joseph Loomis and his family were the only persons of the name who came to Windsor in the early settlement of the town, (as early as 1639)—that he with his family, consisting of himself, wife, five sons and one daughter, emigrated from, at, or near Bristol in England, to New England, in the ship Mary and John, Captain Squid, master, which sailed from Plymouth, England, March 20, 1630, and arrived at Nantasket Point, May 30th the same year. From thence with the Rev. John Warham's church and people, in '36, he emigrated to Windsor, (or with Mr. Hewit in '39.) From all that is known it is quite certain that all the Loomises in this part of the country have originated from this family. The names of the five sons are as follows, viz. John, Joseph, Thomas, Nathaniel and Samuel, and daughter, Elizabeth. They all settled in the town of Windsor, and there remained until after Philip's war. Timothy (in No. 2,) was recorder at a much later period than '39. [Dr. McClure was mistaken as to Timothy's coming to Windsor in '39, with Mr. Huit.] He died in Windsor in 1658—his wife died in '52. Joseph, jr., son of Joseph, sen'r., of Windsor, died in '87. Estate £281. His children were, Joseph, 38 years old, John 36, Mary 34, Hannah 25, Matthew 23, Stephen 20, James 17, Nathaniel 14, and Isaac 9, at his decease. John Loomis was an appraiser of his estate, with H. Wolcott and John Wolcott—perhaps at that time an appraiser could be a relative. John, of Windsor, married Elizabeth Scott, and had John, born in '49, Joseph, Thomas, Samuel, Daniel, James, Timothy, Nathaniel, David, Samuel, Isaac, Elizabeth and Mary. Thomas, married Hannah Fox in '53, and had Thomas, (died) Thomas, Hannah, and Mary. His wife died. He then married a second wife, and had, Elizabeth, Ruth, Sarah, Jeremiah, (died) Mabel, Mindwell, &c. Nathaniel, married Elizabeth Moore, and had 12 children. Samuel married and had five children. John, of Windsor, had a granddaughter, Anna Loomis, daughter of Joseph, born in '78.

Lynde, Nathaniel, was an early settler of Saybrook—his son, Samuel, was a native of the town. Nathaniel, gave the first building for a College at Saybrook. His son, Samuel, was many years a member of the Council and a Judge in Connecticut. The other early settlers found upon record were, the Major, Rev. Mr. Higginson, Peters, Barker, Lieut. Bull, Bushnell, Clark, Lay, Lord, Parker, William Pratt, Post, Champion, M. Griswold, Lee, Wade, Backus, Bliss, Huntington, Hyde, Larrabee, Leffingwell, Breede, Chalker, Waterhouse, Kirtland, Shipman, Whittlesey, Willard, Lieut. Seely, Mr. Higginson, was the first unordained minister at Saybrook. He married the daughter of the Rev. Henry Whitefield, of Guilford, and afterwards became his assistant at Guilford, and about 1660 he moved to Salem to assist his father.

Lyman, Samuel, moved from Northampton to Lebanon, and from thence to Coventry about 1718. Noah Carpenter, son of Benjamin, came from Northampton to Coventry at a later period, 1730.

Lucas, William, owned land in Middletown in 1667—he probably resided there previously.

M.

Maloy, Capt., was ordered in 1637, with Allyn and Ward, to go to Agawam and treat with the Indians for their tribute to defray the expense of the wars, of one fathom of wampum a man, and a fathom and a quarter, for the Wawattock Indians.

Markham, James, Windsor—died in 1698—wife, Elizabeth. He left a large estate to his wife—probably had no children.

Marsh, John, who moved from Hartford to Litchfield—was a descendant of John, of Hartford, (in No. 2.)

Marshall, Samuel, Windsor, married Mary Wilton in 1652, and had Samuel, Thomas, died— Daniel, Thomas, Mary, Elizabeth, John, and one other daughter. Capt. Samuel, of Windsor, (in No. 2,) was killed in battle by the Indians in '75. It was his fifth time in service, under Major Treat. He was a brave officer. Estate £902. (See S. Marshall in No. 2.)

Maskell, Thomas, Windsor, married Betsey Parsons in 1660. Children, Betsey, Thomas, Abigail, Thomas, John, Elizabeth and others.

Mason, Edward, Wethersfield, 1639, (in No. 2,) died in 1640, and left an estate of £121.

Mather, Richard, was one of the four early settlers of the town of Lyme before 1666.

Maudsley, John, Windsor, married Mary Newbury in 1664. Benjamin, born in '66, Margaret in '67, Joseph in '70, and Susannah in '75. A respectable family. He set out the estate of James Enoe to his children in '82.

May, Nicholas, Windsor—died in 1664. Estate £4.

Marwine or Merwine, Miles, in 1684. His children were, Elizabeth, John, Samuel, Abigail and Miles.

Miner, John, son of Thomas, of New London. In 1654, I find the following upon the colony record : " Whereas, notwithstanding former provision made for the conveyance of the knowledge of God to the

Natives amongst us, little hath hitherto been attended, through want of an able interpreter;—this Court being earnestly desirous to promote and further what lies in them, a work of that nature, wherein the glory of God and the everlasting welfare of those poor, lost, naked sons of Adam is so deeply concerned—do order, that Thomas Miner, of Pequot, (New London) shall be wrote unto from this Court, and desired that he would forthwith send his son John to Hartford, where this Court will provide for his maintenance and schooling, to the end he may be for the present, assistant to such Elder, Elders or others, as this Court shall appoint to interpret the things of God to them as he shall be directed, and, in the meantime, fit himself to be instrumental that way, as God shall fit and incline him thereunto for the future." This was the first action in the Missionary cause in Connecticut. Nothing previous to this date, appears from the record, to have been done preparatory to christianizing the Indians, except to suffer them, in small numbers, to attend their meetings for worship.

Mitchell, Nathan, who moved from Stratford or Stamford to Litchfield is supposed a descendant of Matthew, (in No. 2,) who moved to Stamford from Wethersfield, in the early settlement of Stamford. John, of Hartford, died in 1683 His children were, Mary, aged 28, John 25, Sarah 21, Margaret 19, Mabel 17, and Miriam 15. Sarah, of Wethersfield, died in '84, and left brothers and sisters, viz., John, Mary, Margaret, Mabel and Miriam, and £20 estate.

Mix, Rev. Stephen, and John Woodward were appointed scribes for the Convention that formed the Saybrook Platform in 1708. The name of Mix is yet at New Haven.

Moore, Deac. John, had a daughter born in Windsor, 1643, also John in '45. Deac. Moore died in '77. His son John married Hannah Foote in '64—and had John, Thomas, Samuel, Nathaniel, Edward, and twins in '74, Josias and Joseph.

Morton, Samuel, Hoccanum—died in 1668. Estate £4.

Mudge, Francis. The town of Hartford, by their committee, sequestered to the use of said Mudge, six acres of land, if the town admitted him as an inhabitant, 1640.

N.

Nash, Joseph, Hartford—died in 1677-8—wife, Margaret. Sarah was his only child unmarried. Capt John, of New Haven, was his eldest brother. He had no sons, and his other daughters were married at his decease. He left a good estate.

Newbury, Thomas, Windsor—died in 1688. Children, Hannah, 8, Thomas 6, Joseph 4, and Benjamin one year old. He married Ann Ford in 1676. Benjamin, of Windsor, married Mary Allyn in '46, and had nine children.

Newel, Daniel, with Samuel Hall, Ebenezer Smith, John Gaines, Richard Goodale, Samuel Eggleston, John Ranny, Thomas Buck, Thomas Wright, Nathaniel and Joseph White, Jonathan Judd, and others, were the first church members at Chatham. The church was organized there in 1721; Daniel Shepard chosen Deacon; and the first meeting house erected there, 26 by 40 feet, in 1718. Thomas, of Farmington, died in 1689. His children were, John, 42 years old, Thomas 39, Samuel 28, Rebecca Woodford 46, Mary Bascomb 44, Hester Strong 37, Sarah Smith 34, Hannah North 31—John Stanley and Thomas North married two of his daughters. He was an early settler of Farmington. Joseph, of Farmington, died in 1689—was a brother of John, and had five sisters, viz., Rebecca, Mary, Sarah, Esther and Hannah; he was also a brother of Thomas and Samuel. To Esther Woodford he gave a share of his estate—was a brother-in-law to John Stanley, who had a son Samuel. He died unmarried. The name yet continues within the bounds of what was then Farmington.

Nicholas, Siborn, of Witham in the county of Essex, England, Gentleman—in 1664 received a deed, executed in London, of a large quantity of land located in Hartford, Conn., on both sides of Connecticut river, from William Whiting, a merchant then in London, and a son of William Whiting then deceased, of Hartford, which had fallen to him at his father's decease, for which Mr. Nichols paid him £320 sterling. It is doubtful whether the above Siborn ever came to this country. Cyprian Nichols the elder appears to have been the son of Siborn, of Witham, particularly from the fact that the lands deeded by Mr. Whiting in London, went into the possession of Cyprian, of Hartford, yet the lands were never deeded by Siborn to Cyprian, as appears of record. Cyprian was occasionally called Siborn, but generally Cyprian. There were five Cyprian Nichols in this family in succession. Cyprian, sen'r., died at Hartford, a gentleman of great wealth; Cyprian, jr., died in 1745—left his widow, Agnes; Lieut. James and William were also sons of Cyprian, sen'r. In 1711 land was set out on execution by S. Webster, sheriff, to Cyprian Nichols. Capt. Cyprian, in 1720, had daughters, Mary Turner and Sarah Webster, wife of William Webster; he also had a grandson Cyprian, and a grandson William Davenport, to whom he gave £50. There was a Cyprian Nichols as late as 1750, and the name is yet in the same family in Hartford at this time. Siborn was a gentleman of reputation and wealth in England, and in 1664 had the title of gentleman and Mr.—Cyprian, of Hartford, married Mary Spencer, daughter of Samuel Spencer, May, 1705. In the settlement of estates, the name of Siborn Nichols has appeared, which is supposed to have been used for Cyprian. No person by the name of Siborn Nichols died in the Probate District of Hartford for the first 75 years of the settlement of the colony. It appears there was either a young man by the name of Siborn after the death of Siborn, of Witham, or Cyprian was occasionally called Siborn. Adam Nichols of 1681, appears to have been a different family—he had a daughter Hester Ellis—he also had a son and daughter at Haddam. Isaac and Caleb Nichols were located at Stratford as early as 1650.

North, John—died in 1690–1. Children, Thomas, Joseph, Mary and Sarah Woodruff.

Northum, John, Colchester—died in 1732—wife, Hannah. He had a son John, and nine daughters; and a brother-in-law, Nathaniel Pomeroy.

Northend, John, an original settler and proprietor of Stamford in

1641—probably the same to whom Mr. Towsey gave 40 shillings in his will.

Noyes, John, Stonington, 1713.

O.

Olmsted, John, was settled at Hartford, as early as 1639—he probably was the same John Holmsted that afterwards located at Norwich, in 1660. He was a kinsman of the Richard Olmsted family of Norwalk, who went there from Hartford.

Osborn, John, Windsor, married Ann Olday in 1645, and had John, Nathaniel, Samuel, Mary, Hannah, Samuel, Isaac, Sarah, and two other daughters.

Ould, Robert, Windsor, married Susannah Sanford, and had Robert in 1670, and Jonathan in '72.

P.

Palmer, Timothy, Windsor, married Hannah Buell in 1663, and had Timothy, Hannah, Mary, Sarah, died, John, Sarah, Samuel and Martha.

Parsons, Rev. Joseph. In 1700 a church was formed at Lebanon, and the same year Mr. Parsons was ordained there. Several persons settled there from Windsor, Stratford, &c. Thomas, married Lydia Brown, of Windsor, in 1641, and had Betsey, Thomas, died, Abigail, John, Mary, Ebenezer, Samuel, and Joseph. Thomas died in 1680. Isaac, son of John and Phillis, born in 1699, Jacob in 1701, Moses in 1702, Phillis in 1704, Aaron in 1706, and Ruth in 1711. Ebenezer. of Windsor, had a daughter Abigail, born in 1675, Ebenezer in 1677, John in 1678. John Parsons married Phillis Hills in 1698.

Parent, John, Haddam—died in 1686. Children, Mary and Elizabeth—no sons.

Payne, Widow Hannah, Wethersfield—died in 1682, and left children, Hannah, 20 years of age, and Thomas 9. John, of Middletown, died in '81. His children were, Job, 4 years old, Latierce 3, and Abigail 1. Richard Hall, Samuel Hubbard and John Savidge were appraisers.

Peacock, John, settled at Stratford before 1650.

Pease, John. It has generally been supposed by the Pease family, that the first of the name settled at Enfield about 1683; yet Miss Caulkins, in her History of Norwich, has reported John Pease as located at Norwich at a much earlier period, with his name and lot registered in the Town Plat, as a proprietor in the N. W. extremity of the settlement, with John Tracy, John Baldwin, Jonathan Royce, Robert Allyn, Francis Griswold, Nehemiah Smith and Thomas Howard. John Calkins, Hugh Calkins, Ensign William Backus, Richard Egerton, Thomas Post and John Gager. Upon the opposite side of the street she locates, with no river land attached to their home lots, Samuel and William Hide; upon the river, Morgan Bowers, Robert Wade, John Birchard, John Post, Thomas Bingham and Thomas Waterman; around the Plain, Gen. Mason and Rev. James Fitch. After which she gives with like particularity the locations of Lieut. Thomas Tracy, John Bradford, C. Huntington, Thomas Adgate, John

Holmsted (or Olmstead,) Stephen Backus, Thomas Bliss and John Renolds. T. Leffingwell, J. Reed, R. Wallis and Richard Hendys, as the first planters of Norwich. Mr. Pease must have been located in Norwich as early as 1660, as a town book was then commenced, and from that it appears the contract which had been made with John Elderkin in '54, to erect a corn-mill for the town of Mohegan, was now understood to be erected either "on the land of John Pease, or at Norman's Acre," before Nov. '61. Mr. Pease was afterwards found at New London. Farmer says, John Pease was a member and captain of the Ar. Co. in '61. He might have returned to the Plymouth Colony, and from thence removed to Enfield, or he might have removed direct from Norwich or New London to Enfield in '83. As the name and age of the man appears to be the same as that of John Pease who had resided at Salem, there is little doubt he was the same man. He was a good surveyor and a gentleman of education.

Peck, Paul. The name of Paul in the Peck family continued over 100 years—named after Deac. Paul, of Hartford, in 1639. Paul, son of Paul, a great grandson of Deac. Paul, born in 1702, Elisha, in 1704, Thomas in 1709, and Cornelius in 1711. Paul Peck married Loah Morry in 1701. Samuel married Abigail Collier, daughter of Joseph, in 1701. Joseph Hopkins married Hannah Peck, daughter of Paul, in 1699. John and Paul, jr., emigrated to Litchfield after 1717.

Perry, Richard, Fairfield, with the following names are found upon the record of Fairfield, as first settlers, viz. Hon. Nathan Gold, Nathaniel Baldwin, John Tomson, George Starkey, Henry Rowland, Daniel Frost, Robert Lockwood and John Gray, as early as 1641. Fairfield had settlers as early as 1639-40. John Barlow, Samuel Drake, Tho. Sherwood, Richard Bowles, Thomas Dunn and Thomas Sherwington, also in 1650-1. There are no dates of 1650. In 1654, Edward Adams, Hon. Roger Ludlow, John Banks, Andrew Ward, Richard Lyon, Thomas Wheeler, John Nichols, Isaac Nichols. John Cable, Thomas Morehouse and Richard Osborn (and William Hill and Robert Turney in 1654; also in 1654, Philip Pinkney, Thomas Barlow, George Goodwin, Thomas Bearsley; in 1657, Henry Lyon. Many names cannot be decyphered on the first record at Fairfield. The names of Rowland, Starkey, Sherwood, Dunn, Sherwington, Lyon, Morehouse, Turney and Pinkney were peculiarly Fairfield county names, none of which I recollect to have found among the first settlers of the old towns of Hartford, Wethersfield, or Windsor. Many of the above persons emigrated from Wethersfield, and other towns on the Connecticut river.—*S. A. Nichols.*

Pettibone, John, Windsor, married in 1664, and had a son, John, born in '65, a daughter in 67, and Stephen in '69.

Peters, Thomas, at New London in 1645—probably the same Rev. Thomas who came to Saybrook with Mr. Fenwick in '39. Mr. Peters aided Uncas in many respects; he performed the duty of surgeon in dressing the wounds of his warriors after his battles with the Narragansetts. In 1645 there must have been about 50 families at New London.

Pond, Samuel, Windsor, married Sarah Ware in 1641, and had children, Isaac, Nathaniel, Sarah and Samuel.

S.

Savage, John, sen'r., settled early at Middletown—died in 1684— left his wife, Elizabeth, and children, John, 33 years old at his father's death, Elizabeth, 30, Sarah, 28, Mary, 27, Abigail, 19, William, 17, Nathaniel, 14, Rachel, 12, and Hannah, 9. He left a large landed estate to his family. He was often called upon by the town in various stations. He appears to have settled there as his first location in the colony, and was the first of the name in the colony.

Sage, David, sen'r., Middletown—died in 1703. Children, David, John, (two of his daughters married Bull and Johnson,) also Mercy, Jonathan, Timothy—Jonathan died in 1713; David, jr. died in 1712 or '13. His mother resided at Middletown, and owned land there. He left an estate of £753. Thomas Stedman, of Wethersfield, married a daughter of David, jr. Children of David, jr., deceased, Mary and Elizabeth—he had no sons.

Strong, Rev. Nathan. His father early moved from Windsor to Woodbury, where the Rev. Nathan was born in 1716. He first learned the trade of a house joiner, but afterwards graduated at Yale College in 1742, immediately after he studied theology with the Rev. Mr. Graham, of Southbury, who preached his ordination sermon. He was ordained in Coventry in 1745, immediately after the church was formed there. He died in 1795, in the 51st year of his ministry. He married the daughter of the Rev. Mr. Meacham, and a granddaughter of the Rev. John Williams, of Deerfield, who was taken captive by the Indians. Some of the first settlers of Coventry under Mr. Strong, were Nathaniel Kingsbury, John Fowler, Noah and Benjamin Carpenter, Joseph Long, Amos Richardson, Aaron Strong, Ebenezer Brown, John Hackings, John Craw or Crow, Timothy Ladd, Jonathan Shepard, Elijah Hammond, James Hotchkins, and others. The father of Rev. Nathan who moved to Woodbury, was the 14th child in his father's family. Rev. Nathan, of Coventry, was the father of Rev. Drs. Nathan, of Hartford, and Joseph, of Norwich. There are yet at Woodbury several families by the name of Strong, all descendants of John of Windsor. After 1717, Eleazer and Supply Strong moved from Windsor to Litchfield. Rev. Nathan was a lineal descendant of John, of Windsor, who moved to Northampton.

A Catalogue of the Families who emigrated to Massachusetts, in 1659, from Connecticut.

"At a meeting at Goodman Ward's house, in Hartford, April 18, 1659, the company there met, engaged themselves. under their own hands, or by their deputies, whom they had chosen, to remove themselves and their families out of the jurisdiction of Connecticut, into the jurisdiction of Massachusetts, as may appear in a paper dated the day and year abovesaid. The names of the engagers are these:

John Webster, William Goodwin, John Crow, Nathaniel Ward, John White, John Barnard, Andrew Bacon, William Lewis, William Westwood, Richard Goodman, John Arnold, William Patrigg, Gregory Wilterton, Thomas Standley, Samuel Porter, Richard Church, Ozias Goodwin, Francis Barnard, James Ensign, George Steele, John Marsh, Robert Webster, William Lewis, jr., Nathaniel Standley, Samuel Church, William Markum, Samuel Moody, Zechariah Field, Wid. Westly, Wid. Watson, Andrew Warner, Mr. John Russell, jr., Nathaniel Dickinson, Samuel Smith, Thomas Coleman, Mr. John Russel, sen'r., John Dickinson, Philip Smith, John Coleman, Thomas Wells, James Northam, Samuel Gardner, Thomas Edwards, John Hubbard, Thomas Dickinson, Robert Boltwood, Samuel Smith, jr., William Gull, Luke Hitchcock, Richard Montague, John Lattimer, Peter Tilton, John Watson, Richard Billing, Benjamin Harbert, Edward Benton, John Catling, Mr. [Samuel] Hooker, Capt. Cullick, not fully engaged, Daniel Warner."

Of the 60 names on the foregoing list, about one-fourth part never removed to Hadley, and several that did remove returned to Connecticut again some years after. The names of a number that did remove are not on this list.

ADVERTISEMENT.

The three numbers, of which this is the last, is designed to give the information to those who possess any curiosity to learn the first of the name who came into the colony of Connecticut. When it is known who the first progenitor was, there is little difficulty in tracing their ancestry. With most men there exists an anxiety to learn something of those of the same blood who had preceded them, and had aided in building up, and were the pioneers of this great and mighty republic, which has now become one of the three most powerful governments of the world .There will be a satisfaction in recognizing our first ancestor—in learning from whence he came—where he was first located, and his condition and character in life, in this country. If he was poor and homely, so much the more are you indebted to him, for abandoning the land of his nativity, his friends, and all that he held dear, (except his religion) to come to this gloomy wilderness, inhabited only by wild beasts and savage men, where for many years their lives were never safe even with their arms in their hands, and the sweet sleep they had enjoyed in childhood had become a stranger to their eyelids. It will not be forgotten that all these dangers were suffered for you. Since my attention has been particularly called to this subject, I have often been astonished to find so many of the intelligent inhabitants of the State so perfectly destitute of information of their genealogy ; indeed I conversed with one gentleman of whom I enquired the name of his great grandfather, and where he resided—he looked at me with a sort of surprise, and remarked, "Really, Sir, I never thought I had any ancestor previous to my grandfather," and was unable to give the name or place of residence of his grandfather. Thought I, a poor reward this for the hardships of his ancestor—and my informant was a gentleman of $80,000. Nothing is required to find much of every man's ancestry, but patience, perseverance and industry in collecting them from the early records and papers which have been preserved for 200 years.

My object at first was to publish only a list of the names of the Puritans who came to Connecticut during the first 30 years, from 1635 to 1665, while Connecticut stood alone, before the Union of the New Haven Colony with Connecticut; but believing it would be more interesting by adding little historical scraps to names, and giving short biographical sketches of persons, I have done so with as much accuracy as possible. To those who are familiar with the labor of such a work, I need not say, that much time has been bestowed upon these three small pamphlets, as well as considerable money advanced in so imperfectly giving it to the public. Errors there will be, but when it is considered that the numerous facts here collected are drawn from the half obliterated records, imperfectly kept 200 years since, depending mostly upon the colony record, I trust that such errors will be excused until those who find them shall attempt to better the work by their own personal exertions. No towns are included in this compilation, but such as were at some time before 1665 within the jurisdiction of Connecticut. There probably at no period of time was ever as many respectable and educated men emigrated from any country, as from England, to Virginia, Massachusetts and Connecticut from 1635 to 1665—men who were neither inferior to their successors in fervent piety, patriotism, learning, or in sterling integrity. There were, it is true, many needy and avaricious adventurers who quit their country, hoping to better their condition in life; and the fate of time and accident, by the equal laws of our country, has placed the successors of some of the most wealthy of the original pioneers, in humble poverty, while the successors of the most humble emigrants are now found surrounded with every comfort and in the highest walks of life. This is the fate of idleness on the one hand and persevering industry on the other, in most cases. Where the names of families are mentioned, they may perhaps differ from some ancient family records, as some of them are taken from town books, while others are taken from the records of Probate—the former contains all the births, while the Probate record mentions only such as were living at the decease and distribution of the estate of the head of the family. Dates in the ancient records of the colony are difficult to procure with accuracy, as wills often are without date, as are inventories of estates. Not only so, some may be misled in supposing dates incorrect, from the fact, that the first settlers commenced the year on the 25th day of March, instead of the first day of January, and the records for many years are so dated, and time thus divided.

Only 500 copies have been printed in this edition. The language used in describing the facts attached to names, is usually the language, if not the words of the record.

ERRATA.

For "Hon. Henry Wolcott, the first of Windsor," on page 108, 12th line from bottom, read Gov'rs. Winthrop, Welles and Webster.

On page 94, the 5th line from bottom, read Doct. Charles P., instead of H. Welles.

The Errata for the three numbers will be published in the next number.

No. IV.

☞ IF an apology is required for publishing, at my own expense, a Fourth Number, after having remarked in No. 3, that it was the last to be published, I have only to say that there were several names left on hand which had cost considerable labor, and the 3d No. had cost all for which the numbers sold, and could be made no larger without a loss—I have, therefore, rather than to lose the labor, ventured again to trespass upon the public, by publishing a Fourth Number.

The following is a copy of the officers of the first organized General Court of Connecticut, under the compact of 1638, viz :—*Record.*

" April, 1639.   A General Meeting.

John Haynes, Esq. was chosen Governor for this year, and until a new be chosen.

Mr. Roger Ludlow, Deputy Governor.

Mr. George Wyllys, Mr. Thomas Welles, Mr. Edward Hopkins, Mr. John Webster, Mr. William Phelps were chosen to Assist in the Magistracy for the year ensuing ; and all took the oath appointed for them.

Mr. Edward Hopkins was chosen Secretary, and Mr. Welles Treasurer for the year ensuing.

Mr. John Steel, of Hartford, John Pratt, of Hartford, Mr. Gaylord, Mr. Stoughton, of Windsor, Thurston Rayner, of Wethersfield, Geo. Hubbard, of Hartford, Mr. Spencer, Edward Stebbins, of Hartford, Henry Wolcott, of Windsor, Mr. Foard, of Windsor, James Boosey, Richard Crabb" of Wethersfield, were the Committee who composed the House of Deputies.

Inscription on the Monument erected by the Ancient Burying Ground Association of Hartford, in Memory of the First Settlers of Hartford.

Jeremy Adams, Matthew Allyn, Francis Andrews, William Andrews, John Arnold, Andrew Bacon, John Barnard, Robert Bartlett, John Baysey, John Bidwell, Thomas Birchwood, William Bloomfield, Thomas Bull, Thomas Bunce, Benjamin Burr, Richard Butler, Clement Chaplin, Richard Church, John Clark, Nicholas Clark, James

21

Cole, John Crow, Robert Day, Joseph Easton, Edward Elmer, Nathaniel Ely, James Ensign, Zachariah Field, William Gibbons, Richard Goodman, William Goodwin, Ozias Goodwin, Seth Grant, George Graves, Samuel Greenhill, Samuel Hales, Tho's Hales, John Haynes, Stephen Hart, William Heyden, William Hills, William Holton, Thomas Hooker, Edward Hopkins, Thomas Hosmer, William Hyde, Thomas Judd, William Kelsey, William Lewis, Richard Lord, Tho's Lord, Richard Lyman, John Marsh, Matthew Marvin, John Maynard, John Moody, Joseph Mygatt, Thomas Olcott, James Olmsted, Richard Olmsted, William Pantry, William Parker, Stephen Post, John Pratt, William Pratt, Nathaniel Richards, Richard Risley, Thomas Root, William Ruscoe, Thomas Scott, Thomas Selden, Richard Seymour, John Skinner, Arthur Smith, Thomas Spencer, William Spencer, Thomas Stanley, Timothy Stanley, Thomas Stanton, Edward Stebbins, George Steele, John Steele, George Stocking, Samuel Stone, John Talcott, William Wadsworth, Samuel Wakeman, Nath'l Ward, Andrew Warner, Richard Webb, John Webster, Thomas Welles, Wm. Westwood, John White, William Whiting, John Wilcox, Gregory Wolterton, George Wyllys, John Hopkins, William Butler.

The following names were also in Hartford as early as 1640 :—

Andrew Adams, Nathaniel and John Allen, Thomas Allen, Thomas Alcocks, Joseph Aikin, Thomas Burnham, William Butler, Francis Barnard, John Bigelow, John Brunson and Richard, John Barnes, Nathaniel Bearding, John Bliss, sen'r. and jr., Richard Butler, John Bailey, John Cullick, Nathaniel Kellogg, Richard Church, William Clark, Thomas Calder, Thomas Catling, John Carter, Nicholas Disbrough, Davey Fuller, Philip Davis, Nathaniel Eldredge, John Friend, Samuel Fitch, Jonathan Gilbert, Daniel Garriot, John and Thomas Hall, William Haughton, Thomas Hungerford, John and Nicholas Jennings, John Kirbee, Ralph Keeler, William Lewis, Edward Lay, William Markham, John Meigs, James Northum, Nicholas Olmsted, William Phillips, James Richards, Nathaniel Ruscoe, Henry Rowe, Robert Sanford, John Sables, John Savill, Henry and Aaron Stark, James Steel, Samuel Storm, Benjamin Ufford, Thomas Upson, Robert Wade, Henry Wakelee, Henry Walkley, Richard Walkley, Nathaniel Ware, Thomas and Richard Watts, William Webb, William Westley, Samuel Whitehead, George Winterton, Thomas Woodford, Samuel Talcott, Matthew Woodruff, Richard Billings, John Birchard, Thomas Bliss, Robert Boltwood, Richard Case, Thomas Collins, John Jessup, Paul Peck, Henry Stiles, Benjamin Munn, John Holloway, Widow Betts, Clement Chapin, Rev. Thomas Hooker, Gov. John Haynes, and others.

First Settlers of Windsor.

The very few dates to be found for several years in the first records of Windsor, renders it difficult to designate time in all cases, and for three or four of the first years of the settlement there was little or no record.

The following list of names are found in the land record of Windsor, in the hand writing of Bray Rosseter, Town Clerk of Windsor until 1652. Those names which have no date annexed, are entered 1652, though many of them were probably much earlier.

Thomas Marshfield, 1642, Thomas Newell, '42, William Hayden, '42, John Banks, '44, Thomas Gibbard, '44, Richard Lyman, '44, James Eno, '46, Lawrence Ellison, '46, Anthony Dorchester, '49, John Wayt, '49, Owen Tudor, '49, John Bennett, '52, Peter Tilton, '52, Samuel Pond, '52, Thomas Orton, '52, Robert Howard, '46, Jasper Raulins, '52 of Roxbury before '46, Thomas Parsons, '50, Jeffery Baker, '52, John Osborn, '52, Robert Sanford, '52, Richard, Church, '52, John Strong, '51, Edward Griswold, '49, John Browton, 49, Miles Merwin, '49, St. John Nicholas, '49, Matthew Allyn, '47, George Alexander, '46, Thomas Huntington, '56, Walter Lee, '55, Edward King, (an Irishman) '62, Timothy Hall, '64, John Pettibone, '66, Joseph Skinner, '66, George Jeffries, '69, John Millington, '70, John Bartlett, '49, John Case, '64, John Griffin, '48, Humphrey Hydes. '45, Arthur Henbury, '69, Robert Sanford, (Rossiter) '52, Richard Saxton, '53, Josiah Ellsworth, '54, John Moses, '51, John Brooks, '50, John Owen, '57, Henry Curtice, —, John Bancraft, '58, Peter Brown, '58, Edward Elmer, '66, Jonas Westover, '61, Simon Miller, '51, Edward Messenger, '61, Robert Watson, '65, Samuel Wilcoxson, '64, Christopher Crow, '66, Edward Chapman, '67, Samuel Forward, '70, John Maudesly, '64, John Fitch, '43, Robert Haywart, '43, Michael Humphrey, '43, Tho. Rowley, '62, Ambrose Fowler, '50, John Pettes, '66.

The foregoing persons appear at the dates given as land holders in Windsor.—*Hayden.*

Many of these persons are known to have been in the colony several years before the above dates.

Location of some of the Settlers of Windsor.

Some of the following persons were located within the Palisado at the Windsor trading house, and others on the "common street" north, and many of them on the road leading west from Dr. Pierson's house and Joel Thrall's to sandy bank. Tradition says, that as late as 1700, there were more dwellings upon the two roads mentioned than upon main street, viz :

William Gaylord, sen'r., Stephen Terry, John Hoskins and his son, Thomas Hoskins, Thomas Stoughton, Thomas Gunn, Thomas Holcomb, Humphrey Pinney, Josiah Hull, John Rockwell, Thomas Buckland, Joseph Clark, Thomas Dibble, Michael Fry, Philip Randall, Robert Winchell, Joseph Carter, William Hanmer, Eddy Filley, Richard James, George Hull, George Phillips, John Hawkes, Anthony Hawkins, David Wilton, Walter Filer, William Hill, Thomas Ford, Nicholas Denslow, Capt. Mason, Giles Gibbs, Abraham Randall, Ephraim Huit, Henry Fawkes, Matthew Grant, William Hosford, William Hubbard, John Taylor, Eltwed or Edward Pomeroy, Aaron Cook, Elias Parkman, Brigget Egglestone, Francis Gibbs Richard Weller, Simon Hoyte, Thomas Dewey, Thomas Bassett.

Those who settled south of Little River in the vicinity of the mill, and between the mill and the foot of stony hill, were—Rev. John Warham, William Phelps, sen'r., Nathan Gillett, Jonathan Gillett, George Steeaky, Richard Voar, Bray Rossiter, Roger Williams, Tho. Bascome, Nicholas Palmer, William Thrall, John Hillier, Wm. Buell, Henry Wolcott, sen'r., Henry, jr., John Moore, Thomas Moore, John Branker, Thomas Marshall, Richard Birge or Birdge, Benedict Alford, Christopher Wolcott, John Witchfield, William Phelps, jr., George Phelps, John Porter, Joseph Loomis, Thomas Barker, William Filly, Simeon Mills, Arthur Williams, John Youngs, Joseph Newbury, Benjamin Newbury, John Newbury, Sarah Newbury.—*Hayden.*

The First Settlers of Wethersfield.

Richard Belden, Jacob Waterhouse, William Boarman, John Roote, Richard Wastecoat, Jeremiah Jagger, Samuel Barrett, Robert Burrows or Barrows, John Northend, William Bramfield, Robert Beedle, Enoch Buck, John Bishop, Joseph Bennett, John Brundish, Wm. Palmer, Enoch Buckley, Hon. James and Joseph Boosey, Wm. Bascum, Jasper Rawling, Dorothy Chester, Robert Abbott, Leonard and John Chester, Richard Crabb, Robert Coe, Thomas Coop, Amos Williams, George Chappell, Josiah or Joseph Churchill, John Whitmore, Mr. Chaplin, Matthew Mitchell, John Coltman, William Colefax, Richard Park, John Curtice, Thomas Ufford, William Dickinson, Rev. Richard Denton, Rev. Peter Prudden, John Edwards, Rev. Henry Smith, Fracis Kilbourn, John Deming, Joseph Edwards, Abraham Elson, Nathniel Foster, Daniel and John Finch, Nathaniel Foot, Richard Gildersleve, John Johnson, Richard Harris, John Tinker, Thomas Hurlbut, Thomas Hubbard, John Gibbs, Joseph Hollister, John Harrison, Richard Smith, John Kilbourn his father and family, Samuel Ireland, Richard Laws, Mrs. Lattimore, Andrew Landon, Richard

Montague, Andrew Langdon, Matthew Williams, Benjamin Munn, John Nott, John and Edward Pierce, Joseph and John Plumb, Thurston Rayner, John Reynolds, Richard Riley, John Robins, Robert Rose, John Saddler, Lieut. Robert Seeley, Joseph and Samuel Sherman, Thomas Stanton, Thomas Standish, John Stoddar, Hon. Thomas Tracy, Richard Treat, Richard and Matthias Trott, Ephraim Turner, John Wadams, John Miller, Hon. Andrew Ward, Joyce Ward, Josias Willard, Jonas Wood, William Swain, Thomas Wright, Thomas Atwood, William Biggs, George Hubbard, Thomas Couch, Wm. Tailer, Benjamin Crane, Leonard Dix, Thomas Fenner, John Goodridge, John Hilton, John Betts, Alexander Keeney, Thomas Hanset, Edward Mason, Charles Taintor, (1640,) Widow Paine. Not as early, James Boswell, John Russell, jr., Edward Stott, Philip Goose, Hitchcock Lake, Samuel Hale, John Kirbe, John Latemore, John Lilly, John Westfall, Francis Yates.

Where these names are found in Connecticut at this time, it will also be found that in nine cases out of ten that the person of the name found in the above list was their first ancestor in Connecticut.

———

The Proprietors of the Undivided Lands of the Town of Hartford, in 1639, who were probably all settlers in the town at that time—I give a list of their names, viz :

William Andrews, Jeremy Adams, John Arnold, Francis Andrews, Matthew Allyn, Andrew Bacon, John Barnard, Thomas Birchwood, William Butler, William Bloomfield, Richard Butler, Thomas Bull, John Basey, Robert Bartlett, John Crow, John Clark, James Cole, Nicholas Clark, Richard Church, John Cullick, Clement Chaplin, Dorothy Chester, Robert Day, Nathaniel Ely or Elly, Joseph Easton, Edward Elmer, James Ensign, Zachery Field, William Goodwin, William Gibbons, Richard Goodman, Samuel Greenhill, Geo. Graves, Seth Grant, Bartholomew Green, John Haynes, Edward Hopkins, Thomas Hooker, Thomas Hosmer, Stephen Hart, John Hopkins, William Hills, William Heyden, Thomas Hales, Samuel Hales, Wm. Hide, William Holton, John Higginson, Jonathan Ince, Thomas Judd, William Kelsey, William Lewis, Thomas Lord, Richard Lord, John Moody, John Marsh, John Maynard, Joseph Mygatt, James Olmsted, Richard Olmsted, Thomas Olcock, William Pantry, John Pratt, Stephen Post, William Parker, William Pratt, William Ruscoe, Nathaniel Richards, Thomas Root, Samuel Stone, John Steel, Thomas Scott, William Spencer, Thomas Stanley, Timothy Stanley, Edward Stebbins, George Steel, John Skinner, John Stone, Thomas Spencer, Arthur Smith, George Stocking, Thomas Stanton, Thomas Selden, John Talcott, George Wyllys, Thomas Welles, John Webster, William Whiting, William Westwood, Andrew Warner, Nathaniel Ward, William Wadsworth, Gregory Winterton, Samuel Wakeman, Richard Webb, Richard Wrisley, John Wilcox.

In addition to this class of proprietors, there were others who by the courtesy of the town had the privilege of wood and keeping cows, &c. on the common, viz :

John Brunson, John Biddell, (Bidwell) Thomas Barnes, Benjamin Burre, Nathaniel Barding, Thomas Blisse, Thomas Blisse, jr., Widow Betts, Thomas Bunce, William Cornwell, Nicholas Disbroe, Hosea Goodwin, Daniel Garwood, John Ginnings, Thomas Gridley, John Hallaway, John Hall, George Hubbard, Ralph Keylor, Nathaniel Kellogg, Thomas Lord, jr., Benjamin Munn, John Morrice, John Olmsted, John Purcase, William Phillips, John Pierce, Paul Peck, Tho's Richards, Richard Seymour, John Sables, Giles Smith, Thomas Upson, Thomas Woodford, Robert Wade, Richard Watts, Henry Walkley, James Walkley, William Watts, William Westley. Whether Tho's Reed, Thomas Fisher, John Friend, Thomas Goodfellow, Thomas Hungerfoot or ford, Thomas Munson, Renold Marvin, Abraham Pratt, and Samuel Whitehead were there at this time is uncertain—they had owned lots previous to 1639, and had sold them, or not fulfilled the conditions of the grant.

If all these persons were settlers in Hartford at the land division in 1639, and had families, as probably most of them had, there must have been from 500 to 800 settlers in Hartford in 1639.

The following persons, it is supposed, came from England to Massachusetts with Mr. Warham in 1632–3, viz :

Henry Wolcott, William Phelps, George Phelps, John Whitefield, Humphrey Pinny, Dea. John Moore, Dea. William Gaylord, Lieut. Walter Fyler, Matthew Grant, Thomas Dibble, Samuel Phelps, Nathan Gillett, Richard Vere or Voar, Abraham Randall, B. Egglestone and Thomas Ford, all of whom settled at Windsor under the pastoral charge of Mr. Warham.

The following persons who first came to Hartford from Massachusetts, were from the county of Essex, in England, and probably from Braintree, in 1632, viz :

Jeremy Adams, Matthew Allyn, Richard Butler, Edward Elmer, Richard Goodman, William Goodwin, Stephen Hart, John Haynes,

(Thomas Hooker, Chelmsford) Thomas Hosmer, William Lewis, Richard Lord, James Olmsted, Daniel Patrick, John Pratt, William Pantry, Nathaniel Richards, William Spencer, Thomas Spencer, Edward Stebbins, John Steel, Henry Steel, Samuel Stone, John Talcott, William Wadsworth, Andrew Warner, Richard Webb, William Westwood, John White. These men, with others, went to Newton before Mr. Hooker; Mr. Hooker arrived and was settled there in October, 1633.

The following persons, mentioned by the Rev. Mr. Hotchkiss, were the early settlers of Saybrook, viz :

D. Gardner, J. Winthrop, Higginson, Peters, Barker, Bull, William Bushnell, Clark, Lay, Lord, Parker, Pratt, Post, Champion, Griswold, Lee, Wade, Backus, Bliss, Huntington, Hyde, Larrabee, Leffingwell, Breed, Chalker, Waterhouse, Kirtland, Shipman, Whittelsey, and Willard.

Many of these persons must have came directly to Saybrook, as their names do not appear upon any of the records of the three towns first settled ; the remainder of them removed there from Windsor, Hartford and Wethersfield.

An Alphabetical List of the First Settlers of Enfield ; and a Genealogical View, comprising only those persons whose descendants are now settled in that town.

Abbe, Thomas—one of the original proprietors of the town, died 1728, had two sons settled in Enfield. Thomas, b. 1686, married Mary Pease, daughter of Capt. John Pease, 1714, d. 1745, had two sons, (1.) Obabiah, b. 1728, d. 1745 ; (2.) Thomas, b. 1731, married Penelope Terry, daughter of Dr. Ebenezer Terry, d. 1811, aged 81, leaving children ; John, b. 1692, one of the first settlers of the upper part of " King's street," had four sons—John, b. 1717, married Sarah Root, daughter of Timothy Root, of Somers, 1739, settled in the east part of the town, d. 1794, left two sons, who both settled and died in the east part of Enfield. Thomas, b. 1721, and Daniel, b. 1726, both died at Cape Breton, 1745, without children. Richard, 4th son of John Abbe, b. 1735, m. Mary Bement, daughter of Capt. Dennis Bement, 1755, d. 1807, left children.

Allen, John—one of the first settlers of King's street, supposed to have come from Deerfield about 1700, d. 1739, aged 69—had two sons who settled in Enfield. Azariah, b. 1701, m. Martha Burt, of Longmeadow, d. 1787, left one son, Moses, who settled and died in

Enfield. Ebenezer, 2d son of John Allen, was b. 1712, settled and died in the south part of Enfield, left four sons, two of whom settled and died in East Windsor, two in Enfield.

Allen, Samuel—married Hannah Burroughs, 1700, settled in King's street, d. 1735, aged 62—had three sons. Samuel, b. 1702, m. Elizabeth Booth, 1728, settled in E. Windsor, where he died. Joseph, b. 1704, settled and died in E. Windsor. John, b. 1712, m. Abigail Pease, 1737, d. 1791, left one child, settled in Enfield.

Bement, John—first settler on lot now occupied by his descendants —came in 1682, d. 1684, left three sons. John, d. 1703, had two sons—Benjamin, b. 1698, m. Elizabeth Abbe, 1723, removed to Simsbury. John, b. 1701, history unknown. William, 2d son of John, sen'r., m. Hannah Terry, daughter of Capt. Samuel Terry, 1707, settled in the east part of the town, died 1728, left four sons. William, b. 1708, m. Phoebe Markham, and removed to Windham. Samuel, b. 1720. Ebenezer, b. 1723. Joseph, b. 1725, settled and died in Enfield, without children. Edmund, 3d son of John, sen'r., m. Prudence Morgan, 1700 and Priscilla Warner 2d wife, 1703, d. 1745, had three sons ; Jonathan, b. 1705, removed to Suffield, d. in the Cape Breton expedition ; Dennis, b. 1711, m. Mary Abbe, daughter of Tho's Abbe, 1737, d. 1789, had two sons, Dennis and Edmund, both settled and died in Enfield. Edmund, 3d son of Edmund, sen'r., b. 1713, settled in East Hartford.

Booth, Simeon—a first settler in 1680, d. soon after, left two sons ; William, m. Hannah Burroughs, daughter of John B., 1693, d. 1753, aged 89, had two sons ; Caleb, b. 1695, m. Mary Gleason, 1728, settled in E. Windsor, had a numerous family ; one of his sons, Levi, d. in Enfield, 1815, aged 76, without children ; Joshua, 2d son, born 1697, settled first in Enfield, had two sons ; Oliver, b. 1725, and William, b. 1731. Zachariah, 2d son of Simeon Booth, m. Mary Warriner, 1691, and Mary Harman, 2d wife, 1696, d. 1741, had two sons ; John, b. 1697, m. Lydia Chandler, daughter of Henry Chandler, 1727, d. 1778, left two sons ; John, b. 1728, m. Hannah Phelps, 1751, d. in Enfield, leaving children ; Daniel, b. 1744, removed to Ohio in 1811, and died leaving children ; Joseph, 2d son of Z. Booth, b. 1710, m. Sarah Chandler, daughter of Henry C., 1736, d. in Enfield, had six sons ; Joseph, b. 1736, m. Mary Hale, 1762, died in Enfield, and left children ; Isaac, b. 1739, m. Deborah Hurlburt, 1764 ; Samuel, b. 1740 ; Zachariah, b. 1742, settled and died in Enfield, leaving a family ; Henry, b. 1745, and David, b. 1747.

Bush, Jonathan—a first settler, 1680, d. 1739, aged 89, had two sons; Jonathan, m. Rachel Kibbe, daughter of Elisha Kibbe, d. 1746, aged 65, left four sons; Joshua, b. 1712, m. Experience French, 1737, settled in "Terry Lane," d. 1793, had three sons; Joshua, b. 1737, died in Enfield; Eli, b. 1741, moved to New York and died; Jonathan, b. 1747, died also in New York State; Moses, 2d son of Jonathan Bush, jr., b. 1714; Aaron, 3d son, b. 1717, m. Alice French, d. 1805, had five sons; Caleb, 4th son, b. 1725, left town; John, 2d son of Jonathan Bush, sen'r., b. 1685, d. young, left one son, Joseph, b. 1718.

Collins, Rev. Nathaniel—first settled minister of Enfield, began the ministry in 1700, m. Alice Adams, 1701, d. 1756, had four sons; John, b. 1705, m. Mary Meacham, daughter of Isaac Meacham, jr., 1728, d. 1746; Nathaniel, 2d son of Rev. Nathaniel, b. 1709, m. Abigail Pease, daughter of James Pease, 1735, d. 1787, left one son, Eliphalet, b. 1744, settled and died in Enfield; William, 3d son of Rev. Nathaniel, b. 1711, m. Ann Collins, 1734, settled and died in Somers; Edward, 4th son, b. 1713, m. Tabitha Geer, 1736, d. 1796, left descendants who left town.

Chandler, Henry—one of the early settlers of the N. W. part of Enfield, came from Andover, 1723, and purchased 700 acres of land, d. 1737, aged 70, had five sons; Henry, d. 1735, left three sons, who left town; Samuel, b. 1699, d. 1761; Daniel, b. 1701, m. Sarah Keep, 1728, d. 1785, left two sons—Daniel, b. 1732, d. 1805 out of town—Joseph, b. 1738, d. 1816, in Enfield, and left children; Nehemiah, 4th son of Henry Chandler, b. 1702, m. Mary Burroughs, daughter of John B., 1737, d. 1756, aged 54, had five sons—Samuel, b. 1737, Jonathan, b. 1742, died young, Nehemiah, b. 1744, d. 1814, John, b. 1746, died young, Joel, b. 1748, left town; Zebulon b. 1754, left town; Isaac, youngest son of Henry Chandler, b. 1717, m. Abigail Hale, 1741, d. 1787, aged 70, had five sons, Isaac, David, Henry, Nathaniel, and John. Henry Chandler had six daughters—five settled in Enfield. Lydia, m. John Booth, 1728, d. 1780, Abigail m. John Rumerill, 1728, d. 1772, Sarah, m. Joseph Booth, 1736, d. 1777, Deborah, m. Ebenezer Colton, d. 1769, Hannah m. Ezekiel Pease, 1732, d. 1756, Mary, m. Timothy Pease, 1736, d. 1789.

Chapin, Ebenezer—an early settler near Scantic—the son of Japhet Chapin, of Springfield, d. 1772, aged 97, left eleven sons; Ebenezer, b. 1705, m. Elizabeth Pease, daughter of Jonathan P., d. 1751, left two sons, Ebenezer, b. 1735, settled in Enfield, d. 1822, left children, history of the other son unknown; Noah, 2d son of Ebenezer Chapin, sen'r., b. 1707, left town, as also Seth, b. 1709, Moses, b. 1712, and Aaron, b. 1714, m. Sybil Markham, daughter of Daniel M., 1745 ; Elias, b. 1716, died out of town ; Reuben, b. 1718, settled in Salisbury; Charles, b. 1720, died in Western N. Y., 1812 ; David, b. 1722, settled at New Hartford ; Elisha, b. 1725, died unmarried, as also Phineas, b. 1726.

Gleason, Isaac—a first settler, d. 1698, aged 44, left two sons ;— Isaac, b. 1687, m. Mary, daughter of John Prior, 1712, settled and died in the S. E. part of the town, had four sons—Isaac, b. 1715, settled in Enfield ; Jonah, b. 1724, ditto, had a family ; Joseph, b. 1726, m. Hannah Colton, 1746, settled and died in Enfield, left children ; Job, b. 1734, settled in Enfield for a time. Thomas, 2d son of Isaac Gleason, sen'r. b. 1690, supposed to have moved to Farmington.

Hale, Thomas—an early settler, m. Priscilla Markham, 1695, d. 1725, had five sons, who settled in Enfield ; John, m. Mary Gleason, 1716, d. 1753 ,left two sons, who settled in Enfield—Thomas, b. 1727, m. Elizabeth Bush, 1753, died leaving children—David, b. 1732, m. Hannah Warriner, d. 1796. William, 2d son of Thomas Hale, sen'r., died in Enfield, had two sons—William, b. 1724, left town—Jonathan, b. 1729, died in Enfield. Joseph, 3d son of Thomas Hale, sen'r., m. Phoebe Warriner, 1725, had three sons, two died in Enfield. Samuel, 4th son, b. 1698, d. 1774, left one son, b. 1762, died at Greenwich, Mass., 1830. Thomas, youngest son of Thomas, sen'r., died in Enfield about 1759.

Hurlburt, William—an early settler near the south part of the town, d. 1734, had three sons ; William, b. 1698; Obadiah, b. 1703, m. for 2d wife, Esther Colton, 1745, d. 1784, had four sons—William, b. 1731, Obadiah, b. 1738, settled and died in Enfield, 1811, left children, Ebenezer, b. 1747, Job, b. 1750, settled and died in Somers, 1827, Eliphalet, b. 1752. Benjamin, the other son of William Hurlburt, lived in Enfield until he had five sons—Abel, b. 1741, Benjamin, b. 1746, Berijah. b. 1749, Ambrose, b. 1752, Elisha, b. 1756.

Killam, Lot—a first settler in the south part of the town, d. 1683, aged between 40 and 50—the first person who died in the settlement ; left one son, James, who settled and died in Enfield, 1761, aged 84, and had one son, Lot, b. 1717, m. Jemima, daughter of James Pease, 1739, d. 1772, aged 54, left one son who settled and died in Enfield, James Killam had seven daughters—Elizabeth, m. Samuel Vining. 1721, died young, Patience, b. 1701, m. John Osborne, of Ridgefield, 1726, Sarah, b. 1703, m. Ebenezer Morris, of Woodstock, 1728, Hannah, b. 1706, m. Josiah Wood, of Somers, 1724, Ruth, b. 1709, m. Edward Farrington, 1728, Mary, b. 1712, Thankful, b. 1715, m. Israel Meacham, 1737.

Markham, Daniel—one of the first settlers in the east part of the town, m. Deborah Meacham, daughter of Capt. Isaac, 1703, d. 1761, aged 88, had five sons ; Daniel, who moved to Stafford, Israel, m. Ann Spencer, 1733, died in Enfield, had three sons, Nathan, b. 1737, died in Enfield, Barzillai, b. 1740, left town, Darius, b. 1745, died in Enfield. ·Isaac, 3d son of Daniel Markham, sen'r. m. Jemima Pease. 1734, settled in Enfield until he had three sons—Ambrose, b. 1746, Ebenezer, b. 1750, Isaac, b. 1752, died out of town—Jeremiah, another son of Daniel Markham, m. Sarah Hale, 1734, died out of town— Joseph, youngest son of Daniel Markham, m. Abigail Booth, 1740, died of small pox, 1763, had four sons ; Joseph, b. 1742, m. Abigail Meacham, 1761, died out of town—Justus, b. 1744, died in Enfield— Jehiel, b. 1746, died out of town, as also the youngest, Isaac.

Meacham, Isaac—a first settler, d. 1715, had seven sons ; Isaac, d. 1715, left two sons—Benjamin, b. 1701, m. Elizabeth Pease, 1722, d. 1770, had eight sons—Benjamin, b. 1723, d. 1776, left children— Isaac, b. 1725, died at Cape Breton, 1746—James, b. 1728, went to New Hampshire—Abner, b. 1732, died in the French war—Joel, b. 1735, m. Priscilla Simons, 1760—Isaac b. 1746, both died out of town. Samuel, 2d son of Isaac, jr., b. 1703, m. Sarah Pope, 1727, settled and died in Somers. Israel, 2d son of Isaac Meacham, sen'r., d. 1715, without children. Jeremiah, 3d son, d. 1740, aged 75, without children. Ebenezer, 4th son, settled in the N. E. part of Enfield, had three sons born in Enfield—Ebenezer, b. 1721, m. Rachel Hale, 1749 —Jeremiah, b. 1725, and Barnabas, b. 1734. Ebenezer Meacham, sen'r., d. 1744, aged 66. Ichabod, 5th son of Isaac, sen'r., died in Enfield, 1766, had two sons—Ichabod, b. 1725, died in Enfield, left children, John, b. 1728, died in Middlefield, Mass. John, 6th son, settled in the N. E. part of Enfield, died 1765, aged 84, had two sons, Israel, m. Thankful Killam, 1737, died at Salisbury, 1760, Joseph, d. 1794, aged 82. Joseph, youngest son of Isaac, sen'r., b. 1685, settled as first minister of Coventry, 1713, and there died.

Parsons, Benjamin—one of the Proprietors' Committee, died at Springfield soon after the settlement of Enfield, had two sons who settled in Enfield ; Benjamin, first settler near the centre, d. 1728, left two sons, Benjamin, b. 1688, d. 1734, without children, Christopher, b. 1691, m. Mary Pease, 1714, d. 1749, had seven sons, John,

b. 1716, m. Ann Colton, 1740, d. 1773, had one son, John, b. 1744, settled and died in Enfield, and one son, Ebenezer, b. 1746, left town. Christopher, 2d son of Christopher Parsons, sen'r. b. 1717, d. 1789, had two sons, Asahel, b. 1747, and Christopher, b. 1748, both died in Enfield. Ebenezer, 3d son of Christopher, sen'r., died at Cape Breton, 1746, aged 21. Joseph, b. 1724, m. Rebecca Allen, 1751, died out of town, left children. Benjamin, b. 1729, d. 1795, left children. The sixth son b. 1731, history unknown. Noah, b. 1734, died at the north in the French war. Samuel, 2d son of Benjamin Parsons, sen'r. d. 1736, aged 69, had seven sons ; John, b. 1693, m. Thankful Root, 1716, settled and died in Somers—Luke, b. 1696, m. Sarah Osborn, 1716, settled and died in Somers—Hezekiah, b. 1698, settled in Enfield, d. 1748, had five sons, Hezekiah, d. in Enfield, 1815, David, b. 1732, died aged 73, Eldad, b. 1734, m. Elizabeth Meacham, 1763, d. in Enfield, Jonathan, b. 1741, left town, as also, Charles, b. 1742. Nathaniel, 4th son of Samuel, sen'r., b. 1702, m. Mary Pope, 1726, settled in Somers. Moses, 5th son, b. 1707, died in Enfield, 1786, had four sons, Wareham, b. 1737, d. 1802, left children, Daniel, b. 1744, settled and died in Enfield, Caleb, b. 1746, Peter, b. 1752. Samuel, sixth son of Samuel, sen'r., b. 1714, history unknown, and ditto, Aaron, born 1717.

Parsons, Philip—a first settler 1697, d. in Enfield, had five sons ; Philip, b. 1708 ; Nathaniel, b. 1712, m. Alice Collins, 1736, had six sons, Nathaniel, b. 1736, settled in Enfield, Asa, b. 1742, Edward, b. 1745, d. in Springfield, Ebenezer, b. 1748, William, b. 1750, died in E. Windsor, Shubael, b. 1752, died in Enfield, 1819. Shubael, 3d son of Philip Parsons, sen'r., b. 1715, died in Enfield at an advanced age, without children. Thomas, 4th son, b. 1718, died in Enfield, 1811. His eldest son, Elijah, b. 1745, d. 1797. Ebenezer, fifth son, b. 1724, died young.

Pease, John—from Salem, Mass., came to Enfield in 1680, d. 1689, aged 60, left six sons, all of whom settled in Enfield. John, jr. came to Enfield in 1679, m. Margaret Adams, of Ipswich, d. 1734, aged 80 or 82, left three sons and four daughters ; John, b. 1678, at Salem, m. Elizabeth Spencer, of Hartford, d. 1761, aged 83, left one son, John, b. 1726, m. Bathsheba Jones, daughter of Thomas J., 1752, d. 1810, aged 84, left four sons and two daughters. James, 2d son of John Pease, jr., b. at Salem, 1679, came to Enfield, 1679, m. Mary, daughter of Thomas Abbe, 1710, settled in Somers, 1713, there died, had one son, Richard, b. 1717, settled and died in Somers. Joseph, 3d son of John, jr., b. 1693, m. Mary Spencer, of Hartford, 1727, d. 1757, left three sons, Joseph, b. 1728, Stephen, b. 1731, Jonathan, b. 1740, all left town. Joseph died in Suffield. Margaret, eldest daughter of John Pease, jr., b. 1683, first child born in Enfield, m. Josiah Colton, 1709, d. 1775, had two sons and five daughters ; Josiah, b. 1709, Job, b. 1711, Esther, b. 1714, m. Obadiah Hurlburt, 1745, Margaret, b. 1716, m. David Phelps, 1737, Abiel, b. 1718, m. Col. John Bliss, of Wilbraham, d. 1803, Ann, b. 1720, m. John Parsons, 1740, Hannah, m. Joseph Gleason, 1745. Sarah, 2d daughter, m. Timothy Root, 1710, settled in Somers, 1713, d. 1750, had two sons and five daughters, Timothy, b. 1719, Thomas, b. 1726, Elizabeth, m. Ebenezer Spencer, 1733, Sarah, m. John Abbe, 1739. Mary, 3d daughter of John Pease, jr., m. Thomas Abbe, 1714, d. 1746, had two sons and five daughters ; Obadiah, b. 1728, d. young, Thomas, b. 1731, d. 1811, Mary, m. Dennis Bement, 1737, Sarah, m. Nathaniel Chapin, Tabitha, m. Ephraim Pease, 1740. Ann, 4th daughter, m. Jeremiah Lord, 1719, settled in E. Windsor, d, 1753, had two sons and one daughter.

Pease, Robert—second son of John, sen'r., came to Enfield in 1679, d. 1744, aged 88, had four sons ; Robert, b. 1684, m. Hannah Sexton, first wife, had one daughter who married Nathaniel Pease—second wife, Elizabeth Emery, had four sons and one daughter, Robert, b. 1724, Emery, b. 1727, Abiel and Noah, all with their father settled and died in Somers. Samuel, 2d son of Robert, sen'r., b. 1686, m. Elizabeth Warner, 1717, had four sons and four daughters, Samuel, b. 1717, m. Teriah Chapin, settled and died in Enfield, left children, Ephraim, b. 1719, m. Tabitha Abbe, 1740, d. 1801, had three sons who died young, and four daughters, Tabitha, d. young, Sybil, m. Rev. Elam Potter, Nancy, m. Augustus Diggins, Agnes, m. Rev. Nehemiah Prudden. Aaron, 3d son of Samuel, sen'r., m. Anna Geer, 1751, settled and died in Enfield, left children. Nathaniel, 4th son, m. Eunice Allen, 1754, died in Norfolk. Mary, eldest daughter of Samuel, sen'., m. James Gains, had one son and two daughters. Elizabeth, 2d daughter, m. John Allen, had one son and two daughters. Joanna, m. Benjamin Root, had one son and one daughter. Mary, m. Christopher Parsons, had three sons and four daughters. Daniel, 3d son of Robert Pease, sen'r., b. 1692, m. Abigail Fletcher and settled in Somers, had four sons, Daniel, b. 1718, William, Parker and Asa, and four daughters, rest unknown. Ebenezer, 4th son of Robert, sen'r., b. 1698, m. Mindwell Sexton, d. 1743, had two sons, Ebenezer, m. Mary Terry, 1739, d. 1784, aged 70, left children, James, b. 1724, had five daughters, Hannah, m. Shubael Geer, had two sons and four daughters. Abigail, m. George Pyncheon, of Springfield, had three sons and two daughters, Mindwell, m. Amos Bull, 1741, had five sons and four daughters, Catherine, m. Benjamin Hall, 1746, had three sons and five daughters, Martha, m. Caleb Bush, had six sons and five daughters. Abigail, a daughter of Robert Pease, sen'r., m. Israel Phelps, 1703, had one son and three daughters. Hannah, m. David Miller, first husband, had one daughter, second husband, Gershom Sexton, had five sons and four daughters.

Pease, Abraham—third son of John, sen'r., m. Jane Mentor, died 1735, without children.

Pease, Jonathan—fourth son of John, sen'r., m. Elizabeth Booth, daughter of Zachariah, 1693, d. 1721, left three sons ; David, b. 1698, went to the South, Josiah, b. 1706, moved to Massachusetts, Pelatiah, b. 1709, m. Jemima Booth, 1736, d. 1769, had four sons and one daughter—one son, Jonathan, died at Schenectady, 1760. Rebecca, a daughter of Jonathan, m. John Pierce, 1736, had four sons and two daughters. Elizabeth, another daughter of Jonathan, m. Ebenezer Chapin, had two sons and five daughters.

Pease, James—fifth son of John, sen'r., came to Enfield when ten years old, m. Hannah Harman, 1695, d. 1748, left one son and six daughters ; Joseph, b. 1712, d. 1800, had four sons, Noah, b. 1736, Joseph, d. 1758, Gideon settled and died in Enfield, James, d. in Somers, 1830. Hannah, eldest daughter of James, b. 1700, m. Benjamin Terry, 1721, had six sons and three daughters. Elizabeth, b. 1703, m. Benjamin Meacham, 1722, had eight sons and three daughters. Mary, b. 1706, m. Jacob Terry, 1730, had five sons and two daughters. Abigail, b. 1708, m. Nathaniel Collins, 1735, had three sons and six daughters. Sarah, b. 1710, m. Jonathan Terry, had two sons and two daughters. Jemima, b. 1716, m. Lot Killam, 1739, had four sons and six daughters.

Pease, Isaac—youngest son of John, sen'r., m. Mindwell Osborn, 1691, d. 1731, aged 59, left seven sons and two daughters ; Isaac, b. 1693, m. Amie French, 1722, d. 1757, had four sons, Isaac, settled and died in Enfield, left children, Abner, and Jacob unknown, Noadiah, m. Terzah Smith, 1765, went to Sandisfield, Mass. ; one daughter, Ann, m. Ebenezer Hall, 1753 ; Laurani, m. John Gains, 1755. Abraham, 2d son of Isaac, sen'r., b. 1695, m. first wife Jemima Booth, 1719, had three sons and one daughter, Abraham, b. 1721, John, b. 1725, settled in Suffield, one son died young, the daughter m. William

Lord, 1752 ; by his second wife, Abigail Warner, he had nine sons and one daughter, viz : Moses, settled and died in Enfield, aged 91, left children, Samuel, d. 1772, aged 35, left children, Joel b. 1737, Nathan, b. 1740, went to Wilbraham, Gideon, b. 1741, went to Massachusetts, Josiah b. 1744, William b. 1746, died in Enfield, Zebulon b. 1749, d. 1829, one son died young—the daughter m. Nathaniel Parsons. Abraham Pease d. 1750, aged 55. Israel, 3d son of Israel, sen'r., b. 1702, m. Sarah Booth, 1726, d. 1771, had five sons and four daughters ; Israel died in Massachusetts, left a family, David b. 1729, died in Enfield, Hezekiah died in Enfield, Jesse b. 1739, Nathan died in Enfield, Sarah m. Jeremiah Lord, Mindwell m. Ebenezer Terry, Alice m. Thomas Root, Bathsheba m. David Wilson. Ezekiel, 4th son of Isaac, sen'r., b. 1710, m. Hannah Chandler, 1732, d. 1799, had four sons and five daughters, Ezekiel m. Jemima Markham, moved to Vermont, Henry b. 1739, moved to Massachusetts, Isaac died in Enfield, left children, Oliver died young, Hannah m. Job Gleason, had three sons and seven daughters, Abiah m. Samuel Gowdy, 1759, had four sons and three daughters, Jane m. Obadiah Hurlburt, had one son and four daughters, Mahitabel m. Edward Parsons, had two sons and four daughters, Sarah m. Jehiel Markham, had two sons and two daughters. Timothy, 5th son of Isaac, sen'r., b. 1713, m. Mary Chandler, 1736, d. 1794, had three sons and nine daughters, Timothy b. 1737, Edward and James settled in Enfield, Mary m. Wareham Parsons, Abigail m. David Terry, Martha died young, Deborah m. Gideon Pease, Dorcas m. Isaac Pease, Lydia m. Ezekiel Pease, one daughter m. Benjamin King, one Samuel Hale, and one Freegrace Hancock. Cummings, 6th son of Isaac, sen'r., b. 1715, m. Elizabeth Pease, daughter of John, for first wife, had three sons, Cummings left town, Ebenezer, Asa, died in Enfield, and two daughters, Love m. Jacob Hills, and Ruth, David Hale. Cummings m. for second wife Sarah Hale, 1755, had two sons. Isaac Pease, sen'r., had two daughters, Ann m. Nathaniel Prior, 1725, and Abigail, history unknown. Benjamin, youngest son of Isaac, sen'r., b. 1717, m. Abigail Rose, d. 1768, had two sons, Benjamin m. Margaret Prior, died in Enfield, Sharon died in Hartford, two daughters died young, Abigail m. Zachariah Prior, 1759, Lucy m. Reuben Perkins, Rose m. Daniel Kingsbury, Damaris m. Edward Collins.

Phelps, Israel—a first settler near Scantic, married for first wife Mary Pease, 1703, had one son, Israel, who married Hannah Bement, daughter of William B. 1731, had a son Israel b. 1733, left town.

Israel Phelps, sen'r., married for second wife, widow Rachel Jones, 1713, had two sons, David b. 1716, m. Margaret Colton, 1737, d. 1803, left a family, Noah b. 1726.

Pierce, Nathaniel—a first settler in the S. E. part of the town, d. 1755, aged 84, had two sons; Nathaniel b. 1704, Joseph b. 1721, died in Enfield.

Prior, John—settled in Enfield in 1686, married Mary Geer, had six sons; Daniel b. 1697, died at Cape Breton, 1746, Nathaniel b. 1702, m. Ann Pease, 1725, d. 1786, had one son who settled and died in Enfield, Azariah b. 1705, left town, Ezekiel b. 1708, m. Deborah Geer, 1732, settled and died in Enfield, had one son who settled and died in Enfield, left a family, Ebenezer b. 1712, m. Hannah Simons, 1737, left town, and died in Vermont, old. John Prior m. Sarah Pease for second wife, 1721, had one son, John b. 1723, went to East Windsor.

Raynolds, Rev. Peter—settled as minister in Enfield in 1725, died 1768, aged 68, had four sons; Samuel b. 1728, settled as physician in Somers, d. 1774, Peter b. 1730, d. 1777, left two sons, John b. 1738, d. 1812, left children, Edward b. 1740, a daughter Margaret b. 1742, m. Doct. Simeon Field, 1763, died in Enfield.

Simons, William—a first settler, d. 1738, aged 79, had four sons; John b. 1695, m. Sarah Geer, 1722, had six sons, John b. 1724, Paul b. 1726, Ebenezer b. 1731, Asahel b. 1734, settled and died in Enfield, Edward b. 1740, and Titus b. 1744. William, 2d son of William, sen'r., b. 1696, m. Hannah Randall, first wife, and Margaret Parks, second wife, had five sons, William b. 1718, Timothy b. 1720, Stephen b. 1723, Benjamin b. 1731, settled and died in Enfield, 1805, Joseph b. 1729. James, 3d son of William, sen'r., b. 1699, m. Dorcas Foster, 1730. Philip, 4th son, b. 1702, m. Martha Bement, 1727, had one son, Philip b. 1734, Abel b. 1742, one daughter, Esther m. Caleb Jones, 1759.

Terry, Samuel—a first settler, married Hannah Morgan, daughter of Isaac M. 1682—the first marriage in the settlement—died 1730, had seven sons; Samuel b. 1690, went to N. York State, Ebenezer b. 1696, d. 1780, had three sons who settled in Enfield, Ebenezer b. 1722, d. 1817, aged 94, left children, Selah b. 1732, d. 1803, left children, Christopher Healms d. 1770, aged 34, left children. By his first wife, Samuel Terry, sen'r., had two daughters; Hannah m. William Bement, 1707, Rebecca m. John Pasko, 1713. By his second wife Martha Credan, Samuel, sen'r. had five sons; Benjamin b. 1698,

m. Hannah Pease, 1721, died in Enfield, had three sons who settled in Enfield, Benjamin b. 1728, m. Hannah Olmstead, 1756, died in Enfield, left children, Gideon b. 1737, died without posterity, Shadrach b. 1741, d. 1799, left children. Ephraim, 4th son of Samuel, sen'r., b. 1701, m. Ann Collins, 1723, d. 1783, left five sons, Samuel b. 1725, died in Enfield, 1798, left a family, Ephraim b. 1728, d. 1807, left children, Nathaniel b. 1730, d. 1792, left children, Elijah b. 1736, died in Enfield, left children, Eliphalet b. 1742, d. in Enfield, 1812, left children. Jacob, 5th son of Samuel, sen'r., b. 1704, m. Mary Pease, 1730, settled in Terry lane, d. 1779, had four sons, Jacob b. 1731, left town, Joseph b. 1732, died in Enfield, left children, Daniel b. 1743, died in Enfield without children—one son living in 1831, died soon after. Jonathan, 6th son of Samuel, sen'r., b. 1707, m. Sarah Pease, 1738, d. 1793, had two sons and two daughters. Isaac, youngest son of Samuel Terry, sen'r., b. 1713, died in Enfield in 1782, left children.—*Dr. John C. Pease.*

LIST OF FIRST SETTLERS,
Who have few or no Descendants in Enfield.

Abbe, Obadiah—settled in 1682, d. 1732, without children.

Adams, John—settled in 1697, lived in Enfield for some years, history unknown.

Bancraft, Thomas—settled in 1681, had one son, Nathaniel b. in Enfield, d. 1684.

Burroughs, John—settled in 1680, d. 1691, aged 42, had one son who settled in Enfield, and had the following sons born in the town : John b. 1711, Simon b. 1719, David b. 1724, Abner b. 1728, one daughter, Mary m. Nehemiah Chandler, sen'r., and d. 1807, Æ 95.

Bliss, John—an early settler, had one son, John b. in Enfield, in 1695. John Bliss went to Lebanon.

Bliss, Nathaniel—m. Mary Wright, settled in Enfield, 1697.

Bishop, David—an early settler, had one son, Thomas b. in town.

Citron, Benjamin—m. Sarah Bush, and settled in Enfield, 1718, had two sons b. in Enfield ; Benjamin b. 1721, Daniel b. 1723.

Collins, Daniel—a first settler in the south part of the town, d. 1690, aged 42, left one son, Nathan, who went to Brimfield, Mass.

Durell, John—an early settler, had two sons b. in Enfield ; John b. 1721 ; David b. 1723.

Fairman, John—an early settler in the lower part of town, died out of town, had one son, James b. 1683, m. Patience French, 1711, settled in the west part of Somers, died about 1722, had five sons ; James b. 1713, died in Enfield, John b. 1715, went to Wilbraham, Joseph b. 1717, Richard b. 1719, went to Newtown, Benjamin the youngest, m. Hannah McGregory, 1741, first wife, and Abigail Bement, second wife, 1749, died at Havanna.

French, Ephraim—a first settler in the north part of the town, d. 1716, had one son, Richard, who died 1757, aged 83, had three sons ; Ephraim b. 1708, settled in the east part of the town, Richard born 1712, d. at Ticonderoga, 1759, John b. 1716, d. 1775.

Gains, Benoni—an early settler, m. Abigail Fairman, 1700, had three sons ; Benoni b. 1706, d. 1741, John b. 1708, m. Hannah Chandler, 1736, d. 1784, had one son, John b. 1737, m. Lauraina Pease, 1755, left town. James, 3d son of Benoni, sen'r., b. 1710, m. Mabel Pease, had one son, James b. 1741.

Gary, Nathaniel—an early settler from Barnstable, had a large family, five daughters married in Enfield ; Mahitabel m. Ebenezer Jones, 1719, Rachel m. Nicholas Hall, 1721, Mary m. Thomas Whipple, 1722, Rebecca m. Samuel Gibbs, 1731, Abigail m. Gershom Sexton, 1736.

Geer, Thomas—a first settler in the south part of the town, died in 1722, aged 99, had one son, Shubael, who settled in Enfield, m. Sarah Abbe, 1706, had two sons ; Shubael b. 1717, had four sons and four daughters, Thomas b. 1722, m. Hannah Abbe, had two sons, Thomas b. 1746, Elihu b. 1749, died in Enfield. Sarah, eldest daughter of Shubael Geer, sen'r., b. 1704, m. John Simons, 1723, Deborah b. 1707, m. Ezekiel Prior, 1732, Mary b. 1710, m. Roger Griswold, 1731, Tabitha b. 1712, m. Edward Collins, Bathsheba b. 1715, m. Charles Sexton, 1745, Anna m. Aaron Pease, 1751, Elizabeth b. 1720, m. Ebenezer Terry.

Hall, Ichabod, Nicholas and John—three brothers, were early settlers in the east part of Enfield. Nicholas settled at Coal Meadow, had two sons ; Benjamin b. 1723, left town, Joseph died in the Revolution. Ichabod settled on the Somers road, had three sons, Ebenezer b. 1730, went to Tyringham, Moses b. 1732, Elisha b. 1751. John settled near Scantic, d. 1775, aged 51, had six sons, Israel, John, Joel, Azariah, Daniel and Levi, all left town.

Hayward, Thomas—settled in Enfield in 1682, had two sons ; Nathaniel and John. The family lived in Enfield twenty or thirty years, and finally removed to New London and other places.

Hitchcock, David—an early settler, had two sons born in Enfield ;

David b. 1708, Paul b. 1714. David, sen'r. m. Mary Thomas, 2d wife, 1717.

Horton, Nathaniel—an early settler in the south part of the town, afterwards went to Somers, had two sons; Nathaniel b. 1695, m. Hannah Parsons, 1720, d. 1790, had one son, Aaron b. 1733, d. 1806. David Horton, 2d son of Nathaniel b. 1698.

Jones, Benjamin—one of the first settlers of Enfield, and the first settler of Somers in 1706, d. 1718, had six sons; Thomas m. Mary Meacham, daughter of Capt. Isaac, 1708, d. 1763, aged 83, had four sons and four daughters, Mary b. 1709, m. Abraham Whipple, 1731. Jerusha, 2d daughter of Thomas Jones, b. 1711, m. Jonathan Spencer, 1731, settled in Somers. Thomas, b. 1713, died in the Cape Breton expedition, 1746, Israel b. 1716, went to Barkhamsted, Rev. Isaac b. 1717, settled in Mass., Bathsheba b. 1720, m. John Pease, Elizabeth m. David Kellogg, of Westfield, 1747, Samuel b. 1724, d. 1743. Mary, the wife of Thomas Jones, d. 1744./ Ebenezer, 2d son of Benjamin Jones, m. Priscilla Smith, 1713, settled in Somers, Eleazer m. Mahitabel Gary, 1719, settled in Somers, Benjamin b. 1710, Levi b. 1716, one other son, name unknown.

Kibbe, Elisha—a first settler near the middle of the town, died 1735, aged 97, had four sons, Edward, one of the first settlers of Somers, in 1713, had four sons born in Enfield, Edward b. 1694, m. Esther Fowler, 1720, settled in Somers, Elisha b. 1698, m. Mahitabel Felt, 1728, settled in Somers, his eldest son, Elisha b. 1729, d. in Enfield, 1805. Jacob, 3d son of Edward Kibbe, b. 1701, m. Grace Citron, 1723, settled in Somers, Israel b. 1704, m. Sarah Horton, 1725, settled in Somers, left sons. John Kibbe, 2d son of Elisha, sen'r., settled near the centre of the town, had one son, John b. 1699, moved to Stafford, left three sons. James Kibbe, 3d son of Elisha, sen'r., settled in the north part of the town, had four sons born in Enfield; James b. 1707, Isaac b. 1712, Stephen b. 1714, David b. 1723, and one daughter who married Samuel Billings, 1733, and settled in Somers. Isaac, youngest son of Elisha, sen'r.. b. 1683, the first male child born in Enfield, died 1766, had one son, married Margaret Terry, 1755, d. 1779. Rachel, daughter of Elisha, sen'r., b. 1688, m. Jonathan Bush, first husband, d. 1786.

McGregory, John—married Hannah Pease, 1712, one of the first settlers of Somers, afterwards went to the N. E. part of Enfield, and died there, had two sons; John b. 1714, died in Enfield, Ebenezer died in Enfield, left a large family, four sons and seven daughters, (three of the daughters were born at one birth.)

Miller, Andrew—an early settler, died 1708, aged 60, had one son, David, who m. Hannah Miller, 1713, d. 1715.

Morgan, Isaac—settled in 1682, was drowned, November, 1706, aged 56, had one daughter who married Capt. Samuel Terry.

Osborn, Samuel—early settler, died in 1713, aged 60, had one son, Isaac, who married Elizabeth Jones, 1715, one son, Samuel b. 1694.

Pasco, John—early settler, died 1706, had one son, John, who married Rebecca Terry, 1713, and one son, Jonathan b. 1687.

Pease, Robert, 2d—from England, came to Enfield in 1687, married Hannah Warriner, 1691, had three sons ; Nathaniel b. 1702, m. Miriam, daughter of Robert Pease, 3d, 1730, had three sons, Nathaniel b. 1737, left town, Levi b. 1739, settled in Shrewsbury, Ms., and died in 1821, Abel b. 1741. Joseph, 2d son of Robert, 2d., b. 1707. Benjamin, 3d son.

Perkins, Thomas—early settler, married Sarah Richards, in 1694, d. 1709, aged 43, left one son, Thomas b. 1695, m. Widow Mary Allen, 1718, settled in the east part of Enfield, died 1770, had five sons by first wife, Thomas b. 1720, d. 1768, John b. 1723, left town for Massachusetts, as did Israel, Daniel b. 1730, died in Enfield, 1803, Elias moved to Derby. By his second wife Thomas Perkins had two sons, both left Enfield.

Pierce, John—died in 1743, aged 60 ; his eldest son, John married Rebecca Pease, 1736, settled in the N. E. part of Enfield.

Randall, William—an early settler, and one of the original Proprietors of the town, lived in Enfield several years, and had daughters there married.

Rumerill, Simon—married Sarah Fairman in 1692, and settled in Enfield, had three sons born in Enfield ; Simon b. 1696, Ebenezer b. 1701, settled in Enfield, had one son, Ebenezer b. 1729. John, 3d son of Simon, sen'r., b. 1704, settled in Enfield, had one son, John b. 1728.

Sexton, Joseph—early settler, died in 1742, aged 76, had one son, Gershom, who married Widow Hannah Miller, and settled in the east part of Enfield in 1716, had four sons ; Gershom b. 1717, Jonathan and David b. 1725, Asahel b. 1733. Joseph, another son of Joseph, sen'r., m. Sarah Parsons, 1723, had one son, Joseph b. 1724. Daniel, a son of Joseph, sen'r., settled in Somers, had one son, Daniel b. 1737, and Stephen b. 1741, Joseph b. 1743. Charles, a son of Joseph, sen'r., b. 1708, m. Bathsheba Geer, 1738, left town.

Trumbull, John—settled in Enfield in 1691, left town soon.

Trumbull, Joseph—died in Enfield in 1761.

Warriner, Joseph—from Northfield, settled in Enfield in 1791, had two sons; Ebenezer and John, who both settled in Enfield. The last of this family, Samuel, b. 1719, d. 1788.

Weld, Daniel—married Mary Warriner, and settled in Enfield in 1711, had four sons; Daniel b. 1719, Joseph b. 1726, Samuel b. 1728, Edmund b. 1732.

West, Joseph and Benjamin—two brothers, settled in Enfield in 1686. Benjamin married Hannah Haddock, 1692, had one son, Benjamin b. 1692. This family removed to Middletown.—*Dr. Pease.*

CATALOGUE

NAMES OF THE FIRST PURITAN SETTLERS OF
CONNECTICUT.

CONTINUED.

A.

ABBE, Samuel, of Windham, (No. 3, p. 110,) Abraham Mitchell, married his widow, he and Mary Abbe, were administrators on the estate of Samuel Abbe in 1698. John Abbe, of Windham, died Dec. 1700 ; he left a widow and children, and married a widow who had children by her first husband. The name of Abbe is first found in the colony at Wethersfield ; the names of Hebard or Hibbard and Ripley are first found at Windham. (See p. 110.)

Ackley, Henry, settled at Stamford, 1662.

Ackley, Nicholas, of Haddam, died April 29, 1695. He left a widow and children, John, Nathaniel, James, Hannah, Mary, Sarah and Lydia—perhaps another son. He moved from Hartford to Haddam. (For Ashley, p. 13, read Ackley—see p. 110.)

Alderman, William, of Farmington, died about 1697, left a widow, perhaps children.

Allyn, Col. Matthew, jr., of Windsor, grandson of Hon. Matthew, sen'r., married Elizabeth Wolcott, a grand daughter of Hon. Henry, sen'r. An estate had fallen to his wife Elizabeth, from her grand father Wolcott, which was situated in the Parishes of Tolland and Ledyard Lauran, in the county of Sommerset, and at Willington, called Long Forth, in England. In June, 1740, he made a will solely to dispose of this property, without including any of his property in this country. At this time he disposed of his rents in these lands, held by him in right of his wife. His children were, Thomas, (who died before this time and had left a son Thomas,) Henry, (who had but one son Henry,) Josiah, Pelatiah and Matthew. (His wife Elizabeth was deceased.) He gave his rents in England to Henry, jr., grandson of Col. Matthew, to Josiah, son of Josiah, deceased, and to some of his own sons. The death of some of his sons caused him to make a codicil to his will, which somewhat altered the disposal of the property. Estate £1806. (See p. 10.) Col. Matthew died,

June, 1753. His children were, Matthew, Pelatiah, (Thomas died before his father, and left four sons, Thomas, Theophilus, John and Joseph,) Henry, Elizabeth, Eunice and Azuba. His lands at Willington and Torrington he gave to his three living sons, and one fourth to the four sons of Thomas, deceased. He gave £4 to the old church in Windsor. He had three grandsons—the sons of Josiah, viz. Josiah, John and Matthew.

Ainsworth, Tixhall, of Hartford, had a case in court in 1700.

Ashley, Robert, came to Springfield in Mass. in the year 1639, and now appears to have been the only one of the name that came to New England. The name of his wife was Mary—her family name is not known. Their children were as follows, all born in Springfield :

David, born June 8, 1642.   Sarah, born Aug. 23, 1648.
Mary, born April 6, 1644.   Joseph, born July 6, 1652.
Jonathan, born Feb. 12, 1646.

Of these children, all are noticed in their father's will, except Sarah, who probably died young. Mary married John Root, of Westfield. (This branch is not traced.) Robert the first, died at Springfield, Nov. 29, 1682 ; his wife, Mary, died Sept. 19, 1683.

Ashley, David, son of Robert, married Hannah Glover, of New Haven, Conn., in 1663, supposed a daughter of Henry Glover. Their children were,

Samuel, born Oct. 26, 1664.
David, born March 10, 1667.
John, born June 27, 1669.
Joseph, born July 31, 1671.
Sarah, born Sept. 19, 1673, married Thomas Ingersoll, 1691.
Mary,   } twins, born Dec. 14, 1675, died young.
Hannah, }   born Dec. 14, 1675, married Nath'l. Eggleston.
Jonathan, born June 21, 1678.
Abigail, born April 27, 1681, m. Nath'l. Lewis, of Farmington.
Mary, b. March 3, 1683, m. Benjamin Stebbins, of Northampton.
Rebecca, b. May 30, 1685, m. Samuel Dewey.

David removed to Westfield, and died there in 1718. His five eldest children are recorded in Springfield, and two of the same, and the six youngest are recorded in Westfield. The first Mary died young. The other five sons and five daughters were married, and are mentioned in their father's will.

Ashley, Jonathan, 2d son of Robert, married Sarah Wadsworth, the daughter of William Wadsworth, an original proprietor of Hartford,

Conn., a gentleman of wealth and exalted reputation. (See page 86, No. 3.) Jonathan removed to Hartford, and died there, Feb. 1705, and left three sons ând two daughters, and a large estate. (See p. 111.) This branch in Connecticut is not traced.

Ashley, Joseph, 3d son of Robert, lived in West Springfield, and was the ancestor of the West Springfield Ashleys. He married Mary Parsons, 1685, and had children, Joseph, Ebenezer, Mary, Abigail and Benjamin. He died May 19, 1698. This includes the children and grand children of Robert Ashley, (except the Roots, and some of David's grand children.)

Ashley, Samuel, son of David, married Sarah Kellogg, of Hadley, and had children, Mary, born 1687, Samuel, jr., 1688, Daniel 1691, Sarah 1693, Rachel 1695, Jacob 1697, Johannah 1699, Aaron 1702, Ezekiel —, Abigail 1708, and Joseph 1709—this last son graduated at Yale College, 1730, and was a minister at Sunderland, Mass., and died in 1780.

Ashley, Dea. David, son of David, married Mary Dewey, 1688. Their children were, Thomas, born 1690, David 1692, Mary 1694, Elizabeth 1697, Abigail 1700, Moses 1703, Hannah 1706, Israel 1710 —Israel graduated at Yale College in 1730, was a physician, and died in 1758. Dea. David died in 1744. (See Yale Catalogue.)

Ashley, Joseph, son of David, married Abigail Dewey, 1699, died before his father, and left but one son, James born in 1770. He had three other children, who died young.

Ashley, Jonathan, son of David, married Abigail Stebbins, of Springfield, 1699, and had children, Abigail born 1701, Azariah born 1704, Mercy 1707, Lydia 1710, Jonathan 1712, Benjamin 1714, Ebenezer 1717, Phineas 1729. Jonathan, son of David, died 1749. The above Jonathan, the son of Jonathan, graduated at Yale College in 1730, in the same class with three other cousins, viz. Israel, John and Joseph Ashley. This Rev. Jonathan, son of Jonathan, was ordained at Deerfield, Mass., in 1732. He married Dorothy Williams, daughter of Rev. William Williams, of Hatfield. She was born in 1713. He was the second ordained minister at Deerfield, and became a celebrated preacher and divine. Their children were, William, born July, 1737, died in 1737, Jonathan born Jan. 6, 1738, William born 1740, died same year, Dorothy born April 3, 1743, married Dea. William Williams, of Dalton, Mass., Elizabeth born June 9, 1745, married Maj. David Dickinson, of Deerfield, 1783, Solomon born May 25, 1754, drowned Jan. 14, 1823, Elisha (Doctor) born Oct. 12, 1750,

Clarissa born Dec. 1, 1757. Jonathan, son of Rev. Jonathan, graduated at Yale College in 1758, and became a lawyer, and practised at Deerfield. He married Tirzah Field, daughter of Col. Field, of Deerfield, and had three daughters, viz. Tirzah, who married Rufus Saxton, Esq., of Deerfield ; Harriet married Col. E. Gilbert, of Greenfield ; Dorothy married Dr. Roswell Leavitt, of Cornish, N. H., and all had families ; Clarissa, youngest daughter of Rev. Jonathan, married Dr. Moses C. Welch, of Mansfield, Conn., who was a distinguished divine. They had children, Jonathan Ashley Welch, Esq., attorney at law at Brooklyn, Conn. ; he married Mary Devotion Baker in 1819 ; his children are, Ebenezer B., Mary C., Louisa D., Charles A., Joseph, James F., and Elizabeth Jane. Archibald Welch, M. D., of Wethersfield, is also a son of Rev. Moses C., born 1794, President of the Connecticut Medical Society ; he married Cynthia Hyde, of Lebanon, in 1819, and has three sons and two daughters. Rev. Jonathan Ashley died in 1780, aged 68 ; his wife died at Deerfield in 1808, aged 95 years. Elisha Williams, Esq. settled at Wethersfield, and married Mehitabel Burnham, Aug. 24, 1749, and had eight children ; he died in 1784. Samuel W., his son, graduated at Yale College in 1772, and married Emily Williams in 1785, and had eleven children, the last born at Wethersfield in 1806, John Stoddard Williams. Dr. Elihu Ashley, son of Rev. Jonathan, married his cousin, Mary Williams, daughter of Dr. Thomas Williams, of Deerfield, a brother of Col. Ephraim Williams, the founder of Williams College. The children of Dr. Elihu were, Col. Thomas W., born 1775 ; Robert W., a physician ; Mary b. 1790. Col. Thomas W. married a daughter of Rev. Mr. Crosby, of Enfield in 1814, and has children, Jonathan, Josiah, Thomas W. and Abbot, and had others who died. Dr. Robert W., brother of Col. Thomas W. Ashley, now resides at Lyons, N. Y., and has children. Mary, sister of Dr. Robert, married a Mr. Tippets, and died at Geneva, N. Y. It was by the above intermarriage of the Ashley and Williams families that the late Chief Justice Williams, of Connecticut, is descended from this family.

Ashley, John, the third son of David, born in 1667, in Springfield ; had three wives, first, Sarah Dewey, born 1692, she died in 1708 ; he married for his second wife, widow Mary Sheldon in 1708, she died in 1735 ; for a third wife he married Hannah Glover in 1735. The second wife, widow Mary Sheldon, was the relict of Joseph Sheldon, of Suffield, (who went from Northampton) ; she was the daughter of Joseph Whiting, of Hartford, who was the Treasurer of Connecticut for some years. (See William Whiting, No. 3, p. 97—Siborn Nichols, p. 155, No. 3.) This Joseph Whiting resided a few years in Westfield, and married Mary Pyncheon, the only daughter of Col. John Pyncheon, of Springfield, Oct. 5, 1669 ; she was born Oct. 28, 1650. Mr. Whiting had by Mary Pyncheon in Westfield, Mary, born Aug. 19, 1672, and Joseph born 1674, who died young. Mr. Whiting returned to Hartford, and his wife soon after died, and he married a daughter of Col. John Allyn, for his second wife. This Mary Whiting, born 1672, the grand daughter of Col. Pyncheon, (see William Pyncheon, p. 66, No. 2,) married Joseph Sheldon about 1694 ; she had a son Joseph born in Northampton, 1695 ; the other children most or all of them were born in Suffield, Conn., viz. Amy, Mary, Joseph born in 1700, (the first Joseph died,) Rachel born 1703, Benjamin 1705. Joseph Sheldon died July 2, 1708, at Boston, where he was attending the General Court as Representative of Suffield. His widow (the grand daughter of Col. Pyncheon) married John Ashley, Esq., of Springfield. The children of John Ashley, of Springfield, by his wife, Sarah Dewey, were—Sarah born 1693, Hannah 1695, John 1697, (died young) Moses 1700, Ebenezer 1702, Noah 1704, Roger 1705, Lydia 1708. By his second wife, widow Mary Sheldon, he had John born 1709, and Preserved 1711—the latter died young. John Ashley, of Sheffield, was the only child of John Ashley, Esq, of Springfield, by his 2d wife, (Mary Sheldon) who lived. John Ashley, Esq. who had been much employed in public business, and held many responsible places of public trust in Springfield, died April 17, 1759, in his 90th year. Col. John Pyncheon, of Springfield, died in 1703, but his estate, for some reason, was not fully settled until 1737. In that year there was about £8000 of his estate remaining not distributed, which consisted chiefly of land, and two-thirds of this, or £5312 was given by the Probate Court to the heirs of his son John, and one-third, or £2656 to heirs of his grand daughter, Mary Ashley, alias Sheldon, alias Whiting, (so the record reads) ; of this £2656 Joseph Sheldon had a double portion, £758, Benjamin Sheldon £379, Amy, wife of James Warriner £379, Mary, wife of Ebenezer Hitchcock, £379, Rachel, wife of Jedediah Bliss £379—(these were the five Sheldon children), and John Ashley, son of Mr. John Ashley £379—all having the same mother. This John Ashley, who afterwards settled at Sheffield, was a great grand son of the first Robert Ashley ; he was also the great grand son of Col. John Pyncheon, of Springfield.

Ashley, John, Esq., of Sheffield, son of John, Esq., of Springfield,

was born at Westfield, Dec. 2, 1709, emigrated in early life to Sheffield, and located himself there as a lawyer, after he had been admitted to the bar, in 1732 or 3. He held large quantities of land in the
valley of the Housatonic and at Kunkapot, three miles east of the
river. He soon rose in the militia to the rank of colonel, and was
most of his life a magistrate of the county of Berkshire; he was also
a Judge of the County from 1765 until the Court was dismissed during the war of the Revolution in 1781. He graduated at Yale College
in 1730, and died at Sheffield, Sept. 1803, aged 93 years. Hannah,
his wife, died June 19, 1790. He became a gentleman of great wealth,
and left to his son and grand children about 1000 acres of finely cultivated lands and other estate; most of his lands he had held from his
first settlement there, until his death. Colonel or Judge John married
in early life, Hannah Hugaboom, of Claverac, in the State of N. Y.
Her sister married Mr. Van Ness, of Kinderhook, the father of Gen.
Van Ness, late deceased, of Washington, D. C., of Hon. C. P. Van
Ness, former Governor of Vermont, and Minister to Spain, and Judge
Van Ness, deceased, of New York. Judge Ashley had one son and
three daughters, viz. Gen. John, Jane, Mary and Hannah.

Ashley, Jane, the eldest daughter of Judge John, of Sheffield, married William Bull, who lived and died at Sheffield. They had one
son, Dr. William Bull. After the death of her husband, she married
Ruluff Dutcher, of Canaan, Conn., by whom she had several children,
viz. Christopher, John, Ruluff, jr., Washington, and five daughters—
one of the daughters of Ruluff, jr. married Mr. Stirling, of Salisbury,
another married a Mr. Bushnell, and a third married Gen. Francis
Bacon, of Litchfield, a young lawyer of much promise. After the
death of Mr. Dutcher, Jane married for her 3d husband, Judge J.
Porter, of Salisbury, the father of the late Gen. Peter B. Porter, of
Black Rock, or Niagara Falls, N. Y.

Ashley, Mary, 2d daughter of Judge Ashley, married Gen. John
Fellows, of Sheffield. They had four daughters and three sons, viz.
Hannah, Mary, Charlotte, Jane, John, Edmund and Henry. Hannah
married Dr. J. Porter, of Salisbury; Mary married a Mr. Penfield,
who settled the town of Penfield in the State of New York; one of
the daughters of Mr. Penfield married the Hon. Ogden Edwards, of
the city of New York. Mary Fellows, wife of Gen. Fellows, died
Dec. 7, 1797.

Ashley, Maj. Gen. John, born Sept. 26, 1736. He entered Yale
College, and received the honors of that Seminary in 1756, after

which he received a law education, but never followed his profession, and settled in his native town, Sheffield, as a merchant. He served his town many years as Representative to the General Court at Boston, as his honored father had done before him. He rose through the several militia grades to the rank of Major General of the 9th division of the militia of Massachusetts; he also held several civil appointments. Gen. Ashley distinguished himself in the suppression of Shay's rebellion in Massachusetts. He married Louisa Ward, of New Marlborough, May 20, 1762. Their children by this connection, were—Louisa, born March 10, 1763, and John Ashley, born Jan. 11, 1767. Louisa, the first wife of Gen. John, died April 2, 1769. Gen. Ashley, for his 2d wife, married Mary Bollentine, Oct. 17, 1769, daughter of Rev. John Bollentine, of Westfield. She was born in 1744, and died March 8, 1827, aged 83 years. By this marriage his children were, Bollentine born Dec. 2, 1770, Maj. William born Jan. 3, 1773, Roger born March 27, 1775, Samuel born Nov. 21, 1778, Mary born March 20, 1781, Hannah born Sept. 10, 1782, Jane born March 19, 1784, Lydia Ashley born Nov. 19, 1788. Gen. Ashley died Nov. 5, 1799, in the 64th year of his age, and was buried with military honors. Bollentine, son of Gen. John, died single, aged 28 years. Roger and Samuel died young and unmarried. Col. John, son of Gen. John, of Sheffield, half brother of Maj. William, married Aseneth Keyes, a relative of Col. Henry Stanton, U. S. A., and had children, Harry, Louisa, Maria, Emeline, Eliza, Jane, John and Robert. Col. John died Dec. 22, 1823, and his widow, Aseneth, died a few years after him.

Ashley, Louisa, eldest daughter of Gen. John Ashley, by his first wife, married Samuel B. Sheldon, then of Salisbury, who soon moved to Vermont and became the first settler of the town of Sheldon, and gave to the new town his own name. They had two children, Eliza and John—the latter died young. Eliza married Dr. Chauncey Fitch, late of Sheldon. Their children were, Jabez, Samuel S., John, Louisa and Eliza.

Ashley, Maj. William, son of Gen. John, was born Jan. 3, 1773, and was educated at Harvard College, but followed no profession, except that of a gentleman farmer, holding a large estate in lands in Sheffield, where he now resides. When young he married Jane Hillyer, a daughter of Judge Hillyer, of Granby, Conn., Jan 4, 1803, born Aug. 24, 1779. By this connection he had a son and two daughters, viz. Julia H. b. Nov. 29, 1803, and died Aug. 4, 1822, and Jane Pelletrau, b. Jan. 21, 1808. Julia married Horatio L. Warner, Esq., a merchant of Sheffield, June 18, 1821, she died soon after marriage, and left no issue. Jane married Hon. William G. Bates, of Westfield, Mass., October 29, 1830, a lawyer of eminence, and has been two years a member of the Governor's Council of his State, and held other important offices. He was born Nov. 17, 1803—his children, Sarah Barnard b. June 24, 1831, d. Aug. 27, 1831, Jane Ashley b. Feb. 24, 1835, Mary Ashley b. July 28, 1837, d. Sept. 23, 1838, William Ashley b. Jan. 26, 1839, d. May 2, 1839, Sarah Porter b. Oct. 16, 1840, d. April 25, 1841, an infant b. June 17, 1843, d. same day, and Fannie Bulah Bates b. March 4, 1845.

Mary, the daughter of Gen. John, married Dr. John Laffargue, of St. Domingo, in the West Indies—he afterwards located and died at Sheffield. He had only one son, John, who is married and has several children. Mary, the widow, is yet living at Sheffield.

Hannah Ashley, married John Hillyer, son of Judge Hillyer, dec'd. of Granby, Conn., and has several children, viz. Mary A b. July, 1809, Julia b. 1812, William A. b. 1814, John b. 1817, and Jane b. Jan. 11, 1823. William A. married Julia Banker, of New York, January 10, 1815.

Jane Ashley, daughter of Gen. John, married Harry Clark, of Sheffield, and had two children, John B. and Jane M. She then married Dr. Nathaniel Preston, of Sheffield, and had Lydia A., Harriet A., and Sarah B. Sarah died young. John married Miss Graves, a daughter of Judge Graves, of Sherman. Jane married Judge Prentice, of Michigan. Lydia married Jonathan Woodruff, of Lima, Indiana, and left one child, she died in 1846. Harriet married Elijah Deming, of Indiana, June 23, 1847.

Lydia Ashley, youngest daughter of Gen. John, married Royal R. Hinman, Esq., of Hartford, Sept, 14, 1814. (See No. 3, p. 147.)

John Ashley, Joseph Ashley, Israel Ashley and Jonathan Ashley, graduated at Yale College in 1730 ; Jonathan Ashley and John Ashley graduated at Yale in 1758 ; and in 1767, Israel and Moses Ashley also graduated at Yale. Hon. Chester Ashley, the present United States Senator from Arkansas, was born in Massachusetts, and graduated at Williams College in 1813, and is a descendant of Robert Ashley, of Springfield, 1639.

Austin, John, of Hartford, appointed guardian of the minor heirs of Ebenezer Fitch, deceased, of Windsor, 1734. He married Mary Hooker, Dec. 1713.

Ayrault, Nicholas, of Wethersfield, died 1706. He was a physician by profession, a French gentleman. At his decease he left a widow, (Marian) and several children. To his son Peter, he gave his gold buttons. The rest and residue of his property in France and elsewhere, he gave to his widow, Marian. He provided for his children, after either the marriage, or death of his widow. He married Marian Breton or Bretoon, of Providence, R. I. The house which he built, stood on the next lot south and adjoining the residence of Capt. Jesse Goodrich in Wethersfield. He was a gentleman of wealth and reputation, and was connected by marriage to the Dodd family. Marian Dodd, of Hartford, now has a beautiful French box of splendid workmanship, which has descended from Marian Ayrault.

B.

Baldwin, Nathaniel, was a resident at Fairfield as early as 1641.

Barlow, James, of Suffield, and Sarah Huxley, were joined in marriage. James Barlow, the son of James, which Sarah his wife bore to him, born Jan. 27, 1688. James Barlow, sen'r., died March 16, 1689–90. James Barlow, jr., and Mary Harmon, were joined in marriage, April 1st, 1714. Their children were, Mary b. March 17, 1714–15, Sarah b. Jan. 14, 1716–17, Elizabeth b. April 20, 1719, James b. June 16, 1721, Anne b. June 19, 1723, Nathan b. March 26, 1726, Ebenezer b. Jan. 30, 1727–8, Deborah b. Nov. 14, 1729, Edmund b. May 18, 1732. John Barlow, of Fairfield, 1650. Thomas, at Fairfield, 1654.

Bates, Robert, an early settler in Stamford, 1641—whether of the family which settled at Haddam is not known.

Bearding, Widow Abigail, died in 1682, (relict of Nathaniel, p. 17.) She had a daughter, Hester Spencer. Another married Mr. Andrews, and had a son Samuel.

Belden, Richard. Tradition says, that two brothers, by the name of Belden, were among the first settlers of the colony of Connecticut, and that they made their first location at Wethersfield, but that one of them, (William) after a while, on the settlement of Norwalk, removed thither. And this appears nearly certain by the records of the town of Wethersfield; for as early as Feb. 7, 1641, and among the earliest grants, Richard had eight distinct tracts of land allotted to him by the town, and little or no mention is made of William, save that he had three sons, Samuel, Daniel and John born to him, by his first wife,

Tomisin, in 1647, 1648 and 1650, and no trace of them is found afterwards.

Belden, Samuel, a son of Richard, had a daughter Mary, and two sons, Samuel and Stephen, born to him by his wife, Mary, July 10, 1655, April 6, 1657, and Dec. 28, 1658.

Belden, Samuel, jr., son of Samuel, m. Hannah, Jan. 14, 1685. They had issue, Samuel born July 25, 1689, Daniel, Feb. 14, 1691, Gideon, March 24, 1693, Prudence, Feb. 12, 1694, Richard, April 18, 1699, Matthew, June 13, 1701, and Hannah, Sept. 25, 1704.

Belden, Daniel, 2d son of Samuel, jr., married Margaret Clark, widow, daughter of Peter Blin, Nov. 23, 1714. They had issue five daughters, Margaret, Lois, Prudence, Eunice and Thankful b. Sept. 10, 1715, June 14, 1717, Jan. 28, 1719, Mar. 17, 1722, Nov. 10, 1724.

Belden, Samuel 3d, son of Samuel, jr., married Mary Spencer, of Haddam, April 10, 1712. They had issue, Samuel born April 26, 1713, Jared, Jan. 19, 1715, Nathaniel, June 24, 1716, Lydia, May 24, 1718, Asa, April 1, 1720, Mary, Dec. 11, 1721, Ann, Nov. 7, 1723, Seth, Sept. 18, 1725, Daniel, May 19, 1727, Richard, Dec. 30, 1728, Phineas, Sept. 14, 1730, Dorothy, Sept. 6, 1732, Esther, June 22, 1734, and Martha, June 6, 1736.(a.)

Belden, Gideon, 3d son of Samuel, jr., married Elizabeth, daughter of Zachariah Seimer, (Seymour) Feb. 7, 1712. They had issue, Eunice, Elisha born July 22, 1715, Ruth, Elizabeth, Abigail, Hannah, Hezekiah born Oct. 26, 1725, Sarah and Experience.

Belden, John, presumed to be the 2d son of Richard, married Lydia, his wife, April 24, 1657. They had issue, John born June 12, 1658, Jonathan, June 21, 1660, Joseph, April 23, 1663, Samuel, Jan. 3, 1665, Daniel, Oct. 12, 1670, Ebenezer, Jan. 8, 1672, and two daughters, Sarah and Margaret. He was much employed in the public affairs of the town. He died in 1677, aged 46.

Belden, John, jr., son of John, married Dorothy, daughter of Josiah Willard, June 15, 1682. Had issue, Josiah born Feb. 14, 1683, John, Dec. 3, 1685, Benjamin, 1687, Stephen, May 21, 1697, Ezra, Nov. 27, 1699, and three daughters, Lydia, Hannah and Dorothy.

Belden, Josiah, eldest son of John, jr., m. Mabel, daughter of Serg't Samuel Wright, May 1, 1707, and had issue, Josiah, b. June 11, 1713, Ozias, Nov. 18, 1714, Return, Jan. 28, 1721, Solomon, May 22, 1722, and six daughters, Mabel Wright, Dorothy, Rebecca, Abigail, Lydia and Hannah. Died Sept. 5, 1746.

Belden, John, 3d—second son of John, jr., m. Keziah, daughter of

Sergt. Benjamin Gilbert, May 1, 1712. She died Dec. 2, 1712, in premature childbirth, aged 21. For his 2d wife he married Patience, daughter of Josiah Rossiter, Esq., March 22, 1715, by whom he had issue, John born March 1, 1716. His wife died on the 9th of the same month, "aged 24 years wanting one month." He married for his 3d wife, Sarah, daughter of Jacob Griswold, Dec. 16, 1718, by whom he had issue, Ebenezer, born Dec. 6, 1719, Timothy, Dec. 26, 1723, and a daughter Keziah, b. Aug. 21, 1722.

Belden, Benjamin, 3d son of John, jr., married Anne, daughter of Lieut. Benjamin Churchill, Jan. 29, 1714, and had issue, Mary, born Dec. 9, 1715, Benjamin, Feb. 9, 1718, and Charles, March 13, 1720.

Belden, Ezra, 5th son of John, jr., married Elizabeth, daughter of Dea. Jonathan Belden, Feb. 15, 1722, by whom he had issue, Ezra born Nov. 29, 1722, Aaron, Sept. 9, 1725, and a 2d Aaron, Oct. 1, 1731, and three daughters, Elizabeth, Lois and Eunice. From this family descended all the Beldens in Rocky Hill.(b.)

Belden, Lieut., Esq., and Dea. Jonathan, 2d son of John the 1st, was born June 21, 1660. Married Mary, daughter of Thomas Wright, Dec. 10, 1685. Had issue, Jonathan born Dec. 11, 1686, Mary, Sept. 11, 1687, Silas, July 29, 1691, Jonathan, March 30, 1695, and Elizabeth, Oct. 1, 1698. Greatly respected, and much employed in town affairs. He died July 6, 1734.

Belden, Jonathan, his eldest son, died in childhood.

Belden, Silas, his 2d son, married Abigail, daughter of Capt. Joshua Robbins, Nov. 30, 1716. Had issue, Silas, born Nov. 13, 1717, Abigail (married to Thomas Hurlbut, of Wethersfield) Nov. 4, 1720, Joshua, July 19, 1724, Charles, May 4, 1728, Lydia, May 1, 1730, Oliver, Nov. 19, 1732, and Jonathan, Nov. 16, 1737. While he remained in Wethersfield he was much employed in public affairs. Disposing of his property in Wethersfield, he removed to Canaan in the spring of 1741, where he had made purchase of large tracts of choice new land. He made like purchases also in Dutchess county, N. Y., and in Berkshire county, Mass., proposing to make them the future establishments of his children. In the autumn of 1741 he returned to Wethersfield to settle up his affairs and remove his family to his new possessions. At the time a malignant dysentery prevailed in Wethersfield. He was seized with it, and died.

Belden, Silas, jr., his eldest son, settled in Canaan, on a farm inherited from his father.

Belden, Joshua, his 2d son, was liberally educated—graduated at

Yale College in 1743. He studied theology, was settled in the ministry in Newington, Nov. 11, 1747, and statedly discharged the duties of the sacred office until Nov. 1803—56 years. He married Anne, daughter of Lieut. Ebenezer Belden, Nov. 1749, by whom he had issue nine daughters. Martha and Anne, both of whom died in childhood, Abigail married to James Lusk, late of Enfield, Sarah, who died, aged 22, a 2d Anne died in infancy, a 3d Anne, Martha married to Joseph Lynde, druggist, late of Hartford, Octavia married to the Rev. Nathaniel Gaylord, late of Hartland, Rhoda married to the Rev. Silas Churchill, of New Lebanon, N. Y., and one son Joshua, born March 29 1768. His wife, Anne, died Oct. 29, 1773. By a 2d marriage, with Honor Whiting, widow of Capt. Charles Whiting, of Norwich, and daughter of Hezekiah Goodrich, Esq., of Wethersfield, Nov. 14, 1774, he had a son Hezekiah, born Feb. 17, 1778. In 1772 he corrected the erroneous orthography of the family name, from Belding to Belden, at the suggestion of Col. Elisha Williams, then Town Clerk. The Colonel showing him from the records, an original signature of the first John, where the name was spelled as it now is. He effected the change by addressing a Circular, requesting the correction, to all of the name, of whom he had knowledge ; and it was at once, very generally complied with—very few thereafter spelling the name Belding, although there are still a few who adhere to the corrupt spelling. He died, July 23, 1813, in a good old age, and ripe for eternity.

Belden, Joshua, jr., eldest son of Rev. Joshua, graduated at Yale College in 1787—studied medicine and settled as a physician, and after a few years, as a farmer, in Newington. Married Dorothy, daughter of Lieut. Lemuel Whittlesey, Jan. 9, 1797. Had issue, four sons, Lemuel Whittlesey, born Jan. 6, 1801, Joshua, Aug. 3, 1802, Chauncey, Oct. 15, 1804, John Mason, Aug. 26, 1806. He was highly esteemed, and died June 6, 1808, greatly lamented.

Belden, Hezekiah, 2d son of the Rev. Joshua, was liberally educated, and graduated at Yale College in 1796. Was a merchant in New Haven for some years. Married Harriet Halsted Lyon, daughter of Underhill Lyon, Esq., of Rye, N. Y., Dec. 28, 1818. Losing his wife, he removed to Richmond, Va., and in connection with others, became a contractor for the transportation of the U. S. Mail from 1823 to 1842, when he returned to Wethersfield, and is at present town clerk of Wethersfield. He has a son, George Hubertus, born Oct. 12, 1819, who is now an engineer on the New York and Erie Rail Road, and a daughter, Mary Honoria, born Sept. 20, 1821.

Belden, Lemuel W., eldest son of Joshua, jr., graduated at Yale College in 1821. Studied medicine, and settled at Springfield, Mass., as physician. He married Catherine, daughter of Stephen Chester, Esq., May 7, 1829, had issue a son, Donald, born Jan. 21, 1831, who died June 1, 1837. Dr. Belden died, greatly lamented, leaving no issue, Oct. 26, 1839. He was a man of great purity of mind, of amiable manners, and of rare attainments, and was rapidly rising into eminence.

Belden, Joshua, 2d son of Joshua, jr., graduated at Yale College in 1825. Went to St. Louis, Mo., and commenced business as a merchant—was unsuccessful—removed to Glasgow, Mo., and retrieved his circumstances. Married Agnes Morton Graves, widow, daughter of —— Lewis, Esq., of Glasgow, a large landed proprietor, of the ancient family of the Lewises, of Virginia. He is now a land holder and farmer in Glasgow, has the unbounded confidence of the community about him, and has obtained the rare and enviable subriquet of the honest man. He has one surviving daughter, Elizabeth Morton, born April, 1838. His wife died two or three years since.

Belden, Chauncey, 3d son of Joshua, jr., was graduated an M. D. at Yale College in 1829. Settled in West Springfield, Mass., as a physician. Married Lucy B., daughter of Justin Ely, Esq., of that place, Nov. 1834. Had issue, Theodore, born June 8, 1836, Elizabeth, May, 1838, Chauncey Herbert, Feb. 6, 1844. Died in 1846. He was respected both as a physician and a man.

Belden, John Mason, 4th son of Joshua, jr. Married Mary Elizabeth, daughter of Mr. —— Hale, of Glastenbury, June 14, 1838, and is settled as a farmer at Newington, on the old ancestral Belden place. He has surviving issue, three daughters, Mary Elizabeth, Cornelia Hale, Agnes Whittlesey, born Sept. 8, 1839, April 11, 1845, January 18, 1847.

Belden, Charles, 3d son of Silas, was born May 4, 1728. Settled at Dover in Dutchess county, N. Y., on a fine farm inherited from his father. This family has furnished a member of Congress.

Belden, Oliver, 4th son of Silas, born Nov. 19, 1732, settled on a noble farm inherited from his father, in Lenox, Mass. Two of his sons have been Representatives of Lenox in the Mass. Legislature.

Belden, Jonathan, 5th son of Silas, born Nov. 16, 1737. Little is known of him by the Compiler, not even his place of settlement. He undoubtedly shared with his brothers in his father's provident provision for his children.

Belden, Jonathan, 3d son of Dea. Jonathan, born March 30, 1695, married Martha, daughter of John James, Dec. 29, 1715. Had issue David, born Oct. 4, 1716, Jonathan, March 8, 1719, Moses, Dec. 29, 1720, and two daughters. He bore the military title of captain, was a justice of the peace, town treasurer a number of years, and much employed in public affairs. He died Aug. 20, 1768.

Belden, David, his eldest son, married Hepzibah Goodrich, Aug. 3, 1769—had issue, one daughter, born June 29, 1772.

Belden, Joseph, 3d son of John the 1st, was born April 23, 1663, and m. " Mary his wife, Oct. 27, 1693." Had issue, Joseph, b. Dec. 28, 1667, Thomas, Sept. 9, 1700, and four daughters, Sarah, Mary, Esther and Eunice. It is supposed that Joseph died young, or left town, as there is no further mention of him.

Belden, Thomas, 2d son of Joseph, married Mary, daughter of Rev. Stephen Mix, (date of his marriage not given.) Had issue, Thomas, born Aug. 9, 1732, Joseph, Nov. 24, 1733, and Simeon, Feb. 24, 1737, and three daughters, Mary, Rebecca and Lucy.

Belden, Thomas, jr., eldest son of Thomas, married Abigail, daughter of Doct. Ezekiel Porter, Aug. 1, 1753. Had issue, Ezekiel Porter, born Feb. 12, 1756, and James, and two daughters, Mary (married to Frederick Butler, late of Wethersfield,) and Abigail. He was liberally educated, and graduated at Yale College in 1751. He was highly esteemed, took an active part in public affairs, discharged the duties of many of the more important affairs of the town, and bore the titles of Esq. and Colonel. He died May 22, 1782, greatly lamented.

Belden, Ezekiel P., eldest son of Thomas, jr., graduated at Yale College in 1775. The Revolutionary war had commenced, and he soon entered the service of his country, as a lieutenant of light horse in Sheldon's regiment. He continued in the service to the close of the war, and retired from it as captain, with the honorary or brevet title of major. Subsequently he was colonel of militia. He married Elizabeth, daughter of Elisha Williams, Esq., Sept. 26, 1781. By her he had issue, Abigail, married to Justin Ely, Esq., of West Springfield, Elizabeth, married to Daniel Buck, of Hartford, Thomas, born July 29, 1785, died Feb. 24, 1831, without issue. His wife, Elizabeth, died Oct. 30, 1789. Nov. 1, 1790, he married Mary Parsons, of Amherst, by whom he had issue, James, born Oct. 1, 1791, died Sept. 13, 1800, Ezekiel P., born March 18, 1794, died April 2, 1818, Mary, married to Erastus F. Cooke, of Wethersfield, Celia, married to Heman Ely, of Elyria, Ohio, Julia, married to James L. Belden, of

Wethersfield, Hannah, married to George Prior. He was often and repeatedly chosen selectman—was elected town clerk in 1812, and held the office uninterruptedly until his death—was a member of almost all the town committees, a justice of the peace, and representative of the town in the General Assembly forty-nine sessions, and was elected to two more in which he declined serving. He was a man of kind and social feelings, gentlemanly and amiable manners, and ready and active in the transaction of public affairs. He died Oct. 9, 1824, honored and lamented.

Belden, Joseph, 2d son of Thomas 1st, was born Nov. 24, 1733, and graduated at Yale in 1751. It is presumed he removed from the town in early life, as his name does not appear again on the records, or in the doings of the town. It is understood, however, that he had a son Thomas, who died at Hartford, a few years since, leaving a family.

Belden, Simeon, 3d son of Thomas 1st, was born Feb. 24, 1737, graduated at Yale College in 1762—married Martha, daughter of the Rev. James Lockwood, Nov. 3, 1765, had issue, Simeon, born April 27, 1769, settled at Fayetteville, N. C.; Charlotte, married to the Hon. Lewis B. Sturges, of Fairfield, Martha to —— DeWitt, Esq., of Milford, James Lockwood, Joseph, Mary Mix married to Barzillai Deane Buck, of Wethersfield. By profession a merchant—held several of the town offices, and for several years was deputy sheriff. He died Oct. 29, 1820.

Belden, James L., 2d son of Simeon, was born Oct. 15, 1774. By profession a merchant—for a while successful—ultimately the reverse, and lost his property—turned his attention to horticulture, established the Wethersfield Seed Garden, and thereby retrieved his circumstances and accumulated a handsome property. Married Julia, daughter of Ezekiel P. Belden, Esq., Sept. 28, 1819. By her he had issue, three sons and one daughter. The eldest son and daughter died in early childhood. The survivors are, Ezekiel P., born April 4, 1823, and James L., March 23, 1825. Ezekiel P. graduated at Yale in 1844, and is the ingenious modeller in wood of the Cities of New Haven and New York. James L. has a spirit of enterprise and daring, and is a sailor on his first voyage. While at Wethersfield, Mr. Belden was held in high estimation and had much of the public confidence, and was an active and useful member of society. For a number of years he held the office of Post Master in the town ; this he resigned to enable him to enter into the civil concerns of the State—was several times elected a representative of the town in the General Assembly, and was appointed a justice of the peace from year to year. In 1840 he removed to New Haven for the purpose of educating his sons. He was highly respected there. He was a man of sound judgment and of much shrewdness, conjoined with probity of character and great energy in action. He died in New York, Feb. 22, 1847, and has his sepulture by the side of his fathers.

Belden, Joseph, 3d son of Simeon, was born Dec. 29, 1776, graduated at Yale in 1795. Commenced business as a druggist, but after a few years became a general book agent, and by industry and tact made the business profitable both to himself and his employers. Married Hannah, daughter of John Reynolds, of Enfield, Nov. 1813, had no issue, and died in 1826.

Belden, Samuel and Daniel, 4th and 5th sons of John the 1st, born Jan. 3, 1665, and Oct. 12, 1670, it is supposed removed, the one to New London, and the other to Norwalk, (to his great uncle William,) and are the progenitors of the Beldens in those towns.

Belden, Ebenezer, 6th son of John the 1st, was born Jan. 8, 1672. No record of his marriage, but his son Ebenezer, by his wife, Abigail, was born Sept. 7, 1697. He held, at times, nearly all the offices of the town, from hayward and constable to selectman, and bore the military title of sergeant. His son Ebenezer, born as above, married Mary, daughter of cornet Samuel Talcott, Dec. 7, 1720. Like his father he held most of the town offices and bore the military title of lieutenant. He had issue, Martha, born Sept. 24, 1721, John, Anne, married to the Rev. Joshua.

Belden, John, son of Lieut. Ebenezer, like his father, ran the round of the town offices, and enjoyed the military title of colonel. Married Rebecca Rennalls, June 12, 1760. Had issue, Elizur, Rebecca, Mary, John, Ebenezer, Lucy, Ebenezer, Sarah, Nancy and Harriet Man. Time of his birth and death not recorded.

(*a.*) *page* 191. Belden, Matthew, 5th son of Samuel, jr., born June 13, 1701—married Elizabeth, daughter of Samuel Williams, Apr. 16, 1729. Had issue, a daughter, Mercy.

Belden, Samuel 4th, eldest son of Samuel 3d, born April 26, 1713—married Elizabeth, and had issue, Abner, born Jan. 12, 1744, Bildad, Sept. 9, 1745, Seth, Aug. 7, 1747, Moses, June 18, 1749, and three daughters, Prudence, Rebecca and Mary.

Belden, Richard, 7th son of Samuel 3d, born Dec. 30, 1728—married Elizabeth Hurlbut, Oct. 30, 1749—had issue, Amos, b. Oct.

26, 1750, Jeremiah, March 26, 1753, Othniel, March 27, 1755, Caleb, Feb. 10, 1757.

Belden, Phineas, 8th son of Samuel 3d, born Sept. 14, 1730—married Hannah Deming, March 22, 1751—had issue, Charles, b. April 3, 1752, and a daughter, Mary.

(b.) page 192. Belden, Aaron, 3d son of Ezra, born Oct. 1, 1731 —married Mercy, daughter of Matthew Belden, Feb. 1756—had issue, Moses, b. Aug. 14, 1756, Benjamin, Oct. 25, 1757, Ashbel, Sept. 18, 1759, Silas, Dec. 28, 1761, Roswell, Jan. 21, 1763, Justus, Jan. 23, 1767, Aaron, Sept. 14, 1769, and a daughter Elizabeth.

Benjamin, Caleb, sen'r., of Wethersfield—died May 8, 1684. Wife, Mary. His children were, Mary, aged 13, Sarah 8, Samuel 5, Abigail 11, John 6, and Martha 3 years. (See p. 114, 115.) One of his descendants emigrated to Stratford.

Berry, Nathaniel, of Mansfield—died 1719—wife, Elizabeth, and children, Nathaniel, Rachel Fuleham, Ann Fenton, Bethia Gove, Elizabeth, Sarah 14, and Abigail 11 years old.

Betts, John, sen'r., is found in Wethersfield as early as 1648, but removed to Long Island, and died at Huntington on the Island, before 1700. His son John was administrator.

Bevin, Arthur, of Glastenbury—died in 1697. Estate £269. Wife, Mary—children, John, b. 1676, Mary, 1678, Grace, 1679, Mercy, 1681, Thomas, 1682, Desire, 1684, Arthur, 1686, Joanna, 1687, Elizabeth, 1690, Abigail, 1692, Sarah, 1694, and Anna, 1696. Arthur Bevin came early to Wethersfield, before Glastenbury was incorporated as a town. Arthur died at Glastenbury.

Bidwell, John, of Hartford, (in No. 1,)—was in the colony in 1639. Wife, Sarah. He died in 1683. He gave to his son John, his swamp east of Connecticut river, also all his lands and buildings, in Hartford, west of the river. To his son Joseph, he gave £30; to his son Samuel, £20; to his daughters, Sarah House and Hannah Wadams, £20 each; to his daughter, Mary Meekins, half his upper lot, and the other half to his grandson, John Meekins, provided John should live with him and his wife until he became 20 years of age; he gave his wife, Sarah, half of all his estate not disposed of; to his son Daniel, he gave the property which he had devised to his wife, after her decease. He afterwards made a codicil, and added to and altered his will. Estate £419 : 10 : 6.

Bidwell or Biddoll, Jacob—Sarah, his wife—had children, Mabel,

b. March 19, 1766, d. July, 1766, Jacob, jr., Sept. 2, 1767, Jared, Feb. 12, 1769, 2d Mabel, June 23, 1771, Timothy, May 7, 1773, and d. March, 1774, Sarah, March 31, 1774, Lucretia, Oct. 2, 1777, Polly, July 23, 1780, d. Feb. 13, 1781, 2d Polly, Jan. 30, 1782, d. Feb. 4, 1782, 2d Timothy, Dec. 28, 1782, Abner, July 8, 1785, Charles, Sept. 10, 1787.

Bishop, John, of Wethersfield—was in the colony as early as 1648. He died in 1678. Wife, Sarah. Joseph Bishop, settled at Stamford as early as 1662—perhaps the son of Rev. John, who had previously preached there.

Blynn, Peter, of Wethersfield—died in 1724—wife, Mary—children, Peter, James, William, Deliverance, Mary Hurlbut, Daniel, Jonathan, and Margaret Belden. His silver-headed cane, he gave to his grandson, George Blynn. A joiner by trade.

Boarn, John, of Middletown, was supposed to have been lost at sea, and in 1707, administration was taken on his estate by Hannah, his wife. Children, Nathaniel 17, Francis 15 years old, and others.

Boreman, Mary, of Wethersfield—died in 1684. Estate £257— children, Isaac, Samuel, Mrs. Sarah Robbins, Jonathan, Sarah, Daniel, Nathaniel and Martha.

Bowman, Nathaniel, (inn-holder at Wethersfield in 1706–7.) He died unmarried without issue, in 1707, and gave his small estate to Samuel Buck, of Wethersfield.

Brunson, Richard, of Farmington—died, stricken in years, about 1685. His children were, Samuel, John, Hannah, Eddy, Abigail, Mary, and another son. He was the father of John, (see p. 119.) Estate £405 : 8.

Bunce, Thomas, of Hartford—wife, Sarah—died in 1683. Children, John, Elizabeth White, Thomas, jr. Estate £1024 : 3. He gave his son John his house, barn and home lot in Hartford, which he purchased of Thomas Gridley, and 40 acres near Wethersfield line, also his right in a saw-mill built by Mr. Gardner, Stephen Hosmer and himself; also, 16 acres in the south meadow; also, a lot near Mr. Websters. To Elizabeth he gave £20. He left a legacy to each of his grand children; also, to his cousin, Elizabeth White £ ; to his sister, Katherine Clark, £10 ; he also provided liberally for his wife, Sarah. To his son, Thomas, jr., he gave, after the death of his wife, all his housing and lands, not disposed of before, and made his son Thomas, executor of his will. (See p. 16.)

Burnam or Burnham, Thomas, is found at Hartford as early as 1648.

He resided at Podunk at the time he made his will, and at his decease. Wife, Ann. His children were, Thomas, John, Samuel, Richard and William, Rebecca, wife of William Mann—(perhaps the same William Man who settled early in Rhode Island,) the wife of Samuel Gaynes, the wife of William Morton, and the wife of Moore Cook. To his daughter, Rebecca, he gave his dwelling house and barn and other buildings on his home lot, together with the lot at Podunk, &c. He left a grandson, Thomas Gaynes. His will having been secreted by his widow, (Ann) or lost, was proved by the witnesses of the will, in June, 1690, though he died as early as 1688.

Burnham, John, the son of Thomas, died in 1721, and left a widow, Mary, who with his son, John, jr., were his executors. John, jr. had 10 acres of meadow land, bounded south on Samuel Burnham and Richard Gilman, and west on Podunk river, and 17 acres east of the country road ; and left other property to his other children, viz. Jonathan, Jabez, Caleb, Mary Webster, Rachel, Amy, Sarah, Elizabeth, and Silas, b. Nov. 1721. His inventory is dated May 15, 1721, appraised at £487 : 18 : 7. Sarah married Elisha Pratt, and had seven children. Elizabeth married Richard Gilman, March, 1702. Mary married Stephen Webster in 1717.

Burnham, Samuel, son of Thomas, of Hartford, d. 1728. Wife, Mary. His children were, Samuel, jr., Joseph, William, Daniel, Timothy, Hannah Drake, Amy Trumble, Mary Church, and Rebecca. Samuel and Joseph Burnham were his executors.

Burnham, Thomas, jr., son of Thomas, died in 1726. He left a son, Thomas, to whom he gave all his lands in Hartford and Windsor. He also left two daughters, Elizabeth and Esther Burnham—he gave them each £25. Thomas, jr. married a daughter of John Strong, of Windsor, who was his executor. He left three children, and a handsome estate.

Burnham, (another Thomas,) of Hartford, died in 1726. Wife, Naomy. He left children, Thomas, John, Josiah, Charles, Elizabeth Gilman, Sarah Mulford, Naomy Gailor, Mary, Abigail Williams. His son, Charles, was his executor.

Burnham, Capt. William, son of Samuel, a grandson of Thomas, senr., resided at Kensington, (then Farmington.) He died in 1749. Wife, Ruth. Elisha was his only son, to whom he gave half of his estate ; the other half he gave to his two daughters, Sarah and Ruth. He left an estate of £8246 : 10 : 11—distribution on file, 1756, and perhaps he left a daughter Mehitable. Sarah m. Elisha Pratt, 1726.

Burnham, Charles, son of Thomas, jr., of Hartford, died in 1753–4. Wife, Dorothy. Left children, Charles, jr., Freeman, Rachel, Stephen, Mary or Mercy Kilbourn, the wife of John Kilbourn, Anna, the wife of John Risley, and Susannah Burnham. He left a large estate.

Burnham, Caleb, of Hartford, son of John, died in 1750. Sarah, his widow and Caleb, jr., administrators. Account of administration presented by Jabez and Sarah Burnham in 1753. His minor children were, Isaac 12 years old, Sarah 10, Ame or Anne 5, and Jemima 3. He left a large estate.

Burnham, Nathaniel, of Wethersfield, died in 1755. Widow, Mehitabel. Children, Nathaniel, jr., Peter and Mehitabel.

Burnham, Lieut. Richard, of Hartford, son of Thomas, died in 1754. Elisha and Ezra Burnham, of Hartford, administrators. His estate was settled by an agreement on file. He married Sarah Humphrey, June 11, 1680. His children were, Sarah, b. July 11, 1683, Rebecca b. Sept. 20, 1685, Mercy b. April 14, 1688, Richard b. July 6, 1692, Martha Esther b. March 22, 1697, Charles b. July 23, 1699, Susanna b. Feb., Michael b. May 30, 1705.

Burnham, Martha, of Wethersfield, died in 1733. Her children were, Eleazer Gailord, Martha Wilcox, Elizabeth Gailord, Sarah Bissell, Hannah Orvis, and Samuel Gailord. Her son in law, Nathaniel Gailord, was her executor.

Burnham, Freeman, son of Charles, of Hartford, chose his brother in law, John Risley, his guardian in 1753.

Burnham, Jabez, son of John, died in 1760—Cornelius Burnham, of Hartford, was his administrator.

Burnham, Charles, of Hartford, son of Charles, died in 1760. Widow, Elizabeth. Elizabeth and Eastman, of Ashford, administrators.

Burnham, Aaron, of Hartford, died Sept. 14, 1760, supposed son of Richard. Widow, Hannah, who with Ezra Burnham, were his administrators.

Burnham, John, jr., son of John, left children, Silas b. 1721, Mary b. 1722, Stephen b. 1724, Sarah b. July, 1727, Daniel b. Nov. 1730, Mabel b. May, 1734.

Burnham, Rev. William, of Kensington, executed his will upon the 15th day of July, 1748. He died before 1751. His wife died before him. His children were, William, (he was married and resided near his father,) Josiah and Appleton. He gave his house and homested to his youngest son ; his large tracts of land, divided or undivided, in Farmington, he gave equally to his three sons, as well as lands in other towns. He left four daughters, viz. Hannah, wife of Jeremiah Curtiss, of Southington ; Lucy, the wife of Jacob Root, of Hebron ; Abigail, the wife of Lieut. Robert Willis or Welles, of Newington ; and Mary, the wife of John Judd, of Farmington. To his daughters he gave his servants, furniture, money, plate, books, cattle, swine, horses, indeed all his personal property, except his tools for husbandry. His Spanish Indian woman (Maria) he gave liberty to live with any of his children, and made them responsible for her support. His mulatto boy, James, he desired Abigail to take at appraisal—in case she refused, he then required William to take him upon the same terms, and if he refused, then to have him disposed of in one of the families of his deceased wife's children, or her sister's children. Rev. William was a gentleman of great wealth. His son, William, was his executor.

Burnham, Silas, son of John, and grandson of Thomas, b. 1726—daughter Mary, 22 years of age.

Butler, Dea. Richard, of Hartford, died in 1684. Wife, Elizabeth. Made his will in 1677. Children, Thomas, Samuel, Nathaniel, Joseph, Daniel, Mary Wright, Elizabeth Olmsted, and Hannah Green. To Thomas he gave his upper lot in long meadow ; to Samuel all his meadow land in Wethersfield meadow ; to Nathaniel his meadow lot near long meadow gate ; to Joseph his lands in south meadow ; to his son Daniel his dwelling house, buildings and land about it, also his lot called ten acres ; to each of his daughters he gave twenty shillings. Estate £564 : 15. Dea. Butler was a leading amd important man in Hartford. (See p. 16.)

Butler, William, of Hartford, brother of Richard, died in 1648–9. Mrs. West was his sister—he gave her children, in England, £5 each ; he gave his sister Winter's children, who lived in England, £5 each ; he gave Rev. S. Stone, T. Hooker £10 each ; John Steel and William Goodwin £10 each ; he gave three score pounds to the church in Hartford ; to William Gibbons and Mr. John Cullick £3 each ; to his brother, Richard, the remainder of his estate of £429. He appears to have left neither wife or children. (See p. 15.)

C.

Cadwell, Thomas, (in No. 1, p. 20)—had children, Mary b. Jan. 8, 1657, Edward, Nov. 1, 1660, Thomas, Dec. 5, 1662, William, July 14, 1664, Matthew, Oct. 5, 1668, Abigail, Nov. 26, 1670, Elizabeth, Dec. 1, 1672, Samuel, April 30, 1675, Hannah, Aug. 22, 1677, Mehitabel, Jan. 12, 1679.

Cadwell, Edward, son of Edward and Elizabeth, b. Sept. 24, 1681, William, Aug. 24, 1684, Elizabeth, Dec. 5, 1687, Rachel, April 3, 1689.

Cadwell, Matthew, of Hartford, m. Abigail Beckley, a daughter of John, March 25, 1695—and had Matthew, b. June 11, 1696, Abigail, April 28, 1698, Ann, May 6, 1700, John, Nov. 30, 1702, Abel, Nov. 27, 1703.

Camp, John, of Hartford—had children, Hannah, b. Nov. 24, 1672, John, Feb. 13, 1675, Sarah, Feb. 17, 1677, Joseph, Jan. 7, 1679, Mary, June 30, 1682, James, June 23, 1686, Samuel, Jan. 29, 1690, Abigail, July 30, 1699. (See p. 122.)

Catlin, John. His children were, Mary, b. July 10, 1666, Samuel, Nov. 4, 1673, John, April 27, 1676, Thomas, Aug. 1678, Benjamin, 1680. (See p. 123.)

Catlin, John, son of Samuel, married Elizabeth, October 20, 1703. Children, Thomas, b. Feb. 17, 1705–6, Samuel, March 27, —, Isaac, Nov. 11, 1712, Abijah, April 6, 1715, Mary, March 26, 1717, Ebenezer, July 25, 1724.

Chalkwell, Edward, of Windsor—died Dec. 5, 1648. He left no childeren. His legatees were, Nicholas Sensions, John Moses, Rev. Mr. Warham, George Phelps, and the poor of the church of Windsor.

Cheeny, William, of Middletown—died in 1705. Estate £259. He gave Benjamin Hand, of Middletown, 80 acres of land ; he gave Cheeny Clark, son of John Clark, deceased, his son in law, another lot of land of about 327 acres ; he gave Ambrose Clark, his brother, several lots ; he gave all his personal and real property not before named, to the three children of John Clark—Cheeny, Ambrose and Eunice. John Williams, and Abigail, his daughter, executors.

Clark, Samuel, of Wethersfield, in 1640, was of the company who purchased the town of Stamford of the New Haven Company, and settled there among its first settlers.

Clark, Nicholas, of Hartford—died in 1680. Children, Thomas appears to have been his only son. He had two daughters, one of them married Alexander Douglass, the other married Mr. Leister, of New London. He entailed his estate to his son Thomas, son in law Douglass, and grandsons Thomas, Daniel and Joseph Clark, and forbid any alienation by them of any of his estate either by deed or even by mortgage. Estate £243.

Clay, Miles, of Braintree or Brantery, in England, owned a right in the estate of Zachery Sanford, who had lately deceased, in 1678.

John Durant and John Loomis, of Hadley, were grand children of said Clay, either in their own or wives' descent, and were administators of his estate.

Coe, Robert, (in No. 1,) moved to Stamford in 1640 or 41. He was a worthy man, and much respected at Wethersfield, and the ancestor of those of the name in Connecticut. He died at Stamford.— (See p. 19.)

Cole, James, of Hartford, married Ann Edwards, the widow of Rev. Richard Edwards, who had been a minister in London, and died there. Mr. Edwards left a young son, William Edwards, who came to Hartford with his mother and father in law. Mr. Cole located in Cole-street, east of the South Green, in Hartford. Ann, his wife, died Feb. 20, 1678–9. She gave her house and lot to her son, William Edwards, during the lives of William and his wife, then to vest in her grandson, Richard Edwards, the son of William and his heirs forever. Richard was appointed administrator. Estate £103. James Cole had a son, John Cole, who married, and had a son John. John, sen'r., died at Hartford in 1685. Elizabeth married Daniel Sillivant, of New Haven. William, son of Ann, married Agnes Spencer, the widow of William Spencer, of Concord, about 1646, and had a son Richard, born in 1647. This William and his son Richard were the progenitors of the celebrated Edwards family of Connecticut. John, of Wethersfield, in 1640, (page 130,) was not the ancestor of either President Edwards, Pierpont, or either of the Dr. Edwardses.

Cole, John, grandson of James, of Hartford, died before his wife, about 1682 or 3. His son John settled at Farmington, to whom he gave £30. He had daughters, Benton and Wilson, and a son Job, in England, to whom he gave £10. He gave his wife £6 a year during her life, also a cow to be kept summer and winter during the life of his wife, out of his estate. The residue of his estate he gave to his sons Samuel and Nathaniel, except the housing and home lot, which was divided by metes and bounds, to his children. He gave Samuel 20 bushels of apples annually for six years, and gave Nathaniel the remainder, except some privileges to his wife, and 40 shillings to Hannah Yeomans. He was not the husband of Hannah Cowles below.

Cowles, Hannah, (widow of John, of Hartford)—died March, 1683. Estate £107. Children, Samuel, John, Hannah, (wife of Caleb Stanley) Esther Bull, Mary Dickinson, Elizabeth Lyman, and Sarah Goodwin.

Coltman, John, of Wethersfield—died about 1696. He married

Mary, who after his decease, married Mr. Sherman. Estate £142. He left three daughters and no sons. He was in the colony in 1645.

Colton, Rev. Benjamin, of Hartford, married Ruth Taylor, Dec. 3, 1713, died in 1759. He graduated at Yale College in 1710, and was the first minister of West Hartford.

Corbe, Samuel, of Haddam—died April, 1694. Estate £60. Children, Mary 17 months old, and " a posthumous son three months old, named Samuel."

Couch, Samuel, of Fairfield, in the year 1724, purchased of Chicken, an Indian saggamore, (who lived between Fairfield and Danbury,) Ridgefield and Newtown, at a place called Longtown, for the consideration of £12 : 6, all the lands situated between said towns, except such as had been Patented by the Governor and Company of Connecticut—(all unpatented land) Chicken reserved in his deed, to himself and his heirs, the right to hunt, fish and fowl upon the land and in the waters ; also reserved to himself, his children and grand children and their posterity, the use of so much land by his wigwam as the General Assembly should by an indifferent committee deem necessary " for him, and his children's children's children and their posterity."— Acknowledged before Joseph Platt, Justice, 1724. (The above Samuel Couch was a descendant of Thomas, in No. 3. Some of his posterity yet reside in Fairfield county, at Greensfarms.) Record of Patents, p. 31. (See No. 3, p. 127.)

D.

Davenport, Rev. John, of Stamford, was the only son of Rev. John Davenport, one of the founders of New Haven. Rev. John, of Stamford, had a daughter, Sarah, who married Rev. Eleazer Wheelock, D. D., of Lebanon. Dr. Wheelock was known as the " founder of Moor's Charity School for Christianizing the Indians." Sarah married Rev. Mr. Maltby, of New Haven, by whom she had a son and two daughters ; the son became a minister, and settled in Bermuda, in the West Indies, and afterwards settled in Charleston, S. C. ; one of the daughters died young, the other married Doct. Betts, of Norwalk, Conn. After the death of Mr. Maltby, she married Dr. Wheelock, while a widow, and by her 2d marriage had three children, viz. Theodora, Ruth and Ralph. Theodora married Alexander Phelps, Esq., of Hebron, who afterwards removed to Oxford in New Hampshire ; Ruth married Rev. William Patten ; Ralph was also a clergyman, and an assistant of his father in the ministry—and died without children. Ruth was born March 4, 1740. Rev. James Davenport was a brother of Sarah Wheelock. James had a son, John Davenport, who was a minister; Hon. Abraham Davenport, of Stamford, was also a son of John, and brother of James and Sarah. A daughter of Hon. Abraham, married Dr. James Cogswell, a son of Rev. Dr. Cogswell, of Windham—he had but one daughter, who married the Rev. Samuel Fisher. Hon. John, son of Abraham, married a daughter of the Rev. Noah Welles, of Stamford, and one of their daughters married Judge Radcliff, of Brooklyn, Long Island. The 2d son of Abraham, viz. Hon. James, was a gentleman of great ability; three of his daughters married clergymen, viz. Rev. Messrs. Whelpley, Bruen, of New York, and Dr. Skinner, late a Professor in the Theological Institution at Andover. It is supposed by the Compiler, that a sister of Sarah Wheelock married the Rev. Dr. Williams, of Springfield, who had three sons who were ministers, of which Rev. Dr. Williams, of Tolland, was one. By the different marriages into the Davenport family, they are now the relatives of the following families, viz. Pattens, Williams, Cogswells, Fishers, Welles, Radcliffs, Whelpleys, Bruens, Skinners, Storrs, Stebbins, Streets, Barkers, Reynolds, Kirklands, Wheelocks, and many other distinguished families in this country.

Davie, Humphrey, Esq.—inventory presented to court by John Davie, his son, Nov. 6, 1689. He died at Hartford, the 18th day of Feb. 1688. Wife, Sarah. He had two negro servants, both named Mingoe. He owned a small dwelling house with two and a half acres of land at (Beacon Hill) Boston, part of a powder mill at Dorchester, a small orchard at Rumney March, and had some moveables at Boston, and lands at the Eastward not then known. He was a gentleman of high respectability and wealth.

Deane, Hon. Silas, deceased, of Wethersfield, in Connecticut, came from the town of Groton to Wethersfield, about 1762. Oct. 8, 1763, he was married to Mrs. Mahitabel Webb, of Wethersfield, the grand mother of J. Webb, of Hartford. After her death he married a Miss Saltonstall. He had but one child, Jesse Deane, born June 24, 1764. Jesse located himself at Hartford. He married and had an only daughter, named Philura, who married Horatio Alden, of Hartford, at which place they now reside and have several children. Hon. Silas resided at Wethersfield until he received his appointment of Minister to the Court of France. He was a man of fine appearance, of about a middle stature, strong powers of mind, and a true gentleman of his day.

He never returned from his mission, but died in England in 1792. His wife died at Wethersfield in 1767, before he left this country for Europe. Hon. Silas owned two slaves, Pompey and Hagar, and though he had considerable estate at his decease, yet his estate proved to be insolvent—he having received of his country but little remuneration for his services abroad. Silas had several brothers, viz. Barnabas, Simeon, John, Barzillai, Jesse, and a younger brother whose name is supposed to have been David—the latter died young. Silas had also a sister Hannah, who married Josiah Buck, jr., of Wethersfield, whose descendants now reside there. Jesse, son of Silas, died at Hartford in 1828. At his decease he left a large estate to his only daughter, Philura. Hon. Silas Deane graduated at Yale College in 1758.

Deane, Jesse, brother of Silas, died at sea, and left no family.

Deane, Barnabas, also a brother, resided at Hartford, and was never married. He was a wealthy merchant—built and resided in the house where Daniel Buck, Esq. now resides in Hartford. He owned several stores and wharves in the city—was a partner in a large distillery, with John Caldwell, Esq.—and was also a partner with Jeremiah Wadsworth, Esq., and Gen. Green, of Rhode Island, of Revolutionary memory. He made his will in October, 1794, and gave to his nephew, Jesse Deane, his house and home lot where said Barnabas had lived in Hartford, and two gold watches, one of which had been left by his brother Simeon, and the other a French watch. He gave his friend, Jeremiah Wadsworth, his horse and saddle and £10 sterling in money, in testimony of his esteem for him. The residue of his property, real and personal, he directed to be sold, and the avails of the whole of it to be divided between his sister, Hannah Buck, and his nephew, Jesse Deane. The estate of Barnabas was appraised at £10,208 : 11. Another record says, the balance of the estate, after payment of debts, was paid over to Hannah Buck and John Deane, in equal shares.

Deane, John, a brother of Silas, died at sea in 1788. Doct. Caleb Perkins was his executor or administrator. He left no family.

Deane, Simeon, a brother of Silas, of Wethersfield, in April, 1777, being about to make a journey to a distant part of the continent, and to provide against the chance of his return, made his will—and as he had no family, he gave to Jesse, the only child of his brother Silas, all his books and wearing apparel ; he gave to his nephew, Josiah Buck, the 3d son of his sister Hannah, a debt due him from his brother in law, Josiah Buck ; he gave the United States the avails of tickets he held in the U. S. Lottery ; and the remainder to his brother Barnabas, his sister Hannah, and Jesse, his nephew.

Deane, Barzillai, brother of Silas, died at Wethersfield in 1788. Barnabas was his administrator. He left no family.

This family of brothers appear to have originated from the ancestor who settled early at Pequot, and were probably relatives of the Deane families at Stonington, Colchester, and Canaan—the latter moved from Colchester to Canaan many years since.

Deane, John, made his will at Hartford, the 25th day of June, 1791. He appears to have been of a different family. He gave in his will to his brother David Deane, his house, shop and one rood of land, at Flamington, ten miles from Trenton, in New Jersey, for which David was to support his father during his life. He gave to his sister Betsey Armstrong, of New Jersey, £50. ; to his father, the furniture to furnish one room. He ordered his large farm of 270 acres, situated and butted on the Raritan river, one mile in length, together with his stone house and other buildings on the farm and his lot on Limehill, to be sold by his executor, and laid out in farms at Hartford, Conn., for his children. To his wife, Mabel, he gave his moveables in Connecticut, and the use of his children's lands so long as she remained his widow. He ordered collected of his uncle, Doct. Jonathan Deane, 120 hard dollars, and a State note of £50, and $8000 in continental money, for his children. His slave, Jack, he ordered sold in New Jersey, or brought to Connecticut. The names of his children not found at Hartford.

Deane, Jarvis, of Manchester, died in 1824, and left an estate of $2348. His relation to Silas not found—probably of the Groton family.

Deane, William, of Plainfield, had a deed of land of William Blanchard, of Hartford, in 1720. Relation not found.

Deane, Joshua, of New London, married Charlotte Smith, of Wethersfield, June 27, 1830.

Deane, James, married Sarah Parker, June 2, 1697, both of Stonington. Their children were, James, b. Oct. 1671, Sarah, 1676, John, 1678, Nuphirus and Mary, (twins) 1680, William, 1684, and Francis, 1689. James, son of James, had James, b. 1698, Sarah, 1699, Francis, 1701, Christopher, 1702, Elizabeth, 1703, Jabez, 1704, John, 1707, Benajah, 1709, (David, 1711, d. 1711) Thankful, Jan. 1713.— James Deane, son of James, d. 1747 ; Sarah, daughter of James, d. Dec. 20, 1712. James and his children and grand children were of Stonington.

Diggins, Jeremy, resided in Hartford in 1684, and had children, Mary, Elizabeth and Jeremy, jr.

Disbrow, Nicholas, of Wethersfield—died in 1683. He left four daughters, but no sons. One daughter married Obadiah Spencer; one Samuel Egglestone; one John Kelsey, and one Robert Flood. Estate about £300.

Doan, Joseph, of Middletown—died Aug. 27, 1745. Estate £766.

Dodd, Edward, the son of John, of Northamptonshire, in England, was the first of the name that came to Hartford, Conn., and when 18 years of age, about 1682, to accompany his sister, Joanna, who afterwards married Thomas Richards, Esq., only son of Hon. James Richards of Hartford. Edward Dodd married Lydia Flowers, of Hartford, and had ten children, viz. Joanna, (married Joseph Porter,) John, married Dorcas Spencer, Lydia, married Bavil Seymour, Mary, (died young,) Mary 2d, married John Francis, and for her 2d husband married P. Ayrault, Edward, married Rebecca Barnard, Elizabeth, married Nathaniel Porter, son of Solomon, Anna, married Joseph Rockwell, Benjamin,—Timothy, married Abigail Benton. Edward, sen'r., died in 1729. Edward, jr., married Rebecca Barnard, March 14, 1744, and had eight children, Mary his last, b. April 4, 1765, and d. April 9, 1822. John, his eldest son, married first, Sarah Benton, and for his 2d wife, Mary Steel—by his first he had John, Henry and Sally, and by his 2d wife he had James, b. June 10, 1786. His first wife died in 1775, and his 2d wife died March, 1809.

Doolittle, Abraham, of Middletown—died in 1733. Wife, Martha, administratrix. Estate £288 : 7 : 9.

Douglass, Francis, came from the island of Barbadoes to Hartford. He disposed of his property in the West Indies before he left there, to his brother, Lewis Douglass, of London, Gent., sister Elizabeth and Mary Anne Douglass, of London, and Peter Douglass, of Barbadoes, and appointed Capt. Thomas Mapp and Joseph Bailey, of Barbadoes, his executors. He left his will in the hands of John Dallison, of Barbadoes, merchant. In 1731 he made another will at Hartford, and disposed of all his property in New England to Francis Bewithe, of Boston, merchant, and Mrs. Susannah Beuchamp, a daughter of John Beuchamp, of Hartford, Conn. His executors, Samuel Mather, of Windsor, and William Pitkin, of Hartford—they refused, and John Beuchamp was administrator. Mary Douglass, of Coventry, (9 years old) a daughter of Mary Johnson, then deceased, had a guardian appointed June 3, 1712—first of the name found in the Hartford Probate

Office. Francis Douglass, of Hartford, died in 1731. Samuel Douglass, of New Hartford, died in 1766. His administrators were, Samuel and Moses Douglass, of New Hartford. Estate £461 : 17 : 6. Distribution returned to court Oct. 11, 1770—on file.

Dunham, Thomas, (in No. 3,) died in 1717. The heirs to his estate were, John, Elisha, Benjamin, Edward and Ebenezer. Samuel Stetson and Desire Stetson were also heirs. Estate £285 : 17 : 6. (See p. 130.)

Dusee, Abda, alias Jinnings, of Hartford—died before 1710. Wife, Lydia.

Dutton, Joseph, of Haddam, (east society)—died in 1733. Wife, Mary. Samuel Dutton, executor. Children, Samuel, Benjamin, David and Thomas—Matthew Smith, son in law—Rebecca Gates, Ruth Millard, daughters. He had a grandson, William Selby. Will dated 1733. Estate £157 : 11.

E.

Edwards, William, of Hartford. He was a son of Richard Edwards, D. D., of London. After the death of his father, his mother married James Cole in London, and moved to America, and settled in Hartford, when William was young. After a few years William married Agnes Spencer, and had a son Richard, born in 1647. The grand mother of Richard died at Hartford in 1678–9, and gave her estate to her son William and his wife for their lives, and then to vest in Richard and his heirs forever. Richard for his first wife, married Miss Tuttle, and for his second wife, Mary Talcott, by whom he had the following children living at his decease, viz. John, Timothy, Samuel and Daniel—Mary, Abigail, Elizabeth, Ann, Mabel and Hannah. His widow, Mary, was living at his decease, and he provided for his son John, to take charge of his mother during her life. He also directed Daniel to be educated at College—and he graduated at Yale in 1720, and became a Judge of the Supreme Court of Connecticut, and died 1765. Samuel, he directed to be put to a trade, if his overseers thought advisable, and he gave him all his lands in Colchester, (250 acres.) Estate £1125 : 12 : 11. Richard Edwards died in 1718. His son, Timothy, was educated, and settled at East Windsor as their minister. He had a son, Jonathan, who graduated at Yale College in 1720, who became President of Nassau-Hall College, and one of the most celebrated and orthodox divines in New England. President

Edwards died in 1758. His son, Jonathan, D. D., graduated at Nassau-Hall College in 1765, who became President of Union College at Schenetady, and died in 1801. These were among the fathers of the divinity of New England, in the early settlement of the country. Such has been the respect entertained for this family of divines in Connecticut, that as late as 1834, even the step-stone of the door of the Rev. Timothy Edwards' house, in East Windsor, was placed as the corner-stone of the building erected there for the Theological Institute of Connecticut. (See James Cole, p. 204.)

Elson, Abraham, of Wethersfield, left a widow and two daughters, one 3 years, the other one year and a half old. He ordered his lands to be rented for four years to support his children. Estate £221. He gave to his friend, B. Gardner's children, his lot at the meadow gate, and the remainder to his wife, except his house and home lot, which he gave to the two sons of his wife, Benjamin and Job, after her decease.

F.

Farnsworth, Mary, in 1683, complained to the court at Hartford, that her husband had leased his farm and servant, and left her destitute of any means of living. She asked for half the rents of the land and servant.

Fayerweather, Benjamin, of Stratford, and his associates, in 1722, purchased for the consideration of £29 in money, of Waromaug and Nepaloe Peacooke, Indian proprietors of lands situated the east side of Stratford great river, northerly of New Milford, running with the river, one full mile east from the river, and 25 or 30 miles by estimation, to comprise the whole of the Massachusetts swamp. Deed dated March, 1722.

Ferris, John, settled at Stamford in 1640 or 41.

Finch, Abraham, of Wethersfield—died as early as 1640, and left a wife and one child, (Abraham) whom he left in charge of his grandfather, Abraham, who agreed to educate him at his own expense. David Finch, a son or brother of Daniel, (in No. 1) of Wethersfield—one of the purchasers of Stamford, and a first settler there.

Fisher, Robert, of Wethersfield, emigrated to Stamford as early as 1642.

Flood, Robert, of Wethersfield—died in 1689. His widow, Abigail, married Matthew Barry. Robert left several sons and daughters, and a small estate.

Foster, Rev. Isaac, settled in Hartford, in the ministry, in the latter part of 1679, or beginning of 1680, and died in 1683–4. Mehitable Russell, his wife—married about 1679. In 1679, before marriage, the parties formed a jointure, providing that if said Foster should deceaste before said Mehitabel and leave issue of her body, that the estate descend to her and her heirs. She had received one-third of the estae from Daniel Russell's last will, (supposed her father;) this one-third was distributed to the widow, and £200 to Ann Foster, to be paid her when 18 years of age or married, and the remainder of the estate to Mehitabel Woodbridge and her heirs. Estate £1507 : 15 : 4.

Fowler, Jonathan, of Windham—died before 1698. His widow, Elizabeth, administratrix. Children, Elizabeth, Joseph, Sarah and Jonathan.

Fyler, Lieut. Walter, of Windham—died in 1683. Wife, Jane. In his will he gave the use of his estate to his wife, Jane, during her life ; he also gave her £100 in cash to bestow upon *another husband*, or to reserve it to herself to bestow upon whom she pleased. He left two sons and no daughters. His sons were, John and Zerubbabel. He gave his grandson, Thomas, £20, and his other three grand children £5 each. Estate £318 : 6 : 10. Jane, his widow, died in 1690, not having married a second time. She had a grand child, Jane Fyler. The money her husband gave her to purchase a second husband, she carefully saved for her children and grand children. (See p. 26.) Zerubbabel Fyler, of Windsor, son of Walter, died in 1714. Wife, Experience. Children, Thomas, Zerubbabel, Stephen Fyler, Wakefield Dibble, Experience and Elizabeth Fyler, and Jonathan Deming, of Windsor. He left a good estate to his family. John Fyler, of Windsor, son of Walter, died in 1723, and left a large estate—(children not found.) Samuel Fyler, of Hebron, brother of Thomas, of Windsor, died in 1710. He was also a brother in law to Timothy Phelps, of Hebron. Estate £129. Children, Abigail 17 years old, Ann, Samuel, jr., 10 years old, an only son—perhaps other daughters. (See p. 134, No. 3.)

G.

Gardner, George, of Hartford—died in 1679. He had brothers, Thomas and Samuel. He owned an interest in a mill in Salem, Mass., and gave his son, Samuel, his house and land at Salem, where his son Samuel then lived, and his share of the mill there ; he also gave

Samuel his farm and meadow where Thomas Gold then lived. His house and land at Hartford, Windsor and Simsbury he gave to his son, Ebenezer. He had a daughter, Buttolph, also Mrs. Turner, who left children; another daughter, Hawthorn. He gave his daughters £300 each, and gave his cousins, Miriam Hascall and Susannah Hill £5 each; to his sister, Grafton £5; to his servant, Arrah £5. Estate, £3001 : 0 : 6. His widow, Elizabeth, died about 1681. She made her will, June, 1681. She left a grandson, Samuel Sedgwick, and a grandson, John Roberts. One of her family married a Mr. Fitch, another Mr. Butler. Mrs. Fitch had children, Rebecca, Nathaniel and Mary. Mr. Butler had a daughter, Sarah Butler. Her daughter, Elizabeth, married John Roberts, of Hartford. Mrs. Gardner died the widow of Rev. Samuel Stone, of Hartford, by whom she had Samuel Stone, jr. (See p. 135, No. 3.)

Gibbs, Giles, of Windsor—died in 1648. There appears to have been in the early settlement of Windsor, not only Giles, but Francis and Joseph Gibbs, who are supposed to have been brothers. Giles, in his will, directed that his son should be placed as an apprentice to some godly man for five years; and provided if he served out his time, for him to have the lot over the Great River. He gave Samuel, Benjamin and Sarah £20 each; he gave Jacob his house and home lot, and all his lots west of the river, after the decease of his mother. Katherine, his widow, executrix. Estate £76 : 18 : 8. (See p. 125.) Jacob Gibbs, of Windsor, an early settler there, before 1700—died in 1711–12. Widow, Abigail. Left an estate of £778 : 8 : 10. He was the first of the name who died in this colony. Children, Jacob, jr., Ebenezer, John, Abigail, Elizabeth, Mary and Esther. Samuel Gibbs, sen'r., of Windsor, (supposed to be a brother of Jacob,) died in 1716, an aged man. Children, Samuel, jr., his eldest son, Benjamin, Hepzibah, who married a Dickinson, and died before her father, Patience, who married Samuel Denslow, Elizabeth Hayden, Joanna, who married Moses Loomis, Experience Huxley, and Miriam, the wife of Josiah Bissell. He left an estate £111 : 3 : 9. Samuel Gibbs, jr., son of Samuel, died in 1720. No other estate of the name appears in the Probate record at Hartford for many years after this. John Gibbs, aged 17, (a son of Jacob, of Wethersfield, who was deceased in 1764,) made choice of William Morrice, of Wethersfield, for his guardian in 1764.

Gold, Nathan, (in No. 3,) of Fairfield, had a grandson by the name of Nathan, who was Lieut. Governor of Connecticut, from 1708 to

1724, until he deceased, aged 60. Samuel Gold, of Fairfield, died in 1723, aged 77. Col. Abraham Gold, his son, died in 1777, aged 44. He was killed at Ridgefield in the war of the Revolution. Jason Gold, son of Abraham, of Fairfield, died in 1810, aged 39. Abraham had two brothers, Daniel and Abel. Hon. John Gold, State Senator in 1847, is also a descendant of Hon. Nathan, of Fairfield. (See p. 136, No. 3—also p. 28, No. 1.)

Goodfellow, Thomas—died Nov. 25, 1685. Wife, Mary. He resided in the colony as early as 1639. Estate £49.

Goodwin, George, moved from Hartford to Fairfield about 1654.

Gozzard, Nicholas, of Windsor. Widow, Elizabeth—and children, Matthew 16 years old, Eizabeth 4, John 11. (See p. 137.)

Grant, Seth, of Hartford—died as early as 1646. Estate £141.

Gray, Walter, was in the colony in 1644. He died at Hartford in 1684 or 5. He left several children and a small estate. (See p. 138.)

Grimes, Henry, of Hartford—died about 1684. Wife, Mary. Benjamin, eldest son. The widow died in 1685. Children, Benjamin 22 years old, John 19, Joseph 17, Mary 16, Sarah 13, Ellizabeth 10, Susanna 7, Rebecca 4. The widow, in her will, provided for her brother Benjamin to take her second daughter—her brother Joseph the third daughter, and John Watson the fourth, to educate and bring up.

Griswold, Francis, of Norwich, in 1660, appears to have been of a different family from that of Matthew, of Lyme, or Samuel, of Windsor—perhaps the same Francis who was at Cambridge in 1637.— (See Farmer.)

Gross, Josiah, of Hartford, married Susanna, and had Samuel, born Jan. 24, 1719, Susanna, born June 20, 1722.

H.

Hallaway, John—died in 1683–4. He resided alone in his house, and the selectmen made an inventory of his estate—probably left neither wife or children.

Halstead, Henry, of Hartford—died in 1692. He lived with John Meekins, sen'r. He gave what property he had to said Meekins' children, viz. John, jr., Mary and Sarah.

Hamlin, Hon. Giles, an early settler at Middletown. He apparently came from England, and located first at Middletown as early as 1654. (See p. 39.) He had followed the seas some—perhaps as captain—before he came to this country. He was a firm Puritan, a man of good common sense, and soon gained a high standing in the colony, for probity and ability ; and as early as 1673, and for years after, he was an assistant in the colony—was long a magistrate—frequently on important committees—a member of both branches of the General Assembly ; indeed he was one of the pillars of the colony in its early settlement. He married Eunice Crow, daughter of John, of Hartford, grand daughter of elder William Goodwin. He made his will Aug. 30, 1689, in which he gave his son, Hon. John, the home lot, a parcel of land in long meadow, one half of his land at " Gooses Delight," and many other large tracts of land on both sides of the Connecticut river, with £30 in money, one silver platter, one large silver spoon, the largest silver hat-band, one cow, and one breeding mare. He gave to his sons, Giles, jr. and Richard, all his lands at Hartford, and his interest in the mills, by paying their mother, annually, during her life, £14. He gave Giles, jr. a large silver spoon and silver wine cup and one gilt spoon ; to Richard a silver spoon and silver dram cup. For his wife, Hester, he made ample provision. To his daughter, Mary, he gave £100 in money and a share of his furniture ; he also gave to her his servant, Joan, if she needed her, and his widow could spare her ; also a silver spoon and plate. To his daughter, Mabel, he gave £50 in money over and above what he had given her before, and one silver spoon and porringer and goblet, to be divided between Mary and Mabel. He gave a cow to young Samuel Hooker and a small silver spoon. To young John Hamlin, his grandson, he gave a cow and a small silver spoon. The remainder of his estate he gave equally to his sons. The widow and his son John, he made executors of his will. He had grand children, John Hamlin, jr., Giles Southmayd, Samuel Hooker, jr., to each of whom he gave an ewe lamb, and gave the same to each of his negro servants. He died greatly lamented and respected, in 1689 or 90. Estate £2249 : 18: 6.

Hamlin, Hon. John, of Middletown, was the eldest son of Hon. Giles. He posssessed all the abilities and virtues of his father, and had a larger share of public favors. He was a member of the church over forty years, and was an assistant in the colony from 1694 to 1730. In 1715 he was appointed a Judge in Hartford county, and from 1716 to 1721 he was an assistant (or side) Judge of the Supreme Court of the colony. From his early life to his death, in 1733, (aged 75 years) he was greatly esteemed for his many great and good qualities. His wife, Sarah, survived him. He disposed of his great wealth to his family by will. He made provision for his wife so long as she should bear his name, and gave her the use of a part of his house and furniture, unless she should reside with her *own* children, (probably a widow when he married her.) His children were, John, jr., who (though married) died before his father. To John, jr.'s children he gave £340, and the house and homested that John, jr. possessed at his decease, and other lands. The children of John, jr. were, Giles, Mahitabel, Elizabeth and Mary ; to these children he also gave each £60 in silver, besides lands and other property. Hon. John gave to his son, Jabez the house and home lot where he resided, the homested with all the buildings and fences, wharves, warehouse and the grounds—they stood upon the land which had been given him by the town. He also gave him large tracts of land, also his negro, Robbin, the silver tankard, silver hat-band and his seal ring. He ordered his land, located east of Connecticut river, to be immediately sold by his executor, and each of his daughters to be paid £500, viz. Esther, Mary and Sybil. The residue of his real and personal estate, he directed to be divided equally between his four children then living, except Mary King, his grand daughter, was to have a half share with them. One daughter married Mr. Johnson, Sybil married Mr. Dwight, Esther married Mr. Hall, Mary married Mr. Blake or Blague. He gave also in his will, to (his clergyman) Rev. Mr. Russell, £5 ; the church of which he was a member, £5. He had grandsons, Hamlin John Hall, Hamlin Blake, Hamlin Johnson,—to these he gave each, one ewe sheep ; his sealing ring he gave to his grandson, John Hamlin ; to his daughter, Sybil Dwight, he gave his silver salt-cellar ; to his grand daughter, Esther Hall, he gave a silver cup with two handles ; to his grand daughter, Mary Blake, a silver cup with one handle, and to Sybil Dwight, his grand daughter, he gave his silver porringer and dram cup.

Hamlin, Hon. Jabez, grandson of Hon. Giles, and son of Hon. John, became more extensively known and employed by the public than either Giles or John. He graduated at Yale College in 1728. Being mild in his disposition, affable and easy in his deportment, he became greatly respected in the colony and State. He was a colonel of militia, and magistrate in 1733, and was a side Judge in Hartford county from 1745 to 1754, at which latter period he was appointed Chief Judge until 1784. He was also Judge of Probate from 1752 until 1789, and was Mayor of the city of Middletown from its incorporation, in 1784, until his death. He was an assistant from 1773 to 1778. He was frequently a member of the General Assembly and Speaker of the House of Representatives. During the war of the Revolution he was a member of the Council of Safety, and was found in that important body of patriots not only a useful, but a safe adviser in that eventful struggle for liberty. He was a deacon of the first church in Middletown for many years. He died in 1791, at the advanced age of 82 years. He was born, July, 1709. He married for his first wife, Mary Christophers, of New London ; by her he had Sarah, b. Aug. 3, 1730, d. 1799, John, b. Nov. 14, 1731, d. Aug. 28, 1736, Christopher, b. April 25, 1733, d. Aug. 5, 1768, Mary, b. Nov. 21, 1734, d. Sept. 17, 1736, Esther, b. March 22, 1736, d. Jan. 13, 1812. For his 2d wife he married Margaret Phillips, of Middletown ; by her he had John, b. Sept. 5, 1737, and George, b. Feb. 1738. John died in 1750 ; George also died Sept. 15, 1750. He lost his 2d wife, and married Abigail Chauncey, of Durham ; by her he had Jabez, b. Dec. 11, 1752, d. Sept. 20, 1776, Margaret, b. June 22, 1756, d. Aug. 1847, (Mrs. Canfield,) Abigail, b. May 4, 1758. The five sons left no children. For his 4th wife he married Susannah Whittlesey, the widow of Rev. Mr. Whittlesey, of Milford. She was born Jan. 1716. By the last wife he had no children. Mrs. Hubbard, of Middletown, and Mrs. Esther Rainey or Ranny, of New London, are now living, and are grand daughters of Hon. Jabez Hamlin.

Hamlin, William, son of Hon. Giles, of Middletown—died in 1733. His children were, Richard, Nathaniel, Edward, Charles, Susannah and Esther. (Nathaniel died before his father.) William left a grandson, Timothy Cornwell, and a grand daughter, Rebecca Cornwell. He gave Rev. William Russell, his clergyman, £5, and Jabez Hamlin £5. His son Charles, was sole executor of his will. He left a large landed estate.

Hamlin, Nathaniel, grandson of Giles, and son of William—died in 1733, and left Mary, his wife—and children, William, Harris and Sarah. In 1737 the court appointed Richard Hamlin guardian for said William, aged 12, also for Harris, aged 5 years—Nathaniel Baker or Bacor was appointed guardian, at and by said court, for Sarah, 9 years old, children of Nathaniel. After the death of Nathaniel, his widow, Sarah, married for her 2d husband, Nathaniel Baker.

Hamlin, John, son of Hon. John—died young, but left a widow, Elizabeth, and four children, viz. Giles, Mahitabel, Elizabeth and Mary. These children were amply provided for in the will of their grand father. Estate £790 : 19. He left 2 gold rings, 4 oz. of silver buttons, a silver tankard 10 oz., a silver goblet 9 oz., 6 silver spoons 12 oz.

Hamlin, Richard, son of William, married Martha Smith, Nov. 30, 1721, and had Mary, b. July 3, 1722, Esther, b. Oct. 9, 1723, Nathaniel, b. May 29, 1732.

Hamlin, Nathaniel, married Sarah Ware, Sept. 16, 1725, and died Sept. 28, 1731. His children were, William, b. Feb. 11, 1725–6, Sarah, b. April 24, 1728, Harris, b. April 14, 1730, Susannah, b. Jan. 27, 1731.

Hamlin, Charles, grandson of Giles, married Elizabeth Starr, Dec. 18, 1735. By this wife he had Charles, b. Sept. 2, 1736, when his wife died. He then married a 2d wife at Hartford, and had Richard, b. May 12, 1741, John, b. Feb. 23, 1743, William, b. Nov. 17, 1744, and died Sept. 23, 1753, Samuel, b. Sept. 9, 1746, and two sons, twins, b. April 1, 1749, one of which died, aged 5 days. In Oct. 1761 he married Elizabeth Rogers, and had Elizabeth, b. Feb. 5, 1762—she died July, 1762—Elizabeth, b. Jan. 30, 1763.

Hamlin, Nathaniel, of Suffield, died in 1760, and Samuel Kent, jr. was administrator on his estate.

Hamlin, William, son of Nathaniel, married Hannah Allen, June 22, 1750. Their children were, Lucia, b. Sept. 22, 1751, and died Sept. 25, 1751, Hannah, b. Nov. 2, 1752, William, b. Sept. 14, 1754, Lucia, b. May 15, 1756, Susannah, b. July 29, 1757, Sarah, b. Nov. 15, 1758, Elizabeth, b. Sept. 15, 1760, Experience, b. Nov. 10, 1761.

Hamlin, Nathaniel, son of Richard, married Lucretia Ranny, March 9, 1755, and had children, Daniel, b. July 23, 1755, John, b. Jan. 7, 1757, Esther, b. July 10, 1759, Martha, b. May 29, 1761, Lucretia, b. May 3, 1763.

Hamlin, Jabez, son of Thomas, son of Eleazer, lived in Sharon, Ct., from thence he removed to Austerlitz, Columbia county, N. Y., and from thence to Alford, Berkshire co., Mass., where he died, aged 94. His sons were, Solomon, Amasa, Jabez, John, Frederick and Erastus. The four first are deceased—Frederick lives in Elyria, Lorain co., Ohio—Erastus lives in DeKalb co., Illinois. His daughters were, Zilpha, Lucinda, Ruth and Phoebe ; they are all deceased except Lucinda, who now lives in Alford, aged 82. Zilpha married a Mr. Pardee, of Sharon. She had three sons, two of whom are now living, Daniel in New York, and David in Delhi, Delaware co., N. Y. Ruth married, first, a Mr. Johns—second, Samuel Church, of Salisbury, as his third wife, (the father of Chief Justice Church,) by whom she had Nathaniel and Frederick, and two daughters. The sons of Jabez Hamlin, jr. are, Lorenzo F., an attorney, of Elyria, Lorain co., Ohio, John

W., farmer, Aurora, Erie co., N. Y., Hon. Edward S., attorney, Cleaveland, Ohio, Frederick V., merchant, New York, and Cicero J., merchant, Buffalo, N. Y. They are all living. Frederick V. married Catherine E. Hinman, daughter of R. R. Hinman, Esq., of Hartford, March 16, 1847. Jabez's daughters were, Minerva C., married Mr. Hazen, author, N. Y. city, Emeline B., deceased, Harriet, Lucinda L., married Edward Phelps, attorney at law at St. Mary's, Mercer co., Ohio. It appears there were, in the first settlement of New England, two brothers by the name of Hamlin, who emigrated to Massachusetts, one settled about Cape Cod, and the other settled at Middletown, Ct.

Haughton, Richard—died at Wethersfield in 1682—he was building a vessel there at the time of his death.

Hawkins, Sarah, daughter of Anthony—died in 1678. She had an interest in her father's will, also in the will of her brother John Hawkins. Sarah divided her property between her four sisters, viz. Mary, Ruth Hart, Elizabeth Brinsmade, and Hannah Hawkins. Mrs. Ann Hawkins, of Farmington, died in 1680. Her property was distributed to her son, John, Thomas Thompson, Beatrice Parker, Mary Hally or Holly, Hester Gridley and Honor Hawkins.

Heberd or Hibbard, Robert, of Windham—died previous to 1710.

Heber, Christian, of Hartford—died Dec. 1680.

Hilton, John, of Middletown—died in 1686. Children, John, aged 11, Richard 7, Ebenezer 8 months, and Mary 14 years.

Huit, Rev. Ephraim, of Windsor—died in 1643. Estate £633: 19s. The widow survived him. Children—no sons—four daughters. (See p. 41.) The widow married a second time.

Holly, Francis, became a settler in Stamford as early as 1662—was a leading man in the colony, and is supposed to have been the ancestor of a respectable family now of Salisbury. This name is found uniformly spelt Holly and not Hawley.

Hoyt, Thomas, of Windsor, moved to Stamford, and settled there in 1662.

Hungerford, Thomas, of Haddam—died in 1713. Wife, Mary. He gave all his buildings and the grass land adjoining them in East Haddam, and other lands, to his wife; he gave his son, Thomas, one half his land at Stonington which fell to him by his father; he gave his son, John, and his male heirs, his buildings and homested of 80 acres, (except what he gave his wife); to his son, Green Hungerford, he gave half his interest in land in Stonington, and half his land east of eight mile river, and his right in the Moodus meadows on falls river; he gave to his five daughters, Elizabeth, Susannah, Sarah, Mary and Esther, the remainder of his moveable estate, after one-third to his wife; to his grandson, John Churchill, he gave his rights in Lyme; he gave his son Thomas's eldest son, half of his 4th division east of eight mile river. Estate £278. The deceased was a grandson of the Thomas Hungerford mentioned in page 39. This was one of the best names in England, particularly in the days of Oliver Cromwell.

Hungwell, John, in 1682 sued Samuel Collins, at Hartford.

Hurlbut, John, of Middletown—died Aug. 30, 1690. Legatees, John Hurlbut, b. Dec. 8, 1671, Thomas, b. Oct. 20, 1674, Laura, b. Dec. 6, 1676, Mercy, b. Feb. 17, 1680, Ebenezer, b. Jan. 17, 1682, Margaret, b. Feb. 1684, Mary, b. Nov. 17, 1678, David, b. Aug. 11, 1688, and one in March, 1690.

Hutchins, John, of Wethersfield—died in 1681—left a widow and two children, Sarah, 4 years old, and Ann, a year and a half old.— Estate £38.

Huxley, Thomas, of Suffield—died in 1767. Martin Ashley, of Suffield, administrator, also his widow Lois Huxley. Estate £558 : 17s. Thomas Huxley, of Suffield, a minor in 1781, chose Gideon King, of Suffield, his guardian—perhaps a son of Thomas, deceased, above.

J. & K.

Jagger, Jeremiah, in 1640, was one of the purchasers of Stamford, and soon after located there. He had resided, firstly at Wethersfield, and probably moved with Charles Tainter to Fairfield county.

Johnson, Thomas, of Hartford—died in 1641. Estate £10.

Knight, George, of Hartford, (from Great Britain.) Sarah, his wife—had children, Sarah, b. April 27, 1680, married George Sexton, Dec. 25, 1699, Love, b. Sept. 10, 1682, married Thomas Andrews, son of Thomas, Nov. 20, 1702, Elizabeth, b. Dec. 13, 1690, Anne, b. April 16, 1688. George Knight died April 19, 1698. The children of Thomas and Love Andrews were, Thomas, b. Aug. 21, 1703, Elijah, b. March 13, 1705–6, Love, b. Nov. 8, 1708, Samuel, b. Jan. 6, 1712–13. Sarah Knight married Samuel Galpin, Dec. 9, 1715. Jerusha Andrews, daughter of Love, b. June 14, 1716. Love, the wife of Thomas, died Oct. 13, 1718. Moses Ensign, of Hartford, married Love Andrews, daughter of Thomas, Jan. 3, 1730–1.

L.

Lancton, John, jr., of Hartford—died in 1683. Estate £100 : 5. He was a son of Dea. John Lancton, who was administrator. The estate was given to his son, John, to be received at the age of 21 years. In case of the death of John, then to be divided among the children of Dea. Lancton.

Lee, John, of Farmington—died in 1690. Estate £359. Children, John 30 years of age, Mary 26, Stephen 22, Thomas 19, David 16, and Tabitha.

Leete, Hon. William's will was presented to the court at Hartford, May 16, 1683. Gov. Leete gave to his wife, Mary, the use of his hall chamber in his house at Guilford, well furnished, and the rents of half the housing and lands at the island, and of the church housing and land at New Haven, and £6 a year out of his estate during her life. He gave to his lame daughter, Graciana, the remainder of his housing and land in the whole home lot at the town, in fee-simple, &c., to be inherited by his son, John, after her decease ; to his daughter, Ann, (beside former gifts) £100 in his best household stuff.· His sons, Andrew and William were married, also Abigail, to whom he had given their portions ; yet he gave by his will to Andrew and William his farm at Causenchaug, and the property given him at Stonington by Herman Garret, and other lands to his sons. To his daughter, Abigail Woodbridge, he gave £10 in household stuff, &c. ; the remainder he gave to his three sons equally, and made them his executors. Dated Hartford, April 2, 1683. After the above he made a codicil, and made additional provision for his wife. Gov. Leete left a large estate for A. D. 1683. After the Union of the Connecticut and New Haven Colonies, in 1665, Mr. Leete was elected Gov. of Connecticut in 1676, and was continued in the office until 1683, inclusive. He had previously been elected Lieutenant Governor from 1669 to 1675, inclusive. Gov. Leete, previous to the Union of the Colonies, had uniformly held a high standing as a man and a Christian, in the New Haven Colony.

Lothrop, Benjamin, of Hartford—died in 1690. He had property on board the sloop Adventure. Malatya Lathrop, administrator—probably a sailor.

Loveland, Robert, of Glastenbury, made his will in Dec, 1762—he was then an aged man. Sons, Lot and Robert—daughter, Ruth Andrews, Hannah Loveland. Lot and Hannah, executors. Perhaps other daughters.

Lucas, William, of Middletown—died in 1690. William, his eldest son, 23 years old, John 21, Mary 18, Thomas 14, Samuel 11. Left a small estate of about £39.

Lyon, Richard, was at Fairfield in 1654, and is the first of the name found in the colony. Henry at Fairfield in 1657.

M.

Maccoy, Hugh, of Wethersfield—died in 1683—no family found. Alice Maccoy was administratrix of his estate, £100. He had 60 acres of land and a house, and appears to have been a farmer.

Macmin, James, of Windsor—died in 1698. Wife, Elizabeth. Left a handsome estate to his widow, and appears to have left no children.

Marks, Thomas, of Middletown, in 1730. Wife, Sarah—(Sarah Tobe before marriage.) Broughton ran away with a sloop from New London, and carried off the goods of Marks.

Maudsley, Capt. John, of Windsor, (page 153, No. 3,) died in 1690. He owned a mill in Windsor, and an estate of £228; he also had houses and lands at Westfield, appraised at £543.

Merrills, John, of Hartford, had children, Sarah, b. Sept. 19, 1664, Nathaniel, John, Abram, Daniel, Walterton, Susannah, Abel, Isaac and Jacob, b. March 27, 1686.

Miller, John, settled at Stamford as early as 1661.

Mills, Simon, of Windsor—died in 1683. Estate £168. Children, John, aged 14, Simon 5, Mary Humphrey, eldest daughter, 20, Hannah 18, Sarah 13, Abigail 11, Elizabeth 9, Prudence 7. He owned land at Weataug, at horseshoe swamp, at long meadow, and four parcels on the plain.

Minor, Thomas, (in No. 2, p. 54,) of New London, was the first and only person of the name who came to Connecticut. He married Grace Palmer, April 23, 1634. Children, Manasseh, John, Thomas, Clement, Ephraim, b. April 27, 1642, Joseph, Eunice and Marie. John emigrated to Stratford, and from thence he removed to Woodbury in its first settlement, and became the town clerk of Woodbury for about 30 years. From this branch of the family of Thomas, are all of the name descended in Fairfield and Litchfield counties. (See No. 3, p. 153.)

Morecock, Nicholas, of Wethersfield, in 1693.

Morehouse, Thomas, at Fairfield, in 1654. He first settled at Stamford in 1641.

Morrice, Robert, of Hartford, brother of John, of Windsor—died Nov. 19, 1684. In his will he gave Hannah, the wife of Caleb Stanley, some of Baxter's works; to Hannah Pitkin, a daughter of the wife of Caleb Stanley, a book called the "Godly Man's Ark;" to Elizabeth Stanley, her sister, he gave "Abraham's intercession for Sodom;" and other books and property to John Andrews, John Wilson, Samuel Spencer, John Tileston his kinsman, Jeremy Diggins, and Thomas Andrews; to Mary, Elizabeth and Jeremy Diggins, jr., children of Jeremy Diggins and John Wilson, the remainder of his property. He appears never to have been married.

Moses, John, of Windsor—died in 1683. He married Mary Brown, who survived him, and had one-third of his real estate, and £64 personal estate. Distribution of his estate to Timothy £66, to Mary £70, to his four youngest daughters £60 each. Estate £575. Children, John, 28 years old, Timothy 14, Mary 22, Sarah 19, Margaret 17, Martha 12, and Mindwell 7.

Mygatt, Dea. Joseph, of Hartford—died in 1680. For his son, Jacob, he had built a house. He left a wife, to whom he gave an annuity during her life. He had a grandson, Joseph Deming, son of John Diggins, and a grandson, Joseph Mygatt, who was his executor. Estate £368. Ann Mygatt died in 1685–6.

N.

Newman, William, settled at Stamford in 1662. (See Newman in No. 2, p. 57.)

North, John, of Wethersfield—died in 1682. Wife, Susannah.—Children, John, aged 10, Mary 3, Susannah 6. Estate £133. Samuel North, of Wethersfield or Farmington—died in 1682. Estate £188. Children, John, aged 13, Samuel 10, Thomas 8, Hannah 4.

Nott, Serg't. John, of Wethersfield—died in 1680–1. Wife, Ann. Children, Elizabeth Reeves, Hannah Hale, and John Nott.

O.

Ogden, John, a settler at Stamford as early as 1662.

Olderman, William, of Farmington or Simsbury—died in 1697. Mary, his relict. Children, Thomas, 14 years old, William 12, John 3, Joseph 1, Mary 17, Sarah 6. Property at Farmington £42, at Simsbury £53.

Orton, John, of Farmington—died in 1695-6. His widow, Mary, and Thomas Orton, administrators. Estate £486. Left sons and daughters. John and Samuel appear to have been his sons. The maiden name of his wife was Tudor. The estate she received of her father Tudor, she received of her husband's estate as her dower. (See p. 59.)

Osborn, Widow—died in 1689. Children, John, 43 years old, Nathaniel 36, Mary Owen, Samuel Osborn 26, Hester Owen 22, Sarah Wright 20, Hannah Eggleston 24. Richard Osborn, at Fairfield, in 1654. The Osborns in New Haven and Fairfield counties, originated at Long Island, and not from the family at Windsor.

P.

Parents, John, of Haddam—died in 1686. He left a daughter in the care of Nathaniel Chapman, and had another daughter, and no sons. Estate £84. He moved from Hartford to Haddam.

Paring, Samuel, of Windsor—died in 1690. Estate £6. No family.

Patten, Rev. William, was one of the first of the name who settled in Connecticut. He was the son of Nathaniel, of Billerica, near Boston, where he was born. He graduated at Dartmouth College in 1754, and received an honorary degree at Yale in 1759. In 1767, owing to the ill health of the Rev. Elnathan Whitman, who had been settled at the South Church in Hartford, Conn., in 1732, Mr. Patten was settled as his colleague. He married Miss Ruth Wheelock, a daughter of Rev. Eleazer Wheelock, D. D., of Lebanon, afterwards President of Dartmouth College. He finished his collegiate and theological education, married and settled at Hartford when quite young. In 1773 his health began to fail and he left the charge of the church at Hartford, and in 1775, while on a visit at his father's house at Roxbury, Mass., he declined so rapidly that he died there on the 16th day of January, 1775, aged 37. His children were, Eleazer W., Sarah, Rev. William, Ruth, Nathaniel, Mary, Charlotte and George J. Of this family, Eleazer W., Charlotte and Nathaniel died in early life and unmarried. Ruth and Mary are now residing at Hartford, as samples of living piety. Sarah died since 1840, and George J. in 1830, unmarried. Rev. William, D. D., son of Rev. William, of Hartford, graduated at Dartmouth College in 1780, and received the honorary degree of D. D. at Brown University. He was settled in the ministry at Newport, R. I., in 1786, where he preached about 48 years. He married Hannah Hurlbut, of New London, and had the following family, viz. Ruth W., William S., Joseph H., Maryanna, Floride, George W. and Charlotte. Ruth W. married Frederick W. Hotchkiss, a merchant, of Hartford, and had a family of three sons and two daughters, all of whom are now living, except Elizabeth, who died young. William, son of Dr. Patten, is a lawyer at Providence, R. I. Joseph is a lawyer in New York. Maryanna married C. Stockton Halsted, of Brooklyn, N. Y. Floride resides in Brooklyn, N. Y. George W. is a captain in the U. S. Army, and distinguished himself, where he was wounded in the bloody battle at Cerro Gordo, in Mexico, in 1847. Charlotte died recently. Dr. Patten died at Hartford in 1839, aged 76 years, and in the 54th year of his ministry. (See Davenport, p. 205.)

[Rev. William Patten, sen'r., was admitted to Harvard University when about 12 years of age ; within two years after he received his degree. He was licensed to preach, and was ordained before he was 19 years of age, at Halifax, in Mass., where he continued about ten years, when his ill health rendered it necessary for him to ask for a dismission from his society, and was afterwards settled at Hartford. He graduated at Harvard College in 1754, and not at Dartmouth, as stated on the preceding page.]

Peters, Arthur, of Wethersfield—died in 1690, unmarried, and gave his estate to Ephraim Goodrich, of Wethersfield.

Phillips, George, of Windsor—died 1677 or 8—was found dead in his room. Estate £152. No family found. (See p. 63.)

Pierce, Edward, of Simsbury—died in 1693. No estate.

Pinkney, Philip, at Fairfield in 1654.

Piper, Richard, of Haddam—died in 1678. Left no family. Estate £204. Legatees, Susannah Ventriss, John Ventriss, Sarah Gates, 2d, John and Samuel Ackley, John Kinnard and Edward Purfell.

Pomeroy, Eltwed or Edward, (in No. 2)—had a son, Medad, born in 1638, Caleb, b. in 1641, Mary, b. in 1644, Joshua, b. in 1646, and Joseph, b. in 1652. Caleb m. Hepzibah Baker, May, 1664, and had a daughter, Hepzibah, b. in 1666, and probably had other children after he moved to Northampton. Samuel Benton m. Mary Pomeroy, of Northampton, a daughter of Medad. (See p. 65.)

Porter, John, came from England, and settled in Windsor in 1639, and died in 1698. He had a son, Nathaniel, b. at Windsor in 1640, Hannah, b. in 1642. He also had a son, John, who married and had

John, Mary, Sarah, James, Nathaniel, Hannah, Samuel, Rebecca, Hester, Ruth, Hezekiah and Joseph. The last John, in 1669, m. Joanna Gaylord, and had Joanna, Mary, John, Sarah and Ann.

Post, John and Thomas, of Norwich, made free in 1663—probably were brothers, and the sons of Stephen, who settled at Hartford before 1639, and was in the land division of 1639—but left Hartford before he died.

Powell, Thomas, of Windsor—married in 1676, and had Ann, born in 1678, and Thomas, b. in 1680. John Powell, of Windsor, died in 1685, and left an estate of £3 : 9.

Preston, William, of Hartford, in 1642—probably went to Stratford, where the name was soon after found, and some years after at Woodbury. Neither William or Edward Preston died at Hartford. (See No. 2.) The name is yet at Woodbury and Hartford.

R.

Randall, Abraham, of Windsor—died Aug. 22, 1690. Estate £140. He had two wives. He had adopted as a son, his cousin Abraham Phelps, when a child, (who was now married,) and he made him his principal legatee, and provided for his wife, and gave small legacies to Isaac Phelps, of Westfield, and Joseph Phelps, of Windsor. Left no children of his own. William Randall, of Middletown, died in 1684. Estate £18. The Randalls finally settled at Middletown.— William Randall, of Hartford, died in 1684, and gave his estate to Thomas, John and Rachel Grant, the children of his wife. (See No. 2.)

Ranny, Thomas, of Middletown—died in 1713. Wife, Mary. Estate £758. Children, Thomas, John, Joseph, Ebenezer, Mary Savage, Elizabeth, wife of Jonathan Warner, and Esther Savage. He married Mary Hubbard. A good family.

Ray, James, sen'r., of Haddam—died in 1731. Wife, Elizabeth, and sons, James, Peter and Joseph—Anna Dimock, grand daughter, Elizabeth Ray, grandson Isaac Ray, and grandson Samuel Bangs, of Bolton. Estate £255.

Read, Doct. Jacob, of Simsbury—died in 1709. Widow Elizabeth, and John Tuller, administrators. Left a son, Jacob—perhaps other children.

Reeve, Robert, of Hartford—died in 1680. He left a widow and seven children, sons and daughters, with a small estate. (See p. 68.)

Reinolds, John, of Wethersfield—died in 1682. Estate £121.

Widow, Mary. Children, Keziah, aged 16, Anna 14, Rebina 11, John 9, and Jonathan 6 years.

Renolds, John, settled at Stamford among the first settlers of the town. *

Reynolds, John, of Norwich—perhaps the son of Robert an early settler of Wethersfield, and moved to and died at Saybrook as early as 1662—yet more probable was a brother of James and Robert. Robert was employed about the fort.

Richards, Hon. James, died at his house in Hartford, on the 29th day of June, 1680. He married Sarah, the daughter of William Gibbons, Esq., of Hartford. He owned land in England at his decease, and was liberal to his wife in his will. She had received of her father Gibbons a handsome estate in lands before, some of which were located in England, and the rents of which her mother in some measure relied upon for support. Mr. Richards supposed it would prove inconvenient for his mother in law to obtain her distant rents, he therefore made an exchange with her, and took her lands in England and gave her £30, annually, for life, and £200, to dispose of as she pleased for her lands there. His children were, Thomas, Mary, Jerusha, Elizabeth, and one not born at his decease. To his son, Thomas, he gave all his lands and buildings in England, and informed him he could call upon Ralph Ingram, a woolen draper in London, for his deeds; he also gave Thomas most of his lands in Hartford. To his daughter, Mary, he gave his farm at Habuck, east of the river in Wethersfield, to be received when married, or 18 years of age, with the buildings, and £300. To Jerusha, all his lands and buildings west of the river in Wethersfield, and £300. To Elizabeth, all his lands and buildings in and about New London, and £450. He gave to his child not then born, £700. To Thomas Bradford, (his nephew) he gave 10 acres of land and £60, if he should build upon the land. To his brother, John Richards, of Boston, he gave his largest silver tankard and his watch. To the church south of Little River, in Hartford, where he had attended meeting, he gave £10 in silver plate for administering the sacrament. To the Latin school in Hartford, £50. To his pastor, Rev. John Whiting, £15. To the poor of Hartford £20. To Mercy Bradford, his kinswoman, he gave £10; and provided like a true Puritan, that whoever thereafter should hold his lands in Hartford, should pay the ecclesiastical taxes upon them to support the south church in Hartford. His wife, Sarah, and son, Thomas, executors. To his brother, John, of Boston, and Capt. John Allen, of Hartford, he gave

£10 each, and made them overseers of his will. His houses and lands in Boston, he ordered to be equally divided between all his children who were then minors. Estate £7930 : 15. Mary married Benjamin Alford, of Boston ; Jerusha married Gurdon Saltonstall, Esq. ; Thomas married Joanna Dodd, sister of Edward Dodd, of Hartford ; Elizabeth married John Davie, supposed of Boston, (but in 1709, appears to have been the wife of Jonathan Taylor,) she was the wife of Davie in 1691. The child unborn, mentioned in Hon. James's will, proved to be a daughter, and was named Anne—she died before 1691, and the £700 given her in the will was equally distributed to the other children in Oct. 1691. The £200 given to Ursula Gibbons by Hon. James towards her lands in England, were also divided between the children of Hon. James. Sarah, the relict of Hon. James, in 1691, signed the distribution of the personal estate of Hon. James, as Sarah Davie, with her husband, John Davie, together with the children of James. In 1709 " Dame Sarah," relict of Hon. James, was the wife of Jonathan Tyng, Esq., Gent., of Dunstable, in Mass. She gave up to her son, Thomas, her right as executor of his father's will, and quit to him her dower estate in Hartford, signed by herself and Tyng, her husband. Deed dated Boston, March 30, 1709.

Richards, Capt. Thomas, the only son of Hon. James, removed to Boston. He married Joanna Dodd, sister of Edward Dodd, and had two daughters, but no sons. He made his will in 1714, and died in 1715. He owned a shipyard and buildings in Boston, which he gave to his wife, with £500 in money. He gave his niece, the wife of Rev. Sampson Stoddard, of Chelmsford, £50. ; Daniel Alford, of Boston, £50 ; his brother in law, Edward Dodd, of Hartford, £10 ; Rev. Cotton Mather £10 ; Mr. Thomas Buckingham, of Hartford, £5 ; Harvard College £30 ; his servant, John Arcoss, £10 ; the poor of Boston £20 ; his sister, Mary Alford, £10, and her daughter, Sarah, £5. All his other property in England, Boston, Hartford and elsewhere, he gave to his two daughters, Joanna and Mary Richards, conditioned that if his daughters died without issue, the property should fall to William Davie, Sarah Bill, Elizabeth Stoddard and his nephew, Benjamin Alford, on condition that they should pay Edward Dodd £50—another £50, and his niece, Joanna Alford, £30, and the three children of his sister Saltonstall £20 each. (Vol. 3, p. 55, Town books.) His wife was sole executrix—Paul Dudley, Esq. and Samuel Greenwood, merchant, of Boston, trustees of his will. His widow sold a part of his lands in Hartford, for £1108, to Jonathan and Isaac Sheldon, of Northampton. This family closeds the name of Richard on the death of Thomas, as he left no son to perpetuate the high reputation of the family name. It is painful to know that such men as Richards, Hamlin, Gold, Mason, Ludlow and many others, the brilliants of their day and generation, who had figured so largely, morally and politically, in Connecticut, should so soon have been forgotten, not only by the citizens of the State, but by the great mass of their descendants. (See p. 68, No. 2.)

Richards, Thomas, died at Hartford before 1639. His widow had several pieces of land noted in the land records of Hartford, in 1639. He left four children, viz. John, Mary, (married Mr. Peck, of Milford,) Thomas and Obadiah. The widow of Thomas, deceased, died in 1671. John married and had children, Tho's and Samuel. Tho's married Mary Parsons, daughter of Dea. Parsons, of Springfield, in 1691, and had sons, Thomas, Ebenezer, Jedediah, Benjamin and Joseph. Samuel, of W. Hartford, married Mary Graves, daughter of George, sen'r., in Dec. 1665, and had children, Josiah, James and Daniel ; the last Thomas settled at Southington ; Jedediah went to Tolland and from thence to Norfolk, and joined the church there. Joseph, the son of Thomas, settled at Wethersfield. He married and had Joseph and other children. The last Joseph died in 1771. Wife, Lydia, and children, Joseph, Simeon and Eli. He gave Joseph land in Newington, Wethersfield and New Hartford. To Eli and Simeon he gave his homested and some lands in Wethersfield. He had a grandson, Charles Dix, who is supposed to have been the ancestor of Senator Dix, of New York, whose parents removed to Oak Orchard, N. Y., from Torrington. Joseph, a son of Joseph, settled in Berlin— wife, Abigail. He died in 1801. He had a 2d wife, and had children, Thomas, Joseph, Oliver, Joanna and Eli—Lydia, wife of Benajah Deane—Polly, wife of Elias Dilling—Betsey, Sally and Olive. Estate $3767. Obadiah, the son of Thomas, sen'r., appears to have settled at Waterbury, and had children, Benjamin, (died 1714) Obadiah, John, Thomas, Mary, Hannah, Esther and Rachel. Obadiah, jr. settled at Lyme, and died there in 1720. Among the first settlers of Hartford, was Nathaniel Richards, (See p. 68,) who was probably a brother of Thomas, sen'r., and of the father of Hon. James. Nathaniel removed to Norwalk about 1650. The connection of the descendants of the three important families of Richards, is not satisfactorily discovered by the writer. The location, and the names of Thomas, James, John and Samuel, so uniformly given to the children of the different families from one generation to another, is strong presumptive evidence of olden times that they originated from the same common ancestor.

Richardson, Lemuel, of Haddam—died in 1713. Wife, Mahitabel. He owned property at Stonington, which was appraised by Stephen Richardson and James Noyes, of Stonington. Children, Samuel, Lemuel and Mahitabel. Thomas Richardson, of Waterbury, died in 1712. He had a son Thomas. —— Richardson at New London in 1663. Israel Richardson, of Wallingford, died in 1712. His administrators were, John Hopkins and Stephen Richardson, of Waterbury. He had children, Joseph and Hannah. John Richardson, of Waterbury, died in 1712. Wife, Elizabeth. Nathaniel Richardson, of Waterbury, died in 1714. This name was not as early in the colony as many others. Amos, of Coventry, in 1745. Sarah Richardson married Samuel Williams in 1691.

Riley, Jonathan, of Wethersfield, in 1706—was a brother of Joseph, who was then late deceased, of Wethersfield.

Ripley, Joshua, of Windham, was one of the early settlers of the town, and was a commissioner there before 1697. He was a leading man, and well educated. He is the first of the name found in the colony, and was probably the ancestor of those of the name in Connecticut.

Risley, Richard, of Hockanum—died in 1647 or 8. Estate £188. Children, Sarah, 7 years old, Samuel 2, and Richard 3 months.

Rix, Thomas, of Wethersfield—died in 1690—left a wife and £36 estate.

Roath, Robert, of New London—died in 1650. A few years after at Norwich, where the name yet remains.

Roberts, John, of Middletown—died in 1721. Left children, David, aged 20, Mary 17, Jonathan 15, Nathaniel 11, Daniel 8. John Roberts, jr., of Simsbury, died in 1724. Samuel Roberts, jr., of Middletown, died in 1726. Samuel Roberts, the first that I find in the colony, had married Sarah Hinman, daughter of Edward, of Stratford, before 1681, and resided at Woodbury.

Robinson, Samuel, of Hartford. Inventory presented in 1682.— Mary, his widow, administratrix. Estate £55. Children, Sarah, 17 years old, Samuel 14, Mary 10, John 6, and Hannah 3 in 1682.

Rollo, Alexander, of Middletown—died in 1709. Wife, Hannah. William, a son of the deceased, at that time resided at Haddam.

Root, John, sen'r., of Farmington—died about 1685 or 6. Wife, Mary. Children, Joseph, Caleb, Mary, wife of Isaac Brunson, Stephen—perhaps other daughters. Estate £819.

Rose, Nathaniel, resided at Southampton in 1698.

Rowlandson, Rev. Joseph, of Wethersfield—died in 1679. Wife, Mary. Children, Joseph 17 years old, and Mary 13. Estate £290. He also had lands at Lancaster, appraised by Ralph Haughton and Roger Sumner, at £129.

Rudd, Jonathan, (in No. 2, in 1639)—is probably the same Jonathan Rudd who afterwards settled at Norwich.

S.

Sadd, John, of Windsor—died in 1694—and left a son, Thomas, 4 years old.

Sanford, Ann, widow of Robert, of Hartford, made her will in 1682, and died the same year. Her husband's estate was settled in 1776. Children, Zachery, Robert, Ezekiel, Hannah and Abigail. A Zachery Sanford, of Hartford, died in 1713, and Jonathan, Sarah and Abigail Bunce, of Hartford, exhibited his will in court. Nathaniel Sanford appraised the estate at £1100 : 16. Z. Sanford's will was made in 1710, and his children were, Sarah, the wife of Jonathan Bunce, Abigail Sanford and Joseph Bunce. Robert, sen'r., died in 1676. Nathan or Nathaniel Sanford, of Hartford, died in 1687. Susannah, his wife, procured of him a deed to her of all his lands. Deed dated in 1677. Estate £1100 : 16.

Saunders, Christopher, of Windsor, had children, Susannah, born in 1676, Daniel in 1678, and Elizabeth in 1681.

Sawyer, Edward. A settlement began in Hebron in 1704, and the settlers were from Windsor, Saybrook, Long Island and Northampton. Nath'l Phelps, from Windsor, was the first clerk, and Timothy Phelps, Stephen Post and Samuel Palmer, townsmen ; Edward Sawyer, constable. The town was incorporated in 1707. Samuel Curtiss was town clerk there in 1712. Jacob Root resided there.

Scofield, Daniel, came to Stamford as early as 1641. The name of Scofield is common and respectable in the town at this time—perhaps the same name of Scofell or Scoville.

Scovill, Edward, of Haddam—died in 1703. Wife, Hannah. Thomas Shailer and William Scofell appointed guardians of Susannah and Hannah, only children of Edward. His widow married Benj. Smith. The name is spelt upon the colony records, Scofell—at a later period, Scovill. William, of Haddam, died in 1712.

Scott, John, of Ashford or Setauket, L. I., in 1664, was charged of many heinous offences against His Majesty's peace, viz. defaming the King, seditious practices, encouraging the natives in their hostility, usurping the power of the King in pardoning treason, threatening the King's subjects to hang and banish them, profaning the Sabbath, forgery, treachery, claiming power under a pretended commission, and slandering a commissioned officer. A warrant was issued to New Haven, Branford, Milford, Stratford, Fairfield and other towns, to apprehend him. Edmund Scott, sen'r., of Waterbury—died in 1691. Children, Joseph, Edmund, Samuel, George, Jonathan, David, Robert, Elizabeth and Hannah—supposed descendants of Thomas, of Hartford, (in No. 2, p. 71.) Thomas Scott, of Hartford, died as early as 1643. He had only one son, (Thomas) and several daughters. The widow survived him. Estate £174.

Scranton, Nathaniel, of Wethersfield—died in 1693, and gave his estate to William Goodrich, being £36 : 11.

Seaman, John, one of the original purchasers of the town of Stamford, where he settled in 1641. It is supposed he moved from Wethersfield to Stamford.

Seabrook, Mr. was of Stratford in 1650, with Samuel Sherman, Thomas Fairchild, William Judson and three sons, Nicholas Knell, William Wilcoxson and three sons, William and John Curtis, brothers, William Beardslee, John Beardslee, Joseph Hawley, Samuel Wells and three sons, Philip Graves, Rev. Mr. Blackman, Henry Wakelin, Richard Booth, William Burritt, John Brinsmade, Edward Hinman, Daniel Tetherton, John Thompson, David Mitchell, John Hurd, John Beach, Moses Wheeler, Richard Butler, Arthur Bostwick, John Birdseye, Mr. Isaac Nichols, Richard Harvey, John Peacock, Nathaniel Porter, Thomas Sherwood and Mr. Seabrook. These persons, with others, were of Stratford in 1651, and previous—unquestionably many others, who were the pioneers of the settlement, and had either died or removed—are necessarily omitted by the loss of the first records.

Sedgwick, Ebenezer, of Hartford, in 1644, (in No. 2,) who had an ear mark recorded there in 1646, is not afterwards found in the colony. He probably returned to his native country. He was not the progenitor of the Sedgwick family of Connecticut. Robert Sedgwick, who was an early settler at Charlestown, Mass., in 1636 or 7, was the ancestor of this family. Robert at length returned to England in 1654, and died there in 1656. He was made a major general in the days of Cromwell. Gen. Robert had a son, William, who for a while resided in Hartford, and married Elizabeth, the daughter of the Rev. Samuel Stone, of Hartford. He proved to be of a roving character, and spent much of his time in passing to and from the West Indies, in the neglect of his family. His wife became dissatisfied with his absence and negligence, and petitioned the Court of Assistants, in 1674, for a bill of divorce from said William, which was granted the same year. She had but one child by William, which was born after his father left for the West Indies the last time. This child, Samuel, was the only person of the name of Sedgwick in New England then living. His mother afterwards married John Roberts, of Hartford. Mrs. Stone, the grand mother of Samuel, married Mr. Gardner after the death of Rev. Mr. Stone. She left Samuel, her grandson, a small legacy, which was so well managed that at his arrival to manhood, he purchased a valuable farm at West Hartford. He lived where Benjamin Colton now resides, upon the middle road from Hartford to Farmington. Samuel married Mary ———. He became a captain of militia. His children were, Samuel, jr., b. Aug. 22, 1690, Jonathan, b. March 29, 1693, Ebenezer, b. Feb. 25, 1695, Joseph b. May 16, 1697, Stephen b. March 17, 1701. Samuel married Ruth Peck, Feb. 1, 1710–11, Ebenezer m. Prudence Merrills, June 30, 1720, Stephen m. Mary Harriss, Dec. 1725. His children were, Abigail, b. in 1703, Mary in 1705, Elijah in 1708, Thankful in 1710, Mary in 1712–13, Benjamin in 1716. Jonathan was the father of William the father of Timothy. A grand daughter of Stephen, (son of Samuel) is yet living at West Hartford—a fine aged Quaker lady—the mother of Timothy and Levi. Ebenezer had but one son, Abraham, who settled in Lenox, Mass., where his widow and children now reside. Ebenezer's daughter Mary, married John Ensign, and was the grand mother of Chief Justice Church, of Litchfield. Joseph was the father of Samuel, whose descendants reside in Stockbridge, Mass. Benjamin, his youngest son, had his father's homested, but he emigrated to Cornwall in 1744, where he died at the age of 42, in an apoplectic fit, in 1758. He married Ann Thompson, of Wallingford. Abigail, the daughter of Capt. Samuel, married Benjamin Kellogg, Nov. 1721. Mercy married Caleb Merrills in 1733. Capt. Samuel, sen'r., died March 24, 1735, aged 69, and his wife died Sept. 4, 1743, aged 73 years. Samuel, jr. married Ruth Peck, and died before his father, in Dec. 1724, and his father, and Ruth, his widow, were administrators on his estate. In March, 1726, Ruth, his widow, was made guardian of his children, Ruth, 16 years of age, Mary and Jerusha, twins, 13, Daniel 8, and

Thankful 5. The children of Benjamin, who emigrated to Cornwall, were, Sarah, who married Rev. Hezekiah Gold, the mother of Hon. Thomas R. Gold, member of Congress of Oneida co., N. Y., and of Thomas Gold, Esq., of Pittsfield, Mass. John A., the son of Benjamin, was the grand father of Gen. Charles F. Sedgwick, attorney at law in Sharon, and of Albert, the present Sheriff of Litchfield county. The 2d son of Benjamin was Benjamin, jr. The 3d son of Benjamin, of Cornwall, was, Hon. Theodore, who was many years celebrated as a lawyer and judge in Massachusetts. Mary Ann, another daughter of Benjamin, married Rev. Job Swift, D. D., and was the mother of a numerous family, among whom were the Hon. Benj. Swift, U. S. Senator from Vermont, and Hon. Samuel Swift, many years Secretary of the State of Vermont. Lorain, another daughter of Benjamin, married Jacob Parsons, of Richmond, Mass., and from that place he emigrated to Chenango co., N. Y. The children of Col. John Sedgwick were, John A., Sally, Henry, Parnel, Pamelia, Benjamin, Stephen and Roderick. John A. was the father of General Sedgwick and of Albert—perhaps others. Henry was the father of John E., deputy sheriff. Benjamin yet lives upon the old homested in Cornwall, the father of P. C. Sedgwick, of Pennsylvania, clerk of the Supreme Court, also father of Lieut. John Sedgwick, of the U. S. Army, now in Mexico. Stephen, son of John A., is the father of Hon. Henry James Sedgwick, of the New York Senate, and of Charles P. Sedgwick, of Syracuse, N. Y. Roderick yet resides in the city of New York. Hon. Theodore, youngest son of Benjamin, graduated at Yale College in 1766. He held an exalted rank not only in his State, but in the nation. He was Senator and Representative in Congress, and Speaker of the House of Representatives of the U. S., and for many years a distinguished Judge of the Supreme Court of Massachusetts. He died in Februaay, 1813, aged 66 years. His children were, Pamelia, (married Elkanah Watson, of Albany) Theodore, father of Theodore a lawyer of New York, Henry Dwight, Robert, Catherine M., (the authoress) Charles; clerk of the courts in Berkshire county. Catherine and Charles are the only survivors of Hon. Theodore's children. The children of John A., son of Gen. John, are, Gen. Charles F., a lawyer in Sharon, Albert, sheriff of Litchfield county, Mary Ann, married Mr. Noyes, Amanda, married Mr. Bridgman. The children of Gen. Charles F. Sedgwick and his wife, Betsey Swan, are, Elizabeth Swan, John, Marie, Emma, Caroline Swan, Charles H., (died in 1841, 6 years old,) Mary Gould and Robert Adam Sedgwick.

Sedgwick, Abraham, son of Ebenezer and Prudence, was born April 27, 1721, Abigail b. Dec. 2, 1722, Prudence b. Sept. 14, 1724, Mary b. April 29, 1726, Thankful b. April 7, 1728, Eliza b. June 17, 1731, Edward b. March 4, 1734-5. Samuel Sedgwick, son of Joseph, b. April 11, 1725.

Seely, Lieut. Robert, (in No. 2,) had a lawsuit against Wethersfield, in 1636, to compel the inhabitants who held land in Wethersfield, to remove there, or forfeit it, and receive nothing in the land division of the town. The case was tried by a jury, and found for Seely, as he had been an adventurer, the town gave him William Bascum's share. In March, 1637, juror's fees were limited by law to six pence for each action tried by them.

Sexton, John, married Mary Hill in 1677.

Shears, Wid. Sarah, of Windsor—died in 1689. Legatees, Doct. Hasting, the wife of Nathaniel Dickinson, Hannah Palmer, Samuel Forward, Stephen Loomis, Timothy Hosford, John Grimes, and Jacob Gibbs. Executors, Benajah Holcomb and Michael Taynter. Estate £128.

Shepard, Susannah, sen'r., died in 1698. Her daughter, Susannah, married John Pratt ; another daughter married Nathaniel Goodwin. She had three daughters—had a grandson, John Pratt, jr., and grand daughters, Susan and Mahitabel Goodwin. Wittir Goodwin married her daughter. John Shepard, son of John, jr., was born in Nov. 1681, Samuel his brother, b. in 1682, Hannah b. in 1684, Joseph b. in 1688, Timothy b. in 1691, Rebecca b. in 1695. Grand children of John Shepard, sen'r., Timothy, d. in 1716, and Rebecca in 1706. The great grand children of Edward Shepard, of Hartford—Tho's Shepard married Susannah Scott in Sept. 1695, John, jr. married Hannah May in 1680, Thomas Ensign married Hannah Shepard in 1692. Edward Shepard, of Middletown, died in 1713. John, eldest son, Edward, 2d son, Samuel, 3d son. Samuel married Bethia, and had John in 1710, and James in 1714. Serg't. John Shepard, of Hartford, died in 1707, was a cooper. Wife, Martha. Sons John and Thomas his executors. The two sons were also coopers.

Sherman, Samuel, was one of the purchasers of Stamford in 1640, and moved there from Wethersfield in 1640 or 41. (See Sherman in No. 2.) He resided in Stratford in 1650. Joseph Sherman, of Wethersfield, (in No. 2,) Andrew Ward, Joseph Strickland, Robert Coe, Robert Reynold united in the certificate with Jonas Wood to join the church at Wethersfield. (See Jonas Wood.) They soon renewed their covenant publicly before the court and churches, and settled at Wethersfield in 1636.

Sherwington, Thomas, (in No. 2,) resided at Fairfield in 1650.

Sherwood, Thomas, of Fairfield, in 1650. This name has ever since been a Fairfield county name. He was probably the ancestor of Hon. Samuel B. Sherwood, member of Congress, late deceased, of that county, the father in law of Gov. Bissell. Matthew Sherwood, of Fairfield, in 1673, a descendant of Thomas, (in No. 2.) In 1673, the grand committee appointed for ordering the militia of Connecticut, after the Legislature had ordered to be raised 500 dragoons to be ready to march at an hour's warning—appointed Matthew Sherwood ensign, Thomas Fitch, captain, and Jehu Burr, lieutenant for Fairfield troops.

Shippason, Nathaniel, widow Mary, of Hebron. Estate £207. He died in 1718. Children, Johathan, Nathaniel, John, Elizabeth, Mary, Mercy, Joanna and others. (Perhaps Shipman.)

Simking, Vincent, one of the purchasers of the town of Stamford in 1640.

Skinner, Joseph, married Mary Filly in 1666, and had children, Mary in 1667, and Elizabeth in 1669.

Slater, Thomas, of Simsbury—died intestate in 1700.

Slauson, Thomas, first appeared at Stamford in 1662—a firm Puritan and a good man. He was a strong friend of Bell, Holly and Law.

Smead, Richard, of Hartford—died in 1704, intestate. Estate £12.

Smith, Elizabeth, of Farmington—died in 1677 or 8, and left sons, Samuel, Jonathan, William and Benjamin. She had a grandson by the name of Samuel, a son of Jonathan. She had a daughter, Mahitabel, (Elizabeth, her daughter, appeared to have died before her mother,) Susannah. She had a daughter in law, Rachel Smith. Jonathan was a mechanic, and was requested by his mother to teach his brother Samuel his trade. William died before his mother.

Smith, Simon, of Haddam, was one of the twenty-eight original purchasers and settlers of Haddam. He had a son Simon, who had a son David, the father of James. David married Dolly Brainerd, (sister of Rev. David and John Brainerd, missionaries among the Indians,) by whom she had four sons and six daughters, viz. David, James, Hezekiah, Nehemiah, Anne, Jerusha, Dolly, Molly, Esther and Susannah. After the death of his first wife, he married a widow Shailer and died soon after. His son, David, died young, and left a widow and two daughters. James married Mary Hubbard, and had four sons and three daughters, viz. Frederick, James, Hubbard, Nehemiah, Alice, Catherine and Polly. James the first, removed with his family to Harpersfield, Delaware co., N. Y., in the early settlement of that county, where he died in the winter of 1830, aged 93, and left over 250 descendants. He was a captain in the Revolution. Hezekiah married Elizabeth Shailer, and had several children. He removed to Western New York, where his descendants still reside. Nehemiah died young, at sea. Anne married Timothy Towner, and lived in the west part of Haddam. Dolly married Samuel Brooks, and settled in the north part of Haddam, and had a large family. Jerusha married Ezra Brainerd, settled in Middle Haddam, and had a large family. Molly married Joseph Arnold, and resided in Haddam, with a large family. Esther married Ephraim Sawyer, and lived in the north part of Haddam. Susannah married Joseph Selden, and had a numerous family. She settled in West Hartford, where her descendants now reside. Henry Smith, one of the first settlers and purchasers of Stamford.

Soper, Mary, of Windsor, guardian of Pelatiah, 19 years old, Sarah 16, John 13, Abigail 12, Dorcas 7, and Return Soper 4—her children.

Southmayd, William, mariner, of Middletown—died in 1702. Wife, Margaret. He left some daughters, and an estate of £1086.

Sparks, John, of Windsor—died in 1710. Estate £54. Children, Martha, 16 years old, Esther 18, Ruth, John, Anne, Dorothy and Thomas.

Spencer, William, of Hartford—died in 1640. He left a wife and 3 children, viz. Sarah, Elizabeth and Samuel. He was a kinsman of Matthew Allyn, a brother in law of John Pratt and John Talcott. William Spencer was the ancestor of the Hon. Judge Spencer and Hon. John C. Spencer, of the State of New York. He was one of the first Puritan settlers of Hartford. John Spencer, of Haddam, died in 1682. Children, Gerrard, Rebecca, Benjamin, Lydia and Grace. The two eldest children he placed in the care of his sister Hannah, who had married Daniel Brainerd, and allowed Mr. Brainerd the use of the two children's interest in his estate. His son, Benjamin, he placed in the charge of Nicholas Noyes, of Haddam, until he became of age, with the liberty to take the use of Benjamin's share. Lydia he gave to his father Howard, and gave her the old cow and £7 more than her portion, because she had a defective hand. His youngest daughter, Grace, he placed in the care of his brother in law, Kinne, and his sister Rebecca. He left for them to use as a compensation for keeping her, her share, and gave Grace a cow and £5 more than her portion of his estate. The deceased John had taken Tho's Brooks at the age of four years, who had now become 18 years of age, a son of his sister Brooks. This adopted son he directed to respect his mother, (who had married Thomas Shailer,) and gave him his time until 21 years of age ; he also gave him his loom and tacklin for it, and two steers, and directed him to be clothed as well as his own children. He gave the remainder of his property equally to all his children, after dividing to each son £30, and each daughter £20. He allowed 14 shillings to purchase books for his children, and gave Goodwife Smith 20 shillings—his sister Shailer and Thomas Brooks each 20 shillings, for their kind attention in his sickness. He desired Nicholas Royes, George Gates, Daniel Brainerd, Daniel Cone and Thomas Spencer to be overseers of his will. Ebenezer Spencer married Mary Booth in 1699. Garrit Spencer married Hannah Pratt, daughter of John, in 1680. She died in 1692.

Stanclift, James, of Middletown—died in 1712. Wife, Mary. Left two sons, William and James.

Standish, Thomas, of Wethersfield—died Sept. 1735. Estate £396.

Starr, Comfort, was a physician, and the first of the name in New England. He married Elizabeth ——. He came from Ashford, in the county of Kent, in England, and settled at Cambridge, Mass. in 1633. He died at Boston, Jan. 1660—his wife died in 1658. Children, Doct. Thomas, John, Comfort, Elizabeth, Hannah and Maynard.

Starr, Doct. Thomas, son of Doct. Comfort, married Rachel ——, and settled in Charlestown. His children were, Thomas, Comfort, Elizabeth, Benjamin, Constant, (died in 1654,) William b. in 1654, and Josiah b. in 1657.

Starr, Benjamin, son of Doct. Thomas, married Elizabeth Alston in 1675, but left no children.

Starr, Josiah and Thomas, sons of Doct. Thomas, settled at Danbury, and in 1715–16 purchased 100 acres of land of Abraham Adams, located in Danbury. Josiah married and had Benjamin and Comfort.

Starr, John, 2d son of Dr. Comfort, of Cambridge, resided at Boston. He married Martha ——, and had a son, Comfort, b. in 1661.

Starr, Rev. Comfort, 3d son of Doct. Comfort, graduated at Harvard College in 1647. He then returned to England, and after having been settled there, died in 1711.

Starr, Comfort, son of Doct. Thomas, settled at Middletown. He married Rachel Harris, and had children, Comfort, 24 years old, b. in

1670, Mary 22 years old, Joseph b. in 1676, Benjamin b. in 1679, Rachel b. in 1681, Thomas b. in 1684, and Daniel b. in 1689. At his decease Mary was his relict. He died in 1693. Estate £89.

Starr, Joseph, son of Comfort, of Middletown, married Abigail Baldwin, and had nine children, seven sons and two daughters.

Starr, Comfort, son of Comfort, of Middletown, married Elizabeth Hopson, and had eight children, three sons and five daughters.

Starr, Jonathan, son of Comfort, resided at Stonington, married Abigail Cadwell, and had one son and two daughters, the last born in 1750. He died in 1765—his wife died in 1764.

Starr, Jehoshaphat, son of the 3d Comfort, married Elizabeth Ruggles, and had two sons and two daughters. But the record says he settled at Newport, R. I., and his estate at Middletown was about £54. His sister, Elizabeth, married Capt. Thomas Ward. His sister, Hannah, married Mr. Greenfield, of Newport, R. I. He died at sea, in 1717, and his property at Middletown was distributed to his aforesaid sisters. Yet he might have had four children who were deceased at his death—if not, why was his property at Middletown distributed to his sisters instead of his children and widow?—doubtful whether he left children.

Stedman, Samuel—died in 1684. Simmons Stedman, of Farmington, also died—was a brother of Thomas, of Wethersfield. Lieut. John, and his wife, Elizabeth, both died before 1678, and left four small children, with an estate.

Stearns, John's children were, John, Jacob, Josiah, Mary and Hannah Hopkins. This 2d John moved to and died in Northampton or Hadley.

Stevens, Thomas, sen'r., of Middletown—died in 1714, and left a son, Thomas, and other children.

Steward, Alexander, of East Haddam—died in 1732. Margaret, his relict.

Stillman, George, resided in Hadley, Mass. He married Rebecca Smith, daughter of Dea. Philip Smith, in 1685, and lived there until 1703 or 4, and then removed to Wethersfield, Conn. He was a selectman of Hadley in 1696, and a deputy to the General Court of Massachusetts in 1698, and a juror of Wethersfield in 1705, and selectman in 1708. His origin is not known. He was born in 1654, and died in 1728, aged 74 years. He was a merchant at Wethersfield, and left an estate valued at £3622 : 4 : 7. Dea. Smith, the father of his wife, moved to Hadley, one of the first settlers, with Gov. Webster and the Rev. John Russell and others, from Hartford and Wethersfield. His children were, George born in Hadley about 1686, whether he married or not is not known—was living in 1728, and named in his father's will; Rebecca b. Jan. 14, 1688, d. Oct. 19, 1712; Mary b. July 12, 1689, m. Deliverance Blinn; Nathaniel b. July 1, 1791; John b. Feb. 19, 1693; Sarah b. Dec. 28, 1694, m. Mr. Willard, of Saybrook; Martha b. Nov. 28, 1796, d. Oct. 2, 1712; Anna b. April 6, 1699, m. Dea. Hezekiah May, of Wethersfield; Elizabeth b. Oct. 19, 1701, m. Mr. Blinn; Hannah b. Nov. 7, 1702, d. Aug. 9, 1705; Benjamin b. in Wethersfield, July 29, 1705; Lydia m. Rev. Daniel Russell in 1728, minister at Wethersfield; Hannah m. John Caldwell, of Hartford.

Stillman, Nathaniel, 2d son of George, m. Anna Southmayd, daughter of William, of Middletown, for his first wife, by whom he had one child, Nathaniel b. March 10, 1719, Anna, his wife, d. Jan. 6, 1729, aged 37—he then m. Sarah, daughter of Capt. Joseph Allyn, and had the following children: Allyn b. March 20, 1731; Anna b. March 26, 1734, m. Ezekiel Fosdick; Sarah b. Feb. 26, 1736, m. Mr. Burr, of Hartford,; Joseph b. Oct. 21, 1739; Samuel b. March 18, 1741; Mary b. Nov. 18, 1744, m. Appleton Robbins, father of Appleton Robbins, Esq., of Granby; George moved to Machias, Maine—his daughter Elizabeth O., m. Hon. James Savage, of Boston. He has numerous descendants living in Maine and Massachusetts.

Stillman, John, 3d son of George, m. Mary, daughter of Samuel Wolcott, and his wife Judith, who was an Appleton from Massachusetts. His children were, John b. Aug. 9, 1717; Rebecca b. Sept. 17, 1719; Mary b. Dec. 31, 1721; Abigail b. Jan. 22, 1723; Martha b. Aug. 20, 1726; Sarah b. Dec. 2, 1728; Elisha b. Feb. 14, 1730, d. Sept. 23, 1803, aged 73; Abigail b. March 2, 1732; Appleton b. March 23, 1734; Huldah b. April 30, 1737.

Stillman, Benjmin, 4th son of George, m. Sarah, daughter of Capt. Samuel Doty, of Saybrook, for his first wife, and Katherine Chauncey, of Durham, for his second wife. His children were, (those known to the writer,) George b. Nov. 24, 1729; Samuel b. Nov. 28, 1731.

Stillman, Nathaniel, eldest son of Nathaniel and his wife Anna, m. Mahitabel, daughter of David Deming of Wethersfield, June, 1743, and resided in Wethersfield until his death, Feb. 1811, aged 92. His children were, Anna b. Aug. 6, 1748, m. Asa Talcott for her first husband, then m. Abijah Ranney; Mahitabel b. Sept. 23, 1750, m. Peter Deming as his second wife; Nathaniel b. Nov. 27, 1752; Southmayd b. Nov. 3, 1754—lost at sea when young ; Allyn b. Dec. 12, 1757, m. Elizabeth Deming, had no children, and died in 1818 ; William b. Nov. 3, 1759 ; David b. Jan. 3, 1762 ; Simeon b. June 12, 1764 ; Giles b. Jan. 15, 1766 ; James b. Sept. 9, 1770.

Stillman, Allyn, 2d son of Nathaniel and his wife Sarah, was a sea captain in the employ of Congress, or the State, in 1771, and afterwards moved to Enfield, where he has descendants still living.

Stillman, Joseph, 3d son of Nathaniel, m. Huldah Wright for his first wife—was the father of major Joseph Stillman, who entered the army of the Revolution as a drummer, at the age of 16, and afterwards rose to the rank of major in the militia of the State. He was the father of Capt. George, Deac. Timothy and Ebenezer Stillman now living at Wethersfield. He married Sarah Meekins for his 2d wife, by whom he had Otis, a sea captain in the merchant service, who was lost at sea.

Stillman, Samuel, 4th son of Nathaniel, m. Meliscent Riley—was also a sea captain.

Stillman, Nathaniel, eldest son of Nathaniel and Mahitabel Deming his wife, m. Martha Hanmer—was a soldier of the Revolution, and died a pensioner, Aug. 1838, aged 86. His children were, Martha, m. Otis Stillman ; Elizabeth m. William Montague—died at Hartford; Francis, was a sea captain—died in 1838 ; Clarissa ; Charles, lost at sea with Otis Stillman when young.

Stillman, Southmayd, 2d son of Nathaniel, was lost at sea when young.

Stillman, Allyn, 3d son of Nathaniel, m. Elizabeth Deming, and died without issue, Nov. 12, 1818, aged 61.

Stillman, William, 4th son of Nathaniel, m. Mary Goodrich, and removed to Sheffield, Mass., where he died. His children were, Southmayd, Hetty, Samuel, Hopey, Lois, Jared, Allyn and William.

Stillman, David, 5th son of Nathaniel, m. Prudence Hurlbut, and removed to Sheffield, Mass. His children were, Amelia, Thomas, David, Prudence, (m. Mr. Crippen,) and Harriet.

Stillman, Simeon, 6th son of Nathaniel, was formerly a sea captain in the merchant service—m. Rebecca Deming for his first wife, and Nancy Deming for his second wife. He died April 22, 1847, aged 83 years. His children were, Rebecca, m. George Butler ; Simeon, jr., died at the age of two years ; Simeon, Southmayd, Laura, m. Mr. Dickinson ; and Jared A.

Stillman, Giles, 7th son of Nathaniel, died at Cape Francois about 1796, unmarried.

Stillman, James, 8th son of Nathaniel, m. Elizabeth, daughter of John Webster, a descendant of Gov. Webster. He is now living at the age of 77 years. His children were, James b. Feb. 12, 1796 ; Giles b. Aug. 11, 1798 ; Allyn Southmayd b. April 28, 1800 ; Mahitable b. Sept. 26, 1803 ; Elizabeth b. Jan. 15, 1807, m. Benjamin Boardman, of Hartford ; John Webster b. May 10, 1813, and was drowned Jan. 11, 1822, aged 9 years.

Stillman, James, son of James, m. in Augusta, Georgia—his wife died in five or six years after marriage ; William T., and Frances.

Stillman, Giles, 2d son of James, m. Sally Loveland, of Wethersfield, and removed to Farmington—was a captain in the militia, and justice of the peace for several years in the town of Farmington. His children were, Sarah b. July 27, 1823, m. Edward Warren ; Jane Maria b. Oct. 18, 1824, d. at the age of 20 years ; John Webster b. Nov. 21, 1826 ; Walter b. Aug. 27, 1828 ; Giles b. July 9, 1830 ; James Allyn b. Feb. 14, 1833 ; Ellen Elizabeth b. April 22, 1737, died at the age of two years ; Eliza L. b. Feb. 18, 1839 ; Albert b. Dec. 29, 1840.

Sitllman, Allyn Southmayd, 3d son of James, m. Cecilia Andross, of Hartford—was a captain in the militia, has been a representative and selectman of Hartford. His children are, Cecilia A. b. Feb. 23, 1835 ; Charles Allyn b. Feb. 10, 1837 ; Alice Webster b. March 29, 1839 ; Anna E. b. July 28, 1841, d. at the age of two years ; Mary b. Jan. 12, 1846.

Stoddard, John, moved from Wethersfield to Litchfield—was a descendant of Serg't. John, (in No. 2,) and not of Anthony.

Stocking, George, of Hartford—died in May, 1683. He was aged at his decease, and left children, Dea. Samuel, Hannah Benton, the wife of John Richards, and the wife of Samuel Olcott. Estate £257. He had a grandson John, a son of Dea. Samuel. Dea. Samuel Stocking, of Middletown, son of George, of Hartford, died Dec. 30, 1683. Wife, Bethia. Children, Samuel 27 years of age, Bethia Stowe 25, John 23, Ebenezer 17, George, Stephen 10, Daniel 6, Lydia 21. He gave to Rev. Nathaniel Collins, his minister, £3. (See p. 77, No. 2.)

Storrs, Samuel, of Mansfield—died in 1719.

Stoughton, Ancient, was appointed in 1636, with George Hubbard and S. Wakeman, to settle the bounds of Windsor towards the falls near little brook, and upon the east side of the river upon the same line. He with S. Wakeman in Nov. 1636, reported to extend Wethersfield towards Ira, six miles from the south line of Hartford, east of the river, to begin at the mouth of pewter-pot brook and run due east into the country three miles, and then south six miles. (Page 77.)

Stoughton, Thomas, an early and important settler—died in Sept. 1684. He left an estate of £941 to his children, John, Thomas, Samuel, Israel, Elizabeth and Rebecca. This name was formerly spelt Stoton, and afterwards Stoughton.

Stoton, Thomas, of Windsor, married Mary ——, and had John b. in 1657, Mary b. in 1658, Elizabeth b. in 1660, Thomas b. in 1662, Samuel b. in 1665, Israel b. in 1667, and Rebecca b. in 1673.

Stoton or Stoughton, John, of Windsor—died in 1685. Wife, Mary. Estate £909. The use of one-third of his real estate and £100 personal estate was distributed to his widow, and to his children, as follows : To John £199 ; to Thomas £136 ; to Samuel £126 ; to Israel £126 ; to Elizabeth £116, and to Rebecca £116—to be received by the sons at the age of 21 years, and the daughters at 18 years of age. (See p. 77, No. 2.)

Stowe, Thomas, sen'r., of Middletown—died in 1683. Children, John, Nathaniel and Thomas ; he also appears to have had a son in law, Samuel Bidwell, who shared in his estate. The Stowe family settled first at Middletown.

Strickland, Joseph, of Wethersfield, in 1636. Upon the 29th of March, 1636, a dismission from the church at Watertown, Mass., was granted to Robert Coe, Robert Reynold, Jonas Wood, Joseph Strickland, Joseph Sherman and Andrew Ward, conditioned that they should renew the covenant in Connecticut. The court therefore at Hartford on the 26th day of April, 1636, confirmed the certificate, by their promising shortly publicly to renew said covenant, upon notice to the churches. These men settled at Wethersfield, April, 1636.

Strong, John, sen'r., of Windsor, son of John, of Northampton, was one of the early settlers with his father, at Windsor. His children were, John 32 years old, b. in 1663 ; Jacob 25, b. in 1675 ; Josiah 19, b. 1678 ; Mary 40, b. in 1658 ; Hannah Hopkins 36, b. in 1660. Estate £483, Michael Taintor, appraiser. He married Mary Clark in 1656 ; she died in 1663 ; he then married Elizabeth Warner.

Strong, Return, sen'r., of Windsor—died in 1726. Children, Samuel, Benjamin, Sarah, Abigail, Elizabeth, Damaris, Hannah and Margaret. He had grandsons, William Boardman, John Warham Strong, and William Warner.

Strong, Return, jr., of Windsor—died in 1708-9, by trade a tanner, a brother of Samuel. Wife, Elizabeth. Children, John Warham, 7 years old, only surviving son of Return, jr., and Elizabeth, 5 years old in 1713. He married Elizabeth, daughter of Rev. John Warham, of Windsor. Estate £419. The widow was guardian of the 2 children.

Strong, John Wareham, son of Return, jr.,—died in 1752. Wife, Azubah. Left a large estate.

Strong, Samuel, of Windsor, a brother of Return, jr.—died in 1741. Left his widow, Martha, and children, Samuel and Return. He owned land at Torrington, which he ordered to be sold, in his will. He also owned land in Harwinton, which had been laid out to his father, Return. He also had daughters, Mary, Sarah Phelps and Martha Strong. He was a grandson of Rev. John Warham.

Strong, John, son of Return, jr., who deceased in 1726. Wife, Mary, and children, Jonathan, David, John, Hester Clark, Abigail Loomis, Sarah Clark, Elizabeth Burnham and Hannah Strong. David had land in Bolton, and removed there. John died in 1749.

Strong, Asahel, of Farmington—died in 1739, and left children, John, Margaret Root, and Mary Lewis.

Strong, Asahel, of Farmington—died in 1751. Wife, Ruth, and children, Lois 4 years old, Ruth 11, Elnathan 9, Cyprian 7, Elizabeth 4 years old. Estate £1003. Rev. Cyprian, D. D., graduated at Yale College in 1763. He was settled in the ministry at Chatham, and was an eminent divine. He died in 1811.

Sumner, William, of Middletown—died July, 1703. Children, Hezekiah, aged 20, Daniel 15, Sarah 18. This family came late into the colony, but before 1700.

T.

Taintor, Charles, of Wethersfield, in 1644, is found upon the records of lands, and was probably the man who was deputy in 1643 and '46, (in No. 2, p. 79.) Michael Taintor was in this colony, and at Branford and Windsor. As none of the family appear to have died in the probate district of Hartford, Charles probably removed to Fairfield with Jagger, before 1650.

Taintor, Michael, of Colchester, supposed the son of Charles, first of Wethersfield, and afterwards of Fairfield county. Michael's children were, Mary, Sarah, John, Michael and Joseph. His daughters were married at their father's decease. He owned land at Windsor at his death. He had a grandson Michael, and a grandson John, son of Michael, a grandson Michael, son of Joseph, of Branford, deceased. Michael, sen'r., moved from Windsor to Colchester. Wife, Mabel. He died in 1731. Estate £181.

Tomlinson, Noah and Isaac, brothers, were born about 1720. Noah settled at Derby, and married Abigail Beers, of Newtown, and had children, Dan, Nathan, Noah and Beers. Dan lived and died at Derby. He had children, Philo, Abijah, Dan, Eliphalet, Abigail, Susan and Comfort. Philo married Miss Atwell ; Abigail died single ; Dan married Miss Judd, and lives in East Bloomfield, N. Y. ; Eliphalet married Polly Logan, of Washington, where he lived and died. He left children, Christopher, of Canada, married Susan ——— ; Comfort married George Bradley, of Newtown, Conn. This is the family of which Governor Tomlinson is a descendant. The first of the family appears to have settled in Milford or Stratford.

Tomlinson, Thomas, of Hartford—died March 27, 1685. Estate £68. Widow, Elizabeth. Children, Sarah Bishop, aged 20, Mary 18, Ruth 15, Phoebe 12, Elizabeth 10, Hannah 6, and Thankful 1. No sons. In 1727, Henry Tomlinson, of Colchester, died, and left a widow Elizabeth.

Thompson, William, of New London, in 1664, removed to Virginia.

Tomson, John, of Fairfield, in 1641.

Toobe or Tobe, John, of Middletown—(wife, Sarah) died in 1728. Sarah Marks, administratrix, 1730. Son Anthony, aged 15—perhaps other children. His name is spelt Toobe on the record.

Tyler, Isaac, of Haddam—died in 1718–19. Wife, Abigail. Estate £136. Children, Abraham, 13 years old, Abigail 14, Isaac 11, Ann 9, Watchful 8, Israel and Hannah 4.

Tryon, David, of Wethersfield, died as early as 1733. He had a son Benjamin, aged 18 years.

W.

Wade, Robert, of Windham—died in 1696. Peter Cross, administrator. (See p. 86.)

Wait, William, (an Indian man, of Hartford,) died in 1711. Estate £6 : 4 : 5, which was paid him for his expedition against Canada in 1709.

Warner, John, of Waterbury—died while on a visit at Farmington in 1707. Children, John, Ephraim, Robert, Ebenezer, Lydia Brunson, wife of Samuel Brunson.

Waters, Bevil, of Hartford, purchased land of J. Pantry before 1686.

Way, Elizur, of Hartford, (see No. 3, p. 90.) He owned lands at Westfield, Southfield and Rocky Hill. Estate divided by the heirs, March, 1695.

West, Benjamin, of Middletown—died in 1733. Widow, Hannah. He left a daughter, Abigail, and perhaps other children. He moved from Enfield to Middletown. He married Hannah Haddock in 1692. (See p. 181.)

Whitmore, John, son of Thomas, of Middletown—died in 1696–7. Mary, his widow. Children, Thomas, Abigail, Elizabeth 9, Mary 5, John 2, and Ebenezer 3 months old. Some of these may have been the children of his first wife. His widow, Mary, appears to have been the daughter of Andrew Warner. John married Mary for his second wife, she also appears to have married Mr. Savage, for her first husband. John, the deceased, was a brother of Beriah and Joseph Whitmore. (See p. 97.)

Watson, Caleb, of Hartford—died in 1725. Wife, Mary, executrix of his will. He left no children. Samuel Mitchell, administrator with the will annexed. Estate £320. He gave his estate to his sister, Dorcas Adams, of Ipswich, and to his relative Sarah Mitchell, wife of Samuel. In early life he was a school master at Hartford. At the close of his life he was called Rev. He is supposed to have died over one hundred years of age.

Wilcox, Israel—died in 1689. Children, Israel 10 years old, John 8, Samuel 5, Thomas 3, and Sarah 1.

Winchill, Nathaniel, sen'r., of Windsor—died in 1700. Sarah, his relict, and his son Nathaniel, administrators, presented the inventory. Estate £540. Children, Nathaniel 32 years old, Thomas, (deceased when 28 years old, left four children,) Stephen 22, John 20, Sarah 25, and Mary 17.

Wood, Jonas, jr., son of Jonas, of Wethersfield, removed to Stamford in 1640.

Wright, Anthony, of Wethersfield—died in 1679. Wife, Mary, (who had been the widow of Matthias Treat, by whom she had children.) Estate about £200.

Woodruff, Matthew, of Farmington, went there in the early settlement of the town, from Hartford. He lived to old age, and died in 1682. When he made his will he omitted to notice in it, one of his daughters, but the court gave her a share in his estate. His children found, were, Samuel, John, Matthew, Hannah, Seymour, and his daughter, unnoticed by him.

Woodruff, Wid. Sarah—died in 1690. She left two sons, Nathaniel 5 years old, and Joseph 3. (See p. 38.)

Woodruff, Matthew, jr., son of Matthew, sen'r., died in 1691. His children were, Matthew 23 years old, John 19, Samuel 14, Nathaniel 5, Joseph 2, Mary 21, (a cripple,) Sarah 17, Hannah 10, and Elizabeth 12. Estate £324.

Woodruff, John, sen'r., son of Matthew, sen'r., died in 1692. His children were, John aged 23 years, Joseph 13, Mary 25, Hannah 21, Phoebe 16, Margaret 10, and Abigail 8 years. Estate £353. He left a widow. He had a grandson, John Root, son of his daughter Mary.

Woodruff, Samuel, (that hereafter follows, now of Windsor,) was probably the great grandson of Samuel, the son of Matthew, sen'r. ; at all events, Matthew was his progenitor—whether of the fourth or 5th generation.

Woodruff, Samuel, of Southington, long since deceased, was the grand father of Hon. Samuel, of Windsor, who is now living, aged 87 years. Samuel, of Windsor, was long a judge of the County Court— was also an agent to Greece, and published his journey and travels in Europe. The children of Samuel, his grand father, were, Samuel, Isaac, Phoebe, Lois, Rebecca, Sarah and Bulah. Phoebe married Mr. Peck ; Lois married Richard Porter ; Rebecca married Benjamin Dutton ; Sarah married Mr. Peck, and Bulah married Mr. Scott, all of Southington. Judge Samuel, the grandson of Samuel, had children, James, now of Detroit, Michigan, Samuel Henry, Esq., of Tariffville, Sophia, who married Egbert Cowles, Esq., of Farmington, Esther Julia, married Albert Clark, of Enfield. Hon. Samuel married Esther Sloper, of Southington—she died in 1807 ; he then married Chloe Phelps for his second wife, by whom he had one daughter. His son James, of Detroit, married Sophia, daughter of Rev. William Robinson, of Southington, and has children, Anna Mills, Helen E. Anna M. married Theodore Romain, of New York. Helen E. married George H. Tracy, of Troy, N. Y. Samuel H. married Elizabeth M. Root, daughter of Joel Root, of New Haven, in 1812. His children are, Samuel R. born in 1813, William Henry (died an infant,) Sarah S. born in 1818, (died young,) James C. born in 1821, William Forbes born in 1822, Henry Dwight born Dec. 1824, Joel Root Woodruff born Aug. 1828.

PASSENGERS OF THE MAY FLOWER IN 1620.

I have taken the liberty of copying from that most excellent work, which should be in every family in New England, "The New England Historical and Genealogical Register, published quarterly, under the direction of the New England Historic, Genealogical Society," at Boston, Mass., a List of the Names of the Passengers of that noted vessel, the "May Flower," on her first voyage to this country, in 1620, and landed her passengers at Plymouth Rock, (now in Massachusetts,) on the 11th day of December, O. S., 1620.

List of the Names.

John Carver, died in April, 1621; Mrs. Carver, his wife, died in May, 1621; Elizabeth Carver, daughter of Mr. Carver, and afterwards wife of John Howland; Jasper, the boy of Mr. Carver, died Dec. 6, 1620; John Howland; three others of this family died before 1627.

William Bradford; Mrs. Dorothy Bradford, his wife, drowned Dec. 7, 1620.

Edward Winslow; Mrs. Elizabeth Winslow, his wife, died March 24, 1620–1; Edward Winslow, jr., son of Edward; John Winslow, son of Edward; George Soule.

William Brewster; Mrs. Brewster, his wife; Love Brewster, son of William; Wrestling Brewster, son of William; Mrs. Lucretia Brewster, wife of Jonathan, the eldest son of Elder Brewster; William Brewster, son of Jonathan.

Isaac Allerton; Mrs. Mary Allerton, his wife, died February 25, 1620–1; Bartholomew Allerton, son of Isaac; Remember Allerton, daughter of Isaac; Mary Allerton, daughter of Isaac, and afterwards wife of Elder Thomas Cushman; Sarah Allerton, daughter of Isaac, and afterwards wife of Moses Maverick.

Miles Standish; Mrs. Rose Standish, his wife, died Jan. 29, 1620–1. John Alden.

Samuel Fuller; William Butten, his servant, died Nov. 6, 1620.

Christopher Martin, died Jan. 8, 1620–1; Mrs. Martin, his wife, died the first winter; Solomon Martin, son of Christopher, died Dec. 24, 1620; one other of this family died the first winter.

William Mullins, died Feb. 21, 1620–1; Mrs. Mullins, his wife, died the first winter; Priscilla Mullins, daughter of William, and after.

wards wife of John Alden; two others of this family died the first winter.

William White, died Feb. 21, 1620–1; Mrs. Susanna White, his wife, afterwards wife of Governor Winslow; Resolved White, son of William; William White, jr., son of William; Edward Thompson, died Dec. 4, 1620.

Richard Warren.

Stephen Hopkins; Mrs. Elizabeth Hopkins, his wife; Constance Hopkins, daughter of Stephen, and afterwards wife of Nicholas Snow; Giles Hopkins, son of Stephen; Caleb Hopkins, son of Stephen; Oceanus Hopkins, son of Stephen, born at sea.

Edward Dotey.

Edward Leister.

Edward Tilley, died the first winter; Mrs. Tilley, his wife, died the first winter; two others of this family died the first winter.

John Tilley, died the first winter; Mrs. Tilley, his wife, died the first winter; one other of this family died the first winter.

Francis Cooke; John Cooke, (called the younger,) son of Francis.

Thomas Rogers, died the first winter; Joseph Rogers, son of Thomas.

Thomas Tinker, died the first winter; Mrs. Tinker, his wife, died the first winter; one more of this family died the first winter.

John Ridgdale, died the first winter; Mrs. Ridgdale, his wife, died the first winter.

Edward Fuller, died the first winter; Mrs. Fuller, his wife, died the first winter; Samuel Fuller, (called the younger,) son of Edward.

John Turner, died the first winter; two others of this family died the first winter.

Francis Eaton; Mrs. Eaton, his wife, died before 1627; Samuel Eaton, son of Francis.

James Chilton, died Dec. 8, 1620; Mrs. Chilton, his wife, died the first winter; Mary Chilton, daughter of James, afterwards wife of John Winslow, the brother of Edward.

John Crackston, died the first winter; John Crackston, jr., son of John.

John Billington; Mrs. Helen Billington, his wife; Francis Billington, son of John; John Billington, jr., son of John.

Moses Fletcher, died the first winter.

John Goodman.

Degory Priest, died Jan. 1, 1620–1.

Thomas Williams, died the first winter.
Gilbert Winslow, brother of Edward.
Edward Margeson, died the first winter.
Peter Brown.
Richard Britterige, died Dec. 21, 1620.
Richard Clarke, died the first winter.
Richard Gardiner.
John Allerton, (seaman,) died the first winter.
Thomas English, (seaman,) died the first winter.

TOBACCO LAW OF CONNECTICUT IN 1647.

"Forasmuch as it is observed that many abuses are crept in, and committed by frequent taking of tobacko—*It is ordered by the authority of this Courte,* that no person under the age of twenty-one years, nor any other, that hath not already accustomed himself to the use thereof, shall take any tobacko until he hath brought a certificate under the hands of some, who are approved for knowledge and skill in Physick that it is useful for him, and also that he hath received a lycense from the Courte for the same—And for regulating of those who, either by their former taking it, have to theire own apprehensions made it necessary· to them, or uppon due advice are persuaded to the use thereof."

"It is Ordered, that no man within this Collony after the publication hereof, shall take any tobacko publicquely in the street, nor shall any take yt in the Fyelds or woods unlesse when they be on their travill or joyrny, at lest 16 myles or at the ordinary tyme of repast comonly cauled dynner, or if it be not then taken, yet not above once in the day at most, and then not in Company with any other; nor shall any inhabiting in any of the Towns within this jurisdiction take any tobacko in any house in the same Town wher he liveth, with and in the Company of any more than one who vseth and drinketh the same weed with him at that tyme vnder the penalty of six pence for ech offence against this order in any of the particulars thereof," &c.

The foregoing was one of the Public Acts of the Puritanic Legislature of Connecticut, passed in 1647, contemptuously termed *Blue*

Laws. The great and only object of that noble and honest body of men who enacted it, appears uniformly to have been, to do all things without reserve, fear or affection, which they sincerely believed would result in the greatest good, to the largest number of the people of the colony, morally and politically. The disposition so often manifested by a class of men, even of our own citizens, to ridicule the acts of their ancestors, is too often indulged with far less reflection and honesty, than the Puritans manifested in their acts. There had been discovered in this country, a weed which had neither beauty in its form or fragrance agreeable to the senses, but on the contrary, so bitter and nauseous to the taste and smell, that but two living creatures on earth could relish it—one a worm the most filthy and obnoxious of its species —the other a kind of goat which stenched the air where it moved. It had been discovered by the good Legislators, that a disposition had been manifested by some few of their citizens, to level themselves with the worm and the goat in the use of this filthy weed, by snuffing it into their nostrils, to the injury of their smell and voices, by placing it in their mouths, causing an obnoxious breath, injuring the lungs, and destroying their general health ; besides setting their heads on fire by its pestiferous and noxious smoke, or " drinking the weed," as the Indians called smoking ; neither of which could ward off disease, prolong life, or afford nourishment to the body—but on the contrary, laid a sure foundation for disorders, and a certain result in evil consequences—to prevent which, the Puritans enacted the law above. Had the Legislature of Connecticut been alone in its action to prevent the use of tobacco, the enemies of her policy might have sneered at her Blue laws ; but we find that Queen Elizabeth also caused an edict to be enacted against its use ; James I. of England not only enacted laws against its use, but personally attempted to write it down; Charles I. also in his reign made a like attempt. Pope Urban VIII., of Italy, pronounced sentence of excommunication against all who should take snuff at church ; Innocent XII. pronounced his curse upon all who should defile the walls of St. Peters with tobacco. In Russia the penalty for a violation of the tobacco law, was first, the knout, and death for the second offence—and for snuffing tobacco, to slit the nostrils of the offender. In Switzerland, Persia and other Powers in Europe, edicts were passed to prevent the use of this filthy weed under severe penalties. Massachusetts legislated upon this subject, in its early settlement, and made it penal to smoke tobacco within " twenty poles of any house." It was declared by Abbot Nessens

" that the devil first introduced tobacco into Europe." It will in this place be recollected that in the early use of tobacco, a servant of Sir Walter Raleigh entering the room of his master discovered volumes of smoke issuing from his mouth and nostrils, and, supposing his master's head on fire, dashed a pitcher of water into his face to save his life.

Doct. Rogers in his valuable Lecture upon Tobacco, remarks— " that in looking at the history of this plant, (tobacco) we shall see that it has thus advanced to universal sway against the united power of rulers both in church and state. Kings, Sultans and Emperors have opposed its progress; ecclesiastics have thundered their anathemas at the heads of those who should seek in it a gratification, which they pronounced unlawful; the bow-string and the sword and the faggot have been unsparingly used in enforcing their authority; but in spite of edicts and anathemas, it has made its way, until triumphant over its bitterest opponents. Monarchs have now learned to enjoy in it a pleasure in common with their meanest subjects; and nations look to it as one of the most important sources of their wealth and power. And thus (he says) to borrow the words of a writer, 'the whole world finds itself—if I may so speak—tributary to an acrid, filthy, stinking vegetable.' " If, therefore, the Puritans are blameworthy for enacting the foregoing law, or are to be ridiculed for its being in the class termed *blue* laws, I have only to remark, that other countries and states much older, have been as blue and ridiculous in their laws, as Connecticut. Kings, Popes and Emperors, have imitated the Puritans in enacting laws to prevent the use of this noxious and unhealthy weed.

———

The following are some of the First interesting events which occurred in Connecticut during its early settlement.

The first Court held in the colony, was apparently self-constituted, and held at Hartford, April 26, 1636, by five men, before any laws had been enacted, or a government organized—for the trial of Henry Stiles for the offence of selling a gun to an Indian.

The first Law enacted, was to prevent the sale of pistols, guns, powder and shot, to the Indians, April 26, 1636.

The first Military training was ordered by the General Court, held at Wethersfield, in June, 1636. It was then ordered that " each *plantation*" should train once each month.

Juries have attended the trials of cases in the colony previous to its organization as a colony. The first trial by jury was in the case of Serg't. Robert Seely vs. Wethersfield, before the General Court, with a jury, in Nov. 1636.

The first warrant issued and ordered by the Court, was directed to Daniel Finch, of Wethersfield, to summon Richard Gildersleeve to appear before the Court, with the inventory of John Oldham's estate.

The first Probate business done, was in settling the estate of John Oldham, who had been murdered by the Indians, in 1636. Clement Chaplin, first administrator.

George Chappell, Tho's Cooper, and Thomas Barber were the first indentured apprentices, bound by the Court, to Francis Stiles, to serve him four days in each week, to learn the trade of a carpenter, in 1637.

The first session of the General Court, with a Committee or Lower House, was held upon the first day of May, 1637, for the purpose of declaring war against the Pequot Indians; which was also the first declaration of war by Connecticut—the first victory as well as the first and last territory ever held by conquest by the colony, 1637.

The first military draft for soldiers, was for this war in 1637.

The first fort erected by the English was at Saybrook, in 1635-6-7, unless a small fort had been begun at Windsor in 1634.

The Particular Court was the second Court, formed by the General Court, Feb. 9, 1637, O. S., which was principally constituted as a Probate Court, to close the settlement of Oldham's estate, and the business of John Jessup.

Clement Chaplin was the first treasurer, appointed February, 1637. He was also the first collector of rates, with William Wadsworth, Henry Wolcott, Andrew Ward and Jehu Burr, for his sub-collectors, in 1637.

The first tax laid upon the people was for £520, to defray the expense of the war against the Pequots.

The first constables in the colony were, Henry Wolcott, Samuel Wakeman and Daniel Finch, appointed by the General Court in April, 1636.

The first election of the members of the General Court, was in March, 1637. And no evidence of record even then, is found that they were elected by the people; but they attended at the time stated for holding the court, and took their seats.

Thurston Rayner was the first person fined for neglecting to attend the General Court, when elected a member, in 1637—probably few have been fined since for that offence.

Capt. John Mason was the first Major General in Connecticut, with a salary of £40 per annum, paid out of the public treasury quarterly, to train the men ten days each year, 1637.

In 1637 all measures were regulated by law.

The first house built in Windsor, was called the Plymouth house.

The first highway laid out by order of the General Court was located between Hartford and Windsor, and made fit for horse and cart in 1638.

Thomas Stanton was the first public officer appointed to attend courts upon all occasions, General, Particular and meeting of Magistrates, as interpreter between the whites and Indians, (1638) at £10 per annum.

The first formal duty paid, was a duty of one shilling on each beaver skin, half yearly, to the public treasury, (1638.)

Oaths were formed for the Governor, magistrates and constables by law, in 1638 ; before this, the forms used in England, for constables, &c., were used here.

The first General Court legally organized and holden under the Articles of Confederation between the towns of Hartford, Windsor and Wethersfield, was in April, 1639.

The first person who applied to the General Court for remuneration for injuries done to private property by the Indians, was Edward or Eltwed Pomeroy, of Windsor, for a horse killed by the Indians, for which he was allowed, in 1639, £10.

The first case of bastardy punished in the colony, was that of Aaron Stark and Mary Holt, in 1639, (page 75.)

The first writ of attachment issued by the Court against the goods of a debtor, to hold them in security for a debt, was against Thomas James, for five pounds of tobacco, in 1639. This was the first law of attachment in Connecticut.

The first auditors of public accounts, after the Confederation, were Gov. Welles, William Hill and Andrew Ward, in 1639.

Edward Hopkins was the first attorney of record. He appeared in Court for John Woodcock, as plaintiff, in 1639.

Roger Ludlow, Deputy Governor, was fined 5 shillings for being absent from the General Court in September, 1639.

The first court constituted for Poquonnuck, was in October, 1639, to try cases of less than 40 shillings, with the right of appeal.

The first revision of the Laws of the colony was made by Governor Wyllys, Welles, and William Spencer, in 1639.

In 1639 no person could be elected a magistrate unless he had been previously nominated by the General Court.

Previous to Oct. 1639, the towns could not dispose of their lands, except by liberty from the General Court. At this session, liberty was granted ; also the privilege of ordering their towns, making orders, imposing fines and collecting them—with power annually to elect 3, 5, or 7 chief men in each town, one of which should be chosen moderator, and sworn, to meet once in 2 months, as a court to try causes of trespass or debt under 40 shillings, and to administer oaths and issue summonses, with the right of appeal, if aggrieved—and to fine and punish the appellant, if the court should find there was no grounds for the appeal.

It Oct. 1639, the General Court ordered each town in the colony to procure a book for town records, viz. a ledger, with an alphabet. At the same Court ordered town clerks to be elected in each town, to record all deeds of houses and lands, on penalty of 10 shillings per month. All deeds not so recorded, were declared invalid.

In 1656, it was ordered, that all swine over three months old, should be wrung at all seasons of the year, if out of the owner's yard, or within 4 miles of any meeting house—which order extended to all towns in the colony, except Windsor—and there also if found at large, unwrung, within 3 miles of Connecticut river.

A grand list of each town in the colony, in 1652, viz. Hartford, £19,733 : 19 ; Windsor, £14093 ; Wethersfield, £11499 ; Farmington, £5164 ; Saybrook, £3630 ; Stratford, £7040 ; Fairfield, £8850.

The poll tax in 1651 was reduced from 2 shillings 6 pence to 18 pence per poll.

In the year 1653, the General Court of the colony ordered the Hartford Guard, (Governor's Guard) to be allowed a half pound of powder to each man upon Election day, with orders that no enlisted soldier should leave the guard on that day, except by special liberty from the Gov. This appears to have been the company now called the Governor's Foot Guards, who yet attend the Governor on days of Election. It is probable this company has existed as a Governor's guard since the first formation of the colony as a distinct government, in 1639, (on the election of John Haynes, Governor of the colony.) If so, this company is the oldest in the State, if not in the United States, and is still one of the best drilled companies in Connecticut.

ERRATA.

Page 13, top line, for Ashley, read " Ackley."

" 41, top line, omit the word " he."

" 42, read Jonathan Ince for " John Ince."

" 50, line 16th from top, omit " in," and insert took.

" 64, line 4th from bottom, insert " not" before probably.

" 65, death of John Porter, read " 1648."

" 67, line 3d from top, read A. Ward for " H. Ward."

" 78, line 18th from top, for Return, read " John."

" 83, line 9th from top, read Milford, for " Guilford."

" 94, line 5th from bottom, read Dr. Charles P. Wells, for " H. Wells."

" 105, line 2d from bottom, for War, read " the Treasury."

" 108, line 12th from bottom, omit the words Henry Wolcott, the first, of Windsor, and read " Gov'rs. Winthrop, Welles and Webster."

" 145, to the children of Andrew Hinman, jr., add Mary, who married Shadrach Osborn, Esq., and died before her father.

" 159, line 18th from top, read " are," for the 2d " is."

" 184, bottom line, for Elisha, read " Elihu."

" 188, line 2d from bottom, omit the words " a son and."

" 206, line 9th from bottom, insert " grand" before " mother."

" 213, line 12th from top, read " had been," for " died."

" 228, line 18th from top, read " executrix," for " executor."

" 229, line 15th from bottom, for " Oak," read " Indian."

ABBREVIATIONS.

Wid.	for	widow.
d.	"	died.
m.	"	married.
b.	"	born.

ALDEN & KUCHEL, LITH.

R. R. Hinman

1848.

No. V.

A Part of the Early Marriages, Births, and Baptisms, in Hartford, Ct., from Record.

Austin John, m. Mary Hooker, Dec. 8, 1713.

Arnold Jonathan, m. Sarah Jones, Aug. 18, 1715.

Arnold Jonathan, m. Hannah Robinson, Oct. 5, 1709.

Arnold John, m. Hannah Meakins, Jan. 12, 1709–10.

Ashley Jonathan, m. Elizabeth Olcot, May 20, 1703.

Ashley Joseph, m. Mary Mix, Dec. 28, 1709.

Andrews John, m. Hannah Gillet, April 23, 1702.

Andrews Stephen, m. Sarah Gillet, March 29, 1705.

Andrews Thomas, of H. m. Love Knight, dau. of Geo. Nov. 20, 1702.

Barnard Francis, m. Hannah Merrells, Aug. 25, 1644.

Butlar Samuel, m. Mary Gilman, March 2, 1703–4.

Benton Samuel, m. Mary Pomeroy, dau. of Medad, of Northampton, July 2, 1704.

Bigelow Jonathan, m. Mabel Edwards, Dec. 14, 1699.

Bigelow John, m. Hannah Wadsworth, June 30, 1771.

Bracy John, m. Mary Webster, dau. of Jonathan, Feb. 22, 1703–6.

Bull Daniel, m. Hannah Wadsworth, Oct. 26, 1733–4.

Bidwell James, m. Ruth Stanley, Dec. 3, 1713.

Bowne Nathaniel, m. Ellenor Wales, Dec. 1647.

Bushnell Richard, m. Mary Marvin, Oct. 11, 1648.

Barnard Bartholomew, m. Sarah Burchard, Oct. 1647.

Blanchard William, m. Sarah Cowles, Oct. 5, 1718.

Benton Jacob, m. Abigail Carter, July 6, 1724.

Bunce Thomas, m. Eliza Easton, June 2, 1709.

Bidwell Thomas, m. Prudence Scott, March 28, 1710.

Baker Basey, m. Hannah Willet, April 1, 1697.

Bidwell Josiah, m. Martha Butlar, Dec. 1711.

Butlar Thomas, m. Abigail Shepard, Aug. 6, 1691.

Bull Jonathan, m. Sarah Whiting, March 19, 1684.

33

Baker John, m. Rachel M——, Dec. 1702.

Butlar John, m. Mary Marshfield, March 14, 1705–6.

Butlar Jonathan, m. Mary Easton, Sept. 18, 1707.

Bracy Henry, m. Ann Collier, Jan. 30, 1706.

Bunce Joseph, m. Ann Sanford, April, 1708.

Buckland Charles, m. Hannah Shepard, May 22, 1712.

Barnard Samuel, m. Sarah Williamson, Aug. 12, 1714.

Brown Benoni, m. Elizabeth Arnold, Jan. 25, 1715.

Barrett Jonathan, m. Rebecca Whaples, Nov. 12, 1714.

Buckingham Thomas, Mr. m. Ann Foster, dau. of Rev. Isaac, Nov. 29, 1699.

Burnham Richard, m. Sarah Humphries, June 11, 1680.

Belcher Andrew, m. Sarah Gilbert, dau. of Jonathan, July 1, 1670.

Biddoll John, jr. m. Sarah Wells, dau. of Thomas, dec'd of H. Nov. 7, 1678.

Bracy Stephen, m. Sarah Law, March 30, 1701.

Benton Joseph, m. Sarah Waters, Feb. 1697.

Bidwell Thomas, m. Prudence Scott, March 28, 1710.

Bidwell Jonathan, m. Martha Butlar, Dec. 25, 1711.

Bull Thomas, m. Thankful Butlar, June 29, 1720.

Benton Jacob, m. Elizabeth Hinsdall, April 4, 1728.

Bidwell Jacob, m. Sarah Belding, dau. of Mr. Timo. Dec. 31, 1764.

Burlison Job, m. Thankful Gaines, May 3, 1744, and had a son Joel.

Bidwell David, m. Mehitabel Webster, July 8, 1714.

Clark Thomas, m. Elizabeth Burr, April 6, 1698.

Church John, m. Abigail Cadwell, April, 1699.

Cook Aaron, m. Martha Allyn, Jan. 3, 1683.   [5, 1702.

Catlin Samuel, son of John, m. Elizabeth Norton, of Farmington, Jan.

Cole Nathaniel, m. Elizabeth Knight, dau. of George, June 12, 1707.

Cullick Capt. m. Elizabeth Fenwick, dau. of George, May 20, 1648.

Church John, son of Richard, m. Sarah Beckley or Buckley, dau. of Richard, 1657.

Catlin John, son of Thomas, m. Mary Marshall, July 27, 1665.

Church James, m. Abigail Stanley, Dec. 10, 1722.

Chappell Samuel, m. Hannah Cadwell, July 3, 1723.

Cole Nathaniel, m. Lydia Davis, Nov. 1676—died Jan. 25, 1683. He m. for his 2d wife Mary Benton, Oct. 23, 1684.

Clark Daniel, son of Thomas, m. Mary Burr, June, 1693.

Crow Christopher, m. Mary Burr, dau. of Benj. Jan. 15, 1656.

Cadwell Edward, m. Deborah Bunce, dau. of John, Dec. 20, 1704.

Clark Josiah, m. Elizabeth, dau. of Thomas Taylor, March 11, 1703.

Collier Joseph, m. Sarah Forbes, April 15, 1695.

Collier John, m. Elizabeth Humphries, July 4, 1705.

Cadwell William, m. Ruth Marsh, Oct. 31, 1711.

Cadwell Matthew, m. Esther Burnham, Aug. 31, 1720.

Cole Henry, m. Sarah Rusco, Dec. 10, 1646.

Cole Samuel, m. Mary Kingsbury, dau. of James, of Plainfield, Jan. 2, 1693.

Church Samuel, m. Elizabeth Clark, Aug. 17, 1710.

Carter Joshua, m. Mary Skinner, May 21, 1691.

Cadwell Thomas, m. Hannah Butlar, Sept. 23, 1687.

Cole John, m. Elizabeth Goodwin, Sept. 12, 1713.

Dodd Edward, m. Lydia Flower, Aug. 2, 1705.

Dorchester Anthony, m. Martha Richards, Jan. 2, 1650.

Day Thomas, m. Hannah Wilson, dau. of John, Sept. 21, 1698.

Day John, m. Grace Spencer, Jan. 21, 1696.

Deming Jacob. m. Elizabeth Edwards, March 14, 1695.

Dowe Samuel, m. Mary, dau. of Geo. Graves, sen'r. Dec. 12, 1665.

Demmon Benjamin, of H. m. Mary Palmer, of Windham, Nov. 5, 1740—son David b. July 30, 1744.

Davenport William, m. Eliza Yeamans, Dec. 4, 1741—son William b. July, 1744.

Easton John, m. Sarah Butlar, Dec. 11, 1712.

Edwards John, m. Christian Williamson, Dec. 24, 1719.

Ensign Thomas, m. Hannah Shepard, Dec. 1, 1692.

Ensign David, m. Hannah, dau. of Simeon Smith, May 14, 1701.

Ensign David, son of James, m. Mehitabel Gunn, dau. of Tho's 1663.

Ensign David, m. Sarah Moody, April 29, 1726.

Ensign James, m. Lydia Baker, March 20, 1689, d. Sept. 16, 1701.

Ensign John, m. Elizabeth Dickinson, May 13, 1711.

Ensign Moses, of H. m. Love Andrews, dau. of Thomas, Jan. 3, 1730.

Ellery John, of Boston, m. Mary Austin, dau. of John and Mary his wife, of Hartford, July 28. 1737.

Ford Thomas, m. widow Ann Steel, Nov. 7, 1644.

Fitch Samuel, m. Mrs. Mary Whiting, 1650.

Foster Edward, m. Ann Hill, Nov. 15, 1710.

Gillett Joseph, m. Sarah Burr, April 14, 1715.

Gross Jonah, m. Susannah Howard, March 13, 1717.

Goodwin Ozias, m. Martha Williams, June 6, 1723.

Gilbert Joseph, m. Mary Griswold, May 17, 1692.

Gibson William, m. Mary Marshall, (both of Boston) July 1, 1701.

Graves George, son of George, m. Eliz. Ventriss, April 2, 1651.

Grannis Edward, m. Elizabeth Andrews, of Farmington, 1654 or 2.

Graham Benj. m. Abigail Humphrey, Feb. 12, 1684, d. 1697.

Gilbert Samuel, m. Mary Rogers, dau. of Samuel, of N. Lond. Oct. 2, 1684.

Gilbert Jonathan, m. Mary Wright, 1645.

Gilbert John, m. Amy Lord, May 6, 1647.

Gaylord, m. Mary Stebbing, April 29, 1648.

Goodrich, William, m. Sarah Marvin, April 7, 1648.

Graham Benj. m. Sarah Webster, Nov. 20, 1698.

Gross Jonah, m. Rebecca Wadsworth, Aug. 11, 1708.

Gross John, m. Mary Wadsworth, Nov. 17, 1709.

Gilman Richard, m. Elizabeth Burnham, March 4, 1702.

Goodwin Samuel, m. Mary Steel, March 18, 1708.

Gillett Abel, m. Abigail Ensign, May 18, 1731.

Gross Truman, m. Susannah Deming, Jan. 7, 1731–2.

Gurnsey John, m. Sarah Hubbard, Oct. 2, 1728.

Gilbert Joseph, m. Elizabeth Smith, dau. of Joseph, May 8, 1695.

Gridley Thomas, m. Mary ——, 1644.

Goodridge William, m. Sarah Marvin, Oct. 4, 1648.

Galpin Samuel, m. Sarah Knight, dau. of.George, Dec. 9, 1715.

Hosford Benjamin, m. Christian Wetherall, Aug. 22, 1644.

Humphrey Dositheus, m. Ann Griswold, May 23, 1734.

Hopkins Thomas, m. Mary Beckley, March 1, 1616–17.

Hosmer Thomas, m. Susannah Steel, July 18, 1734.

Hosmer Thomas, m. Ann Prentiss, Dec. 24, 1700.

Howard Samuel, m. Alice Hooker, Sept. 20, 1720.

Hayward Henry, m. Sarah Stone, Sept. 28, 1648.

Hopkins Steven, son of Steven, m. Sarah Judd, dau. of Thomas, of Waterbury, Nov. 17, 1686.

Hinsdall Barnabas, m. Martha Smith, Nov. 9, 1693.

Harrison James, m. Mahitabel Graves, Jan. 1, 1701.

Humphrey Nathaniel, m. Agnes Spencer, March 14, 1709.

Hubbard John, m. Agnes Humphrey, Oct. 1715.

Hopkins Ebenezer, m. Mary Butlar, of Wethersfield, dau. of Samuel, Jan. 21, 1691.

Hayward Samuel, m. Susannah Bunce, Feb. 18, 1696.

Hopkins Joseph, m. Hannah Peck, dau. of Paul, April 27, 1693.

Haynes Mr. John, m. Mary Glover, of Springfield, Nov. 7, 1693.

Jennings Joshua, m. Mary Williams, 1647.

Jones Nathaniel, m. Rebecca Pantry, April 30, 1713.

Judd Thomas, m. Hepzibah Williams, Jan. 16, 1708.

Judd Ebenezer, m. Hannah Richards, Nov. 5, 1729.

Judd Joseph, m. Elizabeth R——, Nov. 10, 1726.

Kelsey William, m. Rebecca Messenger, Jan. 5, 1709.

King Thomas, m. Sarah Mygatt, Nov. 6, 1712.

King Joseph, m. Mary Joss, May 2, 1717.

Kellogg Isaac, m. Mary Webster, Dec. 26, 1717.

Kellogg Benjamin, m. Abigail Sedgwick, Nov. 9, 1721.

Kellogg Daniel, m. Deborah Moore, Nov. 27, 1729.

Kelsey Charles, m. Hannah Larkham, of England, May 18, 1729.

Kilbourn Thomas, m. Hannah, dau. of Jos. Hills, of G. Feb. 1, 1699.

Kellogg Samuel, m. Sarah Merrills, Sept. 22, 1687.

Kelsey Stephen, m. Hannah Higenson, dau. of John, of Wethersfield, Nov. 15, 1692, d. 1710.

Kellogg Samuel, m. Hannah Benton, May 11, 1711.

Lord Richard, m. Abigail Warren, Jan. 14, 1692.

Lord John, m. Adrian Basey, May 15, 1648.

Lyman Joseph, m. Abigail Spencer, March 2, 1709.

Lemonge Samuel, m. Sarah Merrills, Sept. 22, 1687.

Milrock John, m. Sarah Wadsworth, Sept. 17, 1646.

Merrills Caleb, m. Mercy Sedgwick, Aug. 1733.

Mygatt Joseph, m. Sarah Webster, Nov. 15, 1677.

Merrills Abraham, m. Prudence Kellogg, April 16, 1699.

Millerton John, m. Martha Rue, or Rice, July 1, 1703.

Merrills Wilterton, m. Ruth Pratt, Jan. 1, 1702.

Morse, m. Ruth Stanley, Dec. 5, 1645.

Milrock John, m. —— Stoughton, Jan. 18, 1649.

Merrills Isaac, m. Sarah Cook, May 22, 1706.

Merrills Abel, m. Mabel Easton, March 15, 1710–11.

Morriss Peter, m. Kezia Ames, March 9, 1718–19.

Merrills Jacob, m. Abigail Webster, May 10, 1710.

Merrills John, jr. m. Sarah Marsh, Sept. 29, 1694.

Moody John, m. Sarah Evetts, April 3, 1700.

Marsh John, m. Susannah Butler, Jan 1, 1707.

Nichols Cyprian, m. Mary, dau. of Samuel Spencer, May 24, 1705.

Nicholson Henry, m. Hannah Spencer, June 8, 1729.

Olmsted Nicholas, m. Mary Hosmer, March 30, 1706.

Olmsted Thomas, m. Ann Webster, Feb. 21, 1716.

Olmsted Thomas, m. Hannah Mix, June 25, 1691.

Olmsted Stephen, m. Sarah Newell, dau. of John, June 27, 1723.

Pratt Daniel, son of Daniel, m. Elizabeth Lee, March 10, 1691.

Peck Paul, m. Leah Morry, Aug. 8, 1700.

Parsons John, m. Phillis Hills, Dec. 1, 1698.

Peck Samuel, m. Abigail Collier, dau. of Joseph, March 6, 1701.

Pratt John, jr. m. Hannah Porter, dau. of John, jr. Jan. 29, 1712.

Porter John, m. Hannah Hopkins, wid. of Joseph, Dec. 3, 1713.

Porter Hezekiah, 2d, m. Sarah Wright, Aug. 25, 1719.

Pammer Nicholas, m. Jane Purchas.

Parsons Joseph, m. Mary Bliss, Nov. 1646.

Peck John, m. Mahitabel Reeve, Nov. 1707.

Parsons John, m. Dorothy Sparks, May 27, 1712.

Pratt Peter, m. Mahitabel Watrous, Sept. 7, 1709.

Pratt Elisha, m. Sarah Burnham, Dec. 7, 1726.

Pratt John, jr. m. Hannah Norton, dau. of John, 1712–13.

Pellitt Thomas, jr. m. Martha ——, March 18, 1730, daughters Phil
    lis and Patience.

Porter Timothy, m. Mary Pitkin, June 14, 1716.

Porter James, m. Mary Pitkin, July 7, 1720.

Ruscoe John, m. Rebecca Beebe, Jan. 2, 1650.

Reeve Robert, m. Sarah Adkins, July 2, 1717.

Richards Samuel, m. Mary Henbury, June 14, 1697.

Russell Mr. John, m. Mary Talcott, June 28, 1649.

Richards Thomas, son of John, m. Mary Parsons, of Springfield, dau
    of Benjamin, Oct. 1, 1691.

Risley Samuel, m. Rebecca Gaines, Aug. 1, 1704.

Richards Thomas, m. Abigail Turner, June 6, 1717.

Roote Joseph, m. Hannah Kellogg, Oct. 20, 1715.

Roby Andrew, m. Abigail Curtiss, Nov. 19, 1690.

Shepard Thomas, m. Susannah Scott, Sept. 5, 1695.

Smith Nathaniel, m. Esther Dickinson, July 9, 1686.

Steel Samuel, m. Mercy Bradford, Sept. 16, 1680.

Shepard John, jr. m. Hannah Peck, May 12, 1680.

Seymour John, jr. m. Elizabeth Webster, Dec. 19, 1693.

Spencer Samuel, son of Samuel, m. Hepzibah Church, Sept. 1696.

Skinner John, m. Rachel Pratt, dau. of Daniel, Feb. 22, 1693.

Spencer Ebenezer, m. Mary Booth, Feb. 28, 1699.

Spencer Garrard, m. Hannah Pratt, dau. of John, Dec. 22, 1680.

Stanley Nathaniel, m. Anna Whiting, Nov. 14, 1706.

Seymour Thomas, m. Ruth Norton, Feb. 29, 1700.

Smith Joseph, m. Lydia Hunt, dau. of Ephraim, April 4, 1656.

Stanley Caleb, m. Hannah, dau. of Samuel Spencer, May 13, 1686, she died Dec. 5, 1702.

Skinner Timothy, m. Ruth Cotton, May, 1738—children, Ruth, Mabel, and Anna.

Stanley Nathaniel, m. Mary Boosey, June 2, 1659.

Sedgwick Josiah, m. Ruth Smith, Jan. 24, 1722.

Sedgwick Stephen, m. Mary Harriss, Dec. 16, 1725.

Sexton Gershom, m. Abigail King, Jan. 20, 1708.

Shepard Thomas, m. Jane North, Oct. 12, 1710.

Sheldin James, m. Elizabeth Pratt, Feb. 1716.

Skinner Joseph, m. Dorothy Hosmer, Jan. 1696, and m. his 2d wife, Eliza Olmsted, Jan. 28, 1707.

Seymour Richard, m. Mary Wilson, Oct. 30, 1707.

Steel Thomas, m. Susan Webster, May 10, 1709.

Sadd Thomas, m. Hannah Grant, dau. of Matthew, Dec. 25, 1712.

Smith Jobannah, m. Sarah Graves, Sept. 26, 1714.

Sedgwick Ebenezer, m. Prudence Merrills, June 30, 1720.

Seymour Jonathan, m. Mary Bull, May 27, 1725.

Seymour Timothy, m. Rachel Allyn, April 27, 1727.

Seymour John, m. Lydia Mason, June 25, 1718.

Steel Jonathan, m. Dorothy Mygatt, May 5, 1715.

Sedgwick Samuel, jr. m. Ruth Peck, Feb. 1, 1710–11.

Stanley Caleb, jr. m. Abigail Bunce, Feb. 15, 1704–5.

Steel John, m. Mary Warner, 1645.

Stebin Samuel, son of George, m. Bethia Loomis, dau. of John, 1652.

Savage John, of H. m. Elizabeth Dublin, 1652.

Stanley John, m. Sarah Steel, Dec. 5, 1645.

Symons Joseph, m. Abigail Spencer, March 2, 1709.

Shepard Thomas, m. Jane North, Oct. 12, 1710.

Seymour Thomas, m. Mary Waters, June 21, 1711.

Sedgwick Jonathan, m. Isabell Stebbins, March 7, 1716–17.

Skinner John, m. Mary Turner, Dec. 24, 1724.

Spencer John, m. Sarah Smith, dau. of Joseph, Oct. 4, 1693.

Smith Richard, m. Elizabeth Cole, Dec. 20, 1705.

Spencer Garret, m. Sarah, dau. of John Day, June 10, 1708.

Shelding John, m. Elizabeth Pratt, April 20, 1708.

Seymour Zachariah, m. Hannah Olmsted, Nov. 24, 1709.

Shepard Samuel, m. Bethia Steel, May 17, 1709.

Smith Philip, m. Mary Robinson, Sept. 1708.

Shepard Joseph, m. Eliza Flowers, June 19, 1711.

Smith Jobannah, m. Mary Flowers, April 16, 1719.

Sedgwick Joseph, m. Ruth Smith, Jan. 24, 1722–3.

Sexton George, m. Sarah, dau. of George Knight, Dec. 25, 1699.

Spencer Garret, m. Hannah Pratt, dau. of John, Dec. 22, 1680.

Shepard John, m. Mary Bigelow, May 18, 1712.

Taylor Jonathan, m. Elizabeth Richards, Oct. 5, 1709.

Taylor Stephen, m. Violet Bigelow, Sept. 1, 1709—he m. Esther
    Richards, Oct. 6, 1703, and died 1705.

Treat Richard, m. Susannah Woodbridge, Aug. 7, 1718.

Thornton Samuel, m. Susannah Whiting, Feb. 12, 1701.

Tomsunn Thomas, m. Anne Welles, 1646.

Turner Ephraim, m. Mary Nichols, May 2, 1700.

Upson Thomas, m. Elizabeth Fuller, 1646.

Ventres Moses, m. Grace ——, 1646.

Wadsworth William, m. Elizabeth Stone, July 2, 1644.

Warner John, m. Ann Norton or Foster, 1649.

Wilcock John, m. Miss Stoughton, Jan. 1649.

Welles Mr. Thomas, son of Mr. Thomas Welles, magistrate, of Weth-
    ersfield, m. Mrs. Hannah Pantry, wid. June, 1654.

Watson John, jr. m. Sarah Steel, dau. of James, Feb. 19, 1707–8.

Wells Hezekiah, m. Mrs. Elizabeth Hobart, dau. of Rev. Jeremiah,
    May 2, 1704.   [1696.

Waters Thomas, m. Sarah, dau. of Benj. Fenn, of Milford, May 19,

Webster Robert, m. Hannah, dau. of John Beckley or Buckley, Sep.
    10, 1689.

Webster Jonathan, m. Esther Judd, dau. of Benj. Dec. 14, 1704.

Webster Joseph, m. Mary Judd, Jan. 23, 1695.

Webster Stephen, m. Mary Burnham, June 6, 1717.

Webster Jacob, m. Elizabeth Nichols, Feb. 16, 1717–18.

Webster Daniel, m. Miriam Kellogg, Nov. 11, 1719.

Webster Joseph, m. Hannah Baker, May 11, 1726.

Wadsworth Ichabod, m. Sarah Smith, Dec. 21, 1720.

Weston Samuel, m. Ann Thornton, May 23, 1728.

Webster Cyprian, m. Elizabeth Seymour, Sept. 25, 1729.

White Nathaniel, m. Sarah Hinsdall, July 29, 1725.

Watson Caleb, m. Hannah Porter, July 5, 1733.

Wells Ichabod, m. Sarah Way, Sept. 4, 1684.

Webster Jonathan, m. Dorcas Hopkins, May 11, 1681.

Whiting William, m. Mary Allyn, dau. of Col. John, Oct. 6, 1686.

Webster Moses, m. Mary Bracy, Dec. 6, 1733.

Wells Samuel, m. Esther Ellsworth, Jan. 1722.

Wadsworth Jonathan, m. Hepzibah Marsh, Nov. 29, 1711.

Webster John, m. Abiel Steel, Dec. 25, 1712.

Williams James, jr. m. Sarah Judd, Dec. 29, 1715.

Whitmore Thomas, m. Sarah Hales, Dec. 11, 1645.

Welles Hugh, m. Mary Rusco, Aug. 19, 1647.

Williams William, m. Fanne Westover, 1647.

Walkley James, m. Alice Boosey, of Wethersfield, 1652.

Welles Thomas, m. Mrs. Sarah Pantry.

Williams James, m. Sarah Richardson, Oct. 2, 1691.

Wright George, m. Mary Harrison, Oct. 1694.

Wilson John, m. Mary Gilbert, Nov. 27, 1707.

Wells Samuel, m. Rachel Cadwell, May 26, 1709.

Watson Cyprian, m. Eliza Steel, Jan. 27, 1715.

Williams Samuel, m. Hannah Hickcox, Nov. 13, 1722.

Watson John, m. Bethia Tyler or Fyler, dau. of Wm. April 30, 1730.

Welles John, jr. m. Sarah Gaylord, Dec. 24, 1735.

Wells Jonathan, m. Ruth Bull, Dec. 15, 1715.

Webster Ezekiel, m. Rebecca Gaines, Jan. 21, 1731-2—children
    Rebecca, Ruth, Ezekiel, Elijah b. May 1, 1742.

Marriages by John Marsh, Esq.

Barnard Joseph, m. Sarah Olcott, March 23, 1739-40.

Clapp Elijah, m. Ann Benton, July 12, 1741.

Charles John, m. Mary Breed, upon special reasons, April 5, 1743.

Handerson James, m. Jerusha White, Jan. 17, 1741-2.

King Joseph, m. Eunice Seymour, of Suffield—for reasons were married without publishing, July 19, 1737.

Messenger Nehemiah, m. Elizabeth Hopkins, Aug. 22, 1739.

Peter, Negro, m. Phebe, Aug. 28, 1740.

Spencer, John, m. Thankful Easton, July 17, 1743.

Shelding John, m. Mary Graham, March 14, 1743-4.

Smith Abiah, of Litchfield, m. Johannah Goodwin, April 18, 1739.

Seymour Zechariah, m. Sarah Steel, April 25, 1739.

Strong Samuel, m. Susannah Brace, Aug. 20, 1739.

Wadsworth Joseph, m. Elizabeth Cooke, May 10, 1742.

Webster Isaac, m. Amy White, Nov. 11, 1739.

Andrews Samuel, son of William, b. Oct. 20, 1645.   [*Record.*]

Andrews John, son of James, bap. Sept. 27, 1646.

Adams Samuel, son of Jeremy, bap. Nov. 23, 1645.

Allcock Elizabeth, dau. of Thomas, bap. Dec. 7, 1643.

Bryant Ebenezer and his wife Mahitabel, had Sarah b. May 11, 1739.
   Elizabeth b. Aug. 26, 1741.   Ebenezer b. Aug. 19, 1744.   Samuel
   b. April 25, 1747.   Timothy b. Aug. 15, 1750.   Jonathan b. Feb.
   6, 1753.   Daniel b. Nov. 24, 1755.

Baysa Elizabeth, dau. of John, bap. Aug. 23, 1645.

Bloomfield John, son of William, bap. Aug. 23, 1645.

Burr Mary, dau. of Thomas, b. Sept. 17, 1645.

Brunson Isaac, son of John, bap. Dec. 7, 1645.

Burr Thomas, son of Benjamin, b. Jan. 26, 1645.

Bartlett Deborah, dau. of Robert, bap. March 18, 1645.

Catling Mary, bap. Nov. 29, 1646.

Desbrow Phebe, dau. of Nicholas, bap. Dec. 20, 1646.

Fellows John, son of Richard, bap. Nov. 1, 1646.

Gibbons Sarah, dau. of William, b. Aug. 17, 1645.

Gozzard Daniel, son of Daniel, bap. Jan. 24, 1646.

Gurnsey John and Sarah, had Sarah b. July 13, 1729.   Elizabeth
   b. Feb. 27, 1730.   John b. Jan. 13, 1732-3.   Lydia b. Dec. 6,
   1734.   Bezaleel b. Nov. 28, 1737.

Hubbard Daniel, son of George, bap. Dec. 7, 1645.

Haynes Mabel, dau. of John, Esq. b. March 19, 1645.

Hollen Samuel, son of William, bap. Nov. 1, 1646.

Hopkins Isaac, son of Ebenezer, b. Nov. 25, 1708.

Ketcherall Hannah, dau. of Samuel, b. Jan. 4, 1645.

Kelsey Abigail, dau. of William, bap. April 19, 1645.

Kerbee Elizabeth, dau. of John, b. Sept. 8, 1646.

Lawes Mary, dau. of William, jr. b. May 6, 1645.

Lawes Philip, son of William, jr. bap. 1646.

Merrells Thomas, son of Thomas, bap. Nov. 1, 1646.

Marsh Joseph, son of John, bap. Jan. 24, 1646.

Newton Samuel, son of Roger, bap. 1646.

Sibly Jonathan, of Windham, died in 1714, and left a son John.

Wadsworth Samuel, son of William, bap. Oct. 25, 1646.

Young Seth and Hannah, had Benj. b. Sept. 23, 1736.   Joseph b.
   Dec. 25, 1738.   Abigail b. Feb. 3, 1740-1.

   Mary, dau. of Arthur Smith, b. 1644.   John, son of William Pratt,
b. Feb. 23, 1644.   Abigail, dau. of Wm. Kelsey, b. April 19, 1645.

Daniel Steel, son of John, b. April 29, 1645, d. 1646. Mary, dau. of William Lawes, jr. b. May 6, 1645. Eliz. dau. of William Wadsworth, b. May 17, 1645. Sarah, dau. of William Gibbons, b. Aug. 17, 1645. Louis, dau. of Timothy Stanley, b. Aug. 23, 1645. Elizabeth Basey, dau. of John, bap. Aug. 23, 1645. John, son of Wm. Blomfield, bap. Aug. 23, 1645. Mary, dau. of Thomas Burr, b. Sept. 17, 1645. Joseph, son of Mr. Wm. Whiting, b. Oct. 2, 1645. Samuel, son of William Patrick, b. Oct. 15, 1645. Jacob, son of John Whight, b. Oct. 18, 1645. Samuel, son of William Andrews, b. Oct. 20, 1645. Samuel, son of Jeremiah Adams, bap. Nov. 23, 1645. Elizabeth, dau. of Thomas Allcock, bap. Dec. 7, 1643. Isaac, son of John Brunson, bap. Dec. 7, 1645. Daniel, son of George Hubbard, bap. Dec. 7, 1645. John, son of Paul Peck, b. Dec. 22, 1645. Thomas, son of Benjamin Burr, b. Jan. 26, 1645. Hannah, dau. of Samuel Kecherall, b. Jan. 4, 1645. Deborah, dau. of Robert Bartlett, bap. March 18, 1645. Mabel, dau. of John Haynes, Esq. b. March 19, 1645. John, son of Thomas Roote, b. June 10, 1646. Thomas, son of Thomas Selden, bap. Aug. 30, 1645. John, son of Thomas Whitmore, bap. Sept. 6, 1646. Elizabeth, dau. of John Kerbee, b. Sept. 8, 1646. Elizabeth, dau. of Robert Sanford, b. Feb. 19, 1645. John, son of James Andrews, b. Sept. 27, 1646. Joseph, son af Mr. Samuel Stone, bap. Oct. 15, 1646. Samuel, son of Mr. Roger Newton, bap. Oct. 1646. Samuel, son of William Wadsworth, bap. Oct. 25, 1646. Samuel, son of Richard Risley, bap. Nov. 1, 1646. Samuel, son of William Hollen, bap. Nov. 1, 1646. John, son of Richard Fellows, bap. Nov. 1, 1646. Thomas, son of Thomas Merrills, bap. Nov. 1, 1646. Mary, dau. of Nicholas Olmsted, b. Nov. 7, 1646. Mary, dau. of John Steel, jr. b. Nov. 7, 1646. Mary Catling, bap. Nov. 29, 1646. Philip Lawes, son of William, jr. bap. Dec. 13, 1646. Phebe, dau. of Nicholas Disbrow, bap. Dec. 20, 1646. ⸺ Tomson, dau. of Thomas Tomson, bap. Jan. 17, 1646. Joseph, son of John Marsh, bap. Jan. 24, 1646. Daniel, son of Daniel Gozzard, bap. Jan. 24, 1646. Sarah, dau. of John Crow, b. March 1, 1646. Joseph, son of Thomas Stanton, bap. March 21, 1646. Samuel, son of Edward Ellmore, bap. March 21, 1646. Sarah, dau. of Wm. Hubbard, b. July 10, 1647. Samuel, son of William Blomfield, b. July 12, 1647. Samuel, son of Thomas Gridley, b. Nov. 25, 1647. Abraham Brunson, bap. Nov. 28, 1647. Steven, son of William Kelsey, bap. Nov. 7, 1647. Sarah, dau. of John Whitmore, b. Dec. 16, 1647. John, son of John Stanley, b. Nov. 3 or 4, 1647. Thomas, son of Francis

Andrews, bap. Jan. 2, 1647. Lydia, dau. of Mr. Samuel Stone, b. Jan. 22 or 25, 1647. Samuel, son of Matthew Marvin, bap. Feb. 6, 1647. Isaac, son of Timothy Standla, b. March 10, 1647. Samuel, son of William Rusco, b. March, 1647. Rebecca, dau. of Nicholas Olmsted, b. March, 1647. Ezerkell Sanford, son of Robert, b. March 13, 1647. John (or Tom,) son of John Gilbert, b. Jan. 16, 1647. Elizabeth, dau. of Thomas Spencer, bap. March 26, 1648. Mary, dau. of Thomas Selden, bap. March 26, 1648. Samuel, son of Wm. Laws, b. Aug. 18, 1648. Richard, son of Richard Risley, bap. Aug. 1648. Sarah, dau. of John Milrock, jr. b. Oct. 3, 1648. Sarah, dau. of Bartholomew Barnard, b. Dec. 3, 1648. Mary, dau. of John Webb, b. Feb. 5, 1647. Abigail, dau. of Nicholas Disbrow, b. Feb. 1648. Johannah, dau. of Gyles Smith, bap. March 25, 1649. Jonathan, son of Thomas Bull, bap. March 25, 1649. A son of Samuel Stone, bap. 1649. John, son of John Cullick, b. May 4, 1649. Mary, dau. of Thomas Catling, bap. May, 1649. Anna, dau. of John Crow, b. July 13, 1649. Joseph, son of John Marsh, bap. July 15, 1649. Elizabeth, dau. of Edward Ellmore, bap. July 15, 1649. Ledea, dau. of James Ensign, bap. Aug. 19, 1649. Philip Judd, son of Thomas, bap. Sept. 1649. Sarah, dau. of Thomas Woodford, bap. Sept. 2, 1649. Mary, dau. of Jonathan Gilbert, bap. Dec. 17, 1649. John, son of Richard Olmsted, bap. Dec. 30, 1649. Rachel, dau. of Matt. Marvin, bap. Dec. 30, 1649. John Allcock, son of Thomas, bap. Feb. 3, 1649. John, son of Nicholas Olmsted, bap. Feb. 3, 1649. Sarah, dau. of William Wadsworth, bap. March 17, 1649. John, son of John Pantree, bap. March 17, 1649. Joseph, son of William Hills, bap. Mar. 17, 1649. Elizabeth, dau. of Richard Seyer, b. June, 1650. Daniel Kelsey, son of William, b. Feb. 1650. Abigail, dau. of Mr. Samuel Stone, b. Sept. 9, 1650. John Russell, son of Mr. John, bap. Sept. 23, 1650. George, son of Geo. Hubbard, bap. Dec. 15, 1650. Joseph, son of Paul Peck, bap. Dec. 22, 1650. John, son of John Milrock, jr. b. Dec. 29, 1650. Thomas Hales, bap. January 19, 1650. Thomas, son of Thomas Gridley, b. first week in Aug. 1650. Mary Fellows, dau. of Richard, b. Feb. 9, 1650. David, son of Tho. Bull, bap. Feb. 9, 1650. Rebecca, dau. of Ralph Keeler, bap. Feb. 9, 1650. Arthur, son of Arthur Smith, bap. 1651. Sarah Whight More, dau. of Thomas, bap. April 20, 1651. Esther, dau. of Thomas Selden, bap. May 3, 1649, d. 1651. John Selden, son of Thomas, bap. 1651. Joseph Selden, son of Thomas, bap. Nov. 1651. John Gilbert, son of John, b. Feb. 19, 1652. Hannah Spencer, dau. of Thomas, b.

April 25, 1653. Dorothy Lord, dau. of Thomas, b. Aug. 17, 1653. Jonathan Gilbert, son of Jonathan, b. May 20, 1648. Mary, dau. of Jonathan Gilbert, b. Dec. 15, 1649—also Sarah, dau. of Jonathan, b. July 25, 1651—also Lydia, dau. of Jonathan, b. Oct. 3, 1654. Mary Seymour, dau. of Thomas, b. May 8, 1655. Mary Graves, dau. of Isaac, b. July 5, 1647. Isaac, son of Isaac Graves, b. Aug. 21, 1650. Samuel, son of Isaac Graves, b. Oct. 1, 1655. Elizabeth Gilbert, dau. of John, b. Feb. 1655. Joseph Grannis, son of Edward, b. March 31, 1656. Martha Spencer, dau. of Thomas, b. Jan. 19, 1657. Tho's Gilbert, son of John, b. Sept. 4, 1658—Amy, dau. of John, b. April 3, 1663—also Joseph, son of John, b. April 3, 1666. Anna Allen, dau. of John, b. Aug. 18, 1654—also Mary, dau. of John, b. April 3, 1657—also Margaret, dau. of John, b. July 29, 1660—also Rebecca, dau. of John, b. March, 1664—Martha also b. July 27, 1667—Elizabeth also dau. of John, b. Dec. 1, 1669.

CATALOGUE

NAMES. OF THE FIRST PURITAN SETTLERS OF CONNECTICUT.

A.

Abbernatha, Caleb, of Farmington (Torrington,) died in 1759. Will exhibited by John Abbernatha, same year. Estate £93 : 12 : 8.

Aights, Abraham, of Simsbury, d. in 1766, and left a son Abraham 14 years old.

Alderman, William, of Farmington and Simsbury, d. about 1697. Mary his widow. He had a son William who resided at Simsbury. Estate £47.

Allis, Nathaniel, of Bolton, d. in 1750. His widow Elizabeth and son David, executors. Children, David, Jonathan, Nathaniel, John, Ebenezer, Timothy, Mary Johns, (she left heirs Benjamin and Stephen Johns,) Jemima Root, Mindwell Rood, and Mary Coleman. He gave to his son David all his lands and buildings in Bolton, if David should pay £1000 in legacies given by the will to his other children within six years after the death of the father, and support his father and mother during their lives. Estate over £2000.

Allyn, Alexander, of Windsor, m. Elizabeth Cross. He was a brother of William and Robert Allyn, who then resided in Scotland. When he died, in 1708, he gave each of them £10 to be expended in Boston in articles, and sent to them in Scotland. He gave £15 to aid in building a school house on the green in Windsor. To the *Scotts' Box* in Boston, he gave £5. He was a merchant at Windsor, and was connected with the Borlands of Boston, in business. He gave Rev. Mr. Mather £5 ; to Rev. J. Marsh £5 ; to Mary Cross, his mother-in-law £5 in specie ; to Sarah Grant, daughter of Thomas, a servant girl, 20s. to purchase for her a Bible. Estate £2706 : 4 : 2. He left children, Fitz-John, Alexander, jr., John, and an only daughter Mary. He gave to her £400 in cash, the remainder to his sons. He had a sister-in-law, Abigail Grant, who married Dr. Mather.

Allyn, Alexander, jr., remained at Windsor, and d. there in 1790. In 1788 he gave Hannah Allyn Hooker, (dau. of Capt. James Hooker)

£1000 in silver out of his estate, and appointed Capt. Hooker his executor. All his estate amounted to £8875 : 9 : 10. Distributed to his children, Feb. 4, 1792, £5990 : 19 : 4—viz. to Increase, Zebulon and Alsan Hoskins in right of their wives, Hannah Allyn and Abigail Ellsworth, a widow, having left no sons.

Alsup or Alsop, Thomas, of Simsbury, d. insolvent, about 1724-5.

Ames, Robert, of Wethersfield, died in 1771. Children, Sarah and John. His wid. Sarah, and son, administrators. Estate £373 : 13 : 7.

Ames, John, of Wethersfield Rocky Hill, son of Robert, was born Nov. 1733, and died July 16, 1790. He m. Abigail Butler, who was b. June 30, 1737, and d. Feb. 23, 1800. They had eleven children, viz. Daniel b. Feb. 1, 1751, and d. Nov. 19, 1822—he lost one of his arms by a pistol ball. He resided in Southington, and taught school for a livelihood after he lost his arm. Philemon b. Oct. 8, 1758, and d. June 9, 1797—m. Ruth Hurlbut, who was b. Oct. 1760. He was a ship-carpenter or builder, and master of the ship yard at Rocky Hill. He was a gentleman of great firmness of character. He died when only 39 years of age, and left but one child, Eunice Ames—she married Frederick Robbins, of Wethersfield. John, son of John, b. Aug. 31, 1760, and died of the small pox, aged 16 years. Benjamin, son of John, b. Oct. 29, 1762, and d. Nov. 1795. Mahitabel, b. March 21, 1765, and d. aged 10 years. William, b. July 31, 1765, d. July 2, 1811. Eunice, b. Sept. 4, 1769, d. in 1775. Robert, b. April 20, 1772, d. in 1775. Abigail, b. June 3, 1774 ; m. Russell Mackee, and was living at Middletown in 1840. She had four children, William the eldest, then lived in Philadelphia ; Henry the second son was a sea captain, and commanded a brig in the West India trade. Abigail died by an injury received by the bursting of the boiler of the steamboat Oliver Ellsworth, when on her way home from Albany, having then recently lost her husband at sea, Capt. Joseph Stocking. She was left a widow with infant twin sons. Joseph was a merchant in N. Y. John Ames, b. May 1, 1777, son of John, died in 1778. Mary Ames, b. June 1, 1780, d. in 1821, making eleven children. This family originated from the Ames family in Massachusetts. Horatio Ames, of Salisbury, Conn. is not of the family at Wethersfield, but came from Massachusetts to Salisbury, where he has a family, and is largely engaged in the iron business. There are but few families of the name in Connecticut at this time.

Anderson, Francis, of Hartford, d. in 1771. Ashbel Anderson, of East Windsor, d. in 1777—Abigail his widow.

Antizell, Lawrence, of Willington, d. in 1759. Estate £186.— Widow Mary. Children, Zeruiah, Mary, Phebe, Lyman or Simon, William, Perez, Phineas, Silas, Dorcas and Sarah. His son-in-law David Fuller, executor.

Ashley, Jonathan, of Hartford, second son of Robert, of Springfield, was born in 1646, and m. Sarah, a daughter of William Wadsworth, of Hartford, where he settled. His children were, Joseph, Jonathan, Samuel, Sarah and Rebecca. Estate £1030 : 19. He died in 1704.

Ashley, Joseph, son of Jonathan and grandson of Robert, died at Hartford in 1754—left no sons. His daughters were, Hannah, who m. Samuel Day ; Ann, m. Samuel Clark, of Windsor ; Mary and Jerusha Ashley. Estate £189. Great grand children of Robert.

Ashley, Jonathan, jr., son of Jonathan, sen'r. and grandson of Robert. He m. —— ——, and had children, Jonathan, Sarah, Elizabeth Olcott, Mary Gaylord, Abigail Ashley, Rachel Tudor, Eunice and Ashley, great grand children of Robert. He died in 1750.

Ashley, Jonathan, grandson of Jonathan, sen'r. of Hartford, d. in 1777. He appears to have left no children.

Ashley, Samuel, the 3d son of Jonathan, sen'r., appears to have removed from Hartford—probably to Plainfield, where he held an estate in lands, by his father's will.

Ashley, Lieut. Ezekiel, of Hartford, m. Hannah ——, and had a son Ezekiel. He d. in 1746. Ezekiel Ashley, jr. m. Elizabeth ——, and d. in 1761, and left issue. The branch of the Ashley family through Jonathan, has now become entirely extinct in Connecticut.

Ashley, Hon. Chester, U. S. Senator from Arkansas, late deceased at Washington, April 29, 1848, was b. at Amherst, Mass. He was the son of William Ashley, who was b. at Leverett, who was the eldest son of Stephen Ashley, who was the son of Rev. Joseph Ashley, of Sunderland, Mass. b. in 1709, who was the son of Samuel, the son of David, and David was the son of Robert Ashley, who settled at Springfield in 1639. Hon. Chester Ashley emigrated with his father's family, from Massachusetts to Hudson, in the State of N. Y. in early life. He graduated at Williams College in 1813 ; after which he read law at the Law School at Litchfield, Conn., under the instruction of those learned jurists, Judges Reeve and Gould. He then went West to seek his fortune in his then future life, and opened a law office for a time in Illinois ; from thence he removed to Arkansas, where he finally located, and his ambition, with wealth and honors, fully gratified in this life. Rev. Joseph Ashley, the great grand father of Hon. Chester Ashley, graduated at Yale College in 1730, m. Miss Ann Dewey, Feb. 16, 1736, and the same year was ordained at Winchester, N. H., but in 1745 was obliged to leave there by danger from the Indians, and was installed over the church in Sunderland, Mass. in 1749, here he died, Feb. 8, 1797, in the 88th year of his age and 61st of his ministry. (See p. 184.)

Aspenwell or Aspenwall, Eleazer, of Farmington (Kensington society,) d. about 1741, and left a good estate. Wife, Mary. Children, Aaron, Mary Adkins, Hamathan and Anna Nott. The three distributors of his estate resided at Middletown.

Atchitt or Adjett, John and Samuel, sons of John. Samuel d. 1712, at Hartford. John d. 1712, at Block Island, and left an estate of £94, which his father then living, inherited as next of kin.

Atwater, Joshua, a merchant at Suffield, died in 1776. Thomas Lee then late of Boston, with David Todd, of Suffield, gave the administration bond with Thaddeus Leavit. Children not found.

Austin, John, of Hartford, m. wid. Mary Hooker, the mother of Capt. Nathaniel Hooker. In his will he gave his wife Mary £300 in money, one cow, the use of one of his servants for life, and the use of half his land and housing in Hartford during her life. He gave to his only daughter, Mary Ellery, the wife of John Ellery, then of Boston, the other half for her life, and at the death of her mother the share given her mother for life. The remainder of his estate he gave his daughter, Mary Ellery. After the decease of his widow and dau. Ellery, he gave all his estate, real and personal, to his grandson Johnny Ellery, except his lands in Litchfield and New Hartford, which he gave to his other grandson, William Ellery for ever. He died in 1743. Will dated 1741-2. William Ellery's daughter m. Major Henry Seymour late deceased, of Hartford. It was her son, Lieut. Col. Thomas H. Seymour, who stript the Mexican standard from the walls of Chepultepec, and hoisted the standard of the U. S., and his aged mother yet lives to witness the bravery of her son. John Ellery, of Boston, m. Mary Austin, dau. of John and Mary Austin, of Hartford, July 28, 1737.

B.

Barrows, Benj. of Windsor, d. in 1763. Goods and chattels £20.

Barton, William, aged 16 years in 1756, chose Josiah Burnham, of Farmington, for his guardian.

Barret, Jonathan, of Hartford, d. in 1752. Sarah, his wid. Estate over £3000. Children, Joseph, Jonathan, Jeremiah, Elijah, Bathsheba Marsh, Dorothy Warren, Sarah Farnsworth, Anna and Mary Barret. He held land at Winchester.

Barringham, Patrick, of Hartford, d. in 1753, and left a wid. Abigail, with a good estate.

Belcher, Samuel, of Windsor, d. in 1756. His will was presented to the Court, by Col. Joseph Richards, of Dedham, Mass. as executor. Mabel, his widow. Supposed to have been killed at or near Crown Point. He left no children, and gave all his estate to his widow and his cousin Belcher Richards, son of Joseph, of Dedham, except small sums to his brother-in-law, Rev. Andrew Tyler and Rebecca Welton. Estate £296.

Beman, Samuel, of Scotland, in Simsbury, d. in 1752. Margaret, his widow.

Benham, Samuel, of Farmington, d. about 1753. Wife Azuba. He had a farm in Southington. Children, Azuba and Luce.

Bingham, John, a minor, son of John, of Windsor—made choice of his brother Ithamer for his guardian, in March, 1756.

Blackleach, John, son of John, of Wethersfield, was an active business man, and a trader at the West Indies. He m. Elizabeth ——, and had children, John and Elizabeth. His daughter m. a Mr. Harris, of Boston. He died in 1703. Estate £1576, besides his property at Antigua. Elizabeth, his wid. d. June 12, 1707. She appears to have left a daughter Mary Olcott, wife of John Olcott, who is not mentioned with his children. Mrs. Harris received £500 of her father's estate. His son John settled at Farmington, where he died young. The Blackleach family for many years were wealthy; few if any of the family now are left in the State by the name. Elizabeth Harris had received of her father her full share of his estate, and the widow gave all her property to her daughter, Mary Olcott.

Blodget, Josiah, of Stafford, d. in 1756. Wife, Margaret. He left a son Josiah and perhaps other children.

Booge, Rev. Ebenezer, of Farmington, was educated at Yale Coll. in 1748, settled in the ministry at (Northington,) and d. about 1771. Left a widow Damaris, also a daughter Damaris, who m. Samuel Bishop. She left no children.

Brewer, Alexander, of Glastenbury, d. in 1750. Thankful, his widow. Children, Thomas, Hezekiah, Joseph, Benjamin, Daniel, Mary Dix, Sarah Goodale, Lydia Loveland and Amy Porter. His son Joseph, administrator. Estate £109 : 8 : 6.

Bullen, David, of Enfield, d. in 1756. His will was presented by his son David. Wife, Abigail. Children, Abigail Pinney, (d. before her father,) Hannah Harden, Juda Richarson and David Bullen.

Burbank, Capt. Abraham, of Suffield, d. in 1772–3. His estate in Connecticut and Massachusetts appraised over £3970. He appears to have left a family.

Burroughs, John, of Windsor, d. in 1757. Abner, his son, executor. He left a widow, Sarah—and children, Mary, Hannah, Sarah, Simon, John and Abner. This name has generally been found at Middletown.

Ball, Robert, of Bolton, d. in 1768–9. Estate £209.

Burton, Samuel, of Middletown, east of the river, d. April 23, 1733. Left a small estate of about £80. Widow Sarah and children.

C.

Cornish, Benjamin, of Simsbury, d. about 1731 or 2. Joseph Cornish administrator. He died insolvent.

Colt, Abraham, the son of Abraham Colt, deceased, of Glastenbury, a minor, made choice of David Hills, of Hartford, for his guardian, in 1730.

D.

Dewolph or Dewolf, Charles, of Middletown, d. in 1731. Wife Prudence. Children, John, Stephen, Symon, Joseph, Prudence, Elizabeth, Sarah, Mary and Rebecca. His land in Glastenbury, he gave to John and Stephen; his lands and house at Middletown, to Symon and Joseph. His land he received of his father in Lyme, he gave equally to all his children. Estate £407 : 4 : 2.

Dixwell, Bathshua or Bathsheba, of Middletown, formerly of New Haven. She resided with her daughter, Mrs. Mary Collins, the wife of John Collins, of Middletown, at her decease in 1730. She had made a will, by which she gave all of the small property she had left, to her dau. Mary Collins and her children, except her late husband's (Dixwell's) Bible—this she gave to her son-in-law, John Collins, a son of the Rev. Nathaniel Collins. Her will is dated June, 1727. From the fact of her mention of her former residence in New Haven, of her christian name, and the christian name of her daughter with whom she resided, and where she died, I am induced to believe she must have been the wid. of Col. John Dixwell, one of King Charles' Judges that signed the warrant for his execution in 1649. He was from the county of Kent, England, and a brother of Mark Dixwell, of Broome, in the Parish of Barham, who was the father of Sir Basil Dixwell. Judge Dixwell, with other judges, abdicated their country to save their heads. Whalley, Goffe and Dixwell came to New England, probably about 1660. Whalley and Goffe were at Hadley, Mass. before 1664-5, at which time Judge Dixwell went there to visit them—how long he remained there is uncertain. At this time and place, Stiles says he assumed the name of James Davids, Esq., (the name of Davids was the maiden name of his mother.) Judge Dixwell must have been at New Haven as early as 1672, at which time he was unmarried, and came there known only as James Davids, Esq. President Stiles says that Col. Davids lived at New Haven in the family of a Mr. Ling and his wife, who were at the time aged and without children. On the death of Mr. Ling, in 1673, he gave his wife all his estate, about £900 by will, and requested Mr. Davids to be kind to his wife, and to aid her in the settlement of his estate. Mr. Davids showed his kindness to the widow by making her his wife. " Mr. James Davids m. Joannah Ling, of New Haven, 1673." His wife did not long survive, and died without children the same year (1673.) James Davids, Esq. was again m. on the 23d day of October, 1677, to Bathsheba ——. By this lady he had three children, viz. Mary b. June 9, 1679; John b. March 6, 1680-1 ; and Elizabeth b. July 14, 1682, in New Haven. His son John Dixwell or Davids, m. Mary Prout, Sept. 1, 1708. Previous to the death of Judge Dixwell he disposed of his estates which he had left in England, to his son John and Mary, &c., which conveyance is yet extant upon the records at New Haven. He died at New Haven, as is now shown on his grave stone there, in these words, viz. " J. D. Esq. deceased March the 18th, in the 82d year of his age, 1688-9." Near by his grave are two other graves—upon the grave stone of one of them are these figures and letters, viz. " 80, M. G." and upon the other, " E. W. 1658," which are supposed to be the graves of Judges Goffe and Whalley— though it is believed they both died at Hadley. It is conjectured that Judge Dixwell caused the bodies to have been brought to New Haven for interment, that they might all be buried in one yard, with only the initials of their names engraved upon their rough monuments. The letters of Dixwell stand both for James Davids, Esq. or John Dixwell, Esq. Judge Whalley d. at Hadley, 1658, and Goffe d. 1680. The time of the death of each of them agrees with the initials and dates upon the tomb stones now standing in the old grave yard in New Haven. Judge Dixwell was known by his true name and character, to the Rev. Mr. Pierpont and others in New Haven, some years previous to his death.

Depestry, Francis, of Hartford, who had removed from the Island of Barbadoes. His property in the West Indies he disposed of by a will he left at Barbadoes, to his brother Lewis Depestry, Gent., of London, and sisters Elizabeth and Mary Anne Depestry, of London, and his brother Peter, of Barbadoes, and made Capt. Thomas Mapp and Mr. Joseph Bailey, of the Parish of St. Phillips, in Barbadoes, executors of his will, of his foreign property. On the first day of April, 1731, he disposed of his property in New England, by will, to Francis Bewithe, merchant, of Boston. To Mrs. Susannah Beuchamp, dau. of Mr. John Beuchamp, of Hartford, he gave his debts due from Stephen Bontiwan and James Boyard, of Boston. All the remainder of his property he gave to Susannah Beuchamp, of Hartford, forever. He appears to have been a merchant in Hartford, and died soon after he made his last will, in 1731.

E.

Eells, Samuel, came when young to this country, and married and settled at Milford, Conn. He had seven sons and one daughter. The daughter married at Long Island. After Samuel lost his wife, he m. for his 2d wife, the widow Hannah ——, of Hingham in Mass. where he afterwards resided. He took with him his youngest son, Nathaniel. This Nathaniel afterwards m. Hannah North, the only child of his mother-in-law. The eldest son of Samuel, sen'r. m. and had a son Samuel, and dau. Esther. She died single. His wife died, and he m. wid. Bryins or Bryant, (maiden name Russell,) by whom he had sons John and Nathaniel. Samuel the eldest son of Nathaniel, m. Deborah Barritt, and had Samuel, Lent, Sarah, Deborah and Esther. John the eldest son of Nathaniel, graduated at Yale College in 1724 or 1755, and settled in the ministry at Canaan, Conn. He m. Hannah Bird, and had a son Bird, and daughters Ann and Hannah; after which his wife died, and he m. a widow Olmsted, and had a son Moses. Moses his son, m. and had Ann and Hannah.

Eells, Nathaniel, son of Samuel, sen'r., m. Martha Stow—she died and left no issue. He then m. wid. Alice White, and had two sons, Nathaniel and Daniel, and three daughters, Martha, Mary and Theodosia. Martha m. Samuel Spencer.

Eells, John, son of Maj. Samuel, m. and had two daughters, Ann and one other. Ann m. Thomas Weldon. His sons died unmarried, except Nathaniel Ells, who was educated and settled in the ministry at Scituate, Mass. His children were, Sarah, Samuel, John, Nathaniel, Edward, Hannah, Mary North and Mahitabel. Sarah, daughter of

Rev. Nathaniel Ells, m. Capt. Benjamin Turner, and had Sarah, David, Hannah and Ann. Sarah Turner m. Ebenezer Hatch, and had Sarah, Abigail and Lucy. He died, and she m. for her 2d husband Isaac Lane, and had a son Benjamin. David Turner, son of Benjamin and Sarah, m. and had Hannah, (who d. single ;) Ann (m. and had two children and died ;) Sarah Hatch m. at Hingham, and had children ; Abigail m. P. Cushing, and had Joseph, Lucy, and one other child. (These facts are taken from old Bibles and tradition.)

Some marriages and deaths of the family, viz. Samuel Ells married Hannah Wetherell ; William Ells m. Sarah Pillsbury ; Robert Linthol Ells m. Ruth Copeland ; Samuel Ells m. Priscilla Palmer ; Hannah North Ells m. George Bennett ; Bradbury Ells m. Benj. Rutson ; John Ells m. Abiah Waterman ; Waterman Ells m. Sarah Tubs ; Hannah Ells m. Anthony Ames ; Abiah Ells m. Mordecai Lincoln ; Lucy Ells m. Churchill Edwards ; Nathaniel Ells, who settled at Stonington, m. Mary Cushing, she d. and he m. Mary D ——— ; Rev. John Ells, who settled at Glastenbury, m. Sybell Huntington, she d. and he m. Ann Welles ; Edward Ells m. Mary Denison ; Mary Ells m. Dr. Joshua Lathrop ; Sarah Ells m. Capt. Nathan Palmer ; Rev. Edward Ells, who settled at Middletown, m. Martha Pitkin ; Edward, jr. m. Sarah Edwards ; Rev. James Ells, who settled at East Glastenbury, m. Mary Johnson, and had a son James ; Rev. Samuel Ells, who settled at North Branford, m. Hannah Butler ; John Ells m. Lydia Lord—she d. he then m. wid. Esther Curtiss ; Pitkin Ells m. Molly ——— ; Rev. Ozias Ells was educated at Yale Coll. in 1779, m. Hannah Ely, and settled at Barkhamsted, and d. in 1813 ; Hannah Ells m. Dr. White of Long Island ; Mary Ells m. Seth Williams ; North Ells m. Ruth Tilden ; Nath'l Ells m. Johannah Turner.

Samuel Ells d. May 9, 1741, in the army on his way from Carthagenia to Jamaica, under the King's pay as Ensign ; Edward b. 1741 ; James b. 1743 ; Samuel b. 1745 ; Ozias Pitkin b. 1747 ; Nathaniel b. 1747, and d. 1747 ; Jane b. 1748, d. same day ; Pitkin b. 1750 ; John was drowned in North Carolina, 1750 ; Nathaniel d. Aug. 25, 1750 ; John b. 1753 ; Ozias b. 1755 ; Hannah b. 1757 ; Patience, who had been the widow of Ichabod Lord, dau. of Rev. Mr. Bulkley of Colchester, was m. to Mr. Ells in 1772 ; John m. Elizabeth Lord, 1773 ; Edward, jr. m. Sarah Edwards, 1763, and for 2d wife m. wid. Abigail Brandegee, 1770 ; Rev. James m. Mary Johnson, 1770 ; Rev. Samuel m. same day, Barnet Butler, at the meeting house ; Lydia, dau. of John, b. 1773 ; Edward, jr. b. 1741, his wife Sarah b. 1740, and m. 1763 ; his son Reuben b. 1764 ; David b. 1765 ; Edward b. 1767; Sarah b. 1769 ; Sarah, wife of Edward, d. 1769; Sam'l b. 1773; Capt. Edward d. of consumption in 1787 ; David son of Capt. Edward, d. in 1796, and left a son Samuel and a widow ; Reuben d. in 1796, and left four children, Joseph, Edward, Pitkin and Sarah—his son Edward d. in 1797 ; Capt. Samuel b. 1773, m. Aura Smith, b. in 1773, m. in 1794 ; son Thomas P., b. Jan. 1795, d. 1796 ; Ralph S. S., b. 1797—he m. Mary C., dau. of Robert Williams, 1819, son Samuel R., b. 1822—his wife d. not many years after ; Ralph S. S., then m. a lady from the West Indies, Miss Maria Mulini, and in 1832 had a daughter b. named Lucy Maria Aurora ; Samuel R. son of Ralph S. S., and Mary b. 1822—he m. Phebe V. Flaster, of Mechanicsville, in Penn. in 1843, and had a daughter, Ann Eliza b. 1845. These scraps of the Ells family are published to aid in some small degree any person who may wish to collect in form, a correct genealogical table of the family. ☞ The name is spelt Eells and Ells.

F.

Flagg, Samuel, of Hartford, d. 1757. Widow, Sarah. He gave his wife one third of his real estate for life, and one third of his chattels absolutely and for ever. Also the entire use of his negro man, London, during her life. Also the use of one half of his homested so long as she should remain his widow. He gave his son Samuel his education free of all charges, with all his school books, horse, saddle and bridle. To his five daughters, viz. Sarah, Abigail, Hannah, Susannah and Elizabeth, he gave half as much of his real estate as he gave his other three sons, viz. Joseph, Jonathan and Benjamin. He made Samuel, with what he had given him, equal in portion with each of his daughters. Mr. Flagg left a handsome estate for his family, of £1152 : 12—£148 : 17—making £1301 : 9. He probably settled at Hartford in early life, about 1700, as his children were born in Hartford.

H.

Higby, John, of Middletown, d. in 1682. Estate £107 : 9 : 3. Wid. Rachel. He left a son Edward—perhaps other children.

[A part of the Hicock family who emigrated first from Hartford to Farmington—some of them afterwards settled at Waterbury and Southbury.]

Hicock, Benjamin, a son of Samuel, of Waterbury, settled at Southbury, was b. in 1656—his wife Hannah was b. in 1678 ; he d.

in 1745, and his wife d. in 1746. They had chidren, David, d. 1727, aged 27 ; Mary, m. Solomon Johnson, 1724—she was burnt in his house, 1735 ; Lois m. Dea. Stephen Curtiss ; Benjamin m. Sarah Stiles, and had four children—Olive, Sarah, Amos and Benjamin ; Silas, brother of Justus, m. and had a dau. Hannah, who m. Bethel Hinman, and had two sons. Justus b. 1714, m. Lois Munn, who was b. 1715—she d. 1781, he d. 1800. Their children were, David, b. 1737, m. Abigail Johnson, b. 1739—he d. 1784, she d. 1833 ; they had a dau. Hannah b. 1776, who m. Zephaniah H. Smith, Esq. who was settled as a clergyman at Newtown, Conn. several years, after which he removed his family to Glastenbury, and settled there as a lawyer, where he d. in 1836, and left one of the most intellectual and learned families in the State, consisting of his wife and five daughters. Gideon m. Hannah Hinman, and had two sons, who removed to Granville, N. Y. ; Reuben removed to Vermont, and d. there in 1777 ; Mercy m. Francis Hinman, and had three daughters ; Justus m. Amy Garrit, and had two daughters, and removed to Castleton, Vt. ; Asa m. Hester Hinman, and had three sons and three daughters—he removed to Pennsylvania ; Annis m. Francis Garrit, and removed to the State of New York.

K.

[King Family of Coventry.]

King, John, came from England in 1645, when 16 years of age. He lived with a Mr. Cole, of Hartford until he was 21 years old, and was then m. to Sarah Holton, dau. of Dea. John Holton, of Northampton, in 1650, to which place they removed at the beginning of the settlement of that town. After the death of his first wife, in 1682, he m. Sarah Whiting. His children were, John, William, Thomas, Samuel, Eleazar, Sary, Joseph, Benjamin, David, Thankful and Jonathan. John King d. December, 1703, aged 74. Jonathan King was b. 1682, and m. Mary French, April 3, 1711, moved to Bolton, May 11, 1727, and d. June 11, 1774—Mary, his wife, d. March 24, 1758, aged 71. His children were, Jonathan b. Jan. 26, 1712 ; Abigail b. Dec. 1, 1713 ; Charles b. July 3, 1716 ; Mary b. May 31, 1718 ; Beriah b. Oct. 2, 1721 ; Seth b. April 18, 1723 ; Oliver b. April 20, 1726 ; Gideon b. Aug. 24, 1729. Jonathan son of Jonathan and Mary King, was m. to Martha Woodward, Feb. 16, 1743, and d. at Coventry, March 16, 1788. Isaac Bronson and Abigail King were m. Nov. 8, 1733—Abigail Bronson d. Feb. 20, 1799. Charles King and Sarah King were m. Sept. 5, 1739—Charles King d. at North Bolton, (now

Vernon) April 7, 1790. Beriah King d. April 10, 1722. Gideon King removed with his family to New Hartford, and d. Dec. 11, 1802. Seth King m. Mary Smith, April 23, 1747, and d. at North Bolton, July 23, 1780—his wife d. at Vernon, March 2, 1811, aged 91. Their children were, Oliver b. March 5, N. S. 1748. Rhoda b. April 16, 1750, and d. August 19, 1750. Joel b. February 8, 1752, and d. at North Bolton, March 21, 1789. Seth, jr. b. June 8, 1754—he removed to and d. in the State of N. Y. Ruth b. Aug. 11, 1756, and d. at Vernon, March 3, 1822. Francis b. Feb. 2, 1759, and d. Oct. 9, 1777, returning from the army in N. Y. Russel b. Dec. 16, 1761, and d. at N. London in the militia service, Sept. 25, 1779. Oliver, son of Seth and Mary, m. Chloe Humphrey, dau. of Hezekiah Humphrey, Esq. of Simsbury, Nov. 21, 1780. Oliver d. at Vernon, July 6, 1818—his wife d. at Vernon, Jan. 24, 1816. Their children were, Francis b. May 12, 1783, and d. at Elizabethtown, N. J. July 16, 1837. Oliver Humphrey King b. Feb. 17, 1787. Joel King b. Feb. 2, 1789.

Kennor or Kennard, of Haddam, d. in 1687. Estate £49 : 8 : 6. He left a widow and one son.

M.

[Mann Family.]

Mann, William, emigrated from Kent county, in England, in the early settlement of Massachusetts, and must have been born about 1607 or 8. He located at Cambridge, and m. Mary Jarrad. His son Samuel was b. in 1647, and in 1665 was educated at Harvard College. William is supposed by the Mann family in Connecticut to have been the first of the name in New England. Rev. Samuel was the only son of William, of Wrentham. He m. in early life, Esther Ware, of Dedham, in May, 1673. He was ordained at Wrentham in 1692. His children were, Mary, Samuel, Nathaniel, William, Theodore, Thomas, Hannah, Beriah, Pelatiah, Margaret and Esther.

Samuel, son of Rev. Samuel, m. Zipporah Billings, in Oct. 1704, and had children, Samuel, Mercy, Ebenezer, Beriah Zipporah, Richard, Josiah, Hannah, Jonathan, Elizabeth, Benj., Esther and Bezaleel.

Nathaniel, son of Rev. Samuel, m. Elizabeth George, Dec. 1704, and had children, George, John, Nathaniel, Mary, Robert, Jeremiah, Joseph, Ezra, Richard and Timothy.

William, son of Rev. Samuel, m. Bethiah Rocket, Dec. 1701, and had children, Bethiah, William, Dorothy, Hezekiah, Michael, Mahitabel, Joseph, Ichabod and Elijah.

36

Theodore, son of Rev. Samuel, m. Abigail Hawes, 1703, and had children, Theodores, Mary, Phebe, Theodore, Abigail, Margaret, Sarah, Daniel, Beriah, Thomas and Jerusha.

Thomas, son of Rev. Samuel, m. Hannah Aldis, Dec. 1709, and had Hannah, Esther, Rachel, Nathan, Ruth, Hepzibah and Mary—no sons.

Pelatiah, son of Rev. Samuel, m. Jemima Farrington, Feb. 1719–20, and had Jemima, Daniel, David, James, Eunice, Jerusha, Melatiah and Lois.

Mary, daughter of Rev. Samuel, m. Samuel Dearing, 1708, and had three daughters, and a son Samuel.

Hannah, daughter of Rev. Samuel, m. Samuel Davies, 1707—but left no children.

Beriah, 3d daughter of Rev. Samuel, m. Daniel Hawes, in 1710, and had Daniel, Samuel, Pelatiah, Moses, Aaron, Ichabod, Timothy, Beriah, Josiah, Joseph and Mary.

Margaret, 4th daughter of Rev. Samuel, m. Nathaniel Whiting in 1711, and had Margaret, Esther, Nathan and Nathaniel.

Esther, 5th daughter of Rev. Samuel, m. Isaac Fisher, in 1719, and had Janathan, Esther, Isaac, Anna, Margaret, Timothy, Experience, Beriah and Hannah.

Thomas Mann, who was a deacon of the Wrentham church, was a son of Theodore. He m. the daughter of James Blake, in 1744, and had nine children.

Ariel, son of Dea. Thomas, d. in early life.

Brownel, grandson of Dea. Thomas, was the son of Jacob Mann.

Nathaniel Mann, who m. Elizabeth George in 1704, came from Massachusetts to what is now Mansfield when it was a wilderness, and being the first settler in the place, it was honored by the name of Mansfield, in memory of its first settler, about 1720. He removed to Hebron, where he purchased another farm, and settled upon it for life—but he died at his son's in Colchester, at an advanced age. Among his children he had a son John, who lived, and died in old age, upon the farm purchased by his father in 1720.

Joseph, son of Nathaniel, had sons, Joel, Zadock, Joseph and James. He died at Hebron in 1798 or 9.

Joel, son of Joel, had Rodolphus, Jeremiah, Samuel, Joel and Doct. Mann who settled in Western N. Y.

Jeremiah, son of Joel, 2d, was the father of Francis Norton Mann, Mayor of the city of Troy.

John, son of Nathaniel, m. Margaret Peters, aunt of Ex-Gov. Peters, of Hebron, had Margaret, Mercy, Mary, Phebe, Hannah, John, Elijah, Nathaniel and Andrew. John died at Hebron in 1806, very aged. Margaret m. Mr. Cross, and settled at Montreal in Canada, and had John and Aaron. Mary m. Jacob Loomis, of Hebron, and had Mary, Jacob and Abigail Phebe m. Mr. Buel. Hannah m. Mr. Baldwin, of Bradford, Vt. Mercy m. Doct. Hanchett, of Ballston, N. Y., and had a daughter, who m. Mr. Plumb, a merchant of Troy, N. Y.

Nathaniel, son of John, sen'r., was educated at Dartmouth College, after which he went to England to perfect his education in his profession of physician and surgeon, and spent some time in the hospital at London. On his return to this country, he m. Miss Owen, and settled and died in Georgia, where he left a family of two daughters, Harriet and Sophia, but left no sons.

Elijah had three sons, Enoch, Elijah and Bemsley—two of them removed and settled at Canandaigua, N. Y. Elijah perhaps is now living near Lake Ontario.

John, jr., son of John, m. Lydia Porter, of Hebron, 19 years old, and moved with her on horseback to Orford, N. H., about 1770, the first settlers of the town. Their children born at Orford were, John, Solomon, Ira, Jared, Aaron, Nathaniel, Benning, Cyrus, Asaph, Joel, Abijah, Lydia, Sally and Phebe.

John, the son of John, jr. is a merchant and farmer in Orford.

Solomon, son of John, jr. d. at Montpelier, Vt., and left a family. Phebe, his daughter, m. Rev. Mr. Hough, a Baptist Missionary at Serampore. Her sister Emily m. Henry Oaks, of Orford, N. H.

Ira is a farmer in the State of N. Y. He has had two wives; first, Miss Bailey, of Piermont, N. H.; second, Miss Scott, and has a numerous family.

Jared, son of John, jr., was a farmer at Orford. One of his sons, a lawyer, settled at Lowell, Mass., where the father and son both died.

Aaron, son of John, jr., is a farmer in Elgin, in Wisconsin, and has a family of sons and daughters.

Nathaniel, son of John, jr., resides in Orford, a farmer. He has two sons and two daughters. One of the daughters m. Hon. —— Wilcox, Member of Congress; the other m. in Brooklyn, N. Y.

Benning, son of John, jr., resides in the city of Hartford—by profession is a lawyer, and is a Justice of the Peace. He has been a State Senator in Connecticut, in 1825, a Judge of the County Court of Tolland county, and now holds the office of Marshal of the U. S.

for the District of Connecticut, and what is most true that can be said of him is, *he is an honest politician.* He m. Phebe Mann, of Hebron, and has three sons and three daughters, viz. Cordelia M., Benning E., Edward M., Catherine Vernon, Margaret Peters and Cyrus N.

Cyrus, son of John, jr., is a clergyman. He received a collegiate education, graduated at Dartmouth College, and was a tutor there. He m. Nancy Strong, of Mass., her brother was a Member of Congress. He preached at Westminster, Mass., about twenty years, but now resides at Lowell, and has a family there, viz. Cyrus S., a physician, Ann Maria and Adelia P.

Asaph, son of John, jr., was a farmer at Orford. He had two sons, one a farmer, the other a lawyer.

Joel, son of John, jr., was educated at Dartmouth College, studied divinity, and settled at Bristol, R. I. He now resides at Salem, Ms. He m. Miss Catherine Vernon, of Newport, and has two sons, Edward and Frederick, and one daughter, Catherine. One of the sons is a merchant in New York. Catherine m. a merchant in Boston, Mass.

Abijah, son of John, jr., d. when young.

Lydia, daughter of John, jr., m. Joseph Pratt, of Orford, N. H., and is the mother of Henry Pratt, a portrait painter in Boston.

Sally, her sister, m. Mr. Rogers, a merchant at Orford, N. H.

Phebe, her sister, m. Samuel Sargent, a farmer at Orford.

Nathaniel, son of Nathaniel, of Mansfield, d. aged 90 years, at Bolton, and left no children.

Abijah moved to the State of N. Y., and had sons, Alexander and Abijah. The grandson of Abijah, sen'r. was a member of Congress from that State. Abijah the elder, d. at Hebron, and left a large family.

Enoch, son of Elijah, d. at Hebron, and left children.

Bemsley, son of Elijah, d. in the State of N. Y.

Andrew, son of John, sen'r., m. Hannah Phelps, and settled at Hebron, upon the old family farm, and left a family, viz. Anna Porter, Reuben, Andrew, Phebe, Cyrus, Manlius, Martha, Hannah and Nathaniel. Hannah, (who m. Doct. Joseph Sibley,) Reuben and Andrew, children of Andrew, all reside at Marshall, Michigan. Phebe m. Benning Mann, Esq. Cyrus resides on the old family farm at Hebron. Manlius d. unmarried in 1808. Martha m. Elihu Wakeman, and d. at Stafford, but left no children. Andrew d. at Hebron.

Ebenezer Mann, son of Samuel, and grandson of Rev. Samuel, of

Wrentham, (who he m. is not known.) His children were, Chloe b. May 15, 1741 ; Lucy b. June 8, 1743 ; Molly b. Nov. 16, 1745 ; Nancy b. May 15, 1747 ; Lucretia b. Oct. 29, 1750 ; Ebenezer, jr. b. July 14, 1753 ; Oliver b. June 5, 1756 ; Peres b. Nov. 30, 1758, and d. Feb. 1, 1843.

Oliver, the son of Ebenezer, was a physician, and settled at Castine, in the State of Maine—to whom m. not known. His children, (by an old family letter) were, Lucy, Polly, Ebenezer, Reuben, Oliver, Lucretia, Harriet and Nancy. Oliver, the father, d. at Castine.

Peres, the son of Ebenezer, was also a physician. He came to Burlington, Conn. in early life. He m. Mrs. Miletee White, Oct. 25, 1786, and settled as a physician there, and had one child, Miletee b. Aug. 23, 1787. His wife d. Nov. 19, 1789, aged 30, and on the 8th of Feb. 1792 he m. for his 2d wife, Frances Treat, and had a dau. Frances b. Jan. 4, 1793. His 2d wife, Frances, d. July 22, 1833. He was a perfect specimen of an honest man, and was respected by all who knew him.

Miletee, the daughter of Peres, on the 6th of July, 1808, m. Doct. Aaron Hitchcock, who settled at Burlington, Conn. He was a gentleman of great originality of character and genius, and shone in his profession. His children are, Jeannette, Peres, Oliver, Roland, Zechariah (died in infancy,) Darwin, Miletee and Helen.

Frances Mann m. Correl Pettibone, July 13, 1815, and had children, Amelia, Frances, Samuel (d. young,) and Lucy.

[Marvin Family.]

The first family of the name of Marvin, who came to New England, consisted of two brothers, Reinold and Matthew, and one sister, Elizabeth. It is not known which of the brothers was the oldest, nor in what year Reinold Marvin came to New England. Matthew, and his family, with his sister Elizabeth, came over from England in 1635, as will be seen by the following statement :

During the summer months of 1842, James Savage, Esq., of Boston, Mass., who was on a visit to England, was chiefly occupied with searching for materials to illustrate the early annals of New England. He was richly compensated for his toil. The result of his investigations was published in the 8th Vol. Mass. Hist. Coll., 3d series, p. 243, and onward, under the title of "Gleanings for New England History." From this article I extract the following items :

" Perhaps the acquisition most valuable, in the opinion of our local antiquaries, is my copious extracts from a MS. volume in folio, at the Augmentation Office, (so called,) where the Rev. Joseph Hunter, one of the Record Commissioners, presides, in Rolls Court, Westminster Hall. It contains the names of persons, permitted to embark, at the port of London, after Christmas 1634, to the same period in the following year, kept *generally* in regular succession. This was found a few months since, and may not have been seen by more than two or three persons for two hundred years."

Under date of " 15th April," 1635, is the following entry :—

"Theis parties hereafter expressed, are to be transported to New England, imbarqued in the Increase, Robert Lea, master, having taken the oath of allegiance and supremacy, as also being conformable, &c. whereof they brought testimony per certif. from the Justices and ministers where there abodes have lately been."

The following names are included in the list above referred to :

		Age.
" husbandman	Matthew Marvyn,	35 yrs.
uxor	Elizabeth Marvyn,	31
	Elizabeth Marvin,	31
	Matthew Marvyn,	8
	Marie Marvyn,	6
	Sara Marvyn,	3
	Hanna Marvyn,	$\frac{1}{2}$"

The common ancestor probably resided in Essex, Co. Eng. His children were, 1. Reinold,[*] who came to New England about 1635. 2. Matthew, b. about 1600, m. Elizabeth ——, came to N. E. in 1635. 3. Elizabeth, b. about 1604, came to N. E. in 1635, m. John Olmsted, of Hartford, and afterwards of Saybrook. She d. without issue, at Norwich.

These brothers were among the original settlers of Hartford, Conn., and both were proprietors of land in that ancient town. Reinold removed to Saybrook before 1639 ; and d. in that town in 1662 or 1663. Matthew resided on the corner of Village and Front streets, Hartford, for some years. He was among the pioneers in the settlement of Norwalk, which town he represented in the General Court in 1654. Matthew, his son or grandson, represented that town in 1694 and 1697; Samuel in 1718 ; and John in 1734 and 1738.

---

[*] This name is spelled in different ways—Reginold, Reinold, Renold, Reynold. I have used Reinold, in this work, as it is generally so spelt on the Colony Record of Conn. •

Reinold Marvin was among the original proprietors of Hartford, Conn. He removed to Saybrook before 1639. He d. in Saybrook in 1662 or 1663. He had two children, Reinold and Mary, and probably other daughters. Sarah Marvin, who m. Capt. Joseph Sill, of Lyme, Feb. 12, 1657, may have been his daughter. A copy of his will is extant, the first clause of which bestows his house and lands on his son Reinold, and the second clause provides that to each of his grand children* " there be provided and given a Bible, as soon as they are capable useing of them." After which he disposes of his personal property.

It is not ascertained at what time, or to whom his son Reinold was married. His daughter Mary m. William Waller, of Saybrook, who was a large landed proprietor, as numerous deeds are on record, of conveyances of land by his widow, after his decease. No record of her children found.

Reinold Marvin, (son of the preceding,) was b. about 1634. He is known on the town records as *Lieutenant* Reinold Marvin. He represented Lyme in the General Court from 1670 to 1676. He was one of a Committee appointed to divide the town of Saybrook, in the year 1665. That part of the town lying east of Connecticut river, was named *Lyme*, from Lyme Regis, in the south-west of England, the native place of the Griswold family, who were large land proprietors in this part of Saybrook. Lieut. Marvin was also a large landholder, and a prominent man in the town. He had three sons,—John, born 1664–5; Reinold b. 1669; and Samuel b. 1671. He d. in 1676, aged 42 years. His remains were interred in the old burial ground in Lyme village—grave about the centre of the burial ground. The following is the inscription on his grave stone :

"1676. Lieut. Reinold Marvin."

John Marvin, first son of Lieut. Reinold, b. in Lyme, 1664–5, m. Sarah Graham, dau. of Henry Graham, (or Grimes,) of Hartford, May 7, 1691 ; d. Dec. 11, 1711, aged 47. His wife d. the relict of Richard Sears, in Lyme, Dec. 14, 1760, aged 91. Their children were, Sarah, Mary, John, Elizabeth, Joseph, Benjamin, Mehitabel and Jemima.—Uriah Marvin, John Marvin, and Alexander Marvin, merchants in Albany, N. Y., are descendants of John Marvin ; as is also Rev. Uriah Marvin. Edward C. Delavan, Esq. of Ballston, N. Y.,

---

* The grand children referred to in the will may have been the children of Mary, or of some other daughter. They were not the children of Reinold, as his oldest child was not born until 1665.

and Prof. John Pitkin Norton, of Yale College, m. female descendants in this family.

Reinold Marvin, second son of Lieut. Reinold, was b. in 1669. He was famous as "*Lyme's Captain.*" He was a deacon in the Congregational church. He represented Lyme in the General Court from 1701 to 1728. He was first m. in 1695, to Phebe ———; she d. Oct. 21, 1707; m. the second time in 1708, to Martha Waterman, daughter of Thomas Waterman, of Norwich; she. d. Nov. 1753, aged 73. He d. Oct. 18, 1737, aged 68, and was interred in the burial ground in Lyme village. The following is inscribed on his tomb-stone :

> "This Deacon, aged sixty-eight,
> Is freed on earth from serving;
> May for a crown no longer wait,
> Lyme's Captain, Reinold Marvin."

The above inscription, as also that on the grave stone of his first wife, was executed by an illiterate artist, and with bad spelling, and the effects of time, is now (1848) rather obscure.

The children of "Lyme's Captain," are as follows : Phebe, Reinold, Lydia, Esther, (by 2d wife,) Martha, Elisha, (d. in childhood,) James, Sarah, Elisha, and Miriam.

Reinold Marvin, first son of *Captain* Reinold, was known and spoken of as *Deacon* Marvin. A great many anecdotes are related concerning "Deacon Marvin"—which have generally been attributed to "Captain Reinold." It is undoubtedly the fact, from a full investigation of the matter, that they all belong to his son Reinold; both being Deacons, and both having the same Christian name, the mistake could easily be made. This son Reinold was unquestionably the poet who composed the epitaphs on his father's and mother's tomb-stones, and the *odd genius* of whom a multitude of anecdotes and queer sayings and rhymes, are still related ;—the most of them are positively known to apply only to the son of Captain Reinold. An aged descendant of this deacon, as also other aged persons now living in the vicinity, insist that this is the fact. Mr. Barber, in his "Historical Collections of Connecticut," has published some of these anecdotes, and attributes them, undoubtedly from hearsay, to "Lyme's Captain." It is to be hoped that in future editions of his work, he may correct the mistake.

The following are some of the descendants of *Captain* Reinold Marvin : Gen. Elihu Marvin, who resided in Norwich, and d. there in 1798. Richard P. Marvin, now a Judge of the Supreme Court in the State of N. Y., and formerly a Member of Congress. William Marvin, now a District Judge of the U. S. Court for the District of Florida.

Dudley Marvin, now a Member of Congress, and formerly for several years a member of the same body. Rev. Elihu P. Marvin, and Rev. Abijah P. Marvin. William Marvin, Esq., of Lyme, for some time Judge of Probate.

Samuel Marvin, third son of Lieut. Reinold Marvin, was b. in Lyme, 1671 ; m. Susannah Graham, of Hartford, May 5, 1699, d. March 15, 1743, aged 72 years. He represented Lyme in the General Court in 1711 and 1722. Children, Samuel, Zechariah, Thomas, Matthew, Abigail, Elizabeth, Nathan, Nehemiah, Mary and a son, twins, who died in infancy.

Henry M. Waite, a Judge of the Supreme Court of Connecticut, is a descendant of Samuel Marvin.

Matthew Marvin, (first) came to New England in 1635, as is stated on page 285. His children were, Matthew, born in England about 1627 ; Mary b. in England about 1629, m. Richard Bushnell, of Saybrook, in 1648 ; Sarah b. in England about 1632 ; Hannah b. in England about 1634, m. Thomas Seymour in 1653 ; Abigail b. at Hartford, m. J. Bouton ; Samuel bap. Feb. 6, 1647–8 ; Rachel bap. Dec. 30, 1649. He removed with his family, to Norwalk, where he died at an advanced age, in 1680.

Matthew Marvin, (second,) son of the foregoing, came to New England with his father in 1635, and was then eight years of age. He was one of the original proprietors of Norwalk, to which place he went with his father. He had six children ; the order or date of birth has not been ascertained, viz. Matthew, who m. Rhoda St. John, and died without leaving issue ; Sarah, who m. Thomas Betts, of Norwalk, in Jan. 1680 ; Samuel ; Hannah, who m. Epenetus Platt ; Elizabeth, who m. Joseph Platt, Nov. 6, 1700 ; John b. Sept. 2, 1678.

(It is very difficult to reconcile the records of the families of the first and second Matthew.)

Elizabeth Marvin, the sister of Matthew, sen'r., aged 31 years when she came with him to this country, in 1635, m. John Olmsted, and d. in advanced age, at Norwich ; the same John Holmsted, (as spelt on the Norwich records,) who first settled at Hartford, as early as 1639.

Mary Marvin, daughter of Matthew, sen'r., m. Richard Bushnell, of Saybrook, in 1648. Their children were, Joseph, Richard, Mary, and Maria, all b. in Saybrook. She was m. the second time, in 1680, to Dea. Thomas Adgate, of Saybrook, and was his 2d wife. Their children were, Abigail, Sarah, Rebecca, and Thomas—all b. in Norwich. Dea. Adgate was one of the original proprietors of Norwich, and d. at that place in 1707, at an advanced age.

Sarah Marvin, daughter of Matthew, sen'r., m. William Goodrich, of Wethersfield, in Oct. 1648. Had sons, John, William, Ephraim, and David; and daughters, who m. Robert Wells, Thomas Fitch, Joseph Butler, and —— Hollister—some of the best families.

Hannah Marvin, daughter of Matthew, sen'r., m. Thomas Seymour, of Norwalk, in Jan. 1653, and had children, Hannah b. Dec. 12, 1654, who m. Francis Bushnell, Oct. 12, 1675; Abigail b. Jan. 1655; Mary and Sarah, twins, b. Sept. 1658; Thomas b. 1660; Marie b. Nov. 1666; Matthew b. May, 1669; Elizabeth b. Dec. 1673, and Rebecca b. Jan. 1675.

Abigail Marvin, daughter of Matthew, sen'r., m. John Bouton, of Norwalk, Jan. 1656, and had children, John, Matthew, Rachel, Abigail, and Mary. John, his son, had two sons, Jakin and Joseph—perhaps others.

Rachel Marvin, daughter of Matthew, sen'r., m. Samuel Smith, of Norwalk, and had children, Rachel, who m. Thomas Benedict, and Lydia, who m. James Lockwood.

The descendants of the first and second Matthew Marvin, are very numerous; but owing to a defect in the early records, it is not easy to trace the descendants of any except those of John, who is supposed to be the youngest son of the second Matthew. Samuel, son of the second Matthew, was probably the father of Matthew, (fourth of the name,) who was b. Oct. 1702, and who was the ancestor of Hon. Charles Marvin, of Wilton, who has repeatedly been Representative and Senator in the State Legislature of Connecticut.

John Marvin, youngest son of Matthew Marvin, (second) was born Sept. 2, 1678, and d. in 1774, at the advanced age of 96. His first wife was Mary Bears, dau. of James, m. March 22, 1704, d. April 17, 1720. His 2d wife was Rachel St. John, daughter of Matthias, m. April 27, 1721. His children were, John, jr. b. July 22, 1705; Nathan b. March 4, 1707; Seth b. July 13, 1709; David b. Aug. 24, 1711; Elizabeth b. Oct. 23, 1713; Mary b. Dec. 29, 1716; Elihu b. Oct. 10, 1719. (By 2d wife,) Hannah b. Dec. 4, 1722; Joseph b. May 29, 1724; Rachel b. Dec. 24, 1725, (she d. an infant); Benjamin b. March 14, 1727-8, (d. an infant); a second Rachel b. March 27, 1728-9; Sarah b. May 18, 1733, and soon died; Ann b. Sept. 7, 1741.   *By T. R. Marvin, of Boston.*

Meakins, John, sen'r., of Hartford, m. Mary Bidwell, and had children, John, Joseph, Samuel, Mary Bidwell, Sarah Spencer, Rebecca and Hannah. He was brother-in-law to Daniel Bidwell. He d. in 1705–6. He had been a respectable and early settler. Estate £480.

N.

Newbury; Maj. Benjamin, of Windsor, d. in 1689, and left children, Hannah 8 years old, Thomas 6, Joseph 4, and Benjamin 1. Estate £563 : 18. Thomas Newbury, of Windsor, d in 1688. Estate over £300. The father of the Newbury family did not himself reside in Windsor.

P.

Peerings, Samuel, of Windsor, died in 1690. Samuel Cross was his only heir—left no children.

R.

[Family of John Robbins, of Wethersfield.]

Robbins, John, had a conveyance of land at Wethersfield, as early as 1638, and was a member of the General Court in 1644. He died about 1666, when his estate was distributed to his children, viz. Mary b. Jan 20, 1641 ; Hannah b. April 30, 1643 ; Comfort b. Oct. 12, 1646 ; John b. April 20, 1649. He gave his eldest daughter, Hannah, land at Naubuck. Estate £579 : 19. It is supposed his father John came with him, and d. at Wethersfield soon after he arrived there. He mentions land owned by his father.

Robbins, John, son of John, m. Mary Denison, and had children, Joshua, Richard, John and Samuel. Mary, his widow. Will made in 1689. He d. in 1698, at which time his children were all minors. He was a cousin of John Chester, jr., and a brother-in-law of Samuel Boarman. His widow Mary appears to have m. a Mr. Davison, and by this name gave her sons, Joshua, Richard and Samuel, land at Long Hill. He left each of his sons a large estate. Joshua had a double portion.

Joshua, the son of John, sen'r., probably d. young, or removed, as he is not found after the death of his father.

John Robbins, son of John, and brother of Joshua and Richard, d. Oct. 6, 1712. He left no children. Estate £391 : 14, which was distributed to his brothers, Joshua, Richard and Samuel.

Robbins, Joshua, sen'r., son of John, and brother of Richard and Samuel, m. in 1709, and d. about 1733. His will was presented in

Court by Sarah, his widow, and Nathaniel Robbins, executors. He was a gentleman of wealth. His children at his decease were, Joshua, jr., Jonathan, Elizabeth Talcott, wife of Nathaniel, Hannah, wife of Joseph Welles, Mary, wife of Joseph Treat, Abigail, wife of Silas Belden, and Comfort, wife of John Coleman. He gave Joshua, jr. his land at Stepney where he lived, also at Newington, at Mile-meadow, at Whirlpool, at Rocky Hill in Stepney, and other places. He gave Jonathan his new house and barns and several pieces of land.

Robbins, Capt. Jonathan, son of Joshua, sen'r. and grandson of John, m. Sarah, dau. of Capt. Robert Welles, in 1728. He d. 1777, and left an estate of £8946, including his farm on which Solomon then lived, the farm Levi sold and the land in Beaver meadow, Bishop meadow, and in Sandisfield, Mass., and other lands. Jonathan Robbins, supposed a son of Capt. Jonathan, m. Miss Stevens, and had Jonathan, Joshua, Solomon, Reuben, Asher, Appleton, Oliver, Robert, Levi, and five daughters. Oliver m. Mary, dau. of John Rose, and had children, Oliver, Robert, George, William, Nancy (m. Moses Griswold,) Mary (unmarried,) Harriet (m. Francis Stillman,) Laura (m. Eratus Holcomb, of East Granby.)

Joshua, son of the above Jonathan, m. and had Asher, (who settled at Newport, R. I. and was United States Senator from that State, and d. in 1845,) Elisha m. Miss Goodrich, and had Rev. Royal, (settled at Kensington,) Elisha and Chauncey, merchants in N. Y., and Henry (who m. Miss Talcott,) Sarah, Julia, Martha, and others who died young.

Solomon, son of Jonathan, settled in Sandisfield, Mass., and m. there, and had a large family. He d. about 48 years since, on a visit to his native town. It was in this family that Archibald Robbins, who was so roughly treated by the Arabs, originated.

Reuben and Asher, sons of Jonathan, probably d. young.

Appleton, son of Jonathan, graduated at Y. C. in 1760, and d. 1824, m. Mary Stillman. Children, Appleton, Allen, George, Mary (d. April 15, 1848, aged 80,) Rebecca (m. Doct. Nath'l Dwight, who d. in 1831 —she d. April 28, 1848, aged 77,) Betsey, Sally and Clarissa.

Rev. Robert, son of Jonathan, m. Ruth Kimberly, of Glastenbury, and after her death, for his 2d wife m. Jerusha Easterbrooks. He d. in 1804, and left issue, Ruth K. (who m. Henry Champion, eldest son of Gen. Henry Champion, deceased,) and is now living at Troy, N. Y; Jerusha E., (m. E. Northam, of Williamstown, Mass.;) Rev. Robert

C., a clergyman—died after preaching a few years ; Samuel W., a farmer, went to the South and married there ; Bela, lived and died at West Chester, in Colchester—was a deacon before he was 21 years of age ; Amatus is now a physician at Troy ; Mandana (m. Mr. Usher) and now lives with her husband at the old Robbins place at West Chester ; Meroa d. unmarried. The children of Henry Champion, jr., were, Rev. George, graduated at Yale College in 1831, was a Missionary, and d. in 1841 ; Maria m. Jonathan Edwards, Esq., of Troy ; Abigail J., m. Mr. Bliss, of New York. Rev. Robert Robbins was a man of great learning, a rigid Calvinist, and considerable *individuality*. He graduated at Yale College in 1760, and was for many years pastor of the church in West Chester.

Levi, son of Jonathan, (m. Miss Kilbourn,) and had a daughter and two sons, viz. Abigail, James and Levi.

Robbins, Joshua, jr., m. Nov. 20, 1707, and had Nathaniel b. Sept. 7, 1708; Zebulon b. Aug. 21, 1710 ; Sarah b. Jan. 25, 1712, and d. 1753 ; John b. March 31, 1713 ; Hannah b. March 3, 1715 ; Joshua b. June 19, 1717, and d. May 30, 1726 ; Elizabeth b. Sept. 1719 ; Abigail b. Oct. 9, 1721. This Abigail Robbins m. for her first husband, Mr. Loomis—after his decease, she m. for her second husband, Hon. Jonathan Trumbull, who was Governor of Connecticut during the War of the Revolution. Nathaniel and John, of Stepney, gave their sisters, Sarah and Hannah, the household property in 1733.

Robbins, Nathaniel, son of Joshua, jr., m. Mary Robbins, sister of John Robbins, Esq., of Rocky Hill, in Dec. 1736. His wife Mary, was b. in 1713, and d. in 1781. They had chidren, Sarah b. Sept. 24, 1738 ; Richard b. Feb. 1740 ; Joshua b. Aug. 8, 1742 ; Sarah b. May 27, 1745 ; Nathaniel b. May 24, 1751 ; Mary b. Aug. 22, 1755, and Eunice. Nathaniel, and his son Richard both d. in 1783, of small-pox. Richard, son of Nathaniel, m. Mary ——, and had Elijah, Enos, Rhoda, Warner, Abigail, Rachel, Roger and Mary.— Joshua and Nathaniel, and their sister Sarah who m. Mr. Deming, (sons of Nathaniel,) moved to Pittsfield, Mass.

Robbins, Thomas, son of Joshua 3d., (wife Prudence,) d. in 1754. Estate about £3000. His children were, Anne, aged 17 at his death, Prudence 15, Abigail 11, Hannah 8. He also had an only son, Unni, the eldest of his children. Thomas d. before his father, and Unni's grand father Joshua, gave Unni a farm at Newington. Prudence, the daughter of Thomas, m. Samuel Wolcott, jr. Thomas resided at Newington. Joshua gave a large share of his estate to the children of his deceased son Thomas. The widow of Thomas d. before the distribution of the estate.

Robbins, Elisha, son of Joshua, and grandson of Jonathan, (wife Sarah, administrator,) d. about 1757, at which time the inventory of his estate was presented to the Court. Estate £489. He left but one child, Sarah, a minor at his decease, and her mother was appointed her guardian, in 1776. The estate was not distributed to the widow and child until 1776. Sarah d. unmarried in 1794. Zebulon Robbins, administrator.

Robbins, Capt. Daniel, son of Joshua, and gt. grandson of John, d. in 1767, (wife Prudence.) Children, Hezekiah, William, Daniel, Roger and Michael. He d. insolvent, as it appears his son Hezekiah held at the time of his death, a bill of sale of all his father's property. Will dated 1761.

Robbins, Joshua, son of Joshua, of Wethersfield, d. in 1796. His son Joshua and Abraham Crane, Executors. Wife Mary, and children, Asa, Richard, John, Eunice (the widow of Solomon Williams,) Mary Crane, Abigail Hart, Sarah Willard, and Elizabeth Wright. He left large tracts of land for his family. Estate £1186.

Robbins, Levi, son of Jonathan, d. in 1793. Estate £133.

Robbins, William, grandson of Joshua, d. about 1786. Estate £412.

Robbins, Prudence, d. about 1764, and the inventory of her property returned to Court by Unni Robbins, in 1765.

Robbins, Joshua, d. about 1763. Wife, Abigail. He left children, Abigail, aged 17, Hannah 13. He notices Prudence, the widow of his son Thomas, deceased; to Unni, the son of Thomas, he gave a farm in Newington; to his son Daniel, to Prudence, the wife of Daniel, he gave a share; his grandson Hezekiah had his house; his son Joshua, his dau. Abigail Bulkley, his dau. Prudence Williams, his grandsons William, Roger, Daniel and Michael Robbins, all shared in his estate. Will made in 1759; the inventory presented to the Court in 1763, and widow Abigail's dower set to her the same year. She had one lot on which her son Joshua then lived.

Robbins, Hezekiah, son of Daniel, grandson of Joshua. His eldest daughter was Mehitabel; his other children were minors in 1777, and their mother then living.

Robbins, Samuel, son of the 3d John, brother of Joshua, Richard and John. Wife, Lucy. He d. in old age, before his wife, and had given his lands by deeds to his sons before he died. He had a son Samuel and other children. All his property not disposed of by deeds, he gave to his wife Lucy for her life, and after her decease to his daughters Lucy, Hannah, Mary and Mehitabel. His son Samuel d. before 1797, and left a son Samuel, for whom Maj. Timothy Russell was appointed guardian in 1797. Widow Prudence and his son Samuel were executors of the will of Samuel, sen'r. in 1753.

Robbins, Samuel, supposed son of Samuel. Wife Mary, and children, Josiah, Samuel, Elisha, Lucy (who m. Nathaniel Crow, of Simsbury,) Hannah (who m. Elisha Treat,) Mary (who m. Joseph Welles,) and Mehitabel (who m. Josiah Belden.)

Samuel, son of Samuel, m. Lucy Wells, and moved to Cannan, and had a son Samuel, and daughter Hester (who m. Rev. Samuel J. Mills, of Torringford, who graduated at Yale College in 1764, and d. there in May, 1833, aged 90, in the 62d year of his ministry.)

Elisha, son of Samuel, m. Miss Willard, and had one child, Sarah, and soon after died. His widow afterwards m. Mr. Robbins.

Josiah, son of Samuel, m. Judith Welles, and had children, Josiah, jr., Samuel, Robert, Judith (m. Seth Welles,) Rhoda (m. Gershom Wolcott for her first husband and Joseph Goodrich for her second husband,) Sarah (m. George Montague.) Josiah, sen'r. had four wives, 1st, Judith Welles, 2d, Wid. Wolcott, 3d, Wid. Wright, (maiden name Buck,) and 4th, Wid. Anna Francis. By his last wife he had a son Samuel, who now resides in Trenton, N. Y. Josiah, jr. m. Christiana Mauley, and had sons Josiah and Elisha. The two sons now reside in Pennsylvania.

Robert, son of Josiah, m. for his first wife Mary Welles, who died soon after her marriage ; he then for his 2d wife m. Cynthia Wood. His first wife had a daughter Mary, (who m. Elisha Wolcott ; by his 2d wife he had Martha b. 1793, (m. Gurdon Montague ;) Rhoda (m. Horace Wolcott and has a son Samuel ;) Cynthia (m. Erastus Deming, of Ohio, and has seven children ;) Rossiter (m. Rebecca Crane,) he removed to Cincinnati, Ohio, but d. in South Carolina in 1830. Robert first, m. Mary Williams, and had Thomas, Mary, Robert, Sarah and Ellen, when his wife died ; he then m. Wid. Humphrey, of Hartford ; Josiah m. Harriet Crane, and has children, Rossiter, Gurdon, Lucy Ann and Frances Cornelia ; Judith m. Timothy Harris, and had children, Donald and Julia—Julia d. young.

Chauncey is yet living, unmarried.

Benjamin m. and had a daughter Virginia. He resides in Greenville, Ohio. Josiah, sen'r. had twelve children.

Robbins, Richard, son of John, and brother of Joshua, John and

Samuel, m. for his first wife, Martha Curtiss. He d. in 1738–9. His children were, Mary, Rachel, Esther, Elizabeth, Experience, Martha and an only son John. He gave his house and homelot at Stepney, and many other large tracts of land, to his son John. His farm at Colchester he gave equally to his seven children. Estate £4400 sterling. Martha, his wife, d. in 1753. Her son John administered upon her estate, out of which property, John received £874 : 17 : 4. Her daughters Mary Robbins, Rachel Stillman, Esther Wright, Experience Hollister and Martha Williams, each received of their mother's estate £437 : 8 : 8. Richard's will dated 1737. He had a farm in Glastenbury. Martha's estate appraised at £3493 : 17 : 11.

Robbins, John, Esq., of Wethersfield, (Rocky Hill,) son of Richard, and grandson of John, m. for his first wife, Martha, daughter of Capt. Jacob Williams, Jan. 13, 1736–7 ; for 2d wife Sarah Wright ; for 3d wife Mary Russell, who was his widow. He d. in 1797–8. His son Wait was his executor. He had a son John, who died before his father, and left a son Justus, to whom his grand father, Esq. John, gave £500 of 3 per cent. stock in the Loan Office, £600 of 6 per cent. stock, and £500 of deferred stocks, and about 600 acres of land east of Connecticut river, which was the balance of the portion of his son John, then deceased. The children of Esq. John were, John b. Jan. 20, 1738–9 ; Sarah b. March 2, 1740, (m. Daniel Warner ;) Eunice b. Feb. 27, 1742, (d. young ;) Wait b. April 1, 1744 ; Jacob b. June 20, 1747 ; Levi b. April 1, 1749 ; Simeon b. Dec. 1, 1750 ; Martha b. March 30, 1754, (m. Mr. Wright,) and d. before her father ; Frederick b. Sept. 12, 1756 ; Samuel and Eunice, twins, b. July 11, 1760, (she m. Mr. Bulkley)—Huldah m. Mr. Riley ; his daughter Martha Wright, who died before her father, left five children, viz. Crafts, James, John, Nancy, and Sally Wright—all noticed in their grand father Robbins' will. He made his will in 1794, in which he manumitted his two slaves, Dell and Amy, at the age of 25 years. He gave Sarah in addition to previous gifts, £175 ; Eunice £215 ; Huldah, wife of John Riley, jr. a farther sum ; to his grand children, the children of his deceased dau. Wright, he gave £331 ; to Wait £2456 : 3 : 6 ; to Levi £2201 ; to Justus, his grandson, £1195 ; to Jacob £2381 ; to Simeon £2657 ; to Frederick £2861, besides the widow's share, about £14,329. Mr. Robbins was probably a gentleman of as great wealth as any in Wethersfield. He was a magistrate, and frequently represented the town at the General Assembly of Connecticut, and held a high standing in the town and State.

Frederick Robbins, the 6th son of John, Esq., m. Mehitabel Wolcott, who was b. June 12, 1759, by whom he had ten children, viz. Mehitabel b. March 9, 1782 ; Frederick b. April 9, 1784 ; Horace W. b. July, 1786; Fanny b. April 10, 1788 ; Ashbel b. March 28, 1790 ; Franklin b. June 5, 1792 ; Roxa b. Feb. 21, 1794 ; Maria b. June 26, 1796 ; Orpah b. April 25, 1798 ; John b. Dec. 24, 1799. His wife died, and he m. Sally Deming who was b. Jan. 5, 1771. By her he had one son, Walter, who d. in infancy, and his mother d. about the same time. Frederick then m. for his 3d wife, Abigail Grimes. By her he had Sarah b. Nov. 18, 1811 ; Caroline b. March 26, 1813; Walter b. June 8, 1814 ; Benjamin G. b. March 26, 1817.

Robbins, John, son of Esq. John, d. before his father, and had a son Justus. Justus's children were, Ira, Justus, Nancy (m. Edmund Bulkley,) Clarinda (m. Mr. Holmes,) Pamelia (m. Mr. West, of Alexandria,) Sarah (m. Daniel Warner,) and had children, Daniel, Frederick, Allen, Sally (m. J. Williams,) Martha (m. A. Collins,) Eunice (m. S. Dimock, Lucy (m. Russel Bull.)

Euince died young.

Wait m. Hannah Robbins, and had children, Wait, Levi, Asher, Samuel (who was killed with his mother, by one of the most destructive hurricanes ever known in this country.) Their daughters were, Lucy (m. J. Griswold;) Hannah (m. Dea. Merriam.) Asher's life was saved by the colored woman's carrying him to the cellar in the hurricane.

Jacob's children were, Elias, Silas (Judge Robbins, of Kentucky,) Austin, Moses, Chloe (m. R. Robbins,) Eunice, unmarried.

Levi's children were, Elisha, Levi, Samuel, John, Frederick, Russel, Sally (m. John Barnard,) Hannah (m. Barzillai Deming, of N. Y.,) Martha (m. Naum Cutler, of Vt.) Levi lived upon, and owned the farm in Hartford, called the Wolcott farm.

Simeon's children were, Simeon, George, James, Mary (m. Josiah Butler,) Sally (m. Eli Goodrich,) Mabel (m. Doct. Daniel Fuller,) Martha (m. a Mr. Willard, of Wethersfield.)

Frederick's children were, Frederick, Horace, Ashbel, Franklin, John, Walter (d. young,) Walter, Benjamin G., Mehitabel m. Washington Willams, Fanny m. Julius Chapman, of E. Haddam, Roxa m. Doct. Bigelow, of E. Haddam—and 2d Joseph Goodspeed, of E. Haddam, Orpah m. Ulysses Butler, Sarah, Caroline m. Edmund Merriam. [These were the children of Frederick, son of John, Esq., son of Richard.]

Eunice m. Charles Bulkley. Their children were, Henry, Ashbel, Archibald, Erastus, Mary m. Mr. Selden, of Haddam, Augusta, Emeline m. S. H. P. Hall now of Binghampton, a member of the Senate of the State of New York.

Samuel, twin of Eunice, d. young.

The children and grand children of Frederick, son of John son of Richard, who was a son of John, jr., son of John who first settled at Wethersfield, viz.

Mehitabel, the eldest, m. Washington Williams. Her children were, Cornelius, Catherine, Maria, Frances and Moses.

Frederick, jr. m. Eunice Ames. His children were, Philemon, Russel, Rowland, Horace, Julius and Louisa.

Horace d. at sea, without heirs. He was an adventurer—was in the Spanish war, and the company to which he belonged were all killed but seven, who fled to the mountains. They afterwards found their way to New Orleans through much suffering; he then enlisted under Gen. Jackson, and was in the battle at N. Orleans. He was a well educated and exemplary man.

Fanny m. Julius Chapman. Her children were, Lavinia, Catherine, Margaret and Laura.

Ashbel m. Elizabeth Rutledge, and d. without heirs, at Warrington, N. C., Nov. 10, 1826, aged 37.

Franklin m. Louisa Glad, of Schenectady, N. Y. Their children were, Edmund, Frederick, Alfred and Adelaide. His wife d. in New York—and he m. for his 2d wife Elizabeth Williams, and had children, Emma and Arthur.

Roxa m. Doct. Jesse Bigelow. Their children were, William and Amelia. She m. for her 2d husband, Joseph Goodspeed, of E. Haddam.

Orpah m. Ulysses Butler, and had one son, Frederick.

John and Maria, unmarried.

Walter, son of Frederick by 2d wife, m. Sophia Wilder, and had children, Frederick, and others.

Sarah, unmarried.

Caroline m. E. Merriam, and had children, Martha, Frances and Horace.

Benjamin, unmarried.

Robbins, John, of Wethersfield, d. in 1768. Wife Mary. Son John, executor. His children, were, Elizabeth Rockwell, Lois Goffe, John, Sarah, Jehiel and Zebulon. He left a good estate. His dau. Elizabeth, who m. Solomon Belden, for her first or second husband, with her brother, Jehiel Robbins, of Lanesborough, Ms., appealed the trial of the will to the Superior Court. Sarah d. in 1784, and her brother Zebulon was her administrator.

Robbins, Josiah, son of John, and grandson of Samuel, d. in 1794. Robert, his son, executor. Estate £1768. His children were, Josiah, Robert, Samuel, Judith Welles, Rhoda Goodrich and Sarah Montague. He gave his son Samuel, and grand daughter Lucy, daughter of Samuel, his lands in Vermont, and other lands; also to Lucy, when she arrived to 18 years of age, £15; to the three daughters of Judith Welles, £5 each, when 18 years old, and what their mother received at her marriage. His widow Mary d. in 1784.

Robbins, Richard, son of Nathaniel, d. in 1783. Estate £2038.

Robbins, Joshua, son of Joshua, d. in 1796. Estate £1186 : 8 : 2.

Robbins, David, d. in 1797, and left a small estate of £55—probably died young.

S.

Simons, Joseph, came from Wobern, Mass., to Hartford, and in 1717 moved to East Hartford *Five Miles*, now Manchester. He m. Agnes ——, and built his house upon the same ground where his grandson Ashna now lives in Manchester. His children were, Joseph, jr., Samuel, Benj., William, Agnes, Sarah and two other daughters.

Samuel, son of Joseph, sen'r., lived and d. in Manchester, in the same house his father built 1717. He m. Eunice Loveland, and had Samuel, jr., Israel, Ashna and Ashbel.

Joseph, son of Joseph, sen'r., m. Abigail Wickham, and had Abigail, Keziah, Ann, Sarah, Hannah, Joseph and Russel.

Benjamin, son of Joseph, sen'r., m. Elizabeth Shepard, of Hartford, and had children, Benjamin, jr., John, Uriah and Betsey. He d. in 1776.

William, son of Joseph, sen'r., m. Rebecca Webster, and had William, Ezekiel, Rebecca, Ruth and Adnis.

Samuel, son of Samuel, m. Miss Evins, and had a family of children. He d. after the War of the Revolution, at Susquehannah.

Israel, son of Samuel, sen'r. and grandson of Joseph, m. a Miss Cleveland, who came with her father from Scotland. They had Martin, Israel, Charles (killed by the fall of a tree upon him,) Sophia and Mary. Israel, sen'r. d. at Manchester.

Ashna, son of Samuel, is now 91 years old, and resides upon the same ground where his grand father Joseph built in Manchester in 1717. He m. Ruth Slate, and had children, James, Stephen, and Henry—all now deceased ; also Therissa, Ruth, Sally, Philamela, Electa, Laura, Almira and Marilda—all now living except Therissa. Ruth and Marilda were never m. Ashna was a soldier in the War of the Revolution, and now draws a pension. Ashbel, a brother of Ashna, d. aged 5 years.

W.

[Hon. William Wadsworth's Family, of Hartford, 1636.]

It is not known whether Captain Christopher Wadsworth, an early settler at Duxbury, or Captain Samuel, of Milton, who was killed by the Indians in 1676, or Rev. Benjamin, his son, of Boston, Mass., were allied by consanguinity, to William Wadsworth, who first settled at Cambridge, and in 1636 removed to Hartford, Conn. From the character of the men, their lofty bearing, and the family names, it may appear that they might have originated from the same common ancestor in England. It appears from Farmer, that William was at Cambridge in 1632, and he is found at Hartford, a member of Mr. Hooker's church in 1636, and holding the office of collector at Hartford, in 1637. Mr. Wadsworth probably was one of the band of pioneers who accompanied Mr. Hooker through the wilderness to Hartford in 1636. In what part of England he was born, or emigrated from, to New England, is yet doubtful. In the Farmer's Journal, giving the biography of Hon. James Wadsworth, of Geneseo, N. Y., he (James) is described as having descended from a native of the County Palatine, of Durham in England. Other places have been designated as the birth-place of William Wadsworth, and his residence in England. Rev. Thomas Hooker was born at Marfield, in Leicestershire, and preached at Chelmsford, England, before he fled to Holland, and had a church at Chelmsford, of which he had the pastoral charge. At this time, or a few years previous, Chelmsford, or this Hundred, contained thirty Parishes ; from which of these Parishes Mr. Hooker and his church were, may be somewhat unsettled. In the reign of Edward the Confessor, Chelmsford was a part of the possessions of the Bishops of London. The Manor which the Bishops of London possessed, was then called the Manor of the Bishops'-Hall or Chelmsford. In whichever Parish Mr. Hooker and his church might have been located, is perhaps immaterial, except as a fact in the history of the

Puritans. His church were fervently attached to him, and after the arrival of his members at Cambridge, they solicited Mr. Hooker to come to this country, and continue to be their minister—with which request he complied. Whether Mr. Wadsworth was one of his members either in England or at Cambridge, is not known to the writer, but as he was a member in 1636, at Hartford, it is conjectured that he had been so previously, and emigrated from Essex county with other members of his church. When Mr. Hooker and his church removed to Hartford, in 1636, from Cambridge, Mr. Wadsworth, from many circumstances, is supposed to have been one of the company. Mr. Wadsworth had probably been married, and was a widower, when he came to Hartford in 1636, as he had a son John, and either a daughter or sister Sarah, who married John Milrock—but as she was not mentioned in the will of Mr. Wadsworth, it is supposed to have been his sister. He gave his son John only £10 in his will, which shows that his son John had received his share of his father's estate before the execution of his father's will.

Mr. Wadsworth was in middle life in 1636. On the 2d day of July, 1644, he married Elizabeth Stone, a sister of the Rev. Samuel Stone, of Hartford. He was an original proprietor of Hartford, and in the land division of the town in 1639. He held several important offices in the town and colony, sustained a high rank with the best Puritan families of Hartford, both in character and wealth. His estate was £1677 : 13 : 9.

The children of Mr. Wadsworth, by his marriage with Miss Stone were, Samuel, Joseph, Thomas, Elizabeth, Sarah, Rebecca, and perhaps Mary. He had by his first wife, a son John, and perhaps Sarah. John settled at Farmington before the death of his father. Mr. Wadsworth died at Hartford in 1675—his widow Elizabeth survived him, and died in 1681-2. His eldest daughter, Elizabeth, was b. May 17, 1645. She m. John Terry, son of Stephen, of Windsor, in 1662, and had children, Elizabeth, Stephen, Sarah, John, Rebecca, Mary and Solomon. His daughter Sarah was bap. in 1649, and m. Jonathan Ashley, son of Robert, of Springfield, Ms. Jonathan settled at Hartford, and d. there in 1704, and left five children, viz. Jonathan, Joseph, Samuel, Sarah and Rebecca. I find John Milrock, of Hartford, m. Sarah Wadsworth, of Hartford, on the 17th of Sept. 1646—she was probably the daughter of William, by his first wife, or his sister who came with him from England, as his was the only family by the name in the colony in the early settlement. Sarah had a daughter Sarah,

b. Oct. 3, 1648, and d. soon after ; and on the 18th of Jan. 1649, Mr. Milrock was again m. to Miss Stoughton. Rebecca, another daughter of Mr. Wadsworth m. a Mr. Stoughton. Little is known of this branch of the family, only that the Stoughton family were among the best families of Windsor. Mr. Wadsworth, in his will, notices his grand daughter Long. It is supposed he had a daughter Mary, who m. Thomas Long, sen'r., who d. in 1711—he left a son Samuel, and other children. Thomas Wadsworth, son of William, sen'r., was provided for in his father's will, by giving him all his lands located east of Connecticut river, with a barn then building upon it. It is therefore presumed that Thomas settled in East Hartford. His children were, John, Thomas, jr., Sarah and Elizabeth. Thomas, jr. m. Sarah ——, who was his executrix, after his decease, in 1717—he d. before his father, and it is not known whether he left children. John, the son of Thomas and his sister Elizabeth, neither of them being married, left no children ; they resided together in Hartford, in the present old brown house directly in the rear of the dwelling house of Doctor Sumner, where they both died in old age, about 1776. She was known as Aunt Betty, for many years previous to her death. Her sister Sarah m. Mr. Burr, of Hartford, and had several children—these children inherited the estate of John and Aunt Betty ; the two last are now distinctly recollected by Mr. Jonathan Olcott, of Hartford, aged 90 years. Thomas d. in 1726.

Samuel Wadsworth, son of Hon. William, was b. Oct. 25, 1646, and d. in 1682. He left neither a widow or children, and gave his estate, (£1108) to his brothers and sisters and his cousin William ; to his brother Thomas particularly, he gave his man servant, for life, and some other property.

It will be discovered in this place that hereafter the name is sustained only by John, Joseph and Thomas, and their male heirs. I shall first trace the branch from John, the eldest of the sons of William, and by his first marriage.

Wadsworth, John, son of William, m. Sarah, daughter of Thomas Stanley, of Hartford, in 1662, and early removed and settled at Farmington, where he resided until his death, in 1689. His widow, Sarah survived him. His children at his decease were, viz. Sarah, wife of Stephen Root, b. 1657, aged 31 ; Samuel b. 1660, aged 29 ; John b. 1662 ; Mary b. 1665—she d. before her father ; William b. 1671, aged 18—had sons, William, Asahel and Gad ; Nathaniel b. 1674 ; James b. 1677—settled at Durham ; Thomas b. 1680, aged 9 years ;

Hezekiah b 1683—had no children. John left an estate of £1398. He gave his widow £100 at her disposal, and the use of his dwelling houses, barns, out-houses, homelot and his negro man, with £12 annually, during her life. His widow, Sarah, d. in 1718. She gave by will, "all her old England money, silver and gold," to her eight children then living. At the decease of John, in 1689, his daughter Root had a son Timothy, 8 years old, and a son John, 4 years old. Mr. Wadsworth was a leading and important man in Farmington. Mr. Wadsworth was a member of what is now the State Senate at the time his brother Joseph seized the Charter and secreted it in the oak tree, in this city.

(In this place I trace the branch of Hon. James, who settled at Durham.)

Hon. James, son of John, sen'r., of Farmington, and grandson of Hon. William, sen'r., of Hartford. In 1708, Maj. James Wadsworth and 34 others, obtained a patent, confirming to them the proprietors of the lands in Durham. Maj. Wadsworth had resided there previous to this time. He is familiarly known as " Col. Wadsworth." He was by profession a lawyer, and enjoyed by his ability and qualifications, as many of the responsible offices of the town of Durham as he desired, and received several appointments of trust and honor from the colony. He was the first military captain, the first justice of the peace, and the first town clerk of Durham. In 1739 he was appointed colonel of the 10th regiment of militia—was a justice of the quorum for some time in New Haven county—and an assistant for many years. In 1724, he with others, were appointed to decide all matters of equity and error which came before the General Assembly by petition, and was for a time a judge of the Superior Court of the colony. Colonel Wadsworth was an important man in the colony. He died in 1756, aged 78 years. He left two sons and one daughter, viz. sons, John Noyes and James. John N. was a farmer in Durham, and the father of John N., Gen. William, and James, grandsons of Col. James, who first settled at Durham. James, the son of Col. James, graduated at Yale College in 1748, and settled in his native town (Durham.) He soon became a gentleman of importance in the colony, and was advanced in military rank. During the war of the Revolution, viz. in 1775, Mr. Wadsworth, who was at this time a colonel, was appointed with Erastus Wolcott and others, a committee to provide for the officers and soldiers and their families, who were prisoners of war at Hartford. In 1776 he was made brigadier general of the battalion of militia raised to reinforce the continental army at N. York. In 1777 he was appointed second major general in the place of Maj. Gen. Huntington. He was one session a member of the Continental Congress. In 1777 he was one of an important committee appointed to revise the militia laws of the State, for the more effectual defence and safety of the country. In 1778 Gen. Wadsworth was again appointed with Cols. Pitkin and Chester, to adjust all accounts of the managers of the lead mines at Middletown. In 1777, upon the passage of the Ten Regiment Bill, Gen. Wadsworth was appointed to command them as brigadier general. He declined marching to Peekskill with the 2000 troops, and Gen. Erastus Wolcott was designated in his stead. In May, 1777, Gen. Wadsworth was ordered to march one-fourth of his brigade, properly officered by his own appointments, to New Haven, to defend the coast. In April, 1778, the Council of Safety directed him to enquire into the state of the guards at New Haven, and to dismiss the militia there in whole or part, at *his discretion*, &c. I might cite many other instances of public confidence in favor of Gen. Wadsworth during the eventful struggle of the Revolution. He was also for a time a member of the Council of Safety. He was Comptroller of Public Accounts for the State. He was also a prominent member of the Governor's Council. Dr. Field says, in 1789 or '90, he became conscientious about the oath of fidelity to the Constitution of the U. S, and retired from public business. He died in Sept. 1816, aged 87 years. He left no children—he had had two, both of whom died in infancy.

John Noyes Wadsworth, sen'r. and John, jr., were both farmers, and remained at Durham, where several of the family reside.

Gen. William and Hon. James Wadsworth cast their fortunes in unison in early life. They were brothers, the sons of John N. sen'r., and grandsons of Hon. James, of Durham, through the Farmington branch of Hon. William Wadsworth, of Hartford. They were both born at Durham. Hon. James was born April 20, 1768, and graduated at Yale College in 1787. During his collegiate life his father died, and his estate was distributed to his three children, which though a fair estate, was not a competency for each ; but their enterprise proved to them far more valuable than a patrimonial fortune, in which they might have spent their lives in idleness, or have become politicians and a blot on the escutcheon of their family shield. The ambition of these two brothers induced them to look farther into the future at that day, than most young men of their age in Connecticut. In 1790 or previous, Col. Jeremiah Wadsworth, of Hartford, a relative of their's, and a gentleman of great wealth, became interested largely in the wild and uncultivated lands in Western New York. In these lands, Col. J. Wadsworth proposed to William and James to become interested, by purchasing so much of them as they might feel enabled, and of the balance to become his agents in that (then) distant wilderness. Gen. William, who was a farmer, might not have been so much startled at the bold proposition of Col. Wadsworth, but to Hon. James, who had been liberally educated, and knew little or nothing of the hardships of a wilderness or a laboring life, must have been terror-stricken at the idea of abandoning the home of so honorable an ancestry, for the many deprivations of a life in the wilderness. Yet looking to the future alone, they started in 1790, full of courage, to reach their purchase on the eastern bank of the Genesee river, where Geneseo is now located. At this time a few detatched pieces of land were cleared west of Little Falls, N. Y. The remainder of the west through which they had to pass was a solitary wilderness, endangered only by wild beasts, or what was worse, the Five Nations of Indians instigated by English traders. They took with them several laborers from Connecticut, to clear away the timber, erect log-houses, and prepare some land to raise crops for the next year. Their provisions for the little band of adventurers had all to be transported, with their implements of husbandry, through the trackless wilderness. They ascended the Hudson—then to Schenectady, through the woods—then in boats upon the Mohawk river, the land but little cleared on either side, until they found a settlement, where they purchased their cattle, and some other necessaries for their future support and for stock. At this point the party divided, and Gen. William with some of his men, took the stock they had purchased, through the forest, while James and his party followed the streams, probably with most of his provisions and implements of husbandry. They again met in safety in an open field, a prarie, near where Geneseo now is. After a long, dangerous and tedious journey they had now arrived to their new home, with their cattle, tools and provisions. The first object was to build a house to shelter them, which they soon did with no other tools than their axes and perhaps an augur. They then attacked the forest, and soon got their crops into the ground. But the fever and ague of the new country, in the autumn, seized their axe men, which hurried them back to their old settlements in Connecticut; but the Wadsworths yet remained there, and in the following spring they replenished their axe men, and continued their clearing. The corn they had raised the first year could now be used by cracking in a rough mortar cut in the stump of an oak, with as rough a pestle—as no mills had yet been built in that section of the State ; but within a few years after they erected a grist and saw-mills at Geneseo. The lands in that region being in market, and the duties of the agency of lands and oversight of the farm having been the duty of both, and as the business of both increased, they divided their labors—James took upon himself the duties of the land office, while William attended to the agricultural labors. The raising of cattle purchased at the east when young, grown and fattened at Geneseo, and then taken to some distant market for sale, was the principal source of profit arising from the farm ; and no market could be obtained for many years for grain or other articles, which had to be transported upon wheels.

At this time the Wadsworths were in the *far West*, and though Hon. James was a most efficient agent, he found it extremely difficult to sell and settle his wild lands, as had been the case with other land companies in that region, and in 1796, Mr. James Wadsworth was solicited by those in interest in western lands, to go to England to interest the capitalists of that country in the lands in Western New York. Being a gentleman tall in stature, a noble countenance and gentlemanly appearance, he was an honor to his birth-place in the best English society, and perhaps the best selection that could have been made for the mission. The immense tract of country held by the two brothers, could not all be cultivated for many years. A part of it was improved by themselves, much of it was leased for years for a small consideration, and other parts cultivated on shares yearly. The great farm upon the Genesee flat adjoining the river, containing over 2000 acres, was cultivated and improved as the *homested* of the Wadsworths. The Messrs. Wadsworths have been, probably, the largest sheep and wool growers in the United States, and ranked with Gen. Wade Hampton, of S. C., as being at the head of all agricultural pursuits in the country ; while Gen. Hampton produced his results by slave labor, Gen. William Wadsworth and James from theirs alone by free labor, on a farm constantly improving.

As has been before remarked, Gen. William was never married, but Hon. James, in 1804, returned to the land of his birth and married Miss Naomi Wolcott, the daughter of Samuel Wolcott, of East Windsor, in this State. In his marriage he was most fortunate. By this connection they had several children, three of whom are now living,

viz. James S. Wadsworth, Esq., who is married, and has children ;
Elizabeth yet unmarried ; William, who was named in honor of the
first Hon. William, of Hartford, is also married, and has one child;
and the unfortunate and accomplished daughter, who married Hon.
Martin Brimmer, former mayor of Boston, died many years since.

Hon. James, by the death of his wife, his brother, Gen. William,
and an affectionate daughter, was greatly afflicted for several of the
closing years of his life—his whose whole life had been one of industry and care. After the sore afflictions in his family in his old age,
he continued his general oversight of his plantations and interests.
He differed from most men of great fortune—though he was econom-
ical in all his acts, yet he was uniformly the poor man's friend, where
industry and merit recommended his wants to Mr. Wadsworth. He
was a gentleman of general science, and was unlike most men whose
elementary education closed in a collegiate degree, if their attention
in after life should by chance be turned to agricultural, mercantile or
any other than literary pursuits. He was, strictly speaking, a scien-
tific planter. No man probably in the United States contributed more
largely with his pen, his influence, and his purse, towards common
schools than did Mr. Wadsworth, for several years previous to his
death. His contributions so often bestowed for erecting school houses
and churches, paying lecturers to instruct the people in his vicinity
upon literary subjects, publishing books, &c., and forming libraries,
must have in so long and fortunate a life been an item in his expenses of
no inconsiderable amount. He was modest and unostentatious as a
public benefactor. Politically, Mr. Wadsworth was in former days a
federalist, but after the political parties abandoned their principles, for
office, and the name of party became synonymous with office, he took
no farther interest in political parties.

Professor Renwick, speaking of Mr. Wadsworth as an improver of
the breed of cattle and sheep, remarks :—"His attention to fine-
wooled sheep was governed by practical and judicious views. He
had no share in the mania, under the influence of which Merino rams
were sought for at the price of thousands of dollars ; but, no sooner
did the price fall to reasonable limits, than he became the possessor
of the largest flock in the State ; and he did not condemn it to the
butcher when the unreasonable expectations of sudden and enormous
profits, which others entertained, were proved to be fallacious.

"Besides neat-cattle and sheep, the breeding of mules formed for
several years an object of his attention.

" It might have been expected that with such extensive concerns to manage as a land agent and landlord, not to mention the great extent of his own farm, cultivation on a small scale could have created but little interest in his breast. But this was not so, for he delighted in directing the culture of his garden, and in propagating the finest descriptions of fruit adapted to the climate, although he eschewed the costly luxury of the forcing-house.

" One peculiarity marks and distinguishes his possessions not only from those of small proprietors, but from those of the greater part of large landholders. This is, the manner in which they are studded with trees, isolated and in clumps, or surrounded and divided by belts. In this respect their aspect is that of the most admired portions of England, with this difference in their favor—that the trees are not planted by the hand of man, but continue to exhibit the grandeur of form and dimensions which they had acquired in the premeval forest. In England, according to his own statement, he learned to love trees, ere it was too late to prevent their entire destruction on his own domains by the unsparing axe of the pioneer of cultivation. He moreover was taught that a time is finally reached in the progress of population when timber is of more value than any other product, even of the most fertile arable soils. With this love of the beauty of trees as a mere object of sight, and sense of their prospective value, he willingly encountered the prejudice which represents them as injuring the meadows, whether for the scythe or for pasture, by their shade. To his surprise he found no diminution in the product of hay in his sheltered savannah, while to his stock, in the summer of our climate, the umbrageous shelter proved of incalculable benefit. More particularly his rich alluvial land, extended in the form of a peninsula from a narrow isthmus, has been protected from encroachment, and from the wash of the river by the native belt of wood which surrounds it.

" Few as are the events which mark epochs in the quiet and successfully industrious life of Mr. Wadsworth, it would be possible to dilate at great length upon these and other points in which his example and experience might be of great value to the proprietor and cultivator land.

" In 1843, Mr. Wadsworth became sensible of a decline in his health. His disorder soon exhibited symptoms which demonstrated its probable incurable nature. The certainty of his dissolution at no distant day became apparent to him, and although he yielded to the wishes of his friends and children, by trying a change of scene and air, he was himself aware how fruitless must be the attempt. The slow and gradual approach of death he awaited with equanimity and fortitude, and although he no longer manifested his accustomed interest in his favorite active pursuits, his intercourse with his friends was not devoid of its usual cheerfulness, which was damped rather by their anxieties than by his own. Returning to his residence at Geneseo, he there died on the 7th of June, 1844."

Gen. William Wadsworth, a brother of Hon. James, was educated a farmer in early life, and pursued it in an easy manner, after a few of his first years, at Geneseo. What is ever unfortunate for all men and the country, fell to his lot—he died a *bachelor*, in 1833. He was a major general in the war of 1812, and was taken prisoner by the British troops at the battle at Queenstown. He gave his large estate to the children of his brother James—which increased the immense estate they received on the decease of their honored father.

John N. Wadsworth, jr., son of John Noyes Wadsworth, sen'r., and great grandson of Col. James the first, of Durham, was a farmer, and settled at Durham. His children were, John N. and Wedworth. John N., jr. died in 1814, aged 55 years. John, the eldest of the sons, was educated at Williams College, and graduated in 1802. He became by profession a lawyer, and settled in New York. He had three children, viz. John W., William M., and Susan Wadsworth. The two sons, John and William M., are deceased. Their father died in 1815, aged 35 years.

Wedworth Wadsworth, son of John N., jr., and grandson of John Noyes, sen'r., now resides at Durham. He has been a member of the General Assembly, and held other places of trust in the State. His children now living, are—Noyes W., Wedworth, Abraham S., William and James ; all farmers except James, who graduated at Yale College in 1841, and is now a lawyer in Buffalo, N. Y. Each of these sons are married and have families, except William. The three eldest are settled as farmers in the State of Michigan. William remains at Durham, and is the present town clerk there.

Wadsworth, Dea. John, jr., grandson of William, sen'r., of Hartford, was born in 1662, and d. in 1718. His brother William was executor of his will. In 1696 he m. Elizabeth Stanley, dau. of John ; she d. in 1713, and in 1714 he m. for his 2d wife Mrs. Mary Gridley, (maiden name Humphries,) who survived him as his widow. His children were, Sarah b. 1697 ; Elizabeth b. 1700 ; John b. 1702 ; Daniel, (Rev.) b. 1704 ; Lydia b. 1706 ; Ruth b. 1711 ; Mary b.

1713—by his first wife. No children found by his last wife. His daughter Sarah m. Mr. Cowles. Mary and Elizabeth probably died before their father, not being noticed in his will. He requested his brother William to act as guardian for his son John—his brother Hezekiah to act as guardian for his son Daniel—his brother James, of Durham, to act for his daughter Lydia, and his brother Thomas to act for his daughter Ruth. In 1718, James the son of John, sen'r., resided at Durham, as he had done some years previous, and was appointed guardian by the court for his niece Lydia, in 1718. At the same court, Thomas was appointed guardian for Ruth. His estate was £857 : 4.

(I here introduce the family branch of Rev. Daniel, son of Dea. John Wadsworth, jr., of Farmington, who settled at Hartford.)

Wadsworth, Rev. Daniel, son of Dea. John Wadsworth, of Farmington, grandson of John, and great grandson of William, sen'r., of Hartford, was b. in 1704, graduated at Yale College in 1726, and was a member of the corporation of that institution from 1743 until his death. He prepared for the ministry, and was settled in the First Society in Hartford, upon the 28th day of Sept. 1732, and became the successor of Rev. Timothy Woodbridge, who d. April 30, 1732. On the 28th day of Feb. 1733–4, he m. Miss Abigail Talcott, daughter of Gov. Talcott, and had children, viz. Abigail b. Jan. 28, 1734-5 ; Daniel b. June 21, 1741 ; Eunice b. Aug. 31, 1736 ; Elizabeth b. July 19, 1738 ; Ruth b. 1746; and Jeremiah b. July 12, 1743. Ruth d. Dec. 27, 1750 ; Elizabeth d. Nov. 15, 1810, aged 72 years ; Daniel, jr. d. Nov. 3, 1750, aged 9 years ; Jeremiah d. April 30, 1804, aged 61 years ; Eunice d. duly 23, 1825, aged 89, years.—*Tomb Stones.* Rev. Daniel died in the prime of life, Nov. 12, 1747, aged 43 years, and left a handsome estate to his family. He had made a will, dated Dec. 19, 1746, and appointed his wife sole executrix. His widow died June 24, 1773, aged 66 years.—*Tomb Stones.* Neither of his daughters were married. Eunice and Elizabeth were living at the decease of their brother, Col. Jeremiah, in 1804. Col. James, who settled at Durham, was an uncle of Rev. Daniel. This branch of the Farmington Wadsworths, has consisted on the male side, of those who arrived to manhood, only of Rev. Daniel and his son Col. Jeremiah and his grandson Daniel, Esq., now living in Hartford. In 1765 the property of Rev. Daniel was divided by the heirs. Col. Jeremiah, Eunice and Elizabeth took the mansion house and lot of one acre on which it stood, in equal proportions—which has ever remained in the possession of the family, until a part of it was so liberally bestowed, in 1842, by Daniel Wadsworth, Esq., for the purpose of erecting, what is now called " Wadsworth Atheneum."

Wadsworth, Col. Jeremiah, son of Rev. Daniel, of Hartford, was b. in 1743. His father d. when Col. Jeremiah was a child ; he was soon after placed by his mother in charge of her brother, Matthew Talcott, Esq., at Middletown, where he continued to reside until after his marriage. When about 17 or 18 years of age he bled at his lungs, and his friends feared his illness might result in consumption. Mr. Talcott being largely concerned in navigation, young Wadsworth was advised by his friends to try a voyage at sea, to improve his health ; he therefore shipped before the mast, as a sailor, in one of his uncle's vessels—his health soon improved, and he continued a sea-faring life for several years, first as a sailor, and afterwards as mate and captain. In the mean time he married Miss Mehetabel Russell, born Nov. 19, 1734, daughter of Rev. William Russell, and grand daughter of Rev. Noadiah Russell, and had three children, viz. Daniel, Catherine, and Harriet. Harriet was a most interesting, elegant and accomplished young lady. She d. at the Island of Bermuda, where she was visiting for her health, previous to the death of her father. After the death of his mother, in 1773, he removed his family to Hartford, where he resided the remainder of his life. His daughter, Catherine, married Gen. Nathaniel Terry, of Hartford, who became an eminent lawyer and member of Congress. He d. in 1844 ; his amiable wife d. Oct. 26, 1841, aged 67. They left children, four sons and three daughters. Col. Wadsworth d. April 30, 1804, aged 61. His widow Mehetabel, survived him, but d. in 1817, aged 82 years. He made a will, and afterwards a codicil, and appointed his wife, his son-in-law Gen. Terry, and his only son Daniel, Esq., executors. He gave to his sisters, Eunice and Elizabeth, a liberal share of his estate during their lives. He provided liberally and kindly for his widow. He gave a handsome sum to his relative, Maj. Decius Wadsworth, of Farmington. Also a conditional sum to the First Congregational Society in Hartford. Also to his cousin Eunice, of Farmington, for her life, the use of the house and land he purchased of Ezekiel Scott; after her decease to descend to his cousin, Daniel W. Lewis, of Litchfield. The remainder of his large estate he gave to his son Daniel, Esq., and his daughter, Mrs. Terry, his only surviving children at his decease.

Col. Wadsworth became a very important man to the State and country during the War of the Revolution. Upon the raising of the six first regiments in Connecticut, in 1775, Mr. Wadsworth and others were appointed commissaries, to supply all necessary stores and provisions for the troops to be raised on a previous order of the General Assembly. In 1776, Mr. Wadsworth with others, were appointed a committee to purchase 5,000 pairs of yarn stockings for the army, in Canada. The same year he was a committee to procure £1800 in specie in exchange for bills, for the use of the Northern army, on request of Congress. The same year Mr. Wadsworth and Col. Fitch were empowered by the Legislature forthwith to furnish a sufficient number of kettles for the use of two battalions then to be raised for New York. The same year the Legislature apprehending there would be large demands for pork, and that great quantities might be clandestinely conveyed to the enemy or engrossed by individuals, which might distress the public and the poor of the colony, therefore the Legislature appointed Mr. Wadsworth and others, to purchase all the pork in the colony at the market price, to be kept in stores for public use, as should be required for the army. Also in 1776 he was appointed commissary of supplies, to receive and deliver over for the troops, then or afterwards to be raised in the colony, all such articles of clothing, refreshments or necessaries purchased and delivered to him by order of the Assembly, and at such places as were ordered by a Resolution of October, 1776. In 1775, the brig Minerva was ordered upon a cruise of six months, by Congress, and Mr. Wadsworth was directed to supply the brig with provisions and warlike stores for the cruise, and to provide 600 pounds of powder for the use of the brig. The prisoners in Hartford having become difficult to manage, and four of the committee being absent in the army—B. Payne and Col. Wadsworth were added to the committee to oversee the prisoners. In 1777 sixteen bales of cloth were forwarded to Mr. Wadsworth to be transported to the clothier general. In 1778 Congress sent an express to Col. Wadsworth and requested his immediate attendance before their Body at Yorktown, on business of great importance to the U. S., and he was advised by the Governor and Council to repair there as soon as possible. It appears from these facts that Col. Wadsworth not only officiated as commissary, but was frequently called upon for any and all purposes that the public interest demanded, and even that Congress held his opinions in high estimation. After the arrival in this country of Gen. de Rochambeau, with the French army, he soon found great difficulty in having a French commissary to purchase provisions for his troops—being neither familiar with our language or country—the high standing of Col. Wadsworth at once recommended him to the French general as a proper man for this purpose; and he being applied to by the General, at once assumed upon himself the duty and responsibility of acting commissary for the French army during the war; in which duty he gave the most perfect satisfaction to the French government, when his account was presented in person in 1783, which was freely and liberally accepted and paid. After which Col. Wadsworth, with his son, visited England, where they remained some time. They then visited Ireland, and made an excursion for a few weeks.

Col. Wadsworth was known as an intimate friend of Gen. Washington, and whenever the General visited Hartford during the war, he made the hospitable mansion of Col. Wadsworth his home, during his stay. History says, that Gen. Washington with Count de Rochambeau, were enjoying the hospitalities of his liberal board when Gen. Arnold was committing treason against his country at West Point, and that Gen. Washington returned there to take a hasty breakfast at Arnold's table, an hour after he had left, immediately before his guilt was discovered.

On the removal of the mansion-house of the Wadsworths, Mrs. Sigourney wrote the following lines, complimentary of the hospitality of Col. Wadsworth:—

"Fallen dome—beloved so well,
Thou could'st many a legend tell
Of the Chiefs of ancient fame,
Who, to share thy shelter, came
Rochambeau and La Fayette
Round thy plenteous board have met,
With Columbia's mightier son,
Great and glorious Washington.
Here, with kindred minds, they plann'd
Rescue for an infant land;
While the British lion's roar
Echo'd round the leagur'd shore."

So high did Col. Wadsworth stand in the estimation of his fellow citizens, that at the time the Constitution of the United States was referred to the several States for their approval or rejection, Col. Wadsworth was chosen a member of the Convention of Connecticut, for this purpose, and proved himself an efficient and firm friend of the Constitution. After this important event, he became a member of the First Congress, and was re-elected to the 2d and 3d Congress; he continued six years in succession in that body, faithfully giving construction and support to the Constitution he had rendered so efficient aid in approving. In May, 1795, he was elected in his native town, a representative to the Geneal Assembly, and also a member of the Council. He took his seat in the Council, where he remained by re-election until 1801, when he declined farther honors. He was a gentleman of great vivacity of spirits—honest in all his motives and purposes—kind to the meritorious poor, and a true friend to his tried friends. Col. Humphreys said of him, " He was always the protector and guardian of the widow, the fatherless and the distressed." His talents for, and dispatch of business, were unrivalled. A French traveller in this country, in 1788, (M. de Marville,) thus speaks of him :— " Hartford is the residence of one of the most respectable men in the United States—Col. Wadsworth ; universally known for the service he rendered the American and French armies during the war ; generally esteemed and beloved 'for his great virtues ; he crowns all his qualities by an amiable and singular modesty. Thus you cannot fail to love him as soon as you see him." In 1796 he received honorary degrees from Dartmouth and Yale Colleges, for the interest he had taken in the literary institutions in the country. " His services at some periods of the war were incalculable."

Wadsworth, Elizabeth, daughter of Rev. Daniel, of Hartford, died Nov. 15, 1810, aged 72 years. Hon. Nathaniel Terry, executor of her will. She gave all her estate to her maiden sister Eunice for life, and after the decease of her sister, to descend to her nephew, Daniel Wadsworth, Esq., and her niece, Mrs. Catherine Terry, with a provision that the mansion-house and lot on which it was located, should go into the ownership and possession of her nephew, Daniel Wadsworth, Esq. She was a most amiable woman, and a devoted Christian.

Wadsworth, Eunice, daughter of Rev. Daniel, of Hartford, was born Aug. 31, 1736, and died July 23, 1825, aged 89 years. She survived the whole family of Rev. Daniel, and died sincerely lamented by all who had the pleasure of her acquaintance, and particularly the widows and fatherless poor.

Wadsworth, Daniel, Esq., of Hartford, son of Hon. Jeremiah, and grandson of Rev. Daniel, in early life married Miss Faith Trumbull, the eldest daughter of the second Governor Trumbull. She was born in Feb. 1769, and died Oct. 19, 1846. She left no issue. Upon the decease of Mr. Wadsworth, the name in this branch of the family will terminate, as he is the only male heir of the descendants of Rev. Daniel, by the name of Wadsworth now living. He has from his childhood been in feeble health. When he was about twelve years of age he accompanied his father in his tour through France, England, and Ireland, near the close of the Revolution, in 1783, to improve his health, but with little benefit, as he has ever since continued feeble. Few gentlemen in Connecticut have more wealth than Mr. Wadsworth ; and none have improved this gift of Providence so constantly for the relief of the needy and distressed. Indeed he has uniformly used his estate as though he was fully aware that it was a gift of Providence to him for his wise distribution for great and good purposes ; and this community will endorse him as having been a most trusty and faithful agent. Among the many great and good deeds of his, was the grant of his father's birth-place, where had stood the family mansion-house for three generations—for the purpose of erecting upon it the beautiful stone edifice, now occupying the west part of the lot, adjoining Main-street, since named " Wadsworth Atheneum ;" an edifice 100 feet long by 70 feet broad. It is probable that the grant of the land, and other grants by Mr. Wadsworth including the lot and towards finishing the building, would not be estimated at less than $20,000. Mr. Wadsworth, to carry his views fully into effect, made a grant in trust to Hon. Messrs. Thomas S. Williams and Alfred Smith, of Hartford, of the land (on which a building has been erected,) about 172 feet in length and 121½ in breadth, for the erection of a building upon it, to be constructed and maintained in three principal divisions, separated from each other by substantial partition walls, extending from the foundation to the roof, as a protection from fire. The central division appropriated for a *Gallery of Fine Arts.* The north division for a *Library, Reading Room,* and other accommodations of the *Hartford Young Men's Institute.* The south division for the *Connecticut Historical Society*—with authority to said Society to grant room in their division for the use of the *Natural History Society* of Hartford. Deed dated March 18, 1842. Messrs. Williams and Smith on the 25th of Nov. 1842, quit-claimed the premises to " *Wadsworth Atheneum,*" and their successors, subject to the conditions and restrictions contained in their conveyance from Mr. Wadsworth to them, March 18, 1842. I take the liberty of saying, that no Historical Society in the United States has a better suit of rooms for their accommodation than the Connecticut Historical Society. This act of Mr. Wadsworth, for the Antiquities of Connecticut, the Natural History, and the general Literature of the State, is worthy of himself. No other gentleman in the State has done as much.

Small acts in a man's life picture to the world his generosity, his amiability, and his goodness of heart, far more clearly than a single great and benevolent deed ; and small favors show the liberality, even of men of great wealth, and their kindness of heart. Some years since, the son of a deacon in moderate circumstances, about thirteen years of age, and of a peculiar genius for invention of machinery, procured a small room between two stores in North Main-street, where by his ingenuity and industry, he invented a small machine for twisting and making fish-lines. The lines when finished cost the boy one cent and five mills each, and were sold for six cents. By his industry in this small business, he soon collected a trifling sum, which he employed in getting other small articles to add to his stock in trade on which he could get a profit. The industry of so small and young a lad attracted the attention of Mr. Wadsworth, and, as he often passed his shop, and saw this little pattern of industry at work there, curiosity induced him to go in and see him. At this time he had finished a machine for another purpose, perhaps at an expense of one dollar. Mr. Wadsworth was much pleased with the ingenuity of the child as well as his industry exhibited in the execution of the work, and to encourage him in well-doing, requested him to make for him a like machine, which he agreed to do. In a few weeks after Mr. Wadsworth called for the machine, and found it completed, and greatly improved, compared with that he had before seen. Mr. Wadsworth opened his pocket book and handed the boy a bill of twenty dollars for the machine. The lad stood astonished at seeing so much money, and remarked, he could not change so large a bill. Mr. Wadsworth replied, I want no change ; I give it all for the machine, and as a reward of your industry and ingenuity—take it ! With joy he received it, and replenished his little shop with trifling articles upon which he could make a small profit. That twenty dollars was the foundation of his present fortune ; for he is now numbered with the wealthy men of Hartford. Several years after, when he had grown to manhood, never forgetful of the favor, and being in New York, he found two pairs of splendid China silk bed spreads, the expense of which might cover the twenty dollars and interest, which he purchased and sent to Mr. Wadsworth without even a reference to his early favor. Mr. Wadsworth replied to him—Sir, you have proved yourself the *man* I thought you would, when a child, in the little shop in Burr-street.— Had all the favors Mr. Wadsworth has in a long life bestowed upon his friends in charity and for good objects, been as well requited as this by this poor boy, his generous disposition would have been fully satisfied. Many similar cases might be related—and should Sully speak of his youthful days, he would or should attribute much of his celebrity as a painter to his kindness.—Here closes the branch of Rev. Daniel Wadsworth.

Wadsworth, Hezekiah, of Farmington, son of John, sen'r., and grandson of William, sen'r. was born in 1682, and there is no evidence found that he was ever married. He d. in 1740. His brother Thomas was executor of his will, to whom he gave all his real and personal estate, except the lot and buildings which had been owned by his brother, deacon John, where Thomas then lived. He also gave Thomas the use of this farm during his life. After the decease of Thomas, he gave the farm to his nephew, Rev. Daniel Wadsworth, of Hartford. He left a good estate.

Wadsworth, Thomas, son of John, sen'r., and grandson of William, sen'r. was born in 1680. In 1745 he married Miriam Beckley, who died in 1759, aged 52. He d. in 1771, aged 92. He left no family.

Wadsworth, Lieut. Samuel, son of John, sen'r., and grandson of William, sen'r. was born in 1660. In 1689 he m. Hannah Judson, of Woodbury, who d. in 1732, aged 75 years. He d. in 1731, and left an estate of £500, and children, Hannah b. 1694, Sarah b. 1695, and Samuel b. 1698.

Wadsworth, Samuel, son of Samuel, and grandson of John, sen'r., of Farmington, m. Susannah Fenn, of Milford, in 1728. She d. in 1732, aged 36 ; and in 1733 he m. Rebecca Porter, grand daughter of Doct. Daniel Porter, who d. in Hartford, 1757. They had children, James b. 1729 ; Samuel b. 1732 ; Asa b. 1735 ; Hannah b. 1736. Samuel and Asa removed to Tyringham ; Hannah m. Asahel Burnham, of Tyringham ; Samuel, jr. d. in 1745, aged 47.

James, son of Samuel, jr., d. in 1773, aged 44. He m. in 1749, Abigail, dau. of Daniel Lewis, of Farmington, who d. 1816, aged 85. Their children were, Fenn b. 1752 ; Luke b. 1754, d. 1759 ; Amos b. 1750, d. 1775 ; 2d Luke b. 1759 ; Susannah b. 1764, d. 1768 ; Orange b. 1766 ; Susannah b. 1768, d. 1777 ; Lucy b. 1772. Amos and Fenn, sons of James, and grandsons of Samuel, jr., were merchants. Fenn was an accurate accountant, and was the principal business man in the Pay Table Office at Hartford, and by his constant attention to business, his health became impaired, and he died unmarried, in 1785. Luke, the son of James, of Farmington, m. Abigail Coles, dau. of James, (her mother was Abigail Hooker.) Their children were, Sukey, who d. single in 1814, aged 31 ; James C., Amos, Catherine, of Geneva, N. Y., single, Laura b. 1791, d. 1808, aged 17, Fenn b. 1793, d. 1795, Harriet and Eliza. James and Amos were merchants at Litchfield. James C. m. a sister of Mr. Delavan for his first wife. Harriet m. Fisher Gay, and d. in 1828, aged 32. Eliza m. Peter Curtiss, of Buffalo. Orange, dau. of James, the son of Samuel, m. Rev. Mr. Osgood, of Gardiner. Lucy m. Amon Langdon, who d. at sea ; he was captain of the vessel in which he died, and his widow now lives with her son Amon L. at Geneva, N. Y.

Sarah, daughter of Dea. John, of Farmington, m. Samuel Cowles, of Kensington, in 1716, and d. in 1786. John, son of Dea. John, d. in 1760. He m. Eunice Porter, dau. of Samuel, in 1734, and had children, Thomas ; Lydia b. 1736, d. 1813 ; Ruth b. 1750, d. 1818, aged 64—both single. Thomas, son of John, m. Miss Gridley, and was unfortunate in his family—he d. poor. His children were, Horace, Abigail (m. David Wright, of New Britain,) and John. John, the son of Thomas, had children, Lewis b. 1797, and d. 1798 ; Eli T., d. aged 25, stage driver in New York ; Thomas b. 1799, d. 1810.

Wadsworth, William, Esq., of Farmington, son of John, sen'r., died in 1751, aged 81. He m. Abigail Lewis, dau. of William, in 1696 ; she d. in 1707, and in 1709 he m. Sarah Bunce, dau. of Dea. Thomas, of Hartford ; she d. in 1748, aged 78. He had children, William b. 1697, d. 1699 ; Mary or Sarah b. 1700, d. 1722 ; Hannah b. 1701, m. Joseph Root, 1726, she d. 1741, aged 41 ; Abigail b. 1702, m. John Smith, 1728, d. 1729 ; Ezekiel b. 1704, d. 1712 ; William b. 1709. William, Esq. was an active and leading man in Farmington, for many years. His son William d. in 1769, aged 61. He m. in 1740, Ruth, the dau. of Thomas Hart, Esq., brother of Rev. John, of Guilford, father of Rev. William, of Saybrook, (she afterwards m. Solomon Whitman, Esq. He had children, William b. 1742 ; Asahel b. 1743 ; Ezekiel b. 1746, d. 1748, and Gad. Gad moved away.— William, the son of William, and grandson of William, Esq., d. 1816, and left an estate of $17,708. He m. Mercy or Mary Clark, dau. of John, who d. 1714, aged 71. He had children, Decius b. 1768 ; Romeo b. 1769 ; George ; William b. 1781, d. 1807, aged 26; Sidney. Decius was educated at Yale College, and graduated in 1785—was a colonel in the ordnance department in the army, and died in 1821, unmarried. Romeo and George resided in the State of New York. Col. Sidney, in 1812, m. Clarissa Buck, and had two children, who died before him. He d. in 1845, aged 59. Asahel, son of William, and grandson of William, Esq., d. in 1817, aged 74. In 1769 he m. Mercy Woodruff, who died, and in 1811 he m. Hannah Wadsworth, dau. of Nathaniel, jr., who d. in 1818, aged 61. His children were, Manna b. 1769; Ruth, who m. Mr. Washburn, of Vermont; and Thomas Hart. Manna, son of Asahel, d. 1796, aged 26, and left a son Frederick M., b. 1796. Thomas H., son of Asahel, of Farmington, m. Sarah North, dau. of Samuel, who d. in 1809, aged 30; he then in 1812, m. Elizabeth Rowe. His children were, Anna Deming, d. in 1809, aged 4 years; Marcus North b. 1805; Lucy b. 1808; Winthrop M.; Adrian R., Esq.; and Elizabeth A. b. 1821, and an infant who d. in 1817.

Wadsworth, Nathaniel, son of John, sen'r., and grandson of William, sen'r., d. in 1761. In 1705 he m. Dorothy Ball, of New Haven, and had children, Eunice b. 1706; Timothy b. 1709, d.; Esther b. 1713; Sarah b. 1717; Nathaniel b. 1718; Mary b. 1720; Hezekiah b. 1722; Timothy b. 1727. Eunice, dau. of Nathaniel first, m. Samuel Bird, in 1730. Esther, dau. of Nathaniel, m. Jonathan Root, of Southington. Sarah, dau. of Nathaniel m. Samuel Gridley, in 1746—he d. in 1764 and left no issue; she then in 1765, m. Thomas Stanley, of New Britain. Nathaniel, son of Nathaniel, d. in 1789, aged 72 years. He m. Hannah Gridley, a sister of the above Samuel Gridley, who d. in 1750, aged 28 years. He m. Esther, who d. in 1775, aged 52. They had children, Eliphalet b. 1747; Abel (died 1756); Hannah b. 1757, d. 1818; Anna b. 1761, d. 1810, and Esther, who d. in 1806, aged 42. All unmarried except Hannah, who m. Ashbel Wadsworth in 1811, at the age of 54.

Nathaniel, son of Nathaniel, jr., d. in 1823, aged 75, and left two daughters. He had m. Mary Youngs, who d. in 1802, aged 50; he then m. Mary Hart, of Berlin. Mary, dau. of Nathaniel, m. Elisha Deming; Hezekiah, son of Nathaniel, m. Lois Judd, dau. of William, who d. in 1801, aged 77 years. He had children, Hezekiah and Elisha (d. young); Huldah d. of small pox, unmarried; Lois m. Israel Jones, of Barkhamsted; Seth b. 1754; Ruth m. Abner Whittlesey, and d. in 1830, aged 80; Sarah d. single. Hezekiah the father, died in 1810, aged 86 years.

Wadsworth, Seth, son of Hezekiah, had two wives; the first died in 1804, aged 50—the 2d d. in 1822, aged 66—he d. in 1830, aged 83 years. His children were, Hezekiah, Elisha Strong, Edwin, Tertius, Timothy and Daniel. Hezekiah, son of Seth, m. Hannah Eells, of Barkhamsted; he d. at New Hartford, in 1813, aged 31, and left one son. Elisha S., son of Seth, d. at Palmyra, N. Y. Edwin m. Livia Judd, and now resides in the State of New York. Tertius, son Seth, resides at New Hartford, and is a gentleman of wealth. He has been twice married. His sons, Elisha and Julius, are extensive merchants at Chicago, Illinois. Mary. Timothy, his son, m. Mary Gillett, and had a large family, and his eldest son John is now of age. Timothy d. in 1841, aged 40 years.

Daniel, son of Seth, has been a judge in Ohio.

Timothy, son of Nathaniel first, m. Mary Cowles, of Southington, in 1750, who d. in 1755, aged 26 ; he then in 1758, m. Heppy Kilbourn. They had children, Theodore b. 1753 ; Rhoda b. 1755 ; Elijah b. 1759, d. 1763 ; Ebenezer b. 1760 ; Esther b. 1762 ; Mary b. 1768 ; Elijah b. 1765 ; Dorothy b. 1769. He lived in Canaan in 1788, and afterwards settled at Tinmouth, Vt.

Theodore, son of Timothy, was a physician, and in 1777 was appointed surgeon's mate in Col. Douglass' regiment, in the place of Doct. Todd, who had resigned continental service. He settled at Southington, and m. Betsey ——, who d. in 1806, aged 49 ; in 1808 he m. widow Asenath Clark, and d. the same year. He lost infants in 1783 and 1796. Daniel died. Theodore, jr. d. in 1804, at Hartford. Nancy (m. Chester Whittlesey, Esq., of Southington, in 1808,) and Harry.

Harry, son of Doct. Theodore, d. in Farmington. He was a physician, and in 1807, he m. Anna Mix, dau. of Judge John Mix—she d. in 1824. They had children, Theodore b. 1807, d. 1808 ; Betsey Mix, died ; Theodore H., b. in 1806, and d. a physician, at Austinburgh, Ohio, in 1843, unmarried.

Rhoda, daughter of Timothy, in 1771, m. Mr. Stanley.

[The following facts are added, not having been received in time to enter them in their proper places in the preceding pages.]

Rev. Daniel Wadsworth, father of Col. Jeremiah, represented the town of Farmington in the General Assembly before he was ordained at Hartford. Ruth, the sister of Rev. Daniel, m. Elisha Lewis, a merchant, and d. in 1776, aged 66.

Wadsworth, James C., who m. a sister of Mr. Delavan, of Albany, has had children, Harriet, James, William, Cornelia (died,) George, Henry and Cornelia.

Amos, of Litchfield, has children, Charles and Lewis.

John, who d. in 1760, left a daughter Eunice, who was living at Hartland, unmarried, in 1824.

Asahel's brother Gad purchased Avon Springs, N. Y., died wealthy, and left four children, viz. Ezekiel, Richard, Betsey (m. Mr. Newberry,) and Henry.

Manna, son of Asahel, was a merchant at Pittsfield, Mass. His son, Frederick Manna, d. single—was a lawyer at Little York, Penn.

Thomas Hart, son of Asahel, was b. 1771 ; Winthrop M. b. 1812; and Adrian R. b. 1815—is now judge of probate at Farmington.

Asahel lost two children in infancy, William and Susannah.

William, who died in 1816, aged 75, lost several children in their infancy.

Col. Decius, died in 1821, aged 53 years. A most complimentary eulogy of him was published in the National Intelligencer, after his decease.

Romeo resided in the city of New York. His children were, Juliette, m. Doct. Scott, of Montreal ; William, now resides in N. Y.

George, it is supposed is living at Burlington, Vt., and has a family.

Samuel, who removed to Tyringham, had children, Reuben, Silas, Ezekiel, James, Amos, Susannah, Sarah, Thankful and Elizabeth.

Reuben, son of Samuel, has children, Sylvester, Archibald, Electa, Olive and Samuel.

Silas has a son Calvin.

Ezekiel has George, Louisa, Hiram and Horace.

Asa left a son Enos, who has children, John, Asa and Betsey.

(This closes the descendants of the branch of the Hon. John Wadsworth, of Farmington.)

————

1. Wadsworth, Thomas, (mentioned on page 302,) was b. in 1651. He was a son of William, sen'r., of Hartford. Since publishing his children, others are found, viz. Rebecca b. 1686 ; Thomas b. 1688 ; Hannah b. 1690, and William b. 1692—William not having afterwards been found, he probably died young.

2. Sarah m. Thomas Burr, d. in 1750, aged 69, and left 10 children.

3. Rebecca m. Jonah Gross in 1708, d. in 1718, aged 32, and left no children.

4. Thomas, son of Thomas 1st, d. in 1716, aged 26. He married Sarah ——.

5. Thomas m. Sarah Arnold, dau. of John—she d. in 1778, aged 62 ; he again m., but d. in East Hartford in 1783, aged 67. Children, Thomas, John, Samuel, Josiah bap. in 1748, William, Jerusha, Sarah, b. in 1754, Rebecca b. 1757, and Elizabeth b. 1761.

6. Thomas, son of Thomas, (5) died in 1810, aged 75. His wife Thankful, d. in 1816, in E. Hartford, aged 74 years, and had children, George bap. in 1762, d. single in 1806; Thomas b. 1763; Thankful b. 1765; David b. 1767, d. at Gainesville, N. Y.; Timothy b. 1770; Solomon b. 1772; Joel b. 1774, d. 1823; Moses b. 1776, d. 1779; Anne b. 1778, d. an infant—another Anne b. 1780; Moses b. 1783.

7. Thomas, Timothy and Moses removed to Whitestown, N. Y. Thomas had a son Norman christened in 1815. Thankful m. David Abbe. Anne m. Asahel Porter, of E. Hartford.

8. Solomon, son of Thomas, (6) of E. Hartford, m. Lucy ——, and had children, Horace, Lucy, Emeline, Laura and Maria.

9. John, of East Hartford, supposed son of Thomas, (5) d. in 1774, aged 32. His widow Jerusha d. in 1804, aged 61 years. A child of Jerusha was bap. in 1772.

10. Samuel, of East Hartford, son of Thomas, (5) d. in 1798, aged 52; his wife Prudence d. in 1822, aged 65, and left children, Molly bap. 1782; Mabel b. 1783; Samuel b. 1784; Oliver b. 1790; Hezkiah b. 1792; Charles b. 1794; Titus b. 1796; Polly b. 1799.

11. Samuel, son of Samuel, (10) m. Hannah Roberts in 1805, and had children, Elizabeth b. 1807; Emeline b. 1810; Stanley b. 1813; Oliver b. 1815; Charles W. b. 1821, d. 1831.

12. Hezekiah, of East Hartford, son of Samuel, (10) m. Maria Jones, who d. in 1835, aged 33, and had children, Maria J. b. 1821; Henry W. b. 1824; Frances P. b. 1826, d. 1831; Louisa M. b. 1828; Anna b. 1830. He m. Heppy Forbes in 1837.

13. Josiah, son of Thomas, (5) m. Susannah ——, and removed to Schenectady, N. Y., and had children, Mary b. 1770; David b. 1772; Wait b. 1773, d.; John b. 1775—a 2d Wait b. 1777; Sarah b. 1779; Josiah, jr., b. 1780; Daniel Marsh b. 1782; Susannah b. 1785.

14. William, of E. Hartford, son of Thomas, (5) d. in 1811, aged 67; his wife Jemima, d. in 1824, aged 67. Their children were, Prudence b. 1772; William b. 1773; Seth b. 1776, d. 1806; James b. 1778; Minea or Mima b. 1780; Leonard b. 1782; Chester; Joseph b. 1786; Anson b. 1788, d. 1826; Abner b. 1790.

Wadsworth, Capt. Joseph, of Hartford, son of Hon. William, sen'r., was born in 1650. He m. for his first wife, Elizabeth, daughter of Bartholomew Barnard, of Hartford; for his second wife he m. Mary, the widow of John Olcott. She had been the widow of Thomas Welles, a grandson of Governor Welles. Her maiden name was

Mary Blackleach, daughter of John, jr. His wife Elizabeth, d. Oct. 26, 1710. His second wife Mary, survived him. His children were all by his first wife, viz :—

Joseph, jr., was born in 1682, and died Aug. 25, 1778.

Jonathan, died young.

Ichabod.

Elizabeth.

Hannah, and

Jonathan.

Capt. Joseph died in 1729. His son Joseph was executor of his will. A jointure was made for his widow Mary, who survived him. To Jonathan he gave lands on the Windsor road, buildings, &c. To Ichabod he gave land in Soldiers' Field, Lower house lot with house and barn, four acres South meadow, sixty acres west of Windsor road, &c. He gave his three grand children, the children of his daughter Elizabeth Marsh, viz. Jonathan, Joseph and Elizabeth Marsh, £10; and a sum to his daughter Hannah Cook, (wife of John Cook.)— Estate over £900 sterling. He made his will in 1723, and gave Joseph, jr. his upper Neck land, where his son Joseph then lived, the upper lot in Long meadow, and four acres of land which joined his brother Talcott's land; also his lands in Coventry, &c.

Before tracing the children of Capt. Wadsworth, I here insert a few of the interesting facts connected with his taking and secreting the Charter given to Connecticut by Charles II., in an oak tree, in Hartford.

CAPT. JOSEPH WADSWORTH—He it was, who, on the night of the 31st of October, 1687, seized and secured the Charter of Connecticut when Sir Edmond Andros came to Hartford in order to wrest it by force from the freemen of this colony.

" The important affair," says Trumbull, " was debated and kept in suspense until the evening, when the Charter was brought and laid upon the table, where the Assembly was sitting. By this time great numbers of people were assembled, and men sufficiently bold to enter-prise whatever might be necessary or expedient. The lights were instantly extinguished, and one Capt. Wadsworth, of Hartford, in the most silent and secret manner, carried off the Charter, and secreted it in a large hollow tree, fronting the house of the Hon. Samuel Wyllys, then one of the magistrates of the colony. The people appeared all peaceable and orderly. The candles were officiously re-lighted, but the Patent was gone, and no discovery could be made of it, or of the person who conveyed it away."—Hist. Conn. Vol. I. p. 391.

A subsequent act of the colony rewards Capt. Wadsworth for the service here described. He was a man of great boldness and energy of purpose. He had practical good sense and a capacity for business. The Records prove that he was frequently elected to represent Hartford in the General Assembly. While still but a young lieutenant in the train-bands of his native town, he served as one of the colonial legislators. He rendered also many important services to the town of Hartford as selectman, and as a member of committees for laying out roads, looking after the ferries and lands, and for many other municipal duties. From his frequent services of this nature, from his plain and popular manners, his ready address and resolute bearing, he seems to have possessed the full confidence of his fellow citizens. His acts prove him to have been an ardent lover of freedom, though he erred sometimes in carrying his own acts into excess when chafed by opposition or dislike. Once he was formally reprimanded, while a deputy in the Assembly, for words used in debate, which were " resented as declaring against the validity of certain acts of the Assembly, which were passed by both Houses separate, for their inconsistency with our Charter"—but he " readily acknowledged his concern that what he had spoken had given any offence to the Assembly, whose Constitution and proceedings he had no intention to reflect upon." On another occasion he was fined ten pounds for using " reproachful words against Mr. Pitkin," one of the Assistants, and saying " in the open Assembly that Mr. Pitkin's proceedings in the case were altogether unjust and illegal." This fine however was formally remitted. Upon still another occasion he was brought before the Court of Assistants, for having threatened, in a certain contingency, " to knock down Mr. Ichabod Wells, sheriff of the county of Hartford." When Col. Fletcher came from New York, Oct. 1691, to usurp the command of the Connecticut militia, Capt. Wadsworth silenced the reading of his commission by ordering the drums of the Hartford train-band to be beaten, and turning to Fletcher, who had interrupted him, said, " if I am interrupted again, I will make the sun shine through you in a moment." He spoke with such energy that no further attempts were made to read or to enlist men. Little accustomed to the spectacle of titled wealth and official arrogance, he was prepared to deem them when they met his eye in the shape of royal governors for Connecticut, as a usurpation on the privileges of his nature. He was just the man to awe Fletcher, and by a quick and daring plot to save the Charter.

He died in the year 1729, being about fourscore years of age, sound in mind, morals and estate. His will and inventory may be found in numbers 11 and 12 of the Probate Records at Hartford. His wife, three sons, and two daughters, survived him, and quite a number of his direct descendants are now living in Hartford. His brother, Hon. John, was sitting at the Council Board when Capt. Joseph took the Charter.

As strangers who visit Hartford, often through curiosity, enquire for the location of the Charter Oak, as the tree is familiarly called, I insert in this place, that it is yet standing in its green old age, (probably 400 years old,) at the South East part of the city, upon that beautiful plat of land purchased by Gov. Wyllys in 1638, and occupied by that noble family while a single male heir remained living. It is now owned and occupied by Hon. I. W. Stuart, whose urbanity of manners and love of antiquities, causes him to treat all strangers with great kindness whose curiosity leads them there to view the oak. He has erected an iron fence about the tree to protect it against depredators.

Wadsworth, Joseph, jr., son of Joseph, and grandson of William, sen'r., was born in 1682, and married Joanna —— ; she died in 1762, aged 68 ; he died in the 96th year of his age, in 1778, and left three sons and two daughters, viz. Joseph b. 1717, d. in 1757–8 ; Daniel b. 1720, d. 1762 ; William b. March, 1723 ; Elizabeth m. Richard Seymour, d. 1759 ; Joanna m. Timothy Goodman, d. 1768, aged 57.

Joseph, son of Joseph, jr., married Jerusha Bissell, of Windsor, dau. of Daniel. He was a merchant and d. aged 37, and his wid. d. Feb. 7, 1762. He resided in Windsor, and had a son Joseph, who d. in 1745, aged six months ; he soon after had another son Joseph B., and in his father's will, which was made after the death of his first infant son Joseph, he directed his only son Joseph B., to be educated at College, and in 1766 he graduated at Yale College. He became a physician, settled in East Windsor, and died in 1784. He had m. Roxana ——, and left her his widow, and an only daughter Roxana. Joseph, who m. Jerusha Bissell, made Jerusha and his father-in-law, his executors. He gave his widow all his household furniture, a horse, cow, his negro man Hazzard, and the use of his house and homelot, so long as she remained his widow ; all the remainder he gave to his infant son Joseph.

Wadsworth, Daniel, son of Joseph, jr., and grandson of Capt. Joseph, sen'r., was born in 1720. He m. and had one son, Daniel, b. Oct. 14, 1762. Daniel, sen'r. d. the same year, and left his only child, an infant. A guardian was afterwards appointed for him, and he resided with his guardian, at Glastenbury. After Daniel, jr. had grown to manhood, he settled at Hartland. His mother d. in 1794.

Wadsworth, William, son of Joseph, jr., and grandson of Capt. Joseph, sen'r., was born in 1723, and m. Mary Cook, July 12, 1751. He had two sons, viz. William b. July 6, 1752 ; Roger b. March 19, 1756. William d. May 29, 1771, aged 47 ; his widow d. in April, 1811, aged 85. Estate £1044 : 10.

Wadsworth, William, jr., son of William, and grandson of Joseph, jr., was born in 1752. He m. Abigail Skinner, but left no children. He d. either in the 34th or 47th year of his age.

Wadsworth, Roger, brother of William, and son of William, was born in 1756. He m. Ann Prior, and had children, viz. Mary b. Aug. 1779, m. James Church, of Hartford ; Algernon Sidney b. June 5, 1781, d. at sea and left no family ; Fanny b. Dec. 1, 1782, m. Joseph Pratt Esq., of Hartford, had a large family, and d. Feb. 14, 1838 ; her sister Charlotte b. July 31, 1797, m. Joseph Pratt, Esq., as his 2d wife, and has no children ; Sukey b. March 23, 1785, died young ; William b. Oct. 23, 1786, now resides at Hartford, unmarried ; Roger, jr. b. Oct. 20, 1789, m. Cornelia Thompson, and resides at Brattleborough, Vt. ; he has had children, viz. Sarah Cornelia (d. young,) Algernon Sidney, and Henry A. ; Jeremiah b. Jan. 21, 1797, d. at the South, unmarried, Aug. 11, 1823 ; Abner Prior b. Jan. 20, 1800, m. Mary Capen. Roger, sen'r. died May 17, 1810 ; his wife Ann died aged 83 years.

Wadsworth, Ichabod, son of Capt. Joseph, sen'r., and grandson of William, sen'r., of Hartford, m. Sarah Smith, Dec. 21, 1720. He had children, Elisha b. Sept. 21, 1721 ; Elihu, Hezekiah and a daughter, who m. William Whiting, of W. Hartford ; another daughter m. Richard Goodman, of W. Hartford, the father of Richard late deceased.

Elihu, son of Ichabod, had children, Elihu, David, Chloe, Jerusha and Esther. Chloe m. J. R. Collins ; Jerusha d. single ; Esther m. James Butler, and removed to Vermont ; Elihu d in 1782.

Elisha, son of Ichabod, b. Sept. 21, 1721, m. Miss Cadwell, and had sons, Elisha and James.

Elisha, jr., son of Elisha, had a son Theodore, who removed to the vicinity of Johnstown, N. Y., and other children.

Hezekiah, son of Ichabod, m. Miss Seymour, of Hartford, and had sons, Jonathan and Hezekiah, and a daughter, who m. Moses Filley, of Windsor. Hezekiah d. in New York during the war of the Revolution, about 1776. The 60 acres of wood land west of mill river, near the Simsbury road from Hartford, given by Capt. Joseph to his son Ichabod, yet remains in the Wadsworth family. Ichabod d. May 5, 1778, aged about 90 years, and is now distinctly recollected by Mr. Jonathan Olcott, of Hartford, who is 90 years old.

Wadsworth, Serg't. Jonathan, the youngest son of Capt. Joseph, sen'r., and grandson of Hon. William, sen'r., of Hartford, married Hepzibah Marsh in 1711. His children were,

Hepzibah b. Sept. 13, 1712, m. Hezekiah Collier—she died Nov. 20, 1770.

Hannah b. July 8, 1714, m. Daniel Bull, Oct. 26, 1733.

Samuel b. Oct. 25, 1716, m. Meliscent Cook, of Harwinton, died in Dec. 1798.

Abigail b. April 10, 1718.

Rebecca b. Sept. 16, 1720, died in infancy.

Helena b. June 2, 1724, died Sept. 23, 1796.

His wife Hepzibah died, and he married for his 2d wife, Abigail Flagg; by her he had

Rebecca b. Sept. 6, 1725—she m. a Mr. Perkins, of Enfield.

Mary b. April 30, 1728.

Jonathan, jr. b. May 9, 1729.

Lydia b. Feb. 1, 1731—she m. John Seymour, of Hartford, and became the grand mother of Harvey Seymour, Esq., of Hartford. He (John) was a sea captain for many years. In early life he was celebrated as an Indian fighter. At the age of 15 years, in 1746, he was drafted to march to an Indian battle; and in 1756 was again drafted to march against the Indians and French; and again fought the British and Indians in 1776. He was a brave soldier and officer; and the sword he wore when a captain in these wars, is now deposited in the Connecticut Historical Society, at Hartford. Serg't. Jonathan, son of Joseph, sen'r., died in 1739. Abigail, his widow, administrator. Estate £991 : 7. His son Jonathan and daughter Lydia, were minors at his death—made choice of Jacob Kellogg, who had married their mother in 1646, as guardian.

Wadsworth, Capt. Samuel, of Hartford, son of Jonathan, and grand son of Joseph, sen'r., was born Oct. 25, 1716. She was b. July 27, 1723. Their children were,

Gurdon and George (twins) b. June 27, 1748. George d. Nov. 22, 1753, aged 5 years.

Hannah b. April 7, 1750—she m. first, John Bigelow, June 30,

1771 ; second, Mr. Tylee, and for her third husband, Capt. James Hillyer. She had five children by John Bigelow—all sons ; one child by Mr. Tylee, (Sally, who m. Daniel Hinsdale,) and no children by Capt. Hillyer.

Eli b. March 3, 1752, married Miss Cadwell.

Nathan b. Aug. 3, 1753, first m. Sally Welles, and for second wife Sarah Bunce.

George, b. Oct. 27, 1755, m. Elizabeth Turner—he d. Feb. 2, 1825.

Samuel, jr. b. May 13, 1757, d. May 28, 1757.

Capt. Samuel was a gentleman of high standing in public estimation ; and in 1775 there was satisfactory proof to the government that a design was formed by the British Ministry to invade the Northern colonies by Canada. At this time Ticonderoga and Crown Point had been taken, and was in the possession of different colonies, and not exclusively held by Connecticut. It was thought to be impracticable for the officers and soldiers to return either to Ticonderoga or Crown Point at that time ; yet that they should be provided for, for the time being—it was resolved that Col. Erastus Wolcott, Capt. Samuel Wadsworth, Col. Fisher Gay, Col. James Wadsworth, and others, should be a committee, or any three of them, to take care and provide for the officers and soldiers and their families, in procuring labor for the soldiers until the Continental Congress; or the Assembly, should take further orders concerning them. Capt. Wadsworth received some other appointments by the General Assembly and Council of Safety during the war. His will was presented to the Court by his sons, Gurdon and Nathan, executors, in 1798. He gave to his two grandsons, (the sons of his son Eli then deceased,) land at Hog river, &c. To his three grand daughters, Lucy, Nancy and Caty, (daughters of Eli,) £30 each. His sister Hellen or Hellena, he provided for during her life. His son Gurdon he had given the trade of a hatter, while Nathan and George, his younger sons, had been upon his farm—he therefore gave Nathan a lot of land at the Neck, east of the Windsor road, and £100 out of his homested, more than he gave Gurdon. To George, his youngest son, he gave £200 over his equal share with Gurdon. His daughter Hannah he provided for. Capt. Samuel died Dec. 29, 1798, aged 82. Meliscent, his wife, died April 24, 1790, aged 67. Estate £3526.

Wadsworth, Capt. Jonathan, jr., grandson of Capt. Joseph, and great grandson of Hon. William, sen'r., was born May 9, 1729. He married Abigail Flagg. In early life he was a sea captain, and during the early part of the Revolutionary war, he was solicited by Col. J. Wadsworth, of Hartford, to take the command of a company, and enter into the service of his country. He consented, though with great reluctance, and was soon after killed near Saratoga, N. Y., on the 19th of September, 1777. Estate £1608. His children were, Henry, Horace, John, Samuel, Jared, Charles and Mary.

Henry, son of Jonathan, jr., m. Betsey Bidwell—she died ; he then m. Lucy Nichols, a sister of Cyprian, Esq. He died in 1821. His children were, Oliver, d. aged 16 ; Abigail, m. Charles Hosmer, Esq., of Hartford—she had two children, viz. James B., d. Sept. 5, 1814, aged 19 months ; Charles, d. Jan. 26, 1815, aged 4 months. Mrs. Hosmer d. Jan. 11, 1816, aged 29 years. Richard, son of Henry, settled at Buffalo, N. Y., and has seven sons. Sally m. Mr. M'Lean, and had a daughter Elizabeth ; he soon after died, and his widow m. Mr. Wells. Frederick died unmarried. Chauncey died unmarried. Samuel m. and had two children in Ohio, and d. 1832. 2d Oliver m. Rosanna Isham, of West Hartford, and has three daughters and no sons. Eliza m. Sylvester Matthews, of Buffalo, N. Y., and has children. Henry Nichols Wadsworth, died at sea, unmarried.

Jared, son of Jonathan, jr., d. at sea, in 1795, soon after he married, and left no issue.

John, son of Jonathan, jr., m. at Utica, N. Y. He died, and left two children.

Samuel, son of Jonathan, jr., died at sea, unmarried.

Charles, son of Jonathan, jr., was a purser in the U. S. Navy. He was aided by Col. Wadsworth, in early life, in getting his education ; he also procured for him his office in the Navy. He was a gentleman of an elegant form and appearance. After he became purser, he located at Alexandria, D. C., where he m. Elizabeth ——, and had three children, now all deceased, viz. Julia Ann, Edwin and Elizabeth. He died at Alexandria in 1834. His mother Abigail, and sister Mary, resided at Hartford. Mary died single.

Horace, son of Capt. Jonathan, jr., m. Abigail Adams. He was many years deputy sheriff of Hartford county. His children were, Henry died a young man, unmarried, in 1830 ; John resides in New York, is married, and has a family of children ; Horace, jr. ; Edward m. Martha Woolly, and resides in Hartford ; Mary and Julia, twins, and Sarah reside at New York, single. Horace, sen.'r, d. in June, 1836, aged 52 years ; his wife, Abigail, d. Dec. 29, 1824. Horace, jr. is living at the South.

Eli, son of Capt. Samuel, and grandson of Capt. Jonathan, m. Rachel Hill, and d. March 1, 1787, before his father. He left two sons, William and Eli, and three daughters, Lucy, Nancy and Caty. These children were provided for in their grand father's will. William, son of Eli, chose Thomas Hanes for his guardian, in 1793. William and Eli, sons of Eli, are both dec'd.

Nathan, son of Capt. Samuel, was b. in 1753, and d. May 28, 1831. He was twice married; first, he m. Sally Wells, who d. Aug. 9, 1796, aged 37 ; 2d wife, Sarah Burr. He had but one child, Ann, and this by the first marriage. Ann m. Elisha Loomis, of Torrington, and afterwards removed to the State of New York.

Samuel, jr., son of Samuel, was b. May 13, 1757, d. May 28, 1757.

George, son of Capt. Samuel, was b. Oct. 27, 1755, d. Feb. 2, 1825. He m. Elizabeth Turner, who d. in May, 1827, aged 63. Their children were, Meliscent, m. Benjamin Allyn, of Windsor, now residing in Illinois ; Elizabeth, d. single ; George, jr., unmarried, resides in Baltimore ; Lucy m. Russel Wildman, of Hartford—she now resides in Norwich.

Gurdon, the eldest son of Capt. Samuel Wadsworth, was a twin brother of George, b. June 27, 1748. George d. when five years old. Gurdon m. Mehetabel Wright, of Wethersfield. She was b. about 1752, and d. Dec. 31, 1793. Their children were, Polly b. Jan. 25, 1776, m. B. Carter, of Warren, Ct., she d. Sept. 1846; Samuel b. Aug. 29, 1777, d. Jan. 21, 1778 ; Sally b. Nov. 26, 1778, d. Sept. 19, 1779 ; 2d Sally b. Oct. 17, 1780, m. Guy Talcott, of Windsor, and d. in Dec. 1817 ; Samuel b. Sept. 6, 1783, m. Catherine Wadsworth, of Hartford, daughter of Reuben ; Harriet b. Nov. 18, 1785, d. April 10, 1794 ; Lydia Wright b. Jan. 23, 1788, unmarried ; Martha b. March 7, 1791, m. John Russell, Esq., of Hartford, now of Pennsylvania—he has several children, and is the father of Doct. Gurdon W. Russell, of Hartford, who has one son, Edward. Mrs. Russell died Jan. 6, 1847.

Samuel Wadsworth, Esq., son of Gurdon, and grandson of Capt. Samuel, m. Catherine Wadsworth, and settled in New Haven, where he now resides. Their children are, Catherine Elizabeth, b. Aug. 9, 1809, m. Russel Hotchkiss, of New Haven, Dec. 25, 1833 ; Henry Stevens b. March 11, 1811, unmarried ; Samuel Wright b. Sept. 23, 1813, m. Sarah C. Sanford, Sept. 18, 1844 ; Charles b. Dec. 31, 1816, d. Nov. 4, 1828 ; Eliza b. Jan. 24, 1824, unmarried ; Edward b. Jan. 27, 1827, and d. Nov. 17, 1828.

Wadsworth, Joseph, jr., son of Joseph, m. Elizabeth ——, who was his widow, and with Daniel Wadsworth, were administrators on his estate in 1760. He had children, Thomas, Joseph, and Timothy—these sons chose their guardians in 1761. His other children were, Elijah 16 years old at the time of his father's death, Ambrose and Reuben.

Thomas, son of Joseph, jr., m. and had a daughter who d. before her father. He d. in 1811, without leaving any children, and gave all his estate to his wife Hannah, and William Stevens Wadsworth, a son of his brother Reuben. Estate $1401 98.

Joseph, third son of Joseph, jr., removed to the State of New York, where he d. and left a large family.

Timothy, son of Joseph, jr., m. and had a son Adna, and one daughter, and d. at Hartford, in Sept. 1826, aged 81. His son Adna moved to Ohio.

Elijah, son of Joseph, jr., m. Miss Hopkins, and removed to Litchfield when a young man. He had one daughter and three sons, viz. Rhoda, who m. Mr. Clark, an attorney at law at St. Mary's, in the State of Georgia, where she d. and left a family of children; Henry m. Miss Bradley, daughter of Aaron, Esq., of Litchfield, where he d.; Frederick and George. Mr. Wadsworth resided many years at Litchfield, but previous to the war of 1812 he removed to Ohio, with his sons, Frederick and George. During that war he was made a general of the militia. And in the war of the Revolution he held an office in Col. Sheldon's regiment. Gen. Wadsworth was a gentleman highly esteemed wherever known.

Ambrose, brother of Gen. Elijah, d. at sea, and left no family.

Reuben, his brother, m. Elizabeth Stevens, and had two sons and four daughters, viz. Horace H., who m. in Pennsylvania, and removed from there to Louisiana, d. in 1847, and left sons and daughters—one of the daughters, Martha A., m. George W. Goodwin, merchant tailor, of St. Louis, Missouri, September 3, 1845, and has one child. William S., the other son of Reuben, now resides in Hartford, married Catherine Bunce in 1816, and has one son and three daughters, viz. Charles R., single, Elizabeth, m. Horatio W. Shipman, of Berlin, and has a son and two daughters—Frances A. m. James E. Terry, of Hartford, in 1847, and Jane, unmarried; Catherine, dau. of Reuben, m. Samuel Wadsworth, Esq., of New Haven; Eliza, her sister, m. Heman Bunce, of Hartford, and had a daughter Elizabeth S., who m. Norman Burr, of Hartford, and has two children; Martha, dau. of

Reuben, m. George Francis, of Hartford, and has four sons and one daughter ; Emeline, dau. of Reuben, d. aged 27. He also had two daughters named Harriet, who died young.

I need not remark to those who peruse this work, that the family of Wadsworths have sustained the name of the first Puritan settler, at Hartford, as well, to say the least, as any other family who settled in the colony, and has produced as many important and useful men.

ADDENDA.

Since finding and publishing the name of Barsheba Dixwell, I have been at the trouble of procuring from Professor Johnson, an accurate Epitaph from her grave-stone, at Middletown, which is as follows :

"Here lyethe the Body of Mrs. Bathsh^a Dixwell, Relict of Mr.
John Dixwell, Esqr. Who departed this life December
ye 27th, 1729, Aged 83 Years."

This is strictly correct, and is verbatim et literatim, though Dr. Stiles, on page 149 says, "that her age at the time of her death was 85, and on her grave-stone 86." It is as here stated upon the grave-stone 83. Dr. Stiles also states that the maiden name of the second wife of Judge Dixwell was Bathsheba How—that by her he had three children, viz. " Mary, daughter of Mr. James Davids, born 9th June, 1679." " John the son of Mr. James Davids and Bathsheba Davids, was born the 6th day of March, 1680–1." " Elizabeth the daughter of Mr. James and Bathsheba Davids, was born the 14th of July, in New Haven, 1682." Also " Mr. John Dixwell and Mary Prout were married, Sept. 1, 1708." In 1685 he was admitted into the church at New Haven, in full communion, by the name of Dixwell as well as Davids. His daughter Elizabeth, died before her father's decease ; and at his death, he left his widow, Bathsheba, and his daughter Mary and son John. Mary married Mr. John Collins, of Middletown, Dec. 24, 1707, and removed there. Afterwards her mother, a part of her time, resided with her daughter, and died there, Dec. 27, 1729, aged 83, (as on her grave-stone.) The children of Mary, by Mr. Collins, were, Nathaniel b. Nov. 17, 1708 ; Mary b. Sept. 23, 1710 ; John b. March 18, 1712, a twin ; Sibbel b. Aug. 16, 1716, and Abigail Collins b. Jan. 4, 1718–19.

The son of Judge Dixwell learned the trade of a goldsmith, and settled in Boston about the time of his marriage, though he became a respectable merchant at Boston, and was a gentleman of good standing and character, and for a time was a deacon of the New North Church in Boston," as appears by the " testimony entered in the records of that church." He died in the 44th year of his age, April 2, 1725, while a deacon of the New North Church. Elder or deacon Dixwell, who married Miss Prout, of New Haven, had children born in Boston, viz. Basil Dixwell b. July 7, 1711, d. in 1764; Elizabeth b. in 1716; John b. in 1718, d. in 1749. After the death of his wife Mary, Dea. Dixwell again married, but died in 1724, and left three children living, by his first wife. John Prout, Esq., of New Haven, Conn., became guardian for the children, and took them to N. Haven, and his mother, Madam Prout, took charge of John Dixwell; Mrs. Mansfield, his aunt, took the charge of Basil, and Mrs. Christophers, of New London, took care of the daughter Elizabeth. Basil settled as a goldsmith at Providence, R. I. He entered the army, and died at Louisburg, in 1746, without leaving issue. John Dixwell, his only brother, became a brazier in Boston, and settled there, where he afterwards became a prosperous merchant. He m. Miss Hunt, of Watertown, Mass., and died in Boston in 1749. He had three children— but Mary, his daughter, only survived him. She m. Samuel Hunt, of Boston. Elizabeth Dixwell, who was educated by her aunt Christophers at New London, was living in 1793, aged 76, the widow of Joseph Lathrop, then deceased, of New London, to whom she was m. April 22, 1739, and by whom she had the following children, viz. Elizabeth Lathrop b. Jan. 23, 1740; Joseph b. Dec. 11, 1741, (died an infant;) John b. June 7, 1743, (had no issue;) Mary b. Feb. 3, 1744; Joseph b. Sept. 16, 1747; Sarah b. Jan. 30, 1752, and Dixwell Lathrop b. July 29, 1753. Mary Collins, a daughter of Mary, and grand daughter of Judge Dixwell, m. a Mr. Caruthers, of Middletown, and moved to Bennington, Vt., and was living there in April, 1793, aged 83 years. This fact is mentioned only to say that the grave of the widow of Judge Dixwell is near by the graves of the Caruthers family at Middletown. A son of Samuel Hunt, in Boston, changed his name to Dixwell.—*Dr. Sitles, Prof. Johnson, Records and Tomb-stone.* (See p. 275.)

Ralph and Alva Mann were sons of Rodolphus. Alva resides in New York, unmarried. Ralph married Judith Phelps, and resides at Michigan. (See p. 282.)

344

On 317th page, 5th line from bottom, after the word "merchants," add, Amos died a lieutenant in the army.

Epitaph in the old Burial Yard at Hartford.

"Here lyeth the body of Mr. David Gardiner, of Gardiner's Island, deceased July 10, 1689, in the fifty fovrth year of his age. Well, sick—dead, in one hovrs space.—Engrave the remembrance of death, on thine heart, when as thov dost see how swiftly hovrs depart.— Born at Saybrook April 29, 1636, the first white child born in Connecticut."

(It is doubted whether his father was at Saybrook as early as April 29, 1636, or Gardiner's Island known by that name as early.)

A few Families of Windsor, from Record.

Nathaniel Bissell m. Mindwell More, Sept. 25. Children, Mindwell b. Oct. 3, 1663; Nathaniel b. Jan. 7, 1665; Jonathan b. July 1668, d.; Hannah b. Jan. 12, 1670; Abigail b. Sept. 14, 1673, d.; 2d Jonathan b. Feb. 14, 1774; 2d Abigail bap. 1776; another dau. born in 1678.

Jeffery Baker m. F. Rockwell, Nov. 15, 1642. Children, Samuel b. May 30, 1644; Hepzibah b. May 10, 1646; Mary b. July 15, 1649; Abiell b. Dec. 23, 1652, d.; Jeffery, jr. b. June 18, 1655. Son Samuel m. Sarah Cook, June 30, 1670.

William Burd m. Nov. 18, 1640. Children, Samuel b. Sept. 2, 1641; Peter b. Aug. 19, 1644; Mary b. Sept. 3, 1642; Hannah b. Jan. 8, 1646; Hepzibah b. Dec. 11, 1649; Sarah b. May 21, 1651, and Abigail.

Samuel Buell m. Debra Griswold in 1662, and had a son Samuel b. July 20, 1663.

Thomas Bassom's children were, Abigail b. June 7, 1640; Thomas b. Feb. 20, 1641; Hepzibah b. July 14, 1644.

John Brooks m. Susannah Hanmore, May 25, 1652, and had children, John b. May 16, 1660, d.; Samuel b. Jan. 6, 1662; Elizabeth b. June 27, 1664; Mary b. May 21, 1665; Joanna b. Feb. 2, 1668; 2d Mary b. Nov. 25, 1670; Lydia b. Aug. 7, 1673, and Susannah.

Daniel Clark m. Mary Newberry, June 13, 1644. Children, Josias b. Jan. 21, 1648; Elizabeth b. Oct. 28, 1651; Daniel, jr. b. Aug. 4, 1654; John b. April 10, 1656; Mary b. Sept. 22, 1658; Samuel b. July 6, 1661; Sary b. Aug. 7, 1663; Hannah b. Aug. 29, 1665, d.; Nathaniel b. Sept. 8, 1666.

John Cass's children were, Mary b. June 22, 1660 ; John, jr. b. Nov. 5, 1662 ; William b. June 5, 1665 ; Samuel b. June 1, 1667 ; Richard b. Aug. 27, 1669 ; another b. in Aug. 1676.

Thomas Dewey m. Miss Clark, May 22, 1638—had four sons, and a daughter Anna.

Thomas Dibble m. in 1635, and had four sons, and two daughters. Ebenezer, son of Thomas, m. Mary Wakefield, Oct. 27, 1663, and had three sons and two daughters ; Samuel, son of Thomas, m. Hepzibah Bartlett, Jan. 29, 1665, and had three daughters, and two sons, Samuel and another.

Job Drake m. Mary Wolcott, June 25, 1646, and had two sons, and five daughters.

John Drake m. Hannah Moore, and had five sons and six daughters.

Peter Brown m. Mary Gillett, July 15, 1658, and had 13 children.

Henry Curtis m. Elizabeth Abel, May 13, 1645, and had Samuel and Nathaniel.

John Ffyler m. Elizabeth Dolman, Oct. 1637.

William Filly m. Margaret, in 1642, had 3 sons and 4 daughters.

Ambrose Fowler m. J. Alvord, May 6, 1646, and had 6 children.

Joseph Griswold m. Mary Gaylord, July 14, 1670, had a son and daughter.

John Gaylord m. Mary Drake, Nov. 17, 1653, and had 2 sons, and 2 daughters.

John Griffin m. Anna Bancraft in 1648, had 4 sons, and 6 daughters.

Jacob Gibbs m. Elizabeth Andrews in 1657, and had 6 children.

Samuel Gibbs m. Hepzibah Dibble in 1664, and had 8 children.

Benajah Holcom m. Sarah Ennos, April 11, 1667, had 2 sons.

Mirall Humfrey m. Priscilla Grant, Oct. 14, 1647, and had 2 sons, and 5 daughters.

REMARKS.

In collecting materials for No. 5, it will be noticed that T. R. Marvin, Esq., of Boston, has meritoriously assumed upon himself the labor and responsibility of collecting the genealogy of his family, which is found in this Number. I am under many obligations to Mr. Philemon Robbins, of this city, for facts relating to the John Robbins family, of Wethersfield, here published. The large number of similar names in the different branches of this family, particularly John, Samuel and Joshua, render it difficult in many cases to decide to which branch of the family the person found may have been a member ; and little light can generally be gained by applying to relatives as to their ancestors previous to 1700 or even 1750. It is not a rare occurrence to find, even in this enlightened community, men well informed on most subjects, who cannot give the name of their great grand father, or even their grand father, or at what places they resided. It will not be expected that in a genealogical publication of this kind, it will be either full in all the branches of the numerous families, or strictly correct in every date, when it is known that even records and tomb-stones differ in some cases. These publications are made to induce those who have a more direct family interest, to perfect their own genealogy, or at least to correct errors, and make such additions in families as are here omitted. There are generally some few in a large family who will have sufficient curiosity to know their ancestry, at least to learn the name of their great grand father. It is indeed a lamentable fact, that many persons conduct upon this subject as if they feared an investigation of their ancestry, lest they should find some great grand father or uncle, who had been executed upon the gallows, or whipped at the post. Otherwise, experience proves that past generations will not suffer by a comparison with the present, either in morals or intelligence.

This Number, containing 80 pages, closes the volume, which per-haps may at some future day, be better arranged and corrected, with such additions as may be found worthy of publication.

ABBREVIATIONS.

m.	for married.	dau.	for daughter.
wid.	" widow.	b.	" born.
d.	" died.	bap.	" baptized.

ERRATA.

Page 52, No. 2, Hannah, Mary and Sarah Marvin, were not the daughters of Reinold.

" 122, Mary Marvin, who m. Richard Bushnell, of Saybrook, was the daughter of Matthew, jr., and not a sister of Reinold.

" 158, on the 15 line from the top, for " Woodbury," read Northampton.

" 282, add to the bottom line, " and Mercy, who m. Mr. Plumb, of Troy, N. Y."

" 283, on the 7th line from the top, after m., read " Joel Mann, who had a daughter Mercy who m."—and erase the 8th line from the top.

" 318, on the 17th line from the top, after the word " Lewis," add Jennett.

INDEX.

Bates, Jane Ashley, 189
John, 113, 127
Jonathan, 113, 127
Mary Ashley, 189
Robert, 150, 190
Samuel, 127
Sarah Barnard, 189
Sarah Porter, 189
Solomon, 113
Wm. Ashley, 189
Wm. G., 189
Baxter, 52
Bridget, 41
Mrs. Bridget, 113
Thomas, 113
Baylding, Mary, 149
Baysa, Elizabeth, 266
John, 266
Baysey, John, 161
Beach, John, 112, 232
Sarah, 126
Beale, Thomas, 13
Bearding, wid. Abigail, 190
Nathaniel, 16, 162, 190
Beardslee, 128
John, 113, 232
Beardsley, 118
Joseph, 113
Samuel, 149
William, 113, 232
Bears, James, 290
Bearsley, Thomas, 113, 157
Beaumont, Wm., 14, 113
Beckley, Abigail, 203
Hannah, 264
John, 264
Mary, 260
Miriam, 317
Richard, 113, 258
Sarah, 258
Beckwith, Jerusha, 113
Job, 113
Joseph, 113
Matthew, 14, 113
Nathaniel, 113
Patience, 113
Sarah, 113
Stephen, 14, 113
Beebe, James, 126
John, 15
Rebecca, 262
Beebie, John, 14
Beedle, Robert, 14,164
Beers, Capt., 113
Abigail, 245
Daniel, 113, 114
James, 114
Joseph, 113
Josiah, 114
Lewis, 114
Seth P., 114
Thomas, 16, 113
Zechariah, 114
Belcher, Andrew, 258
widow Mabel, 274
Samuel, 274
Belden, Aaron, 192, 198
Abigail, 191, 192, 193, 195
Abner, 197
Agnes Whittlesey, 194

Belden, Amos, 197
Ann, 191, 193, 197
Asa, 191
Ashbel, 198
Benj., 191, 192, 198
Bildad, 197
Caleb, 198
Celia, 195
Chas., 192, 194, 198
Chauncey, 193, 194
Chauncey Herbert, 194
Cornelia Hale, 194
Daniel, 190, 191, 197
David, 195
Donald, 194
Dorothy, 191
Ebenezer, 191, 192, 193, 197
Elisha, 191
Eliza, 197
Elizabeth, 191, 192, 194, 195, 198
Elizabeth Morton, 194
Esther, 191, 195
Eunice, 191,192,195
Experience, 191
Ezekiel, 191
Ezekiel P., 196
Ezekiel Porter, 195
Ezra, 191, 192, 198
George Hubertus, 193
Gideon, 191
Hannah, 191, 196
Harriet Man, 197
Hezekiah, 191, 193
James, 195
James L., 195, 197
James Lockwood, 196
Jared, 191
Jeremiah, 198
John, 190, 191, 192, 195, 197
John Mason, 193, 194
Jonathan, 191, 192, 194, 195
Joseph, 191, 195, 196, 197
Joshua, 192, 193, 194, 197
Josiah, 191
Julia, 195, 196
Justus, 198
Keziah, 192
Lemuel W., 194
Lemuel Whittlesey, 193
Lois, 191, 192
Lucy, 195, 197
Lydia, 191, 192
Mabel Wright, 191
Margaret, 191
Martha, 191, 193, 196, 197
Mary, 191, 192, 195, 198
Mary Elizabeth, 194
Mary Honoria, 193
Mary Mix, 196
Matthew, 191, 197, 198
Mehitabel, 295
Mercy, 197, 198

Belden, Moses, 195, 197, 198
Nancy, 197
Nathaniel, 191
Octavia, 198
Oliver, 192, 194
Othniel, 198
Ozias, 191
Phineas, 191, 198
Prudence, 191, 197
Rebecca, 191, 195, 197
Return, 191
Rhoda, 193
Richard, 14, 164, 190, 191, 197
Roswell, 198
Ruth, 191
Samuel, 190, 191, 197, 198
Sarah, 191, 193, 195, 197
Seth, 191, 197
Silas, 192, 194, 198, 292
Simeon, 195, 196, 197
Solomon, 191, 299
Stephen, 191
Thankful, 191
Theodore, 194
Thomas, 195, 196
Timothy, 192
Tomison, 190, 191
William, 190, 197
Belding, 193
Daniel, 114
Ebenezer, 114
John, 114
Jonathan, 114
Joseph, 114
Lydia, 114
Margaret, 114
Samuel, 114
Sarah, 114, 258
Bell, 236
Francis, 114, 150
John, 114
Robert, 114
Thomas, 114
Mary, 114
Beman, Widow Margaret, 274
Samuel, 274
Bement, Abigail, 178
Benjamin, 168
Dennis, 167, 168, 173
Ebenezer, 168
Edmund, 168
Hannah, 175
John, 168
Jonathan, 168
Joseph, 168
Martha, 176
Mary, 167
Wm. 168, 175, 176
Benedick, Thos. 114
Benedict, Thos. 290
Benfield, 114
Benham, Azal, 274
Hannah, 114
Luce, 174
Rebecca, 114
Richard, 114
Samuel, 274
Benjamin, Abigail, 15, 115, 198
Caleb, 114, 115, 198

Benjamin, David,115
Edwin, 115
Gideon, 115
John, 114, 115, 198
Jonathan, 115
Martha, 198
Mary, 15, 115, 198
Richard, 115
Samuel, 15, 114, 115, 198
Sarah, 198
Bennet, James, 114
Thomas, 114
Bennett, James, 149
John, 16, 163
Joseph, 15, 164
Samuel, 53
Bennite, Henry, 114
Benton, 204
Abigail, 209
Andrew, 114
Ann, 265
Dorothy, 114
Ebenezer, 114
Edward, 114, 159
Hannah, 114, 261
Mrs. Hannah, 242
Jacob, 257
John, 114
Jos., 81, 114, 258
Lydia, 114
Mary, 114, 258
Samuel, 114,225,257
Sarah, 209
Berding, Mrs. Abigail, 17
Elizabeth, 17
John, 17
Nathaniel, 17
Thomas, 17
Berry, Abigail, 198
Ann Fenton, 198
Berthia Gove, 198
Elizabeth, 198
Nathaniel, 198
Rachel Fuleham, 198
Sarah, 198
Beswick, Geo., 115
Betts, Dr., 205
John, 16, 115, 165, 198
Thomas, 115, 289
Widow, 16, 115, 102, 166
Beuchamp, John, 209, 277
Susannah, 277
Mrs. S., 209
Bevin, Abigail, 198
Anna, 198
Arthur, 198
Denre, 198
Elizabeth, 198
Grace, 198
Joanna, 198
John, 198
Mary, 198
Mercy, 198
Sarah, 198
Thomas, 198
Bewithe, Francis, 209, 277
Biddell, John, 166
Biddoll, Abner, 199
Charles, 199
Jacob, 198, 199
Jared, 199
John, 16, 258

344

Griswold, G., 40
George, 139
Gov., 28
J., 297
Jacob, 126, 192
John, 117, 138, 139
Joseph, 139, 335
M., 52, 54, 153
Mary, 139, 259
Matthew, 28, 80, 105, 138, 139, 214
Moses, 292
Roger, 105, 138, 178
Samuel, 90, 139, 214
Sarah, 192
Gridley, Thomas, 139, 166
Gross, John, 260
Jonah, 259, 260, 321
Josiah, 214
Samuel, 214
Susannah, 214
Truman, 260
Grouts, G., 30
Groves, Philip, 75, 139
Simon, 139
Guildersleeve, Richard, 139
Gull, Wm., 139, 159
Gunn, Deborah, 139
Elizabeth, 139
Jasper, 31
John, 139
Joseph, 139
Mehitabel, 139, 259
Thomas, 27, 139, 164, 259
Gurnsey, Bezable, 266
Elizabeth, 266
John, 260, 266
Lydia, 266
Sarah, 266
Gutteridge, John, 30
Gwin, Paul, 139
Gymnys, John, 30
Hackings, John, 158
Hackleton, Hannah, 37
Hackwell, Robert, 134
Haddock, Hannah, 181, 246
Hagborn, Samuel, 37
Haines, Joseph, 37
Haizen, Thomas, 140
Hakes, Elizabeth, 139
Elizur, 139
Isaac, 139
Joanna, 139
John, 139
Mary, 139
Nathaniel, 139
Sarah, 139
Hale, Abigail, 169
David, 170, 175
Mrs. Hannah, 223
John, 31, 35, 170
Jonathan, 170
Joseph, 170
Mary, 168
Mrs. Naomi, 151
Nathaniel, 31, 35
Rachel, 171
Samuel, 31, 165, 170, 175
Sarah, 171, 175

Hale, Thomas, 35, 165, 170
Wm., 170
Hales, Samuel, 162, 165
Sarah, 265
Thomas, 162, 268
Hall, Azariah, 178
Benjamin, 174, 178
Cornelius, 35
Daniel, 178
Ebenezer, 174, 178
Edward, 181
Eli, 146
Elisha, 178
Mrs. Elizabeth, 127
Esther, 216
Ichabod, 178
Israel, 178
Jedediah, 148
Joel, 178
John, 31, 35, 125, 162, 166, 178
Joseph, 178
Levi, 178
Hamlin, John, 216
Mary, 64
Mrs. Mary, 91
Moses, 178
Nicholas, 178
Richard, 85, 156
Samuel, 85, 154
Sarah, 35
Stephen, 85
Thomas, 31, 162
Timothy, 35, 163
Hallaway, John, 31, 166, 214
Hallet, James, 31
Hally, Mary, 219
Halsted, C.Stockton, 225
Halstead, Henry, 214
Hamlin, 229
Abigail, 217
Amasa, 218
Charles, 217, 218
Christopher, 217
Cicero J., 219
Daniel, 218
Edward, 217
Edward S. 219
Eleazer, 218
Elizabeth, 216, 217, 218
Emeline B., 219
Erastus, 218
Esther, 216, 217, 218
Experience, 218
Frederick, 218
Frederick V., 219
George, 217
Giles, 39, 133, 214, 215, 216, 217, 218
Hannah, 218
Harriet, 219
Harris, 217, 218
Mrs. Hester, 215
Jabez, 216, 217, 219
John, 215, 216, 217, 218
John W.. 218, 219
Lorenzo F., 218
Lucia, 218
Lucinda, 218
Lucinda L. 219
Lucretia, 218
Mabel, 215

Hamlin, Mahitabel, 216, 217
Mary, 215, 216, 217, 218
Margaret, 217
Minerva C., 219
Nathaniel, 217, 218
Phœbe, 218
Richard, 215, 217, 218
Ruth, 218
Salomon, 218
Samuel, 218
Sarah, 217, 218
Mrs. Sarah, 215
Susannah, 217, 218
Sybil, 216
Thomas, 218
William, 217, 218
Zelpha, 218
Hammon, Wm., 31
Hammond, Elijah, 158
Hampton, Wade, 306
Hanchett, Doct. 283, 336
Hancock, Freegrace, 175
George, 33
Hand, Benjamin, 203
Handerson, James, 265
Hanes, Thomas, 330
Hanford, 80
Rev. Thomas, 33
Hanmer, Martha, 241
Wm. 37, 164
Hanmore, Susannah, 334
Hanset, Thomas, 165
Harbert, Benjamin, 159
Harden, Mrs. Hannah, 275
Hardy, Richard, 27, 31, 35
Thomas, 61
Harman, Hannah, 174
Harmon, Mary, 168, 190
Harris, Andrew, 37
Daniel, 189
Lieut. Daniel, 34
Elizabeth, 189
Mrs. Elizabeth, 118, 274
Hannah, 139
John, 37, 123, 139
Mary, 139, 263
Rachel, 238
Richard, 31, 37, 164
Samuel, 139
Thomas, 37, 139
Timothy, 295
Toleration, 87
Wm., 125, 139
Harrison, James, 260
John, 31, 41, 164
Joseph, 31
Kateram, 41
Martha, 76, 91
Mary, 31, 41, 265
Rebecca, 31
Sarah, 31, 41
Thomas, 31
Harries, Mary, 233
Hart, Mrs. Abigail, 294
John, 34, 53, 318

Hart, Elisha, 39
Mary, 319
Ruth, 318
Mrs. Ruth, 219
Stephen, 31, 34, 162, 165, 166
Thomas, 34, 318
Wm., 318
Hartshorn, David, 140
Harvey, Edward, 31
John, 42
Richard, 139, 232
Harwood, James, 31
Hascall. Miriam, 213
Hastings, Dr., 235
Hastlewood, Richard, 31
Hatch, Abigail, 288
Amy, 81
Ebenezer, 278
Joseph, 81
Lucy, 278
Sarah, 278
Thomas, 108
Haughton, Morton, 35
Ralph, 231
Richard, 219
Wm., 35, 162
Haward, Robert, 31
Hawes, Abigail, 282
Daniel, 282
Hawkes, John, 165
Hawkins, Mrs. Ann, 219, 331
Anthony, 31, 42,80, 127, 140, 164, 219
Elizabeth, 31, 37, 219
Hannah, 31, 37, 217
Honor, 219
John, 31, 37, 140, 219
Mary, 140, 141, 219
Ruth, 31, 37, 140, 219
Sarah, 31, 37, 219
Hawks, John, 31
Hawley, 219
Mrs. Ann, 98
Jared, 146
Joseph, 100, 139, 140, 232
Samuel, 31, 189
Hawly, Samuel, 17
Hayden, 213
Daniel, 41, 140
Hannah, 140
Levi, 41
Mary, 140
Nathaniel, 41, 140
Samuel, 41
Wm.,11, 31,41,140, 163
Hayes, Daniel, 34
David, 34
Jacob, 31, 34
Jonathan, 34
Nicholas, 34
Samuel, 34
Haynes, 62, 94
Gov. 25, 33, 38, 48, 50, 77, 78, 92, 108
Hezekiah, 87
John, 37, 118, 187, 161, 162,165, 166, 255, 260, 266, 267
Gov. John, 86

354

Loveland, Lydia, Mrs., 274
Robert, 49, 221
Ruth, 221
Sally, 242
Thomas, 49
Loveridge, 49
Lovering, Wm., 152
Lucas, John, 222
Mary, 222
Samuel, 222
Thomas, 222
Wm., 153, 222
Ludlow, 50, 94, 229
Mr., 14, 36, 75, 92, 100, 113
Roger, 6, 63, 157, 161, 254
Hon. Roger, 48
Lusk, James, 193
Luxford, Reuben, 49
Stephen, 49
Lyman, 204
John, 48
Joseph, 261
Phillis, 48
Richard, 48, 162,163
Robert, 48
Samuel, 153
Sarah, 48
Lynde, Joseph, 193
Nathaniel, 153
Samuel, 153
Lyon, Harriet Halsted, 193
Henry, 49, 157, 222
Richard, 49, 157, 222
Underhill, 193
Maccoy, Alice, 222
Hugh, 222
Mackee, Abigail, 271
Henry, 271
Joseph, 271
Russell, 271
Wm., 271
Macnim, Mrs. Elizabeth, 222
James, 222
Maloy, Capt., 153
Maltby, Mr., 205
Man, Wm., 200
Manderly, John, 163
Manley, Christiana, 295
Mann, Aaron, 282
Abigail, 282
Abijah, 283, 284
Adelia P., 284
Alexander, 284
Alba, 333
Andrew, 283, 284
Ann Maria, 284
Anna Porter, 284
Ariel, 282
Asaph, 283, 284
Bemsley, 283, 284
Benjamin, 281
Benning, 283, 284
Benning E., 284
Beriah, 281, 282
Bethiah, 281
Bezaleel, 281
Brownel, 282
Catharine, 284
Catharine Vernon, 284
Chloe, 285
Cordelia M., 284

Mann, Cyrus, 283, 284
Cyrus N., 284
Cyrus S., 284
Daniel, 282
David, 282
Doct., 282
Dorothy, 281
Ebenezer, 281, 284, 285
Edward, 284
Edward M., 284
Elijah, 281, 283, 284
Elizabeth, 281
Enoch, 283, 284
Esther, 281, 282
Eunice, 282
Ezra, 281
Frances, 285
FrancisNorton,282
Frederick, 284
George, 281
Hannah, 281, 282, 283, 284
Harriet, 283, 285
Hepzibah, 282
Hezekiah, 281
Ichabod, 281, 282
Ira, 283
Jacob, 282
James, 282
Jared, 283
Jeremiah, 281
Jerusha, 282
Joel, 282, 284, 336
John, 281, 283, 284
Jonathan, 281
Josiah, 281, 282
Lois, 282
Lucretia, 285
Lucy, 285
Lydia, 283, 284
Mahitabel, 281
Manlius, 284
Margaret, 281, 282, 283
Margaret Peters, 284
Martha, 284
Mary, 281, 282, 283
Melatiah, 282
Mercy, 281, 283, 336
Michael, 281
Miletee, 285
Molly, 285
Moses, 282
Nancy, 285
Nathan, 282
Nathaniel, 281, 283, 284
Oliver, 285
Pelatiah, 281, 282
Peres, 285
Phebe, 282, 283, 284
Polly, 285
Rachel, 282
Ralph, 333
Reuben, 284, 285
Richard, 281
Robert, 281
Rodolphus, 282, 333
Ruth, 282
Sally, 283, 284
Mason, 149
Samuel, 281, 282, 284, 285
Sarah, 282
Solomon, 183
Sophia, 283
Theodore, 281, 282

Mann, Theodore, 282
Thomas, 281, 282
Timothy, 281, 282
William, 200, 281
Zadock, 282
Manning, Sarah, 145
Mansfield, Mrs., 333
Manvill, Matthew, 52
Mapes, Thomas, 85
Mapp, Thomas, 209, 277
Marcum, Mrs. Priscilla, 30
Marzeson, Edward, 250
Markham, 92
Ambrose, 171
Barillas, 171
Daniel, 170,171
Darius, 171
Ebenezer, 171
Mrs. Elizabeth, 153
Isaac, 171
Israel, 171
James, 153
Jehiel, 171, 175
Jemima, 175
Jeremiah, 171
Joseph, 171
Justus, 171
Nathan, 171
Phœbe, 168
Priscilla, 170
Sybil, 170
William, 52, 162
Markum, William, 159
Marks, Richard, 53
Thomas, 222
Marsh, Mrs. Bathsheba, 274
Elisabeth, 323
Hepzibah, 365, 327
J., 270
John, 52, 92, 126, 152, 159, 162, 165, 261, 265, 266, 267, 268
Jonathan, 323
Joseph, 266, 267, 268, 323
Ruth, 259
Sarah, 261
Marshall, Ann, 53
Bethia, 99
Daniel, 53, 153
Deacon Daniel, 53
David, 53
Eliakim, 53
Elizabeth, 53, 153
James, 11, 53
John, 53, 153
Lydia, 53, 100
Mary, 53, 153, 258, 260
Samuel, 53, 100, 153
Thomas, 53, 100, 153, 164
Marshfield, Mary, 258
Thomas, 53, 163
Martin, Anthony, 52
Christopher, 248
Elizabeth, 52
John, 52
Mary, 52
Samuel, 52, 142
Solomon, 53, 248
Thomas, 52
Marville, M. de, 314

Marvin, Abigail, 289, 290
Abijah P., 289
Alexander, 287
Ann, 290
Benjamin, 287, 290
Charles, 290
David, 290
Dudley, 289
Elihu, 288, 290
Elihu P., 289
Elisha, 288
Elizabeth, 285, 287, 289, 290
Esther, 288
Hannah, 52, 289, 290, 336
Jemima, 287
James, 288
John, 286, 287, 289, 290
Joseph, 287, 290
Lydia, 288
Martha, 288
Mary, 52, 122, 257, 287, 289, 290, 336
Matthew, 52, 69, 119, 162, 268, 285, 289, 290, 336
Mehitabel, 287
Miriam, 288
Nathan, 289, 290
Nehemiah, 289
Phebe, 288
Mrs. Phebe, 288
R., 127
Rachel, 268, 289, 290
Reginald, 286
Reinold, 28, 52,122, 285, 287, 288, 289, 336
Renold, 166, 286
Reynold, 286
Richard, 52
Richard P., 288
Samuel, 268, 286, 287, 289, 290
Sarah, 52, 260, 287, 288, 289, 290, 336
Seth, 290
Thomas, 289
T. R., 290, 335
Wm., 288, 289
Uriah, 287
Zechariah, 289
see Marvyn
Marvyn, Elizabeth, 286
Mrs. Elizabeth, 286
Hanna, 286
Marie, 286
Matthew, 286
Sara, 286
see Marvin
Marwine, Abigail,153
Elizabeth, 153
John, 153
Miles, 89, 90, 153
Samuel, 153
Mascall, Thomas, 52
Maskell, Abigail, 33, 53
Betsey, 153
Elizabeth, 53, 153
John, 53, 153
Thomas, 53, 153
Mason, 42, 94, 229
Ann, 51

358

Pomeroy, Caleb, 65, 225
Edward, 65, 164, 225, 254
Eldad, 65
Eltwed, 11, 65, 164, 225, 254
Hepzibah, 225
Joseph, 65, 225
Joshua, 65, 225
Mary, 225, 257
Medad, 100, 225, 257
Nathaniel, 65, 157
Ralph, 65
Pond, Isaac, 157
Nathaniel, 65, 157
Samuel, 157, 163
Sarah, 157
Thomas, 65
Pope, Mary, 172
Sarah, 171
Porter, Abigail, 195
Amy, Mrs., 274
Ann, 135, 226
Anna, 65, 284
Asahel, 322
Daniel, 47, 65, 317
Dorothy, 140
Dr. J., 187
Eunice, 318
Ezekiel, 195
Hannah, 225, 226, 262, 264
Haynes, Lord, 37
Hester, 226
Hezekiah, 226, 262
J., 187
James, 65, 226
Joanna, 226
Jonathan, 65
John, 4, 95, 164,226, 256, 262
Joseph, 65, 209, 226
Joshua, 65
Lydia, 283
Mary, 65, 226
Nathaniel, 65, 209, 225, 226, 262
Rebecca, 65,226,317
Rose, 65
Richard, 247
Ruth, 226
Samuel, 65,159,226, 318
Solomon, 209
Sarah, 100, 140, 226
Timothy, 262
Thomas, 112, 140
Porwidge, Wm., 65
Post, 49, 153, 167
Abraham, 139
John, 65, 156, 226
Stephen, 65, 162, 165, 226, 231
Thomas, 65,156,226
Potter, Elam, 123
Phineas, 173
Powell, Ann, 226
John, 226
Thomas, 226
Pratt, 167
Abraham, 66, 166
Daniel, 262
Elisha, 200, 262
Elizabeth, 263
Hannah, 238, 262, 264
Henry, 284

Pratt, John, 55, 66, 161, 162, 165, 167, 235, 237, 238, 262, 264, 266
Joseph, 284, 236
Peter, 262
Rachel, 262
Ruth, 261
Thomas, 66
Wm., 66,97,131,153, 162, 165, 266
Prentice, John, 66
Judge, 189
Prentiss, Ann, 260
Presson, Edward, 66
Preston,Edward,123, 226
Emma, 143
Harriet A., 189
Jehiel, 141, 142
John, 66
Lydia A., 189
Nathaniel, 189
Sarah B., 189
Wm., 66, 226
Price, 106
John, 66
Wm., 66
Priest, Degory, 249
Prior, Ann, 326
Azariah, 176
Daniel, 176
Ebenezer, 176
Ezekiel, 176,178
George, 196
Humphrey, 66
John, 137, 170, 176
Margaret, 175
Mary, 131, 170
Nathaniel, 137, 175, 176
Zachariah, 175
Prout, John, 333
Mary, 276, 332, 333
Provost, David, 66
Prudden, Nehemiah, 173
Peter, 32, 66, 164
Purfell, Edward, 225
Pulford, Mr., 146
Purcase, Elizabeth, 122
John, 66, 166
Purchas, Jane, 262
Purchase, Elizabeth, 122
Purchis, John, 66
Purkis, 61
Putman, Elias, 66
Pyncheon, 104
George. 174
John, 186
Mary, 186
Mr., 53
Wm., 66, 186
Pynchion, John, 24
Wm., 24
Pyne, James, 66
Quimby, John, 67
Radcliff, Judge,22,206
Rainey, Mrs. Esther, 217
Ralph, 44
Ramon, 67
Randall, Abraham, 11, 68, 164,166,226
Hannah, 176
Miss, 63
Philip, 63, 68, 164

Randall, Wm., 180, 226
Randolph, 193
Ranney, Abijah, 240
Ebenezer, 226
Esther, 217, 226
John, 154, 226
Joseph, 226
Lucretia, 218
Mary, 91, 149, 226
Thomas, 226
Raulins, Jasper, 163
Rawling, Jasper, 164
Rawlins, Joseph, 68
Ray, Elizabeth, 226
James, 113, 226
Isaac, 226
Joseph, 226
Peter, 226
Rayner, 114
Thurston, 67, 88, 112, 128, 129, 161, 165, 253
Raynolds, Edwin,176
John, 176
Margaret, 176
Peter, 176
Samuel, 176
Raynor, Thurston, 150
Read, Widow Elizabeth, 226
George, 68
Giles, 68
Jacob, 226
Ralph, 68
Wm., 68
Reed, J., 157
Thomas, 166
Reemes, Joseph, 68
Reeve, Judge, 272
Mahitabel, 262
Robert, 226, 262
Wm., 65
Reeves, Mrs. Elizabeth, 223
Robert, 68
Reinolds, Anna, 227
John, 226, 227
Jonathan, 227
Keziah, 227
Widow Mary, 237
Rebina, 227
Remmington, 68
Rennalls, Rebecca, 197
Renolds, Mrs. Hannah, 129
James, 68
John, 68, 150, 157, 227
Renwick, Professor, 307
Reynold, Robert,235, 243
Reynolds, 49, 206
Hannah, 68, 197
James, 227
John, 165, 197, 227
Mary, 68
Reinold, 68
Robert, 68, 227
Rice, Mrs. Ann, 124
Jonathan, 68
Martha, 261
Michael, 68
Richards, Anne, 228
Belcher, 274
Benjamin, 143, 229

Richards, Betsey,229
Daniel, 229
Ebenezer, 229
Eli, 229
Elizabeth, 227, 228, 264
Esther, 229, 264
Hannah, 110, 229, 261
James, 68, 78, 162, 209, 227, 228, 229
Jedidiah, 229
Jerusha, 227, 228
Joanna, 228, 229
John, 68, 108, 110, 227, 229, 242, 262
Joseph, 142, 229, 274
Joshua, 228
Josiah, 229
Lydia, 229
Martha, 259
Mary, 68, 227, 228, 229
Nathaniel, 68, 162, 165, 167, 229
Obadiah, 68, 229
Olive, 229
Oliver, 229
Polly, 229
Rachel, 229
Sally, 229
Samuel, 68, 229, 262
Sarah, 180
Simeon, 229
Thomas, 68, 166, 209, 227, 228, 229, 262
Widow, 68
Richardson, Amos, 158, 230
Hannah, 230
Israel, 230
John, 230
Joseph, 230
Mrs. Juda, 275
Lemuel, 230
Mahitable, 230
Nathaniel, 230
Samuel, 230
Sarah, 230, 265
Stephen, 230
Thomas, 230
Ridgdale, John, 249
Ridgebell, Mr., 93
Riley, Grace, 69
Isaac, 69
Jacob, 69
John, 69, 296
Joseph, 69, 230
Jonathan, 69, 230
Mary, 69
Richard, 68, 165
Sarah, 69
Rinsdel, Robert, 148
Ripley, 182
Joshua, 230
Rising, James, 68
Risley, John, 201
Richards, 162, 230, 267, 268
Samuel, 69, 230,262, 267
Sarah, 230
Rix, Thomas, 230
Rood, Mrs. Mindwell, 270
Roath, 128
Robert, 203

363

Talcott, 90, 149, 237, 323
Abigail, 310
Asa, 240
Benjamin, 81
Dorothy, 78, 79
Elizur, 81
Gov., 50, 130, 310
Guy, 330
Hannah, 81
J., 59, 78
Jerusha, 79
John, 32, 70, 78, 79, 81, 102, 133, 134, 137, 162, 166, 167
Joseph, 79, 81
Mary, 81, 197, 210, 262
Matthew, 311
Miss. 292
Mr., 70
Nathaniel, 81, 292
Rachel, 81
Samuel, 78, 79, 81, 162, 197
Tanner, Rebecca, 81
Tappin, Thomas, 79, 112
Taylor, Elizabeth, 259
George, 79
John, 11, 79, 164
Jonathan, 228, 264
Mercy, 81
Patience, 81
Ruth, 205
Stephen, 79, 81, 96, 264
Thomas, 259
Wm., 79
Taynter, 79
Michael, 235
Terre, Mary, 30
Richard, 109
Stephen, 11, 79
see Terry
Terry, Abigail, 81
Benjamin, 174, 176, 177
Catharine, 314
Christopher H., 176
Daniel, 177
David, 175
Ebenezer, 167, 175, 176, 178
Elijah, 177
Eliphalet, 177
Elizabeth, 80, 81, 86, 301
Ephraim, 177
Gideon, 177
Hannah, 168, 176
Isaac, 177
John, 79, 80, 81
Jacob, 174, 177
James E., 331
John, 301
Jonathan, 174, 177
Joseph, 177
Margaret, 179
Mary, 80, 81, 173, 301
Nathaniel, 79, 177, 311, 314
Penelope, 167
Rebecca, 80, 176, 180, 301
Richards, 79, 81
Robert, 79
Samuel, 81, 168, 176, 177, 180

Terry, Sarah, 80, 81, 83
Selah, 176
Shadrach, 177
Solomon, 80, 301
Stephen, 79, 80, 81, 164, 301
Thomas, 79
Tetherton, Daniel, 232
Thomas, Mary, 179
Serg't, 80
Thompson, Ann, 140, 283
Capt., 142
Cornelia, 326
Edward, 249
Thompson, Elizabeth, 140
Ezekiel, 137
John, 80, 82, 232
Thomas, 80, 82, 140, 219
Wm., 80, 245
John, 80
Thornton, Ann, 264
G., 82
Mrs. Hannah, 82
Samuel, 82, 264
Thomas, 11, 82
Walter, 94
Thrall, 105
Abigail, 81
Deborah, 81
Elizabeth, 81
John, 81
Joseph, 163
Martha, 81
Mehitable, 81
Moses, 81
Miss P., 148
Phillis, 82
Samuel, 81
Thomas, 81
Timothy, 81, 82, 114
Wm., 82, 164
Throcmorton, 82
Tilden, Ruth, 278
Tilerton, John, 223
Tillerson, Abigail, 80
Elizabeth, 80
John, 80
Mary, 80
Tillerton, Daniel, 82
Tillay, Edward, 249
John, 249
Tilliston, John, 80
Tillotson, John, 80
Hannah, 138
Tilly, Capt., 82
Tilton, Peter, 11, 159, 163
Tinker, 91
Amos, 82
John, 82, 164
Mary, 82
Mr., 74
Rhoda, 82
Samuel, 82
Thomas, 249
Tippets, Mr., 185
Tobe, John, 245
Sarah, 222, 245
Todd, David, 273
Doct., 320
Tomlinson, Abigail, 245
Beers, 245

Tomlinson, Christopher, 245
Comfort, 245
Dan. 245
Eliphelet, 245
Elizabeth, 83, 245
Goy., 245
Hannah, 83, 245
Henry, 245
Isaac, 245
Mary, 83, 245
Nathan, 245
Noah, 245
Phebe, 83
Philo, 245
Phœbe, 245
Ruth, 83, 245
Sarah, 83, 245
Susan, 245
Thankful, 83, 245
Thomas, 83, 245
Tomson, John, 157, 245
Thomas, 267
Tomsunn, Thomas, 264
Toobe, Anthony, 245
John, 245
Sarah, 245
Toppin, 136
Thomas, 79
Topping, John, 187
Toucey, Gov., 84
Towner, Timothy, 237
Towsey, Elizabeth, 82
Miss, 124
Mr., 156
Thomas, 83, 84
Tracy, Albert H., 80
George H., 247
John, 156
Thomas, 28, 49, 61, '80, 111, 156, 165
Uriah, 80
Treat, Mrs. Dorothy, 88
Elisha, 295
Frances, 285
Trumbull, Gov., 83
Treat, Henry, 83
James, 82, 83, 124
Jemima, 83, 124
Jerusha, 83
Joseph, 83, 292
Katherine, 83
Mabel, 83
Major, 153
Mary, 107, 246
Matthias, 107, 246
Rebecca, 83
Richard, 82, 83, 112, 124, 137, 165, 264
Robert, 68, 82, 134
Salmon, 83
Samuel, 83
Thomas, 83
Trill, Thomas, 82
Trott, Matthias, 83, 165
Richard, 83, 165
Trumble, 200
Annie, 83
John, 83
Joseph, 83
Trumbull, Faith, 314
Gov., 314

Trumbull, John, 180
Jonathan, 293
Joseph, 181
Tryon, Benjamin, 245
David, 245
Tubs, Sarah, 278
Tucker, 114
Amos, 84
John, 84
Mary, 84, 129
Rhoda, 84
Samuel, 84
Tucky, George, 84
Tudor, Elihu, 84
Mary, 224
Owen, 11, 84, 163
Rachel, 272
Samuel, 84
Tuller, John, 226
Tully, John, 84, 139
Turner, Abigail, 262
Ann, 278
Benjamin, 278
Capt., 84, 85
Daniel, 84
David, 278
Elizabeth, 328, 330
Ephraim, 84, 165, 264
Hannah, 278
Jonathan, 278
John, 249
Mary, 84, 155, 263
Mrs., 213
Nathaniel, 84
Sarah, 278
Robert, 85, 157
Tuthill, John, 85
Tuttle, Miss, 210
Twitchel, Samuel, 141
Tylee, Mr., 328
Sally, 328
Tyler, Abigail, 245
Abraham, 245
Andrew, 274
Ann, 245
Bethia, 265
Hannah, 245
Isaac, 245
Israel, 245
Watchful, 245
William, 265
Tylerton, Daniel, 85
Tyng, Jonathan, 228
Ufford, Benjamin, 85, 162
Thomas, 85, 164
Underhill, 84
Capt., 50, 60, 67
John, 85, 150
Upson, Stephen. 85
Thomas, 85, 162, 166, 264
Usher, Mr., 293
Robert, 85
Vandict, Gisbert, 86
Van Nep, C. P., 187
Gen., 187
Judge, 187
Mr., 187
Vantrue, Cornelius, 86
Varlet, Jasper, 85
Veats, Francis, 86
Ventres, Grace, 264
Moses, 264
Ventris, Grace, 86
Mary, 6

RECOMMENDED READING
from NEHGS

The Great Migration Study Project
Books • Quarterly Newsletter • Tours
By Robert Charles Anderson, FASG
shop.AmericanAncestors.org/collections/great-migration

The Original Lists of Persons of Quality, 1600–1700
By John Camden Hotten, foreword by Robert Charles Anderson, FASG
NEHGS • 6 x 9 pbk, 616 pp. • $27.95

Genealogical Notes: First Settlers of Connecticut and Massachusetts
By Nathaniel Goodwin
NEHGS • 6 x 9 pbk, 382 pp. • $24.95

New England Marriages Prior to 1700
By Clarence Almon Torrey
NEHGS • 8½ x 11, 2,400 pp. in 3 vols • $84.95 pbk, $124.95 hcvr

The Founders of New England
Originally Collected for and Published in
The New England Historical and Genealogical Register
By Samuel G. Drake
foreword by Henry B. Hoff, CG, FASG
NEHGS • 6 x 9 pbk, 272 pp. • $21.95

New Englanders in the 1600s
A Guide to Genealogical Research
Published Between 1980 and 2010
EXPANDED EDITION
By Martin E. Hollick
NEHGS • 6 x 9 pbk, 272 pp. • $21.95